THE PSYCHOLOGY OF LEARNING AND MOTIVATION

Advances in Research and Theory

VOLUME 42

THE PSYCHOLOGY
OF LEARNING AND MOTIVATION

Advances in Research and Theory: Cognitive Vision

EDITED BY DAVID E. IRWIN

DEPARTMENT OF PSYCHOLOGY AND
BECKMAN INSTITUTE
UNIVERSITY OF ILLINOIS AT URBANA-CHAMPAIN
CHAMPAIGN, ILLINOIS

BRIAN H. ROSS

BECKMAN INSTITUTE AND
DEPARTMENT OF PSYCHOLOGY
UNIVERSITY OF ILLINOIS AT URBANA-CHAMPAIGN
URBANA, ILLINOIS

Volume 42

ACADEMIC PRESS

An imprint of Elsevier Science

Amsterdam Boston Heidelberg London New York Oxford
Paris San Diego San Francisco Singapore Sydney Tokyo

This book is printed on acid-free paper. ∞

Academic Press
An imprint of Elsevier Science.
525 B Street, Suite 1900, San Diego, California 92101-4495, USA
http://www.academicpress.com

Academic Press
84 Theobald's Road, London WC1X 8RR, UK
http://www.academicpress.com

International Standard Book Number: 0-12-543342-5

PRINTED IN THE UNITED STATES OF AMERICA
03 04 05 06 07 08   9 8 7 6 5 4 3 2 1

CONTENTS

MEMORY AND LEARNING IN FIGURE–GROUND PERCEPTION

Mary A. Peterson and Emily Skow-Grant

SPATIAL AND VISUAL WORKING MEMORY: A MENTAL WORKSPACE

Robert H. Logie

SCENE PERCEPTION AND MEMORY

Marvin M. Chun

SPATIAL REPRESENTATIONS AND SPATIAL UPDATING

Ranxiao Frances Wang

SELECTIVE VISUAL ATTENTION AND VISUAL SEARCH: BEHAVIORAL AND NEURAL MECHANISMS

Joy J. Geng and Marlene Behrmann

CATEGORIZING AND PERCEIVING OBJECTS: EXPLORING A CONTINUUM OF INFORMATION USE

Philippe G. Schyns

FROM VISION TO ACTION AND ACTION TO VISION: A CONVERGENT ROUTE APPROACH TO VISION, ACTION, AND ATTENTION

Glyn W. Humphreys and M. Jane Riddoch

EYE MOVEMENTS AND VISUAL COGNITIVE SUPPRESSION

David E. Irwin

WHAT MAKES CHANGE BLINDNESS INTERESTING?

Daniel J. Simons and Daniel T. Levin

CONTRIBUTORS

Numbers in parentheses indicate the pages on which the authors' contributions begin.

Marlene Behrmann (155), Department of Psychology, Carnegie Mellon University, Pittsburgh, Pennsylvania 15213

Marvin M. Chun (77), Department of Psychology, Vanderbilt University, Nashville, Tennessee 37203

Joy J. Geng (155), Department of Psychology, Carnegie Mellon University, Pittsburgh, Pennsylvania 15213

Emily Skow-Grant (1), Department of Psychology, University of Arizona, Tucson, Arizona 85721

Glyn W. Humphreys (223), Behavioural Brain Sciences Centre, University of Birmingham, Birmingham, B15 2TT, United Kingdom

David E. Irwin (263), Department of Psychology, University of Illinois, Champaign, Illinois 61820

Daniel T. Levin (293), Psychology Department, Kent State University, Kent, Ohio 44242

Robert H. Logie (77), Department of Psychology, University of Aberdeen, Aberdeen AB24 2UB, United Kingdom

Mary A. Peterson (1), Department of Psychology, University of Arizona, Tucson, Arizona 85721

M. Jane Riddoch (223), Behavioural Brain Sciences Centre, University of Birmingham, Birmingham, B15 2TT, United Kingdom

Philippe G. Schyns (191), Department of Psychology, University of Glasgow, Glasgow G12 8QB, United Kingdom

Daniel J. Simons (293), Department of Psychology, University of Illinois, Champaign, Illinois 61820

Ranxiao Frances Wang (107), Department of Psychology, University of Illinois, Champaign, Illinois 61820

PREFACE

Much of the information we obtain from the world is through vision. We see objects or scenes in the world and use that information to augment our knowledge, decide on our actions, and keep track of our environment. Even with our eyes closed, we can remember various visual and spatial representations, manipulate them, and make decisions about them.

The role of perception in a full cognitive theory has changed over the last 25 years. The early assumption that there is a clear dividing line between cognition and perception has increasingly met with cases in which the alleged dividing line seems to be violated. We often see that processes thought to be prior to cognitive influences show effects of cognition and, in turn, affect cognition. In addition, recent evidence shows that action, as well as cognition, has influences on visual processing.

Volume 36 of this series examined perceptual learning. The aim of that volume was to highlight research in which perceptual units that underlay cognition were thought of not as fixed building blocks, but rather as adaptive, flexible units that were learned as a function of the goals of the perceiver and constraints of the task.

The goal of this volume is to examine a variety of ways in which cognition interacts with visual processes and visual representations. The first few chapters address the importance of prior knowledge in perceiving, in using working memory, and in visual search. In the first chapter, Peterson and Skow-Grant demonstrate that the perceptual process of figure–ground assignment is strongly influenced by memory and learning, contradicting the long-held belief that early visual processes are impenetrable to higher-level cognition. Logie provides a broad review of research on spatial and visual working memory and argues that working memory does not contain raw sensory information but rather representations that are based on prior knowledge and past experience. Chun describes how regularities in the visual environment are learned through perceptual experience so as to facilitate behaviors such as object identification and visual search.

The next two chapters address the importance of representations and processes on fundamental tasks of navigation and visual search. Wang discusses the structure of spatial representations in memory and how they are used for encoding visual information and for tasks, such as navigating through the environment. Geng and Behrmann discuss the behavioral and neural mechanisms that underlie selective visual attention and visual search.

An important aspect of visual cognition is how it operates when there is rich categorical knowledge. Schyns argues that the memory-driven categorization of a stimulus influences the availability of visual information about that stimulus and henceforth the way in which it is perceived. Humphreys and Riddoch propose that vision directly activates categorical actions to objects independently of conceptual/semantic knowledge, and that action representations in turn affect visual selection.

The volume ends with two chapters that address surprising findings in visual cognition. Irwin describes how one form of action, eye movements, actually interferes with some forms of cognition, specifically visuospatial cognitive operations. Finally, Simons and Levin discuss the phenomenon of change blindness and how it demonstrates an important fallacy in people's beliefs about vision and visual memory.

As is probably clear from the above, rather than restricting ourselves to a particular aspect of the interaction between vision and cognition, we invited contributions from a diverse set of researchers working at the cutting edge of this discipline. We hope that this variety provides a sense of the richness and importance of the interactions between cognition, perception, and action.

Brian H. Ross and David E. Irwin

MEMORY AND LEARNING IN
FIGURE–GROUND PERCEPTION

Mary A. Peterson and Emily Skow-Grant

I. Introduction

It has long been debated whether or not a clear dividing line can be drawn between perception and memory; the debate continues to this day. Nevertheless, since the turn of the twentieth century, it has been assumed that certain visual processes occur sufficiently "early" so as to be impenetrable by memory and other higher level processes. An example of one such early visual process is figure and ground assignment.

Figure–ground assignment occurs when two regions share a common border (as the black and white regions do in Figure 1A–C). One region—the figure—is typically seen as shaped by the border. The other region—the ground—is seen as shapeless near the border it shares with the figure; it typically appears to continue behind the figure as its background.[1] The Gestalt psychologists held that figure assignment imposes shape onto unorganized visual input; shaped entities simply do not exist prior to figure–ground assignment. On the Gestalt view, the shaped entities in the visual field (the figures) provided the substrate for matches to shape or object memories. Thus, it was impossible to access shape or object memories until

---

[1] There are some situations in which both regions can be perceived as figures, and there are other situations in which a contour itself can be perceived as the figure. However, the most likely outcome is a figure–ground outcome.

THE PSYCHOLOGY OF LEARNING
AND MOTIVATION VOL. 42

1

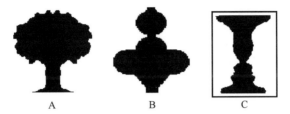

Fig. 1.   Displays illustrating figure–ground segregation. The black regions of (A) and (B) are enclosed, symmetric, and smaller in area than their surrounds. (A). A deciduous tree. (B). A novel object. (C) Rubin's vase/face display.

after shape had been assigned. Following figure–ground assignment memories were accessed only by the shaped entities (the figures), and not by the shapeless entities (the grounds). Throughout this chapter, the assumption that figure–ground assignment precedes access to object memories will be called the "figure–ground–first assumption."

The Gestalt figure–ground-first assumption arose as a counterargument to the Structuralist view of visual perception. The Structuralists held that past experience (memory) imposed shape onto unorganized, pointillistic, visual input. For instance, in the Structuralist framework, one perceives a tree in Figure 1A because one has seen trees before. This past experience with trees both groups the features and parts of the tree together and specifies that the black region is the shaped entity at its border with the white region. The Gestalt psychologists questioned how the proper memory could be chosen to organize a particular array if no organization had yet been imposed on the visual input. They reasoned that some prior organization of the visual input was necessary to constrain the memory matching process. This prior organization had to be based on cues that were innate. Excluding memory from the process of organizing the visual input into shaped and shapeless entities also allowed the Gestalt psychologists to account for the perception of novel shapes, shapes for which memory matches were destined to fail.

How, then, does figure assignment occur? According to the Gestalt psychologists, figure assignment is determined by any of a number of "configural" cues that can operate without accessing memory. Examples of the configural cues are closure, symmetry, convexity, and area. Regions that possess these attributes are more likely to be seen as figures than regions that are open, asymmetric, concave, and larger in area, respectively. The black regions of both Figure 1A and B possess all of the configural cues. The Gestalt psychologists would argue that in both cases, the black regions are seen as shaped entities—figures—because they possess these attributes. In the Gestalt framework, the fact that Figure 1A also portrays a well known object—a tree—is irrelevant for figure assignment.

The Gestalt school had a revolutionary impact on the field of visual perception in the early 1900s. As a consequence, it has long been thought that access to shape/object memories can occur only after the visual field has been organized into figures and grounds. That is, it has been assumed that figure–ground assignment is immune to influences from memory, even from memories that are intrinsically visual (e.g., memory for shape or object structure). Of course, the figure–ground-first assumption entails the belief that a line separating perception and memory can be drawn somewhere between figure assignment and memories of shape or object structure. Research in Peterson's laboratory has shown that the Gestalt-based figure–ground-first assumption is incorrect, however. Some form of shape/object memory is accessed before, and contributes to, figure assignment.

In this chapter, we begin by showing that the evidence that long served to support the figure-ground-first assumption is really quite weak (Section II). Section III reviews Peterson and her colleague's early work revealing shape and object memory effects on figure assignment. In this early work, observers reported their subjective impression of where the figure lay with respect to the border of interest; in other words, figure–ground perception was assessed via direct report. In Section IV, a number of questions are reopened by the findings of Peterson and her colleagues, questions for which answers generated within the figure-ground-first assumption are no longer valid. We review some research conducted to answer these questions and introduce a new model of figure assignment (Peterson, 2000; Peterson, de Gelder, Rapcsak, Gerhardstein, & Bachoud-Lévi, 2000). In this model, memory of shape/object structure serves as one of an ensemble of figure cues, along with the Gestalt configural cues. This model does not represent a return to the Structuralist tradition where past experience was the only organizing factor, or even the dominant organizing factor. In Section V, we describe some recent experiments testing the competitive model. In these experiments, processes involved in figure assignment are assessed indirectly via a priming paradigm. In Section VI, we review an experiment showing that a single past experience with a novel border exerts a measurable influence on figure assignment the next time the border is encountered. The chapter ends with some remarks on learning, memory, and perception.

II. Phenomena Taken as Evidence for the Figure-Ground-First Assumption

Three lines of argument and evidence have long been taken to support the figure-ground-first assumption, but the support they provide is weak at best.

The first line of evidence is based on demonstrations that the perception of novel shapes can be accounted for by the operation of the Gestalt configural cues. From demonstrations showing that shape *could* be imposed on the visual input using only configural cues (e.g., Figure 1B), the Gestalt psychologists concluded that shape was *always* imposed on the visual input using only configural cues (i.e., the figure-ground-first assumption).

The figure-ground-first assumption does not follow as a logical conclusion from demonstrating that configural cues can account for shape perception when past experience cannot (because the displays are novel). Such demonstrations do not support the conclusion that past experience cannot affect figure assignment when familiar shapes and objects are present (Peterson, 1999). To reach this latter conclusion, one must conduct investigations involving familiar shapes and show that large variations in familiarity do not affect figure assignment when the configural cues are held constant. Neither the Gestalt psychologists nor their descendents conducted stringent tests using this strategy.[2]

Another line of support for the figure-ground-first assumption arose from a neuropsychological investigation conducted by Warrington and Taylor (1973). They presented a visual agnosic patient who, although quite poor at object and shape identification (as visual agnosics are), performed figure-ground assignment correctly. Marr (1982) interpreted the patient's pattern of impaired and spared performance within a serial hierarchical model of vision and took it as evidence that object memories are accessed only after figure assignment has been determined. Marr argued that the patient's lesion must be located higher than the brain region responsible for figure assignment but lower than the brain region where memories of objects are stored.

However, naming responses, such as those recorded by Warrington and Taylor (1973), can only index whether or not conscious recognition and identification have occurred. They do not necessarily reveal whether some form of object memory was accessed in the course of figure assignment (Peterson et al., 2000). To address this latter issue, it is necessary to compare figure assignment for regions that are matched for Gestalt configural cues but mismatched in the degree to which they fit the shapes of known objects. Such tests might reveal that for visual agnosics as well as for normal perceivers, borders may be more likely to be seen as boundaries of regions (or portions of regions) portraying known objects rather than novel objects. (For further discussion and a relevant experiment, see Section IV.)

---

[2] Some tests of this assumption were attempted, but they were neither straighforward nor stringent. The Gestalt point of view was the Zeitgeist; consequently, evidence consistent with the Gestalt view was sought and obtained. See Peterson (1995, 1999).

A third phenomenon of evidence for the figure-ground-first assumption is the well-known coupling between figural status and conscious recognition, illustrated by the Rubin vase-faces display in Figure 1C. The vase can be recognized when the central black region appears to be the figure at the border it shares with the adjacent white region, but not when it appears to be ground to the surrounding white region. Likewise, the faces can be recognized when the surrounding white region appears to be the figure at the vertical borders it shares with the black region, but not when the white region appears to be ground at those borders. This coupling between figural status and recognition led many vision scientists to accept the figure-ground-first assumption. A coupling cannot provide unequivocal evidence for a serial sequence, however.

Surprisingly, until the initial tests conducted in our laboratory were published in 1991 (Peterson & Gibson, 1991; Peterson, Harvey, & Weidenbacher, 1991), there were very few direct tests of whether past experience contributed to figure assignment. A few experiments had suggested that aspects of past experience might affect figure assignment (Schaffer & Murphy, 1943; Rubin, 1958). These results were dismissed based on procedural criticisms, desultory attempts (and failures) to replicate, and alternative interpretations that did not fit the data any better than the original interpretation did (for review, see Peterson, 1995, 1999). The Gestalt arguments against the Structuralist tradition continued to exert a strong hold on perception psychologists who, despite evidence that memory and past experience affected many other visual processes, continued to believe that figure–ground assignment lay far enough below an implicit line dividing perception from memory to be immune to influences from memory.

III. Review of Peterson's Research Revealing Object Memory Effects on Figure Assignment

Peterson and her colleagues directly tested whether memories of well-known shapes were accessed in the course of figure assignment. They began using the displays shown in Figure 2A and B, originally drawn by Julian Hochberg. The displays were biased toward a center-as-figure interpretation by the Gestalt configural cues of smallness of relative area, enclosure, and symmetry (or partial symmetry). The monocular depth cue of interposition also favored the interpretation that the black region lay in front of the white region in Figure 2B. In addition, the observers fixated the center region, which increases the likelihood that a region will be seen as figure (Hochberg, 1971; Peterson & Gibson, 1994a). The vertical borders between the black

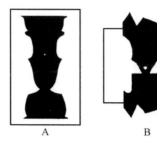

Fig. 2. Displays used by Peterson, Harvey, and Weidenbacher (1991) are biased toward
the interpretation that the black center region is the figure. Portions of known objects
are sketched along the white side of the vertical black–white borders in both stimuli, portions
of standing women in (A) and face profiles in (B). Adapted from Peterson, Harvey, &
Weidenbacher (1991).

and white regions sketched portions of known objects on the white side
(standing women in Figure 2A, and face profiles in Figure 2B). Peterson
et al. (1991) showed these displays to observers who viewed them for long
durations (30–40 seconds) and reported continuously whether the black or
the white region appeared to be figure by pressing one of two keys.

Observers viewed all displays in both an upright orientation, as shown in
Figure 2, and in an inverted orientation (which can be seen by turning the
book upside down). Changing the orientation from upright to inverted did
not change the Gestalt configural cues: the center black region is enclosed,
symmetric, and smaller in area than the surrounding white region both when
the display is upright and when it is inverted. Nor did it change the
monocular depth cue of interposition in Figure 2B, or the fact that observers
fixated the black region on all trials. However, when the display is upright,
the known object sketched on the white side of the black–white border is
portrayed in its typical orientation, whereas when the display is inverted, the
known object is disoriented from its typical upright.

Access to shape and object memories is orientation specific. For instance,
it takes longer for observers to identify objects and pictures of objects that
are disoriented from their typical upright orientation (Jolicœur, 1988; Tarr
& Pinker, 1989). Perrett, Oram, and Ashbridge (1998) have shown that it
takes longer for a population of cells coding an object to reach some
threshold if the object is shown in an atypical orientation. The orientation
specificity of object recognition led Peterson and her colleagues to
hypothesize that changing the orientation of the displays might reveal
object memory effects on figure assignment by modulating them.
Specifically, if object memories affect figure assignment, their influence
should be larger for upright displays than for inverted displays. Therefore,

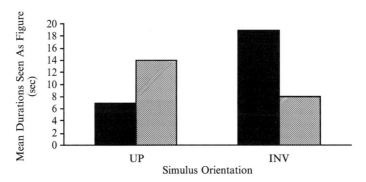

Fig. 3. Mean durations that the two regions of the displays in Figure 2 were maintained as figures in upright versus inverted displays. The black bars denote the center black regions; the striped bars denote the surrounding white regions. Adapted from Peterson, Harvey, & Weidenbacher (1991).

Peterson et al. (1991) reasoned that object memory effects on figure assignment would be implicated if the figures appeared to lie on the white side of the vertical black–white borders in Figure 2A and B more often when the displays were upright than when they were inverted.

Their results, shown in Figure 3, supported this prediction. Observers saw the white surrounds as figures for longer durations in the upright orientation than in the inverted orientation. Taken alone, this finding could simply indicate that regions portraying familiar objects could be *maintained* as figures longer once they had obtained figural status. Importantly, observers saw the black centers as figures for *shorter* durations in the upright orientation than in the inverted orientation. In other words, reversals out of the black center as figure interpretation and into the white surround as figure interpretation were more likely when the displays were upright than when they were inverted. This finding suggested that object memories affected the likelihood that the organization would *reverse into* the surround as figure interpretation, as well as the likelihood that the surround would be maintained as figure once it was perceived as such.

Peterson et al. (1991) found that the order in which upright and inverted displays were presented did not matter. What mattered was that the parts of the well-known object were presented in their proper spatial relationships, both with respect to the upright and also with respect to each other. Peterson et al. also tested conditions in which the parts were rearranged (scrambled) so that the object was no longer recognizable. The effects of object memories on figure assignment were diminished, as they were for inverted stimuli.

Importantly, Peterson et al. (1991) found that knowledge could not overcome the effects of changing the orientation or rearranging the parts. The orientation effects were obtained even if observers knew that the displays portrayed inverted women or inverted face profiles; the same was true for the effects of scrambling the parts. This finding indicated that knowledge of any type could not produce these effects; access to memories of object structure via the visual input was necessary (see also Gibson & Peterson, 1994).

The results obtained by Peterson et al. (1991) indicated that memories of object structure (at least) are accessed in the course of figure assignment and affect its outcome. It was clear in the original experiments that semantic knowledge alone was insufficient for these effects, the proper structure of the object was necessary. Peterson and Gibson (1991, 1994b; Gibson & Peterson, 1994) showed that the Peterson et al. (1991) results extended to masked displays exposed for brief durations (as short as 28 ms).

The initial results showing that object memories affected figure assignment were obtained using displays that were biased against seeing the figure lying on the side of the border where a well-known object was sketched. Later, Peterson and Gibson (1994a; Gibson & Peterson, 1994) tested whether object memories affected figure assignment using displays, such as those in Figure 4A, in which object structure was the only cue that reliably distinguished between the regions on either side of a central border. They found orientation effects for these displays as well: Observers were more likely to report seeing the figure on the side of the border where the well-known object was sketched when the displays were upright rather than inverted. Thus, object memory effects on figure assignment were evident both with displays that should have been unambiguous if only the traditional Gestalt cues were taken to be relevant to figure assignment (e.g., the displays in Figure 2) and with displays that were ambiguous in that configural cues were equated for the two adjacent regions (e.g., displays like those in Figure 4A).

The next question addressed by Peterson and Gibson (1994b) was how the memory of object structure cue fared when it was placed in competition with a single other cue, such as the Gestalt configural cue of symmetry. Consider displays in which a symmetric region shares a vertical border with an asymmetric region. The asymmetric region portrays a known object, whereas symmetric region does not. When viewing inverted versions of such stimuli, where the object memory cue was absent or diminished, observers were significantly more likely to report seeing the symmetric region as figure. When viewing upright stimuli, there was a substantial and significant increase in reports that the figure appeared to lie on the side of the border where a well-known object was sketched compared to inverted stimuli. Importantly, the object memory cue did not dominate the symmetry

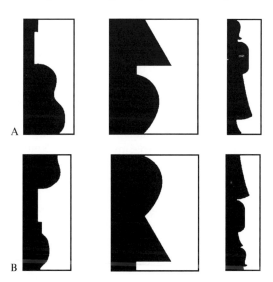

Fig. 4. (A) Sample figure–ground stimuli in which two equal-area regions share a border; a known object was sketched on one side of the central border. These stimuli portray a guitar, a lamp, and a standing woman, respectively. Although the known objects are always shown in black on the left side of the border in this figure, in the displays used in the experiments, they were shown equally often in white and in black and on the left versus the right of the border. (B) "Scrambled" versions of the stimuli in (A). To create the scrambled versions, the objects in (A) were separated into parts at the concave cusps, and those parts were reassembled so that the new arrangement did not portray a known object. Adapted from Gibson & Peterson (1994); Peterson *et al.* (1998).

cue in the upright orientation; instead, the two cues seemed to compete with each other on a roughly equal footing. This finding led Peterson and Gibson (1994b) to suggest that the object memory cue is one of many cues that determines figure assignment; it neither dominates the other relevant cues nor is dominated by them.

In a different series of experiments, Peterson and Gibson (1993) added binocular disparity to displays like those in Figure 4A in which object memory favored seeing the figure on one side of a border, but Gestalt configural cues did not reliably distinguish between the two sides. Binocular disparity indicated that the figure lay either on the same side or on the opposite side of the border as the known object. Peterson and Gibson expected that when both object memory and binocular disparity specified that the figure lay on the same side of the border, the displays would be unambiguous. The stimuli in which object memory and binocular disparity specified that the figure lay on opposite sides of the border were the interesting case. If the addition of binocular disparity rendered the displays unambiguous, then the figure should always appear to lie on the side across the border from the known object. Alternatively, if object memories always overpower binocular disparity, the figure should always appear to lie on the known object side of the border.

Peterson and Gibson (1993) found that object memories did affect figure assignment in these critical displays, but they did not dominate the binocular disparity cue. Instead, for the range of disparities Peterson and Gibson tested, the object memory cue appeared to compete with binocular disparity on a roughly equal footing, as it had with symmetry (see also Peterson, 2003b). The figure was seen to lie on the side of the border where the well-known object was sketched approximately half the time, and on the opposite side, favored as figure by binocular disparity, the rest of the time.

The results of these experiments, showing that object memories affect figure assignment in both two-dimensional and three-dimensional displays, challenged the figure–ground-first assumption. They also raised anew a number of questions, for which answers based on the figure-ground-first assumption were now inadequate. We address those questions in the next section.

IV.   Questions Raised by Evidence Challenging the Figure–Ground First Assumption

A first set of questions is the following. How can object memories be accessed before figure–ground organization has been imposed on the visual field; that is, before shaped figures have been separated from shapeless grounds? What serves as the substrate for access to object memories? Must we return to the Structuralist claim that past experience can be accessed by completely unorganized pointillistic input?

In response to these questions, Peterson and Gibson (1993, 1994b) proposed that at least the initial stages of edge extraction precede access to object memories and that edges, rather than shaped entities or even whole regions, were the substrate for matches to shape and object memories. They argued that edge-based access to memories of object structure could occur at the same time that the Gestalt configural cues are being assessed. This would allow memories of object structure to serve as one more figural cue (i.e., to add to the traditional ensemble of Gestalt configural cues).

Further, Peterson and Gibson (1993) argued that not all edges could support object memory effects on figure assignment. One critical requirement is that edges must be extracted early in processing; only such edges can support quick access to object memories. Evidence that object memories must be accessed quickly if they are to affect figure assignment comes from the orientation effects. Inverted stimuli do access memories of familiar objects; they just take longer than upright stimuli to do so. The additional time required is sufficient to render object memory effects on figure assignment less likely for inverted displays than for upright displays. This is because figure assignment occurs early in the course of visual processing. Therefore, any factor that delays access to object memories can remove or diminish their effects on figure assignment. If edge extraction takes too long, edge-based access to object memories will not occur quickly enough to affect figure assignment. Consistent with this argument, Peterson and Gibson (1993) failed to observe effects of object memories on figure assignment using random-dot stereograms, where edge extraction takes some time.

Peterson (1995, 2003a; Peterson & Hector, 1996) proposed further that object memories could be accessed by portions of edges, rather than by whole continuous edges or borders.[3] Thus, like the Gestalt psychologists, Peterson and her colleagues assume that *some* organization is imposed on the visual input before object memories are accessed; thus, they do not support a return to Structuralism. However, Peterson and her colleagues clearly assume that a lot less organization has been imposed before object memories are accessed than did the Gestalt psychologists and their followers.

A second set of questions that was raised by Peterson and colleague's challenge to the figure–ground-first assumption concerns the behavior of visual agnosic patients, such as the one tested by Warrington and Taylor (1973). If tested with displays designed to reveal object memory effects on figure assignment, will visual agnosics behave like normal observers or will they fail to show effects of object memories on figure assignment? If a visual agnosic cannot identify the objects portrayed in figure–ground displays, yet shows spared object memory effects on figure assignment, that would suggest that impaired identification responses cannot be taken to support a serial view of the relationship between figure–ground assignment and access to memories of object structure.

To address these questions, Peterson et al. (2000) tested a visual agnosic patient, A.D. They assessed A.D.'s object recognition/identification abilities via a battery of standard tests, including the Boston Naming Test, the impossible objects subtest of the Birmingham Object Recognition Battery (the BORB, Riddoch & Humphreys, 1993), and the Visual Object and Spatial Perception Battery (VOSP, Warrington & James, 1991). These tests require either a naming response or a decision regarding whether a depicted object is a familiar object or a novel (or impossible) object. The VOSP

---

[3] Hence, there is no need to distinguish between contours that are intrinsic versus extrinsic to the object before object memories are accessed (see Peterson, 2003a). This is important because the figure–ground-first assumption has been used to separate such contours.

subtest uses silhouettes of objects, which were particularly relevant to our displays. A.D. performed considerably below age-matched control observers on all of these tests. This type of performance is typical for visual agnosics, so performance on these tests partially confirmed that A.D. was a visual agnosic and did not simply have name-finding problems.

Other tests indicated that A.D.'s semantic knowledge regarding those objects she could not identify was intact. She could define objects and give a reasonable description of what they looked like. However, it seemed that this knowledge regarding objects could not be accessed by visual inputs, at least as indexed by naming responses or by overt judgments regarding the familiarity/possibility of objects. Again, this is a typical pattern of performance for visual agnosics.

Peterson et al. (2000) also assessed A.D.'s ability to use the Gestalt configural cues of convexity and symmetry to perceive figure–ground relationships in novel displays. A.D. performed well within normal limits on these tasks. Thus, A.D.'s performance on these initial identification tests and figure–ground tests was similar to that shown by the patient reported by Warrington and Taylor (1973).

Next, Peterson et al. (2000) performed the critical test of whether object memories could affect figure assignment even in a visual agnosic. They asked A.D. to report which region was the figure (i.e., which region appeared to stand out as having a definite shape at the central border) in 48 displays like those shown in Figure 4. These displays were constructed from two equal-area regions separated by a central articulated border. Half of these displays were "experimental" displays in that a portion of a familiar object was sketched along one side of the central border separating black and white regions (the displays in Figure 4A). The critical side on which the familiar object was sketched was the left for half of the experimental displays and the right for the other half; the critical region was black in half the displays and white in the other half of the displays. The rest of the displays were "control" displays in which the central border did not sketch a known object on either side. The control displays had critical regions that were formed by rearranging (scrambling) the parts of the familiar objects portrayed by the critical regions in the experimental displays such that they were no longer recognizable (the displays in Figure 4B). Thus, the critical sides of the control and experimental stimuli were matched in part structure, but not in spatial structure. Therefore, they were not matched in the degree to which they provided a good fit to memories of object structure. None of the Gestalt configural cues consistently favored seeing one of the two halves as figure in the experimental displays compared to the control displays.

Peterson et al. (2000) reasoned that if object memories affect figure assignment even in the absence of conscious recognition and identification then, like non-brain-damaged participants, A.D. should report seeing the figure lying on the critical side of the central border more often in experimental displays than in control displays. Their results supported this prediction: Like non-brain-damaged age-matched controls, A.D. reported seeing the figure lying on the critical side of the central border significantly more often in experimental stimuli (75%) than in control stimuli (46%). As expected of a visual agnosic, A.D. was not able to identify the objects portrayed by the critical regions of the experimental displays, even though she clearly saw them as figure. Her performance deviated from that of the age-matched controls in this respect.

Thus, conscious identification is not necessary for object memories to affect figure assignment. The data obtained from A.D. show that it is erroneous to conclude that figure assignment precedes access to object memories based on a pattern of intact figure assignment and impaired identification. Instead, A.D.'s performance is consistent with the proposal that quick, unconscious access to memories of object structure can occur and can contribute to figure assignment even when conscious recognition and identification are impaired.

A third set of questions raised by the claim that object memories affect figure assignment is the following: If object memories are accessed in the course of figure assignment, how can one account for the fact that regions that would portray familiar objects were they to be seen as figures appear shapeless when they are perceived to be grounds? Recall that Peterson et al. (1991; Peterson & Gibson, 1993, 1994b) showed that when other configural and depth cues compete with object memories, the figure does not always appear to lie on the side of the border where the known object is sketched. In such cases, if object memories matching the ground region were accessed in the course of figure assignment, why don't we recognize the familiar object sketched on the ground side of the border? More specifically, why do we generally not perceive both the vase and the faces in the Rubin vase-faces display? Why do we typically perceive only one of these shaped entities at a time? On the traditional figure–ground-first view, grounds were shapeless because they were not matched to object memories.[4] The Parallel Interactive Model of Configural Analysis, introduced by Peterson and her colleagues (Peterson, 2000; Peterson et al., 2000), provides an explanation for the perceived shapelessness of grounds while assuming that memories of object structure are accessed in the course of figure assignment.

---

[4] The traditional view can account for why familiar shapes can't be seen in grounds. However, it never went far enough to account for why even novel grounds appear locally shapeless.

The Parallel Interactive Model of Configural Analysis (PIMOCA) is illustrated in Figure 5. PIMOCA assumes that as soon as edges are detected in the visual field, portions of those edges are assessed for configural cues *on both sides simultaneously*. In PIMOCA, memories of object structure are considered to be configural cues because previous experiments in our laboratory have shown that the parts of the familiar object must be correctly configured in order for the object memory cue to be effective (Gibson & Peterson, 1994; Peterson, 2003a; Peterson, Gerhardstein, Mennemeier, & Rapcsak, 1998; Peterson et al., 1991, 2000). Given that configuration matters, it seems appropriate to include object memories among the configural cues.

According to PIMOCA, configural cues present on the same side of an edge cooperate with each other, whereas configural cues present on opposite sides of an edge compete with each other. When the cues are unbalanced, the cues on the more weakly cued side are inhibited by the cues on the more strongly cued side.[5] The inhibition of configural cues on the more weakly cued side of a border accounts for the perceived local shapelessness of the region lying across the border from a more strongly cued side. Peterson (2003b; Peterson et al., 2000) argued that in two-dimensional displays, such as those used in our experiments, one perceives shape by perceiving properties such as symmetry, convexity, area, enclosure, familiar object structure, etc. If those cues are inhibited on the relatively weakly cued side of an edge, shape simply cannot be seen in that local vicinity (provided that configural cues are the only cues present). The cross-border inhibition proposed in PIMOCA accounts for the fact that regions adjacent to strongly cued figures are perceived to be locally shapeless, both under conditions where a portion of a known object is sketched on the more weakly cued side of the border, and under conditions where the more weakly cued side is convex or symmetric.

On the more strongly cued side, continued cooperation among cues leads ultimately to the perception of shape, and interactions between the configural cues and semantic and functional knowledge lead ultimately to recognition, if the shape is familiar (barring brain damage).

In Figure 5 boxes of the same size portray all of the configural cues. By representing the cues in this fashion, we do not mean to imply that all of the configural cues are equally potent. We know that is not the case. Kanizsa and Gerbino (1976) showed that convexity is more potent than symmetry, for example. Likewise, the configural cues all appear to lie on one plane in

---

[5] In any competitive system, cues will inevitably be unbalanced. In PIMOCA, any slight advantage for the cues on one side of the edge will be amplified by the cooperative and competitive interactions.

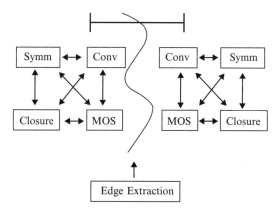

Fig. 5.   The Parallel Interactive Model of Figure Assignment proposed by Peterson et al. (2000). Shortly after edges are detected (e.g., the curvilinear edge in the center of the figure), figural features such as Symmetry (Symm), Convexity (Conv), Memory of Object Structure (MOS), and Closure are assessed for both sides. Features on the same side of the edge cooperate (as indicated by double-headed arrows). Features on opposite sides of the edge compete (as indicated by the horizontal end-stopped line crossing the edge). From Peterson *et al.* (2000).

Figure 5. By presenting all of the configural cues in this way, we do not mean to imply that they are all computed at the same level of processing. Indeed, there is some suggestion that these cues may be assessed at different levels. For instance, cells that respond differentially to convex and concave shapes have been found in V3 (Pasupathy & Connor, 1999). And, based on work by Tanaka (1996), Peterson (2003) has hypothesized that the relevant object memories may be found in the human analogue of V4. The figure is designed to imply that the configural cues (including the memory of object structure cue) are accessed in parallel, and that configural cues accessed on the same side of a border cooperate with each other, whereas those accessed on opposite sides compete with each other.

In PIMOCA, figure and ground assignment is a local outcome of a cross-border competition. It is not a stage of processing through which visual inputs must pass before object memories can be accessed (Peterson, 2002). Nor must figure and ground necessarily be assigned consistently to the same side across a continuous border; figures can be assigned to different sides along different extents of a continuous border (Hochberg, 1962; Peterson, 1995, 2003a; Peterson & Hector, 1996). There is evidence that figure and ground assignment is affected by the global context in which a border is found (Kim & Peterson, 2001, 2002; Peterson & Kim, 2001b). We are currently working on integrating context effects into the model.

PIMOCA is one of a class of competitive models of figure assignment (see also Keinker, Sejnowski, Hinton, & Schumacher, 1986; Sejnowski & Hinton, 1987; Vecera & O'Reilly, 1998). PIMOCA is unique in

- Assuming that memories of partial object structure are accessed via edges rather than via regions or shapes. (Sejnowski and colleagues did not consider a role for object memories, and Vecera and O'Reilly proposed a holistic, region-wide match to object memories.)
- Assuming that memories of partial object structure are accessed in parallel with assessments of the Gestalt configural cues.
- Treating figure–ground segregation as simply an outcome of the cross-border competitive process rather than as a stage of processing.
- Accounting for the perceived shapelessness of grounds via cross-border competition.

V. Tests of the Parallel Interactive Model of Configural Analysis

Peterson and Kim (2001a) tested PIMOCA's predictions regarding the inhibition of cues on the relatively weakly cued side of a border. To do so, they isolated the memory of object structure cue on the white side of a black–white border where the majority of cues favored assigning figural status to the opposite, black side. Those cues included the configural cues of symmetry, convexity, enclosure, and smallness of relative area, along with other cues such as fixation and expectation. Peterson and Kim's (2001a) stimuli were black silhouettes like those shown in Figure 6. Because more configural cues favored assigning figural status to the black side of the border and because previous evidence indicated that the memory of object structure cue did not dominate the other configural cues, Peterson and Kim (2001a) expected that the figure would appear to lie on the black side of the border. They predicted that the object structure memory accessed on the white side of the border would be inhibited.

All of the black silhouettes were novel shapes. Silhouettes like those in Figure 6A to C were shown on 75% of the trials; these were control silhouettes. Silhouettes like Figure 6D, where a portion of a familiar object was sketched on the white side of the border, were shown on 25% of the trials; these were experimental silhouettes (see below). The silhouettes were exposed briefly, for 50 ms.

Observers saw the bounded black regions as the shaped entities; they saw the white regions as shapeless grounds, even for the experimental silhouettes. The stimuli were designed to be seen this way, because (1) a larger number of configural cues favored seeing the figure on the black side

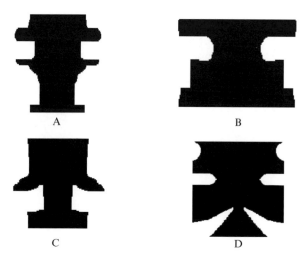

Fig. 6. Sample black silhouettes used as primes by Peterson and Kim (2001a). All silhouettes were novel. The figure was seen on the black side of the black–white border because a larger number of cues favored assigning the figure to that side than to the other side (e.g., symmetry, enclosure, smallness of area). (A–C) Control primes; the borders of control primes did not sketch a known object on either the inside or the outside of the silhouette. (D) Experimental prime. In all experimental primes, the vertical borders sketched a portion of a known object along the outside (the white, ground, side). A portion of an anchor is sketched on the white side of the black silhouette in (D). Hence, for experimental primes the memory of object structure cue is present on the white side of the black–white border.

of the border rather than on the white side, (2) the experimental stimuli were embedded among many control stimuli in which there was no familiar object sketched on either side of the black–white border, and (3) the silhouettes appeared on the point where the participants were fixating.

Observers made no response to the silhouettes; they were asked to simply look at them. Their task was to judge quickly whether a line drawing shown after each silhouette portrayed a familiar object or a novel object. The silhouettes served as primes before the line drawings. The critical trials were those involving familiar line drawings. As shown in Figure 7, half of the line drawings of familiar objects were preceded by experimental silhouette primes in which a portion of the same basic level object was sketched on the white (ground) side of the black silhouette. These were the experimental trials. The other half of the line drawings of familiar objects was preceded by control silhouette primes with no familiar object sketched on the ground side (control trials). Control silhouettes preceded all line drawings of novel objects. The experimental and control silhouettes were matched for size, area, convexity, and curvilinearity so that observers could

Control   Experimental

Fig. 7. Examples of prime and line drawing matches for familiar line drawings. Line drawings shown on experimental trials were preceded by silhouette primes in which an object from the same basic level category was sketched on the ground side. A sample experimental trial is shown in the right panel. Line drawings shown on control trials were preceded by silhouette primes that sketched novel shapes on both sides of the black–white border. A sample control trial is shown in the left panel.

not distinguish between them.[6] A different unique silhouette was shown on each trial.

The dependent measure was participants' latency to correctly categorize the line drawings as familiar or novel objects. We were primarily interested in participants' responses to the familiar line drawings. If the inhibition proposed in PIMOCA occurs, then object memories accessed for the white side of the experimental silhouette primes should be inhibited. This is because, according to PIMOCA, when the cues for seeing the figure lying on one side of the border are stronger than the cues for seeing the figure lying on the other side (as they are in the silhouette primes), configural cues (including memories of object structure) accessed on the more weakly cued side are inhibited. Peterson and Kim (2001a) hypothesized that evidence of this inhibition would be revealed if response times (RTs) to correctly categorize familiar line drawings were longer following experimental primes rather than control primes. This prediction supposes that the line drawing following the experimental prime must access some of the same memories of object structure as the object sketched on the more weakly cued side of the border of the prime because it is drawn from the same basic-level category. If those memories are inhibited because of the cross-contour competition

[6] Even if observers had been able to distinguish between experimental and control silhouettes, they could not have predicted the response to the subsequent line drawing, since control silhouettes appeared before half the line drawings of familiar objects.

occurring during the perception of the prime, then responses to the line drawings shown on experimental trials should be slowed, provided that the inhibition lasts long enough to be probed by the line drawing. (No familiar object was sketched along any portion of the border of the control primes; hence, no inhibition of specific object memories was expected.)

It is important to point out that although the familiar line drawings shown on experimental trials portrayed an object from the same basic level category as the portion of a known object sketched on the ground side of the silhouette, the contours of the line drawing were not the same as the contours of the silhouette. We made the contours different because we wanted to be sure that any RT differences we observed reflected access to previously established memories of known objects in the course of figure assignment and not simply memory for the specific shape of the border of the silhouette (see Section VI). Indeed, it could be argued that the participants had not seen the particular borders of the silhouettes before, although they had certainly seen similar borders bounding objects from the same basic level category (or at least portrayals of such objects). We designed these experiments to assess whether previously established memories of known objects were accessed in the course of figure assignment and were inhibited if they were accessed on the more weakly cued side of a border.

The novel line drawings were included just so the participants had to categorize the line drawing targets. Although the borders of the control silhouettes shown before the novel line drawings sketched novel objects on both the figure side and the ground side, no attempt was made to match the shapes of the novel silhouettes to the shapes of the novel objects. Hence, responses to the novel line drawings will not be discussed further, except to say that observers took longer to correctly categorize the novel line drawings than the familiar line drawings.

Peterson and Kim (2001a) reported two experiments. In Experiment 1, the silhouette primes were exposed for 50 ms and the line drawings were displayed following an interstimulus interval of 33 ms. In Experiment 2, the silhouette primes were exposed for 50 ms and the line drawings were shown immediately afterward. In both experiments, the line drawings remained on until a response was made. As can be seen in Figure 8A, the results supported the predictions generated from PIMOCA. In both experiments, observers took significantly longer to correctly categorize the familiar line drawings on experimental trials than on control trials.[7]

---

[7] Only observers who responded quickly showed these effects. Results obtained from observers whose RTs on control trials exceeded a threshold set by the experimenters were excluded from the analysis. (For details, see Peterson & Kim, 2001a.)

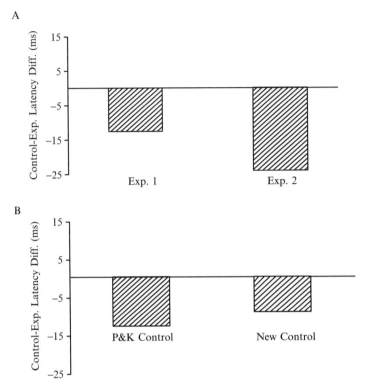

Fig. 8. Latency differences between accurate responses to line drawings of familiar objects shown on control and experimental trials obtained by Peterson and Kim (2001a) (A) and Peterson et al. (2003) (B). In (B) the results obtained replicating Peterson and Kim's experiment under masking conditions (i.e., no known object was sketched on the ground side of the control primes) are shown on the left. The results obtained using the new control condition are shown the right. Negative difference scores indicate that RTs were longer for experimental trials than for control trials. (A) From Peterson & Kim (2001a).

Peterson and Kim's (2001a) results provide indirect evidence that object memories are accessed in the course of figure assignment. Until these experiments were conducted, the evidence supporting the proposal that object memories were accessed in the course of figure assignment was based on participants' direct reports regarding their phenomenological experience. Some investigators had wondered whether our observers were indeed reporting the first figure–ground organization they perceived, as we had assumed. Driver and Baylis (1995) suggested that our observers might have been responding to some implicit demand to try to find familiar objects in the figure–ground displays. If so, they might have reversed the first figure–ground organization of the displays in search of familiar objects, and may have reported them when they found them. In the latter case, our direct report evidence could not be taken as inconsistent with the figure–ground first assumption. That Peterson and Kim (2001a) obtained evidence for the inhibition of object memories matched by the more weakly cued side of a border even though the experimental task did not direct participants to make figure reports regarding the silhouettes provides converging evidence that, contrary to the figure–ground-first assumption, memories of object structure are accessed in the course of figure assignment.

Before the Peterson and Kim (2001a) results could be taken to reflect the cross-border inhibition as predicted by PIMOCA, a few questions remained to be addressed. One question stems from the fact that a known object was sketched on the white side of the silhouette primes shown on experimental trials, but not those shown on control trials. As a consequence, more cross-border competition occurred for experimental than control silhouettes. This increased competition may have led to longer resolution times for experimental silhouettes than for control silhouettes. The differences in RTs may reflect differences in the time required to resolve the figural status of the silhouette primes rather than differences in the state of the object memory matching the line drawing itself.

Peterson, Skow-Grant, and Kim (2003; Skow-Grant, Peterson, & Kim, 2002) tested this alternative *resolution time hypothesis* against the *inhibition hypothesis* by altering Peterson and Kim's (2001a) design such that known objects were sketched on the white sides of both experimental and control silhouettes shown before familiar line drawings. Whereas the known objects sketched on the white side of the silhouettes shown on experimental trials were from the same basic level category as their paired line drawings, the known objects sketched on the white side of the silhouettes shown on control trials were from a different category (e.g., living versus nonliving) than their paired line drawings. Thus, in this experiment, the competition for figure assignment was equated for all silhouettes preceding line drawings of familiar objects. The time required to resolve the figure assignment in the silhouettes should be equated as well. (As in Peterson and Kim's experiment, no familiar objects were sketched along the borders of the silhouettes shown before line drawings of novel objects.)

Peterson et al. (2003) reasoned that if the slower responses to experimental line drawings than to control line drawings reported by Peterson and Kim (2001a) reflected longer resolution times for the silhouettes shown on experimental versus control trials, then that pattern of results should not be obtained in their experiment. Indeed, there should be no differences in the latencies to respond to familiar line drawings shown on experimental versus control trials. However, if the slowed responses to Peterson and Kim's

(2001a) experimental line drawings reflected the inhibitory component of PIMOCA (and if inhibition is specific to the category of the known object sketched in ground), then responses to line drawings shown on experimental trials should be slower than responses to line drawings shown on control trials.

In the experiment designed to examine the resolution time hypothesis, silhouettes were displayed for 35 ms and were followed by a 70-ms mask (to ensure that participants could not use the silhouette to predict the line drawing type). Because they added a mask to the sequence of stimuli preceding the line drawings, Peterson et al. (2003) tested two groups of observers. One group was tested with a control condition like that used by Peterson and Kim (2001a) (i.e., for these participants the contours of the control silhouettes did not sketch a familiar object on the ground side). A second group was tested with the new control condition (in which the contours of the control primes sketched an object from a different category than the line drawing shown afterward). Including both of these conditions allowed Peterson et al. to compare the magnitude of the difference scores obtained with the different types of control primes under similar presentation conditions.

The results were consistent with the inhibition hypothesis rather than with the resolution time hypothesis. As can be seen in Figure 8B, RTs on experimental trials were longer than RTs on control trials for both groups of observers, even though the competition for the borders of experimental and control silhouettes was equated for the observers in the new control condition, whereas it was not equated for observers in Peterson and Kim's (2001a) control condition. The differences between the results obtained using the two different control conditions were not statistically significant. It appears that any differences in the competition occurring for experimental versus control primes is not evident in responses to the line drawings used in these experiments.

An alternative interpretation arising from an attentional framework remained to be considered before these results could be taken as supporting the PIMOCA model, however. Suppose that the longer RTs obtained on experimental trials compared to control trials reflect the fact that participants *ignored* the silhouette primes. After all, the silhouette primes were irrelevant to the participants' task, which concerned the line drawings. Milliken, Joordens, Merikle, and Seiffert (1998) showed that when observers ignored primes shown immediately before target stimuli, they responded more slowly to matched than to mismatched target stimuli. On this alternative *attention hypothesis*, the withdrawal of attention from the silhouette primes accounts for the RT differences, rather than the fact that the side of the border where the known object was sketched was seen as the ground. In other words, the slowed responses to the line drawings may not have reflected the fact that the memory of object structure cue was accessed on the more weakly cued side of a border. They may simply have reflected the fact that the prime was ignored.

To test the attention hypothesis, we altered the silhouette primes so that the regions seen as grounds in the silhouettes used by Peterson and Kim (2001a) and Peterson, et al. (2003) would now be seen as figures. We report this experiment here. If the attention hypothesis is correct, the RTs should be slower on experimental trials than on control trials even when memories of object structure matching the experimental line drawings were accessed by regions determined to be figures rather than grounds in the prime. Alternatively if the previous results reflect the ground status of the side of the contour where the known object was sketched, they will not be replicated here. Indeed, a prediction generated from numerous priming experiments conducted by others (e.g., Dell'Acqua & Grainger, 1999) is that RTs will be faster when line drawings are preceded by figures portraying an object from the same category.

We created new figure silhouette primes from the silhouette primes used in the previous experiments (henceforth called "figure" primes and "ground" primes, respectively). Sample figure primes are shown in Figure 9 along with the ground primes from which they were generated. Figure primes were matched to ground primes on a number of dimensions that could influence the results. For instance, the contour sketching the known object was presented in approximately the same location in the figure primes as it had been in the ground primes. This was important in case differences between the locations of

Fig. 9. Sample figure primes are shown on the bottom and the "ground primes" from which they were generated are shown above them. The known object depicted is a face profile on the left and an anchor on the right. The figure primes were created to match the ground primes on several dimensions including location and portion of known object visible. The gray boxes were intended to portray surfaces that might be occluding the rest of the known object.

the known objects sketched in the prime versus the line drawing affected the magnitude of the priming. In addition, we took care to portray the same portion of the known object in the figure prime as was portrayed in its associated ground prime. This was important because if the new "figure" primes portrayed the *entire* object whereas the old "ground" primes portrayed only a *portion* of the known object in the ground, then any differences in the results might reflect those differences in the amount of the object portrayed rather than the change from ground to figure status of the prime. To portray a portion of a known object effectively as a figure prime without introducing any spurious edges that could interfere with recognition (Gerbino & Salamaso, 1987), we added gray boxes to the figure primes positioned in such a way that they would appear to be occluding the rest of the known object.

In these experiments, half of the figure primes portrayed portions of known objects; the other half portrayed portions of novel objects. We did not mask the primes in these experiments, so we expected that observers might see the differences between the figure primes portraying known objects versus novel objects. Therefore, we designed this experiment so that line drawings of both familiar and novel objects were preceded equally often by primes portraying familiar and novel figures.

As in the previous experiments, our predictions concern responses to the familiar line drawings. The familiar line drawings were divided into experimental and control sets based on whether they were preceded by figure primes portraying known objects from the same basic level category as the line drawing or figure primes portraying novel objects, respectively.[8] If the delayed responding found on experimental versus control trials in the previous experiments was a consequence of inhibition induced by ignoring the primes, then we should obtain the same pattern of results using figure primes rather than ground primes. This is because, as in Peterson and Kim's (2001a) experiments, on experimental trials, the object portrayed in the figure prime matches the basic level category of the object portrayed in the line drawing whereas there is no match on control trials. However, if the previous results reflect the inhibition of the memory of object structure cue accessed on the side of the prime seen as the ground, we should not observe longer RTs on experimental trials than on control trials in experiments using figure primes. Instead responses might now be faster on experimental trials compared to control trials.

---

[8] For this experiment, the familiar objects were divided into three sets so that none of the control line drawings portrayed an object from the same basic level category as any of the figure primes. In any given experiment, two sets were shown as line drawings, one as control and one as experimental. The experimental line drawings were preceded by silhouette primes portraying an object from the same basic level category. The third set of objects was shown as figure silhouettes before novel line drawings. These three sets were balanced across these conditions.

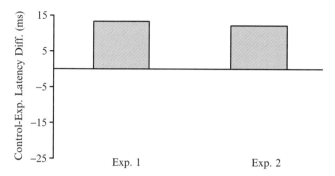

Fig. 10. Latency differences between accurate responses to line drawings of familiar objects shown on control and experimental trials we obtained in experiments using figure primes. Positive difference scores indicate that the RTs were shorter on experimental trials than on control trials.

We conducted two experiments using figure primes, using slightly different exposure durations. In the first experiment, the figure prime was displayed for 50 ms and was followed by an interstimulus interval (ISI) of 33 ms. In the second experiment, the figure prime was displayed for 35 ms, followed by an ISI of 35 ms.[9] In both experiments, the line drawing was shown after the ISI; it remained on the screen for 646 ms in the first experiment and for 660 ms in the second experiment.

As can be seen in Figure 10, our results provide no support for the attention hypothesis. An ANOVA conducted on the RTs for correct responses to familiar line drawings showed that in contrast to the results reported by Peterson and Kim (2001a), responses on experimental trials were *faster* than responses on control trials, $F(1, 27) = 4.36, p < .05$ for the first experiment, and $F(1, 33) = 4.00, p = .054$ for the second experiment. Thus, on experimental trials, when the figure prime portrayed an object from the same basic level category, responses to the target line drawings were faster than on control trials where the prime was a novel figure. The silhouette primes were equally irrelevant in these experiments as they were in Peterson and Kim's (2001a) experiments; yet here RTs were faster on experimental trials than on control trials. Therefore, it does not appear to be the case that the irrelevance of silhouette primes is responsible for the slower RTs recorded on experimental trials versus control trials by Peterson and Kim (2001a) and by Peterson et al. (2003). The critical difference between the present experiments and the previous experiments appear to be that the matching known objects were sketched on the figure side of the border of the

---

[9] The difference in the length of time for the interstimulus interval (ISI) was due to computer monitor replacement between the experiments.

prime in the present experiments and on the ground side of the border of the prime in the previous experiments.

Based upon the results of the experiments we have summarized here, including the new experiment utilizing figure primes, we are confident that the slower RTs obtained on experimental trials by Peterson and Kim (2001a) and by Peterson et al. (2003) reflect the cross-border competition and inhibition proposed in PIMOCA. Thus, these experiments provide support for PIMOCA; especially for the proposals that configural cues (including memory of object structure) lying on opposite sides of a border compete and that cues on the relatively weakly cued side of the border are inhibited. Therefore, it is conceivable that cross-border inhibition accounts for the apparent shapelessness of ground regions in the vicinity of more strongly cued figures.

VI. Learning: How Much Past Experience Is Necessary before Memory for the Structure of an Object Can Affect Figure Assignment?

In our initial work investigating whether object memories affected figure assignment, we used stimuli in which well-known objects were sketched along one side of a border (e.g., objects such as standing women, table lamps, or guitars). On the basis of those experiments, we knew that memories of objects could be accessed in the course of figure assignment, but we did not know how much past experience was required with an object before memory of its structure could affect figure assignment.

We avoided the learning question in part because other research using initially novel displays had failed to find any influence from past experience on figure assignment following a single past exposure to the novel object (e.g., Rock & Kremen, 1957). In those previous experiments, investigators had tested for effects of past experience on figure assignment some time after the experience was induced. Therefore, the results confounded questions concerning how long memories of novel objects last with questions concerning whether past experience affects figure assignment. In addition, Rock and Kremen (1957) measured direct reports about figure and ground relations; they did not record RTs, which might have permitted them to assess whether memories of newly learned objects compete for figural status with other cues, even if they do not dominate them.

Recently, Peterson and Lampignano (2003) found that a single prior exposure to a novel shape was sufficient to observe its influence on figure assignment the next time a portion of the border of the shape was encountered. They obtained these results using a paradigm initially used by Treisman and DeSchepper (1996, Experiment 6). Treisman and DeSchepper had adapted a negative priming paradigm for use with novel displays. Using this paradigm, they obtained some results that they took to be evidence that even though the ground of a novel figure–ground display was phenomenologically shapeless, its shape was nevertheless stored in visual memory along with an "ignore" tag. Peterson and Lampignano thought that Treisman and DeSchepper's results could be better interpreted within PIMOCA than within a negative priming framework. In particular, Peterson and Lampignano thought that Treisman and DeSchepper's results might show that a single prior experience with a novel figure was sufficient to establish a memory that affected figure assignment the next time the border was encountered. We describe Treisman and DeSchepper's paradigm in some detail so that Peterson and Lampignano's variant of it, and the alternative conclusion they reached, can be understood.

Treisman and DeSchepper (1996, Experiment 6) showed observers paired prime-probe trials. On the first, "prime," trial, an ambiguous figure–ground display was shown on a gray field above a fixation cross (see Figure 11A). The ambiguous display had a central articulated border shared by a black region and a white region. Observers were instructed to match the (standard) black region in the figure–ground display shown above fixation to a black comparison shape shown below fixation. They assumed that in order to perform the shape-matching task, observers perceived the black region as the shaped figure and the white region as the shapeless ground in the prime figure–ground display.

On the next "probe" trial, two separated shapes, one black and one white, appeared above fixation, and a second white comparison shape appeared below fixation (see Figure 11B). The left–right arrangement of the black and white shapes above fixation was the same as that of the black and white regions in the prime figure–ground display. On the probe trials, however, the two shapes above fixation did not share any borders. The observers' task on probe trials was to determine whether the standard white shape shown above fixation was the same as the comparison white shape shown below fixation. (The black shape shown on the probe trials was a distractor with a novel border.) On experimental probe trials, the standard white shape was the white region isolated from the prime figure–ground displays (the region that was perceived as a shapeless ground on the prime trial).[10] On control probe trials, the standard (and comparison) white shapes had novel borders that had not been seen previously.

In Treisman and DeSchepper's experiment (1996; Experiment 6), observers took longer to respond on experimental probe trials than on

---

[10] On same experimental probe trials, the white region isolated from the prime figure–ground display was shown both above and below fixation.

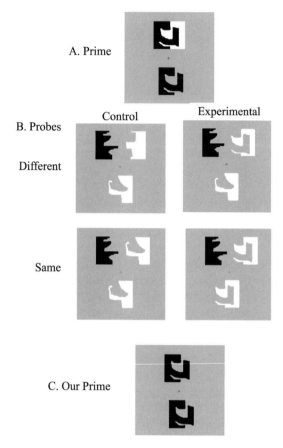

Fig. 11. (A) The prime display used by Treisman and DeSchepper (1996, Experiment 6). (B) Sample probe displays. Half of the probe trials were experimental trials; the other half were control trials. On experimental probe trials, the white "standard" probe shape shown above fixation was the same as the bounded white ground region of the prime figure–ground display. On control probe trials, the standard white shapes were novel shapes. On half of the probe trials of both types, the white shapes shown above and below fixation were the same; on the other half of the trials, they were different. In the experiment, a given distractor was seen only once and a given white shape was seen on only one probe trial. The shapes are repeated here for illustrative purposes only. (C) The prime display used by Peterson and Lampignano (2003).

control probe trials. These results led them to conclude that before figure and ground are determined, equivalent memories are established for the whole shapes of the figure and the ground, regardless of the fact that these regions are perceived quite differently (i.e., the figure is perceived to be shaped by the central border whereas the ground is perceived to be shapeless in the vicinity of that border). Treisman and DeSchepper explained the fact

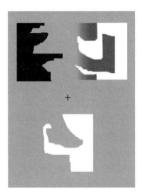

Fig. 12. A sample prime on the left and an experimental probe on the right. The probe has been altered to highlight the fact that a portion of the shape of the black prime figure is sketched along the gray side of the border of the white standard probe shown on experimental trials.

that they obtained longer latency responses on experimental compared to control probe trials as reflecting an "ignore" tag attached to the memory of the shape of the ground.

Peterson and Lampignano (2003) pointed out that in reaching this conclusion, Treisman and DeSchepper (1996) neglected to consider a critical aspect of their displays. As can be seen in Figure 12, when the shape of the region seen as ground was extracted from the prime display and repeated on the probe display, the shape of the region seen as the figure in the prime was necessarily sketched along the outside of its articulated border. Therefore, any slowing on experimental trials compared to control trials may just as well have reflected competition from a memory of a portion of the figure seen on the prime trial as an ignore tag attached to the shape of the ground. Peterson and Lampignano favored the former interpretation because it is consistent with a competitive model of how figure assignment occurs, such as PIMOCA, and because of its exciting implications that one previous experience with an object was sufficient to establish a memory that could exert an influence on figure assignment. They did not favor the latter interpretation (Treisman and DeSchepper's interpretation), both because it did not take the process of figure–ground segregation into account, and because it implied an inconceivably large capacity for shape memory. To distinguish these two interpretations for the original results Peterson and Lampignano (2003) changed Treisman and DeSchepper's (1996) design in two ways.

First, they decreased the similarity between what Treisman and DeSchepper would consider the global shape of the ground on the prime trial and the white standard shape shown on the probe trial. They did this by removing the white region from the prime figure–ground display and by presenting the black region alone on the larger gray ground in the standard prime display (see Figure 11C). Their probe displays were the same as those used by Treisman and DeSchepper (1996, Experiment 6). In the probe display, the standard was a closed white shape. Except for the repetition of the articulated border of the prime, the shape of the standard probe was quite different from the ground in the prime display.

Priming effects are larger when the shapes of prime and probe stimuli are the same rather than different. Therefore, Peterson and Lampignano reasoned that this manipulation would diminish the latency differences between experimental and control trials if those differences reflect memory for the shape of the ground, as Treisman and DeSchepper claimed. Alternatively, this manipulation should not diminish the latency differences if those differences reflect cross-border competition for figural status. All that is necessary for competition is the repetition of the border of the prime figure on the probe trial. The competition hypothesis predicts that the memory of the structure of the figure seen on the prime trial will compete with the cues favoring seeing the figure on the inside of the probe shapes. This competition might increase the time required to resolve the figural status of the experimental probes, and consequently, could be responsible for the longer RTs observed on experimental probe trials compared to control probe trials. Note that the competition hypothesis does not require that memories of the structure of the figure seen on the prime trial dominate the perception of the probe stimuli. More cues favor the interpretation that the figure lies on the inside (white side) than the outside of the border of the probe display.

Second, Peterson and Lampignano (2003) attempted to obtain evidence for the competition hypothesis by examining the consequence of adding a second cue that favored assigning the repeated articulated border to the outside rather than to the inside of the standard white probe. This second cue—partial closure—was manipulated by positioning the distractor near to or far from the white probe shape, as shown in Figure 13. Partial closure is a variant of the Gestalt configural cues of closure. Gillam (1975) had shown that partial closure served as a grouping cue; Peterson and Lampignano reasoned that it might also serve as a figural cue.

Peterson and Lampignano (2003) found robust slowing on experimental compared to control trials, despite the decreased similarity between the probe shape and the prime ground. They also found that the distance to the distractor mattered more in the experimental condition than in the control condition, suggesting that the addition of another cue, partial closure, favoring assigning the border to the same side as the shape memory

Fig. 13. The near- and far-distractor conditions. The distances shown in this figure are approximations of those used in the experiment.

cue increased the competition for the border. A second experiment showed that the mere repetition of the border of the figure seen on prime trials was sufficient for these effects; the presence of distractors was not necessary.

Thus, it seems that Treisman and DeSchepper's (1996, Experiment 6) results are better interpreted within a competitive model of figure assignment than within a negative priming paradigm. Peterson and Lampignano's results show that a single past exposure is sufficient to establish a memory that enters into the competitive figure assignment process the next time the border is encountered. Future research will have to test how long this memory lasts and whether its longevity is affected by exposure to other, similar, novel shapes. In the paradigm used by Peterson and Lampignano, the interval between presentation of the novel stimulus and test was on the order of 1700 ms. Longer intervals (with and without the introduction of new stimuli) must be tested in order to determine how long these new memories last.

Peterson and Lampignano (2002) interpreted their results as evidence of cross-border *competition* rather than cross-border *inhibition* for a number of reasons. First, the stimulus onset asynchronies (SOAs) they used were much longer than those at which consequences of cross-border inhibition have been observed. The longest SOA over which Peterson and Kim (2001a) and Peterson et al. (submitted) observed inhibitory effects was 105 ms; they failed to find evidence for inhibition using SOAs of 200, 350, 500, and 650 ms. In addition, Treisman and DeSchepper (1996, Experiment 6) obtained longer latencies on experimental probes than on control probes even when the experimental probes were shown three trials after their associated primes. The cross-border inhibition predicted by PIMOCA is expected to be short-lived, and, therefore, unlikely to be observed over long SOAs. In contrast, new object memories may last (and can potentially influence figure assignment) for an unlimited duration of time. Second, the articulated border shown in the prime display was repeated on the probe display in Peterson and Lampignano's experiments and in Treisman and DeSchepper's experiment, whereas it was not repeated in the experiments conducted by Peterson and Kim (2001a; Peterson et al., 2003; Skow-Grant et al., 2002). Thus, Peterson and Lampignano assayed memory for a particular novel border that had been seen only once before the probe trials (i.e., on the prime trial), whereas Peterson and Kim (2001a; Peterson et al., 2003; Skow-Grant et al., 2002) assayed the consequences of accessing preexisting memories of portions of similar basic-level objects. The mechanisms mediating short-lived inhibition and memory for past experience with a previously seen border may be different. They certainly seem to follow a different time course. Future experiments will investigate the relationship between inhibition and competition in more depth.

VII. Concluding Remarks

The body of research reviewed here shows that past experience affects figure assignment. One reason many scientists sought to exclude past experience from inclusion among factors that might affect early perceptual processes was the belief that were past experience to have an effect, it would necessarily dominate other cues. The cue competition experiments show that object memories do not exert a dominating influence; instead they constitute just one more among many configural cues used by the visual system.

The results showing that past experience does affect figure assignment raised a number of questions that had been answered under the old figure–ground-first assumption. Peterson and her colleagues offered new answers to these questions in the form of the Parallel Interactive Model of Configural Analysis (PIMOCA). They provided some empirical support for predictions arising from the model. But the model must be tested further before its full value can be known.

The surprising results reviewed in the last section showing that a single past experience with a border is sufficient to establish a memory that is accessed the next time the border is encountered suggest that memories of object structure are remarkably plastic. These results were observed in RT measures; they would not have been evident in direct reports regarding what was seen as figure because the past experience cue did not win the cross-border competition. Thus, these experiments attest to the importance of using measures that can reveal the course of figure assignment rather than simply its outcome.

The research reviewed here opens up many avenues for future research using computational, physiological, and behavioral techniques. One important question is where in the stream of visual-cognitive processes these memories lie, as well as where the configural cues are assessed. The answer to these questions will be valuable, not for finding the place to draw a line dividing visual perception and memory, but rather for understanding both the nature of object memory and the nature of the interactions that determine figure assignment.

REFERENCES

Dell'Acqua, R., & Grainger, J. (1999). Unconscious semantic priming from pictures. *Cognition, 73*, B1–B15.

Driver, J., & Baylis, G. C. (1995). One-sided edge assignment in vision: 2. Part decomposition, shape description, and attention to objects. *Current Directions in Psychological Science, 4*, 201–206.

Gerbino, W., & Salmaso, D. (1987). The effect of amodal completion on visual matching. *Acta Psychologica, 65*, 25–46.

Gibson, B. S., & Peterson, M. A. (1994). Does orientation-independent object recognition precede orientation-dependent recognition? Evidence from a cueing paradigm. *Journal of Experimental Psychology: Human Perception and Performance, 20*, 299–316.

Gillam, B. (1975). The evidence for "closure" in perception. *Perception & Psychophysics, 17*, 521–524.

Hochberg, J. (1962). The psychophysics of pictorial perception. *Audio-Visual Communication Review, 10*, 22–54.

Hochberg, J. (1971). Perception I: Color and shape. In J. W. Kling and L. A. Riggs (Eds.), *Woodworth and Schlossberg's experimental psychology*. (3rd ed., pp. 395–474). New York: Hold, Rinehart & Winston.

Jolicoeur, P. (1988). Mental rotation and identification of disoriented objects. *Canadian Journal of Psychology, 42*, 461–478.

Kanizsa, G., & Gerbino, W. (1976). Convexity and symmetry in figure-ground organization. In M. Henle (Ed.), *Vision and artifact*. New York: Springer Publishing Co.

Kienker, P. K., Sejnowski, T. J., Hinton, G. E., & Schumacher, L. E. (1986). Separating figure from ground in a parallel network. *Perception, 15*, 197–216.

Kim, J. H., & Peterson, M. A. (2001, May). *Contextual modulation of the strength of the Gestalt configural cues*. Poster session at the first annual meeting of the Vision Sciences Society, Sarasota, FL.

Kim, J. H., & Peterson, M. A. (2002, May). *Contextual modulation of the strength of Gestalt configural cues*. Poster session at the second annual meeting of the Vision Sciences Society, Sarasota, FL.

Marr, D. (1982). *Vision*. New York: W. H. Freeman and Company.

Milliken, B., Joordens, S., Merikle, P. M., & Seiffert, A. E. (1998). Selective attention: A reevaluation of the implications of negative priming. *Psychological Review, 105*, 203–229.

Pasupathy, A., & Connor, C. E. (1999). Responses to contour features in macaque area V4. *Journal of Neurophysiology, 82*, 2490–2502.

Perrett, D., Oram, M. W., & Ashbridge, E. (1998). Evidence accumulation in cell populations responsive to faces: An account of generalization of recognition without mental transformations. *Cognition, 67*, 111–145.

Peterson, M. A. (1994). Shape recognition can and does occur before figure-ground organization. *Current Directions in Psychological Science, 3*, 105–111.

Peterson, M. A. (1995). *The relationship between depth segregation and object recognition: Old assumptions, new findings, and a new approach to object recognition*. Unpublished manuscript.

Peterson, M. A. (1999). On the role of meaning in organization. *Intellectica, 28*, 37–51.

Peterson, M. A. (2000). Object perception. In E. B. Goldstein (Ed.), *Blackwell handbook of perception.* (Chapter 6, pp. 168–203) Oxford: Blackwell Publishers.

Peterson, M. A. (2003a). Overlapping partial configurations in object memory: An alternative solution to classic problems in perception and recognition. In M. A. Peterson and G. Rhodes (Eds.), *The perception of faces, objects, and scenes: Analytic and holistic processes.* New York: Oxford University Press.

Peterson, M. A. (2003b). On figure, grounds, and varieties of amodal surface completion. In R. Kimchi, M. Behrmann, and C. Olson (Eds.) *Perceptual organization in vision: Behavioral and neural perspectives.* Hillsdale, NJ: Erlbaum.

Peterson, M. A., de Gelder, B., Rapcsak, S. Z., Gerhardstein, P. C., & Bachoud-Lévi, A. C. (2000). Object memory effects on figure assignment: Conscious object recognition is not necessary or sufficient. *Vision Research, 40*, 1549–1567.

Peterson, M. A., Gerhardstein, P. C., Mennemeier, M., & Rapcsak, S. Z. (1998). Object-centered attentional biases and object recognition contributions to scene segmentation in right hemisphere- and left hemisphere-damaged patients. *Psychobiology, 26*, 557–570.

Peterson, M. A., & Gibson, B. S. (1991). Directing spatial attention within an object: Altering the functional equivalence of shape description. *Journal of Experimental Psychology: Human Perception and Performance, 17*, 170–182.

Peterson, M. A., & Gibson, B. S. (1993). Shape recognition contributions to figure-ground organization in three-dimensional displays. *Cognitive Psychology, 25*, 383–429.

Peterson, M. A., & Gibson, B. S. (1994a). Object recognition contributions to figure-ground organization: Operations on outlines and subjective contours. *Perception & Psychophysics, 56*, 551–564.

Peterson, M. A., & Gibson, B. S. (1994b). Must shape recognition follow figure-ground organization? An assumption in peril. *Psychological Science, 5*, 253–259.

Peterson, M. A., Harvey, E. H., & Weidenbacher, H. L. (1991). Shape recognition inputs to figure-ground organization: Which route counts? *Journal of Experimental Psychology: Human Perception and Performance, 17*, 1075–1089.

Peterson, M. A., & Hector, J. E. (1996). *Evidence for the piecemeal nature of pre-depth object recognition processes.* Paper presented at the Annual Meeting of the Psychonomic Society, Chicago, IL.

Peterson, M. A., & Kim, J. H. (2001a). On what is bound in figures and grounds. *Visual Cognition. Special Issue: Neural binding of Space and Time, 8*, 329–348.

Peterson, M. A., & Kim, J. H. (2001b). *Context modulates the Gestalt configural cue of convexity.* Paper presented at the Annual Meeting of the Psychonomic Society, Orlando, FL.

Peterson, M. A., & Lampignano, D. W. *Implicit memory for novel figure ground displays includes a history of border competition. Journal of Experimental Psychology; Human Perception and Performance,* (In press).

Peterson, M. A., Skow-Grant, E., & Kim, J. H. (2003). *Inhibition of object memories accessed on the side of a border perceived to be ground.* Manuscript in preparation.

Riddoch, M. J., & Humphreys, G. (1993). *Birmingham Object Recognition Battery* (test 6). Washington, DC: Psychology Press.

Rock, I., & Kremen, I. (1957). A re-examination of Rubin's figural after-effect. *Journal of Psychology, 53*, 23–30.

Rubin, E. (1958). Figure and ground. In D. Beardslee and M. Wertheimer (Ed. and Trans.). *Readings in perception.* (pp. 35–101). Princeton, NJ: Van Nostrand. (Original work published in 1915).

Schafer, R., & Murphy, G. (1943). The role of autism in a visual figure-ground relationship. *Journal of Experimental Psychology, 32*, 335–343.

Sejnowski, T. J., & Hinton, G. E. (1987). Separating figure from ground in a Boltzman machine. In M. Arbib and A. Hanson (Eds.), *Vision, brain, and cooperative computation.* Cambridge, MA: MIT Press.

Skow-Grant, E., Kim, J. H., & Peterson, M. A. (2002, May). *Tests of a competitive interactive model of figure assignment.* Poster session at the Second Annual Vision Sciences Society Meeting, Sarasota, FL.

Tanaka, K. (1996). Inferotemporal cortex and object vision. *Annual Review of Neuroscience, 19,* 109–139.

Tarr, M. J., & Pinker, S. (1989). Mental rotation and orientation-dependence in shape recognition. *Cognitive Psychology, 21,* 233–282.

Treisman, A., & DeSchepper, B. (1996). Object tokens, attention, and visual memory. In T. Inui & J. McClelland (Eds.), *Attention and performance, XVI: Information integration in perception and communication.* (pp. 15–46). Cambridge, MA: MIT Press.

Vecera, S. P., & O'Reilly, R. C. (1998). Figure-ground organization and object recognition processes: An interactive account. *Journal of Experimental Psychology: Human Perception and Performance, 24,* 441–462.

Warrington, E. K., & James, M. (1991). *The Visual Object and Space Perception Battery.* Suffolk, UK: Thames Valley Test Company.

Warrington, E. K., & Taylor, A. M. (1973). The contribution of the right parietal lobe to object recognition. *Cortex, 9,* 152–164.

SPATIAL AND VISUAL WORKING MEMORY: A MENTAL WORKSPACE

Robert H. Logie

I. Introduction

Working memory refers to the means by which human beings maintain, manipulate, and reinterpret, on a moment to moment basis, information that is required for successful performance of a range of everyday tasks from mental arithmetic (e.g., Ashcraft, 1992; Furst & Hitch, 2000; Logie, Gilhooly, & Wynn, 1994) through reasoning and problem solving (Gilhooly, Logie, Wetherick, & Wynn, 1993) to planning a route (Garden, Cornoldi, & Logie, 2002). Working memory appears also to play important roles in acquiring new knowledge and in some aspects of retrieving previously acquired knowledge. It deals with the manipulation and the temporary storage of information and handles memory for appearance, object location, and movement sequences, as well as words, letters, and numbers. As such, working memory enjoys a much broader role in cognition than does the more traditional concept of short-term memory. The latter has focused on immediate recall of sequences of verbal items, based on tasks akin to remembering a new foreign word long enough to repeat the phoneme sequence in the correct order (e.g., Baddeley, Papagno, & Valentine, 1991).

Working memory is more complex than verbal short-term memory but has helped cognitive psychologists understand important aspects of everyday cognition as well as account for a range of phenomena observed in the laboratory. Its utility has been shown in the study of both healthy adult cognition and cognitive impairments that arise from some forms of brain damage, as well as brain diseases. This chapter will provide a broad overview of some current theoretical arguments regarding working memory, focusing particularly on visuospatial cognition, and will illustrate how a multiple-component working memory model has been particularly fruitful in the study of visual short-term memory function as well as in a range of mental visual imagery tasks performed by healthy adults and by brain-damaged individuals with impairments of visuospatial cognition.

II. Theories of Working Memory

The first definitive discussion of working memory was published almost 30 years ago in the same book series as the current volume (Baddeley & Hitch, 1974). Currently, several contrasting theoretical frameworks refer to the concept of working memory; a comprehensive discussion is presented in Miyake and Shah (1999). All of the frameworks described in Miyake and Shah assume that working memory incorporates elements of temporary storage and some form of processing. However, the frameworks differ in whether processing and storage might be supported by a single, general purpose resource, or supported by multiple resources that separate processing from storage or involve a range of domain-specific temporary storage devices.

Figure 1 illustrates one view of working memory as a single, general purpose mental resource that can be used as a temporary memory store, for directing attention, as the recipient of activated prior knowledge and stimulus input via the sensory systems, and for manipulation of the information it holds. This is an approach of research teams that focus on the study of individual differences in working memory capacity and the extent to which aspects of on-line cognition such as language comprehension or simple mental arithmetic are predicted by a single measure that combines immediate memory performance with some form of ongoing processing load (e.g., Engle, Kane, & Tuholski, 1999; Just & Carpenter, 1992). Working memory capacity is measured by tasks that involve some processing of stimulus material, such as reading a sentence or solving an arithmetic problem, coupled with memory for presented items, such as the last word of each of a series of sentences that have just been read (Daneman & Carpenter, 1980, 1983). Working memory capacity is the number of items recalled in the order of presentation. One implication of this framework is that as more of the working memory resource is required for memory storage, less is available for directing attention or for manipulating information and vice versa.

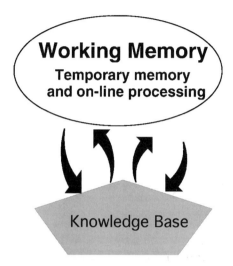

Fig. 1.   Working memory as a single, general purpose resource supporting both processing and temporary memory.

Recent work on individual differences in working memory capacity has suggested that there might be domain-specific capacities for verbal and for visuospatial functions. For example, Shah and Miyake (1996; see also Miyake, Friedman, Rettinger, Shah, & Hegarty, 2001) employed a task in which the processing involved a series of decisions about whether letter shapes in different orientations were shown in the usual form or as mirror reversed. Participants were then asked to recall the sequence of letter orientations, and recall performance was taken as the capacity measure. The same participants were assessed in their capacity for the sentence processing plus verbal recall version for the task. The analyses indicated low correlations between working memory capacity for letter orientation and for final word recall, pointing to domain-specific working memory capacities, with visuospatial and verbal capacities being quite independent. If this turns out to be the case, then there are some interesting implications for the link between visuospatial working memory capacity and other views of visuospatial working memory derived from experimental manipulations or studies of brain-damaged individuals rather than from individual differences in the healthy population. However, there remains a debate as to whether working memory capacity is domain specific or domain general (e.g., Miyake, 2001). There also remain questions about whether processing and storage rely on a single system or on separate systems (e.g., Duff

& Logie, 2001; Towse, Hitch, & Hutton, 2000, 2002). Despite these debates, the individual differences approach has shown working memory capacity to be correlated with a wide range of cognitive abilities such as reading comprehension, control of attention, and other tasks that require on-line processing of information. In this sense it may offer a relatively simple means to measure a robust mental ability that differs between individuals and might determine the factor structure and relationships between measures of working memory capacity. The focus of discussion in the chapter will be on experimental manipulations that have explored visuospatial working memory function as a separable component of the cognitive system. However, it is notable that the work of Miyake and colleagues is accumulating evidence from an individual differences perspective that is consistent with the idea of domain-specific working memory resources for visuospatial on-line cognition.

An alternative theoretical perspective is that working memory is not a separate component of the cognitive system, but broadly comprises the currently activated elements of information stored in the knowledge base that is derived from past experiences (e.g., Cowan, 1995, 1999; Ericsson & Delaney, 1999; Ericsson & Kintsch, 1995). In particular, Ericsson and Kintsch point to various studies of remarkably high working memory capacity linked to expertise. For example, expert chess players can play multiple games of chess while blindfold, suggesting that they can retain and update detailed information about the position of pieces on several chess boards. They also point to the study demonstrating that an individual can be trained to encode and recall random sequences of up to 80 digits. This kind of evidence seems to undermine the idea of a limited capacity working memory system for visual arrays or for verbal sequences. Although there are compelling arguments to support this view, there are even more compelling arguments to suggest that there remains a requirement for a separate working memory system. For example, the chess experts are no better than chess novices at remembering digit sequences, and the individual with a digit span of 80 demonstrated that capacity only with sequences of numbers (Ericsson, Chase, & Falloon, 1980). That is, expert knowledge and strategies can be learned and employed to boost performance on immediate memory tasks for specific kinds of material, but there remains a limited capacity for material that is novel or outside the range of expertise. In the remainder of this chapter, I shall discuss evidence suggesting that there is indeed a separate limited capacity working memory system, but that it draws on domain-specific temporary memory systems and also draws on support from stored knowledge.

III. Working Memory as a Multiple Component Mental Workspace

In the remainder of this chapter, I shall discuss a body of evidence to suggest that the framework indicated in Figure 1 might be misleading. This conclusion arises from a wide range of experimental studies with healthy adults and children, from reports of very specific cognitive deficits following brain damage, and patterns of brain activation detected by brain imaging techniques such as position emission tomography (PET) or functional magnetic resonance imaging (fMRI). All of this evidence points to a human working memory system that comprises a range of specialized mental systems each of which deals with memory for particular kinds of information or with information manipulation (e.g., Baddeley & Hitch, 1974; Baddeley & Logie, 1999). One view of this "multiple component" working memory is illustrated in Figure 2. One pair of components, the visual cache and the inner scribe, are thought to support respectively temporary memory for the visual appearance and layout of a scene together with pathways or movements through the scene. A second pair of components, the phonological store and "inner speech," offer, respectively, temporary memory for the acoustic and phonological properties of words, letters, and numbers together with serial ordered, subvocal (mental) rehearsal of those items. The component labeled "executive functions" comprises a range of functions, including the coordination of the memory and rehearsal systems, and for manipulation of information that is held in the temporary memory systems or is generated from the knowledge base of skills and information acquired from past experience (for reviews see Baddeley & Logie, 1999; Logie & Della Sala, in press).

Although presented as a set of separate components, it is clear that in the healthy brain and for most everyday cognitive tasks, the systems within working memory act in concert. For example, if we are trying to imagine what our living room would look like with the furniture rearranged, then we would hold in mind the names of the items of furniture and their shape and location, but would also have some idea from our past experience of how heavy these items are, how easily they could be moved, and some information about the costs of buying new furniture or the potential health care consequences of unsuccessful attempts to shift the piano. Therefore, what appears to be primarily a visuospatial manipulation task involves verbal information and a great deal of prior knowledge, as well as the processes of mentally imagining the potential appearance of the room following its reconfiguration.

This observation that working memory incorporates some of our existing knowledge raises an additional important feature of Figure 2, namely that there is no direct link between working memory and the processes involved

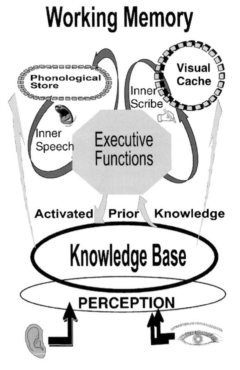

Fig. 2. Working memory as a multiple component cognitive system with contents derived from activated prior knowledge.

in perception of the current environment. In particular, the contents of working memory incorporate some form of interpretation based on prior knowledge. Working memory does not handle raw sensory patterns of edges, contours, shades, and textures directly from the environment. Rather, it deals with objects and shapes that have been identified by the processes of perception and that draw on our knowledge base of past experience. Therefore, in looking at my desk, the contents of working memory comprise a telephone, a computer screen, a small world globe, several paperweights, and a range of books and paper. The identification of these objects is possible only if the patterns of light and shade, edges, textures, and contours in the visual field have been successfully perceived as specific objects, and successful identification relies on my previous experience of these objects and objects of this kind. This process of identification could not be so readily accomplished by a newborn baby who would have a very limited knowledge base. Identification of the objects also would present something of a challenge to people who had never experienced computer technology or electronic communication systems. In sum, perception involves the activation of previously stored knowledge in response to a particular configuration of stimuli from the environment. Much of perception, including object identification, is automatic and requires no direct involvement of working memory. As healthy adults, what we deal with in working memory is the product of what has been activated from our knowledge base, and working memory provides a "mental workspace" within which the activated material is retained and manipulated.

This rather distant, and indirect link between perception and working memory is somewhat controversial, since a great deal of research in cognitive psychology is predicated on the assumption that there is a fairly intimate relationship between perception and mental representations, such as mental images. Moreover, many undergraduate psychology students are still taught that perception feeds information from the environment through a temporary buffer or working memory, and some of the information is subsequently retained in the long-term knowledge base. However, there is growing evidence that the contents of working memory, such as mental images, are interpreted, and this can be possible only if perception has first activated the contents of long-term memory. It is then those activated contents that are dealt with in the mental workspace referred to as working memory (e.g., Denis, Beschin, Logie, & Della Sala, 2002; Beschin, Cocchini, Della Sala, & Logie, 1997; Chambers & Reisberg, 1985, 1992; Cornoldi, Logie, Brandimonte, Kaufmann, & Reisberg, 1996; Logie, 1995).

This view of working memory as a mental workspace provides not only an understanding of healthy adult cognition, but also offers insight into the cognitive impairments that arise from some forms of focal brain damage, as well as from more widespread damage resulting from brain diseases. This chapter will report the results of experimental research that illustrate how the multiple task working memory model has been particularly fruitful in the study of visuospatial cognition as it constrains as well as supports some aspects of creative thinking, offers a means to interpret visual and spatial temporary memory, and accounts for some forms of mental representation deficits in brain-damaged individuals.

IV. Constraining the Generation of New Knowledge from Old

When individuals generate a new idea or a new physical artifact such as a drawing or new object, one means by which this is accomplished is to recombine or reinterpret some aspects of their existing knowledge. If it is the case that the contents of working memory are interpreted at some level, then this could act to inhibit the generation of new interpretations. This is one possible reason why creative thinking is difficult for many people, and why few individuals can excel in this endeavor.

A.   AMBIGUOUS FIGURES AND INHIBITING REINTERPRETATION

One striking example of a failure to dispense with an initial interpretation of a stimulus was described by Chambers and Reisberg (1985, 1992), who explored the ability of volunteers to interpret and reinterpret a range of ambiguous figures. In their initial experiments, volunteers were shown a drawing of an ambiguous figure, for example, the "duck-rabbit" shown in Figure 3. Each volunteer was allowed to view the drawing for just 2 seconds, after which they were to report from memory what the drawing depicted. Roughly half of the volunteers reported that they had seen a drawing of the head of a rabbit. The other half reported seeing the head of a duck. When asked if they could see the figure as depicting anything else, none of the volunteers was able to report the alternative interpretation. However, when asked to draw the figure from memory, they could then report the alternative interpretation from looking at their drawing, even though they could not do so from their imagery. Chambers and Reisberg carried out a number of follow-up studies all of which led to the same conclusion, that volunteers had great difficulty in changing their initial interpretation which was associated with immediate memory for a recently viewed drawing. So, not only was there an interpretation linked to their representation in working memory, but removing or altering that interpretation was extremely difficult when based on the representation in working memory alone.

Subsequent studies by other researchers have shown that some volunteers can report alternative interpretations of ambiguous figures, if some measures are taken to try to prevent the initial interpretation being formed. For example, Brandimonte and Gerbino (1993) asked volunteers to suppress articulation by means of repeating aloud an irrelevant word during the brief time that they were viewing the ambiguous figure. This resulted in

Fig. 3.   Example of the "duck-rabbit" ambiguous figure.

somewhere between 15% and 30% of individuals able to report the alternative interpretations of the figures from their images. Moreover, Brandimonte, Hitch, and Bishop (1992a,b) showed that figures that are easy to name are more difficult to reinterpret in mental imagery than are items that are difficult to name. Brandimonte and colleagues also demonstrated that overt suppression of articulation removed some of the effects of "nameability." In other words, when a stimulus can be readily identified from initial perception, this interpretation forms part of the representation in working memory. Articulatory suppression can act to inhibit some aspects of this initial interpretation, thereby increasing the possibility that novel or alternative interpretations can be generated (for a detailed discussion see Cornoldi et al., 1996).

Although the above studies demonstrate that the interpretation in working memory can be made more flexible, it is striking that only a minority of participants show the benefit of these manipulations in their performance. Therefore, these findings do not undermine the general thesis that "first impressions" have a major effect on the contents of working memory, and can act to inhibit our ability to think about our recent experiences in new and different ways.

B.   Mental Synthesis and Inhibition of Mental Discovery

The findings from studies with ambiguous figures echo those from studies of mental synthesis tasks. In these tasks, volunteers are given the names of a small number of familiar, canonical shapes, such as a circle, a triangle, and a square. They are asked to generate a mental image of these items and to combine the shapes mentally such that they form a recognizable object (Finke & Slayton, 1988). An example of a production from experiments reported by Barquero and Logie (1999) is shown in Figure 4. One crucial feature of these experiments is that volunteers are asked to generate a name for the mental image that they form before they draw their image. After drawing the image, they are then asked if they wish to change the name that they generated. The drawings, together with their names, are then shown to independent judges who are asked to rate the degree of correspondence between each name and the drawing given. The judges rated the second name (produced after drawing) as having a greater degree of correspondence with the drawing than did the first name given. In other words, the volunteers were better able to interpret their newly generated object forms if they could inspect their own drawing of the mental image than if they relied on the mental image alone.

In a further experiment, Barquero and Logie (1999) asked volunteers to combine mentally shapes of real objects, such as a trash can, a rugby ball, and a tennis raquet. Again, they were given the names of the shapes and were asked to combine these, shapes to form a recognizable object that was different from the component parts. A successful attempt from one volunteer is shown in Figure 5. However, many volunteers had difficulty

Mountain

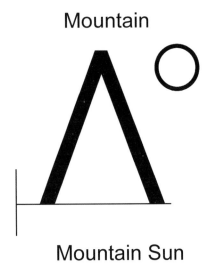

Mountain Sun

Fig. 4.   Example participant drawing from mental synthesis of a triangle, a circle, and the letter "T" (Barquero & Logie, 1999).

Loudspeaker

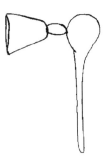

Man talking through loudspeaker

Fig. 5.   Example participant drawing from mental synthesis of the shapes of a trash can, a rugby ball, and a tennis racquet (Barquero & Logie, 1999).

performing this task, and when productions were judged independently, the ratings given were significantly poorer than those that had been allocated to the drawings and names derived from the canonical shapes. It appeared that volunteers had difficulty divesting the object identity from its shape to allow mental manipulation and combination of the shapes to form different objects. That is, the component objects to be combined had a form of "semantic baggage" that was difficult to shake off.

The results above might be interpreted as suggesting that mental manipulation is simply a demanding cognitive task, and the problems that participants experienced arose from simply holding the shapes in memory while they were combined in the absence of external stimulus support. Perhaps real object shapes are more complex visually than are canonical shapes such as circles, squares, and triangles, and are therefore more difficult to hold in mind. However, if this were the case, we would have expected volunteers to miss some of the objects altogether, and there was no evidence that this was any more likely with the real object shapes than with the canonical shapes. Increasing the number of shapes (canonical or depicted objects) to be held and combined resulted in participants forgetting to include some of the shapes. However the number of shapes had no impact on the judged correspondence between drawing and name; correspondence ratings were no different for successful combinations of five shapes than they were for combinations of three shapes (see also Pearson, Logie, & Gilhooly, 1999). That is, number of shapes places a load on the storage capacity of working memory, but it does not appear to enhance or to inhibit the process of mental discovery. What does affect mental synthesis performance is the extent to which the images have associated meaning. These additional observations reinforce the view that it was the semantic interpretation of the items that was crucial for inhibiting mental synthesis, not their complexity or number.

C. STIMULUS SUPPORT AND MENTAL DISCOVERY

Support for mental discovery may comprise mental strategies or acquired skills, prior knowledge of previous, personal discoveries, as well as the characteristics and limitations of working memory. Support also may take the form of external aids such as sketching, or computer-aided design packages. However, the utility of each of these external design tools generally has been assumed rather than formally assessed, and this raises the question as to whether mental discovery is enhanced or inhibited by their use. For example, Anderson and Helstrup (1993) showed that imaging along with paper and pencil support (sketching) can result in either no benefit or even in less creative thinking than using imagery alone, at least for variations of the mental synthesis task. One possible reason for this is that paper and pencil drawings and diagrams cannot convey *dynamic* manipulations, and therefore they may not provide a suitable medium for creative synthesis. In contrast, computer-based graphical packages allow for dynamic manipulations to be carried out that may be similar to those that occur during visual imagery. Where paper and pencil seemed to help was as a memory aid, allowing the volunteers to remember which items they had to combine mentally.

A more recent series of as yet unpublished experiments by Pearson and myself explored further the potential impact of a range of possible external aids in mental synthesis tasks. These experiments followed the general procedure used by Pearson et al. (1999) and Barquero and Logie (1999). Volunteer participants with no specific design training were shown a set of 15 two-dimensional generic and familiar shapes, each of which was associated with a verbal label (i.e., circle, capital "D,") number 8, triangle, etc.). They were asked to learn the precise appearance of the shapes so that they could be accurately imaged and drawn in response to each verbal label.

During the experimental phase of the standard "imagery alone" version of the task participants were presented with a set of the verbal labels for three to six shapes drawn randomly from the total pool of 15. Participants were required to form a mental image of a recognizable object or pattern that included all of the shapes named for that trial. In so doing, the imaged shapes could be manipulated into any size or orientation, but could not be distorted; for example, a circle had to retain a circle shape and could not be used as an oval. Participants were given a period of 2 minutes in which to generate a completed pattern. After this period participants were first asked to give a short verbal description of the resulting imaged pattern, and then to draw their imaged pattern onto a sheet of paper. This procedure was adopted to ensure that the verbal naming of the imaged pattern was not influenced by the stimulus support benefits of being allowed to draw the synthesized image as discussed earlier (Pearson et al., 1999; Barquero & Logie, 1999). If participants were unable to generate a synthesized pattern within the allotted 2 minutes, they were instructed to write "no pattern" for the verbal label, and then to draw as many of the presented shapes as they could remember. This procedure allowed for a measure of memory that was independent of whether the participants could generate a recognizable pattern on every trial.

All participants performed the synthesis task using imagery alone, and then in one of three secondary task conditions. In one condition, participants were asked to carry out the synthesis task while attempting to draw in the air with their preferred hand as a form of stimulus support. In a second condition, participants were given a pencil and a pad of blank paper, and were asked to sketch their various attempted combinations while carrying out the synthesis task. Finally, in a third condition, participants performed the synthesis task using CorelDraw!, a commercially available computer-based graphics package that allows two-dimensional displays to be transformed and manipulated dynamically on screen.

Figure 6 shows the number of trials on which participants generated legitimate patterns, that is patterns that included all the shapes presented for that trial and with no distortions of any of the shapes. It is clear from Figure 6 that drawing in the air resulted in no benefit compared with imagery alone. There was a modest increase in the number of legitimate patterns obtained with paper and pencil support and with the graphics package, although only the effect for the graphics package was statistically reliable. In addition, participants were less likely to forget to include all of the shapes on each trial if they were allowed to use paper and pencil support or computer graphics support. In a follow-up experiment we examined the same set of tasks and forms of stimulus support but with shapes that were more complex visually. Again, the graphics package and paper and pencil support resulted in fewer shapes being omitted from the participant's drawings, but showed only a modest improvement in whether the participants could generate legitimate combinations of the shapes. These findings all support the idea that external aids might provide an aid to memory, but do not necessarily aid the design process, at least with healthy, well-educated individuals who have no particular training in the principles and techniques of design.

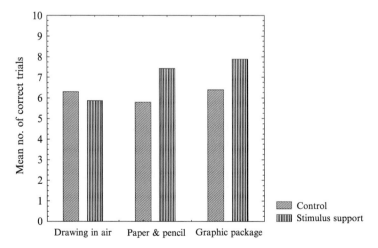

Fig. 6. Mean number of trials on which all presented shapes were included in drawings generated by participants in mental synthesis based on imagery alone, and with three forms of external stimulus support.

D. CREATIVE THINKING: A RAISON D'ÊTRE FOR WORKING MEMORY

Thus far, I have argued that working memory appears to play a role in creative thinking, although the discussion has focused on how the interpreted contents of working memory might inhibit the reinterpretation necessary for creative design. Another part of the discussion has argued that external aids might relieve only the memory load involved in mental manipulation of elements of a design, but not necessarily enhance the creative aspects of design. Of course, if working memory is burdened less with storing details, then one argument could be that the use of external memory aids might free working memory resources to focus on the process of mental manipulation, reinterpretation, and creative thinking.

If working memory deals with interpreted representations, then some of the findings described above suggest that reinterpretation might require active inhibition of the current interpretation. It is also likely to require activating other knowledge from prior experience that is not immediately available from perception of the object. An initial glance at the drawing in Figure 3 may result in the initial identification of the head of a rabbit. To reinterpret the figure as anything else, we have to have some way of activating other knowledge from our previous experience of objects and creatures that we have encountered. We could do this by looking again at the external drawing, turning around the paper, moving it closer or further away. Mentally, we might generate hypotheses as to what else it might be— an object shown from an unusual view perhaps, or the head of a different animal, and we might adopt a top-down approach to focus on the left or the right of the figure. Also, we have to try and inhibit the initial interpretation of the figure as a rabbit. Eventually through a combination of changing the external experience, generating hypotheses, and a mental search process, we can reconfigure and reinterpret the item. In some cases, this process of hypothesis generation, manipulation, and mental search might occur successfully without an external stimulus, and indeed, the external stimulus may interfere with the mental processes. In other cases, as for the duck-rabbit example, the external stimulus may be essential.

Throughout this process, I would argue that working memory provides the mental workspace for the hypothesis generation, inhibition, mental manipulation, and mental search. At a theoretical level, working memory therefore cannot be an input filter between perception and long-term memory, as it is often portrayed in introductory textbooks on memory. It must deal with the product of activated representations in long-term memory (Logie, 1995, 1996). Where the activated information is incomplete or has to be reinterpreted, working memory acts as the workspace to manipulate the information and seek some means to resolve ambiguities or generate new knowledge. This points to one possible reason why we have evolved with a working memory. If we can make sense of a sensation, scenario, or experience from our current knowledge, this can happen effortlessly by activating the relevant knowledge that allows us to act appropriately for the current context. However, if we are confronted by ambiguity, by implication this means that the knowledge activated by perception from the long-term store is insufficient. What knowledge is activated can be manipulated and transformed within working memory to help resolve the ambiguity. That is, working memory can generate new knowledge from old and as such would have significant evolutionary value.

This same argument can be applied to how we might start to acquire knowledge from birth. The neonate is confronted by what William James (1902, p. 7) referred to as "pure sensations," in that there is no knowledge base that can offer an interpretation of perceptual input beyond pain, pleasure, and satiation of hunger or thirst. Empirical developmental studies since that time have demonstrated that babies may have considerably more knowledge than James assumed. However, it might be interesting to explore the concept that working memory in the neonate can generate new knowledge by mentally manipulating whatever information is activated from their limited knowledge base in response to their current environment. By this means, the process of mental discovery from activated current knowledge could be seen as a way to bootstrap knowledge in the early periods of childhood. Some empirical support for this idea comes from work with rather older children. For example, Gathercole and Baddeley (1989) have shown that the system associated with mental subvocal rehearsal in working memory may play an important role in repeating speech sounds and this process of repetition contributes to the acquisition of vocabulary. In other words the children acquire new knowledge through temporary storage and manipulation of the products of perception.

In this scenario, we can all use working memory to generate new knowledge, and the fact that we have a working memory has allowed us to acquire and use the knowledge that we already have available. Therefore, the properties and the exploration of working memory offer a vehicle and a set of experimental methodologies to help understand, and to help develop the human capacity for creative discovery and creative design.

V. Visuospatial Working Memory as Temporary Memory

A. Visual Memory for Visual Stimuli

One major function that is assumed for working memory is to provide support for temporary retention of recently presented stimuli. In the case of the present chapter the discussion will focus on the visual appearance of objects and scenes, of pathways among objects, and the movements associated with our interactions with those scenes. A simple means to demonstrate that we have some form of temporary visual memory is briefly to glance at the array of objects currently within your reach, then close your eyes and attempt to pick up one of the objects. The fact that this task is possible suggests that we must have some means to retain the layout of the objects and their location relative to our hand. Also we have enough information about the object to know that it is small and light enough for us to lift, and we know enough about its shape to adjust our grip appropriately. In other words, the representation that we have of the array of objects is not just a set of lines, contours, edges, and colors. The contents of that representation have associated meaning drawn from our previous experience with such objects, suggesting, as in the previous section of this chapter, that the temporary representation that we hold is the result of activating information in our knowledge base, and is not a transit area between sensory input and long-term memory.

Early evidence for use of a visual short-term memory system was reported by Phillips and Baddeley (1971), who examined retention of individual visual matrix patterns. They observed accurate recognition memory for such patterns after unfilled delays of up to 9 seconds. Subsequently, Phillips and Christie (1977a,b) reported one item recency effects in recognition memory for sequences of abstract matrix patterns. Broadbent and Broadbent (1981) also showed recency effects for abstract wallpaper patterns or sets of irregular abstract line drawings. Later, Walker, Hitch, and Duroe (1993) obtained single item recency effects with a probed memory test for random block patterns. These results are difficult to interpret in terms of the use of verbal labels for the stimuli concerned, and the limited time course of the phenomena suggests that a temporary rather than a long-term memory system is being employed.

Evidence also arises from the report of visual similarity effects in the developmental literature. Hitch, Halliday, Schaafstal, and Schraagen (1988) reported visual confusion errors occurring in young children's recognition memory. The children in these studies were shown a series of pictures, some of which were visually similar to one another such as a brush, a rake, and a pen, while other items were visually distinct such as a pig, a ball, and a pen. Five-year-old children showed poorer recognition memory for items from the visually similar set (see also Walker, Hitch, Doyle, & Porter, 1994). With older children, however, the effect of visual similarity appeared only if they were required to suppress articulation (repeat aloud an irrelevant word) and thereby rely more heavily on visual rather than verbal codes (Hitch, Woodin, & Baker, 1989). Hitch and colleagues argued that younger children rely on visual codes spontaneously, whereas older children rely more on subvocal rehearsal of the picture names, unless that rehearsal is blocked by suppression.

The case for a visual temporary memory system gains support from studies of immediate recall with brain-damaged individuals who have very specific and severe deficits in their ability to recall sequences of verbal items such as KF (Shallice & Warrington, 1970), IL (Saffran & Marin, 1975), or PV (Basso, Spinnler, Vallar, & Zanobio, 1982). Memory span in these individuals for visually presented verbal sequences is much higher than their pathological span for aurally presented sequences. This is the converse of the pattern for healthy adults who typically show higher spans for aurally presented than for visually presented verbal sequences (e.g., Conrad & Hull, 1964; Logie, Della Sala, Laiacona, Chalmers, & Wynn, 1996). Patients with specific impairments of visual short-term storage with relatively intact verbal immediate recall also have been reported (e.g., Beyn & Knyazeva, 1962; De Renzi & Nichelli, 1975; Warrington & Rabin, 1971).

Studies of healthy adults using measures of brain activation add to the body of data supporting a separate short-term visual coding system. For example, Jonides, Smith, Koeppe, Awh, Minoshima, and Mintun (1993) used PET imaging to demonstrate an anatomical dissociation between visual and spatial short-term memory tasks. Jonides et al. tested two groups of subjects, one performing a location task and the other performing an object memory task. In the spatial task, three dots were shown briefly on a computer screen and the subjects were requested to indicate whether a subsequently specified location corresponded to a location of one of the previously presented dots. In the object memory task, subjects were shown abstract patterns for a brief period of time and then were requested to recognize whether it matched a subsequently presented pattern. These two tasks gave rise to different patterns of brain activation. Similar results were obtained in a more recent study by Courtney, Ungerleider, Keil, and Haxby (1996) in which short-term memory for faces gave rise to different patterns of brain activation from short-term memory for face location.

B. Visual Coding in Verbal Memory Tasks

Among the first studies to suggest the use of specifically a visual in contrast to verbal or phonologically based temporary memory for verbal stimuli were Posner and colleagues (e.g., Posner, Boies, Eichelman, & Taylor, 1969; Posner & Keele, 1967), who developed a visual letter-matching task in which pairs of letters were shown in their upper case (e.g., AB) or lower case (e.g., aa) versions or a mixture of both (e.g., Bb). The subjects' task was to respond on the basis of whether the letters in the pair had the same name (e.g., Aa) or had different names (e.g., Ab). When the letters were both in the same letter case and were physically identical (e.g., AA), subjects responded much more quickly than if the upper and lower case versions were different. The advantage for physically identical letters remained when letters in each pair were shown one after another with interletter delays of up to 2 seconds. This suggested that subjects were relying on the visual code for the letters during the delay, after which a name code was being used for the decision. These studies were extended by Parks, Kroll, Salzburg, and Parkinson (1972), who demonstrated that if the retention interval was filled with an auditory shadowing task, then evidence of a visual trace could be found after delays of 8 seconds.

Visual similarity effects in temporary memory for letters appeared in an early report by Wolford and Hollingsworth (1974), who presented participants with visual strings of five letters for immediate recall. The experiment involved a display time of 15 to 25 ms, followed by recall of as many of the letters as possible in their correct position in the display. Wolford and Hollingsworth observed numerous visual confusions in recall coupled with very few acoustic confusions. This suggested that retention following offset of the brief display probably did not rely on phonological codes for the letters. However, because the presentation was very brief it is possible that some of the visual confusions could have arisen from perceptual failures rather than from memory failures. More convincing evidence came from Hue and Ericsson (1988), who found visual similarity effects in immediate retrieval with longer display times and for unfamiliar Chinese characters that would most likely have to rely on visual codes. Yik (1978) also used Chinese characters in an immediate recall task, but with readers for whom the characters were familiar. Yik observed both phonologically based and visually based confusions suggesting the use of both forms of code with this kind of material and participant sample. However, other studies of free recall using visually presented upper case letter stimuli from the English language alphabet have failed to find effects of visual similarity (e.g., Conner & Hoyer, 1976). One possible reason for this was suggested by Manning (1977), who collated ratings of auditory similarity and visual similarity of letter pairs, and concluded that upper case letters in the English language are inherently more distinct visually than they are acoustically. Therefore, acoustic confusions are much more likely to arise with letter stimuli.

Some more recent studies by Logie, Della Sala, Wynn, and Baddeley (2000) showed evidence of visual coding in serial written recall of letter sequences. In these experiments, participants were shown sequences of four letters, with the letters appearing one at a time in either upper or lower case, for example, V k c W. The task was to recall the letter, its position in the list, and, most pertinent to the current discussion, to recall the case in which each letter had been presented. The materials took advantage of the fact that for some letters, the upper and lower case versions look similar, namely Vv Kk Pp Cc Ww Ss, while for other letters, the upper and lower case versions look quite different, namely Bb Ll Dd Rr Gg Qq. Half of the lists were devised using letters for which the upper and lower case versions were similar, such as in the example above, while the other half of the lists involved lists for which the upper and lower case versions were distinct, for example, r G q B. Items were controlled for phonological similarity and for letter frequency. Participants had more difficulty with the similar sets in recalling whether they had seen, for example, an upper "C" or a lower case "c" in the third position of the first example list given above, than for recalling that they had seen a lower case "q" rather than an upper case "Q" in the third position of the second example list above that comprises letters with distinct upper and lower case versions. For some of the lists, participants were asked to undertake articulatory suppression while performing the task as a means to suppress the use of phonological coding, and this resulted in a slight enhancement of the effects of visual similarity in recall of letter case. However, the effect appeared whether or not the task was accompanied by articulatory suppression. The effect was replicated in a further experiment with different letter sets.

Additional experiments in the Logie et al. (2000) paper reported visual similarity effects with word lists. The selection of materials took advantage of the vagaries of English spelling to generate items that were visually quite distinct but phonologically similar: GUY THAI SIGH LIE PI RYE. Recall of lists drawn from this set was contrasted with recall from a set in which the items were visually and phonologically similar FLY PLY CRY DRY TRY SHY. The phonological similarity in both lists should make phonological coding rather less effective, and the issue is whether this might result in evidence for the use of visual codes. Results clearly demonstrated that participants were more accurate in recalling lists of words when the items were visually distinct, and this effect was replicated with further contrasting word sets (WHO BLUE TOO EWE THROUGH FLU versus HEW PEW NEW FLEW FEW THREW).

These results are consistent with the assumption of a visual store that can hold sequential information comprising either letters or words as well as the patterns used in experiments discussed earlier. The visual similarity effect appeared to operate throughout the list, suggesting that it is not limited to the storage of a single presented complex pattern. It could reflect the means by which a sequence of visually presented items might comprise pattern elements in a stored complex pattern. Items could then be added to the pattern as they are presented. In storing letter case information, the kind of mental representation might be analogous to the silhouette of a city skyline, holding visual information about contour and letter shape, but only limited detail about the identity of the objects making up that contour. Retention of information about item identity might then be supported by some other part of the cognitive system, for example as a phonological code. The results also suggest that visual codes are used even when phonological codes would be available, and provide further support for the argument that participants may rely on more than one code when recalling verbal sequences. (For discussions as to which other codes might be employed see Baddeley, 2000; Hulme, Maughan, & Brown, 1991; Logie et al., 1996; Wetherick, 1975.)

The evidence discussed thus far is consistent with the idea that there is some form of visual short-term memory system that would support retention over brief delays of material for which participants have no obvious verbal label, such as unfamiliar Chinese characters or abstract patterns. The data suggest that both visual and phonological codes might support temporary retention of visually presented letters, and that serial recall of letter sequences appears to be possible when phonological coding is minimized. There also is evidence that subjects may use more than one form of coding when given verbal serial recall tasks. Logie et al. (1996) presented 252 participants with word sequences that consisted of short words or long words, and phonologically similar or phonologically distinct words. When items were presented visually, the aggregate data across all participants showed a clear advantage in immediate serial ordered recall for the lists of short words over the long words and for the phonologically distinct words over the phonologically similar words. These effects were no surprise and typically are interpreted as the signatures of a phonologically based store coupled with a subvocal rehearsal system (e.g., Baddeley, Thomson, & Buchanan, 1975; Baddeley, Lewis, & Vallar, 1984; Larsen & Baddeley, in press; although for alternative interpretations see, e.g., Jones, Farrand, Stuart, & Morris, 1995; Macken & Jones, in press; Neath, 2000; Neath, Farley, & Surprenant, in press). What was more surprising in the Logie et al. (1996) data was that a substantial minority of participants failed to show the effects of phonological similarity and word length, particularly with visual presentation. For example, around 50 participants recalled as many visually presented items in correct serial position from long word lists as from short word lists. Moreover, participants who failed to show these effects performed no more poorly overall than did the majority who showed the typical effects. Participants not showing these effects subsequently reported using a range of other codes to support retention, such as a semantic, first letter rather than whole word, or the visual appearance of the word.

In an earlier study, Della Sala, Logie, Marchetti, and Wynn (1991) demonstrated that the effects of word length and of phonological similarity could be removed or observed simply by instructing individual participants to use visual codes, semantic codes, or phonological codes (subvocal rehearsal) to aid their encoding and recall, although the precise nature of any possible visual codes was unclear. However, what does seem to be suggested from the collection of studies reviewed here is that visual codes can be used for retaining serial order as well as item information in immediate retrieval of visually presented verbal material as well as of pictorial stimuli.

VI. The Disruption of Visuospatial Temporary Memory

One approach that has been used widely in the development of the concept of working memory has been to examine the possible selective effects of performing a main memory task with a concurrent secondary task that has been chosen to employ specific cognitive resources. The use of articulatory suppression was described earlier as a means selectively to disrupt immediate serial ordered recall of verbal sequences. Verbal serial recall tasks are not disrupted by other, nonverbal secondary tasks, such as arm movements (e.g., Farmer, Berman, & Fletcher, 1986) or irrelevant visual input (e.g., Logie, 1986). In contrast, arm movements disrupt memory for pathways among targets, while irrelevant visual input has been shown to disrupt some kinds of visual memory tasks. Neither path memory nor visual memory tasks appear to be sensitive to articulatory suppression or other verbal secondary tasks. The links between memory for pathways and movement sequences will be discussed below, but first will be a discussion of the impact of irrelevant visual input.

Logie (1986) asked participants to retain and recall list of words either using rote rehearsal or using the mental imagery based peg-word mnemonic technique. This latter technique involves imagining the meaning of the words to be recalled in an unusual or bizarre mental image along with an object that can later be used as a cue for recall. The technique typically results in much higher recall performance than does rote rehearsal. In a series of experiments, recall using the imagery mnemonic was shown to be disrupted by concurrent presentation of irrelevant line drawings of common objects, or changing color patches, but was unaffected by presentation of irrelevant speech streams. Use of the rote rehearsal strategy was unaffected by this irrelevant visual input, but was affected by the presentation of irrelevant speech (Salamé & Baddeley, 1982; for a recent discussion of the effects of irrelevant speech see Larsen & Baddeley, in press).

This effect of irrelevant visual input on use of the peg-word mnemonic was studied in detail in a series of papers by Quinn and McConnell (e.g.,

McConnell & Quinn, 2000; Quinn & McConnell, 1996, 1999), who developed a technique that they describe as dynamic visual noise. This is somewhat similar to the pattern that appears on a television screen that is not tuned into a particular channel, and comprises pixels on the computer screen being randomly on or off. They have shown this to be a robust means to disrupt recall of the imagery-based memory strategy and have demonstrated the precise parameters of the display required to maximize its selective effects on the peg-word mnemonic, showing that its effects are not simply due to some general attentional distraction.

Quinn and McConnell interpreted their results as suggesting that dynamic visual noise disrupts visuospatial working memory through a direct link between perceptual input and a temporary visual memory store. Other researchers have shown that the effects of dynamic visual noise generalize to other memory tasks. For example, Smyth and Waller (1998) demonstrated that the ability of rock climbers to image a route up a difficult rock face was disrupted by dynamic visual noise. The disruptive effect on the peg-word mnemonic also has been replicated by Andrade, Kemps, Werniers, May, and Szmalec (2002). Baddeley and Andrade (2000) also demonstrated that dynamic visual noise affected vividness ratings of images generated of scenes that were familiar to the participants. However, Andrade et al., (2002) showed that dynamic visual noise appears to affect use of the peg-word mnemonic but does not appear to have any effect on a range of tasks involving immediate recall of visually presented material. Pearson and Sahraie (in press) have also shown that retention of observed targeted movement sequences is insensitive to the effects of dynamic visual noise.

The most robust effects of dynamic visual noise appear to be associated with tasks that involve the generation of images, drawing on knowledge in long-term memory, such as is required for using the peg-word mnemonic or imagining a familiar scene or building. The evidence that it does not affect visual short-term memory tasks is beginning to point toward the idea that its effects may not be directly on temporary visual memory, but rather on the process of retrieving visual knowledge from long-term memory. This general idea fits with the notion that perceptual input does not have direct access to the contents of working memory, as discussed earlier, but instead results in the activation of stored knowledge, and it is the product of that activation that is stored and manipulated in working memory. If information is already in working memory, it appears to be insensitive to the effects of irrelevant visual input (e.g., Andrade et al., 2002). If the task involves generation of images from stored knowledge, such as for the peg-word mnemonic or for generating images of familiar scenes (Baddeley & Andrade, 2000), then perceptual input may disrupt that generation process. This interpretation is admittedly somewhat speculative, and requires further empirical test in which dynamic visual noise is employed across a range of visual and spatial temporary storage tasks and across a range of tasks that require image generation. However, it is an interpretation that is consistent with the apparently contrasting results that have been reported for dynamic visual noise as well as offering an account of the mental discovery literature discussed earlier. This is a topic to which I shall return later in the chapter.

VII. Visual or Spatial Temporary Memory

Thus far, I have discussed evidence that points to the concept of a specific temporary store for retaining visual material that may consist of single patterns of varying complexity or of a series of visually presented items. However, there are other crucial aspects of the visual environment, namely the location of objects relative to the observer and relative to one another, and also sequences of movement or pathways among objects and locations. There is a growing literature that has explored whether the cognitive functions that appear to be linked to retention of visual appearance might also retain more dynamic information such as a pathway or a sequence of movements. The nature of immediate memory for spatial, dynamic information owes much to tasks involving recall of sequences of movements among targets arrays. In one widely used task the experimenter points to series of nine wooden blocks that are arranged randomly on a board. The participant then is required to touch the series of blocks in the same order as presented. In a common version of the task the length of the block sequence is gradually increased until the participant can no longer accurately recall the sequence in the correct order. The task was originally designed as a means to assess the extent of visuospatial immediate memory deficits in neuropsychological patients (De Renzi, Faglioni, & Previdi, 1977; Milner, 1971), and commonly is referred to as the "Corsi block task," although variations of the task exist. An earlier version comprising just four blocks in a row, with sequences that moved back and forward repeatedly between the blocks, was developed by Knox (1914) as one of the tests used to assess potential immigrants to the United States at Ellis Island. It functioned as a test of mental ability that did not rely on a knowledge of the English language. Both versions of the task rely on encoding, retention, and reproduction of a sequence of arm and hand movements to a series of specified targets.

One source of evidence that dynamic spatial and more static visual immediate memory might reflect distinct cognitive functions came from a developmental study by Logie and Pearson (1997) in which groups of children aged 5, 8, and 11 were tested on their memory span for a version of the random array block sequence task described above, and on their memory span for visually presented matrix patterns. Performance on both tasks improved across age groups. However, performance on these tasks correlated very poorly within each age group, and memory span for the more static visual matrix patterns increased with age much more rapidly than did memory span for the sequence of movements to random blocks. Similar results from a developmental study with different spatial and visual tasks were reported by Pickering, Gathercole, Hall, and Lloyd (2001; see also Pickering 2001). This technique, known as "developmental fractionation" (Hitch, 1990), indicates that the cognitive systems responsible for the two tasks seem to develop at different rates and to have little overlap within a given age group.

Earlier studies with adults by Logie and Marchetti (1991) and by Tresch, Sinnamon, and Seamon (1993) both showed that retention of visual appearance such as color shade or geometric form was disrupted by concurrent presentation of irrelevant visual input or color discrimination, while retention of the location of objects presented at different positions on a screen was disrupted by a concurrent arm movement or a movement discrimination task (for further reports of this distinction in healthy adults see Della Sala, Gray, Baddeley, Allamano, & Wilson, 1999; Hecker & Mapperson, 1997).

Neuropsychological evidence also speaks to this visual–spatial fractionation. A case study with selective impairment of visual but not of spatial immediate memory was reported by Farah, Hammond, Levine, and Calvanio (1988). Their patient, LH, as a result of an automobile accident, suffered brain damage in both temporal/occipital areas, in the right temporal lobe and in the right inferior frontal lobe. He performed well on tasks concerned with memory for locations and for pathways, such as letter rotation, three-dimensional form rotation, mental scanning, and recalling a recently described pathway, but had severely impaired memory for colors, for the relative size of objects, and for shapes of states in the map of the United States. Wilson, Baddeley, and Young (1999) reported a similar case of patient LE, a professional sculptress, who, following diffuse damage to both the cortex and the white matter, was unable to generate visual images of possible sculptures. She also had a severe visual short-term memory deficit, including very poor performance on the Doors test (Baddeley, Emslie, & Nimmo-Smith, 1994), a recognition memory task among pictures of doors that are similar in appearance, and on retention of black and white matrix patterns (Della Sala, Gray, Baddeley, & Wilson, 1997). However she could draw complex figures that did not rely on memory, and performed within the normal range for recall of targeted movement sequences.

Several cases have been reported with the converse pattern of impaired immediate spatial memory and intact visual memory. Luzzatti, Vecchi, Agazzi, Cesa-Bianchi, and Vergani (1998) described the case of patient EP who was affected by a slowly progressive deterioration of the brain in the anterior part of the right temporal lobe, including the hippocampus. Her performance was flawless on visual imagery tasks, such as making judgments about relative animal size, or the relative shapes or colors of objects. On the other hand, she was impaired on a range of topographical tasks such as describing from memory the relative locations of landmarks in her home town. A similar pattern was reported for patient MV (Carlesimo, Perri, Turriziani, Tomaiuolo, & Caltagirone, 2001), who had damage in the right dorsolateral frontal cortex. MV performed within the normal range on judging from memory, the shapes, colors, and sizes of objects and animals, but had pathologically poor performance on mental rotation tasks, on span for random targeted movement sequences, and on immediate memory for the Brooks (1967) matrix task. Hanley and Davies (1995) described a patient, Mr. Smith, who suffered from a right internal carotid artery stenosis. He had great difficulty with navigation and was unable to find his way around his own house. He also had difficulties in getting dressed with a mismatch between orientation of the clothing (e.g., sleeves) and the position of his body parts. His spatial knowledge and ability to manipulate objects mentally were impaired. However, his ability to perceive and represent visual features of objects and scenes was intact. For example, he had no difficulty in comparing the colors or forms of objects, and had no difficulty in making mental size comparisons between objects and animals when presented with their names. He could readily identify the shapes of countries from silhouettes, but was unable to move these silhouettes into their correct relative geographic position. Finally, he performed very poorly on recall of targeted movement sequences, and on a series of mental rotation tasks.

It appears then that the notion of a single visuospatial working memory system may be overly simplistic. Although a visual store might hold information about the spatial layout of a static array, a different component of the cognitive system supports retention and manipulation of more dynamic spatial material such as movement sequences or pathways.

VIII. Spatial Working Memory and Executive Control

Although the evidence above suggests some dissociation between the cognitive functions for visual and for spatial immediate memory, there are several indications that at least one feature of this dissociation lies in the requirement for attentional or executive control in some of the spatial tasks. For example, Miyake et al. (2001) demonstrated that measures of individual differences in spatial working memory capacity appear to load more heavily on general fluid intelligence than do measures of verbal working memory capacity.

Using a more experimental approach, Smyth and Scholey (1994) demonstrated that recall of a sequence of targeted movements was disrupted by concurrent shifts of spatial attention in which subjects detected and pointed to the sources of tones presented in spatially separated locations. Some disruption also was observed if the spatially separated tones were presented but required no motor response, and even if the shifts of spatial attention occurred without eye movements (Smyth, 1996). From these and similar results, Smyth and colleagues concluded that spatial attention was crucial to the encoding and retention of a sequence of locations. However pointing to targets as a secondary task generated a much larger decrement, suggesting that aspects of action planning and production may be important in dynamic spatial memory as well as control of attention.

In some recent experiments, Pearson and Sahraie (in press) also have shown that retention of sequences of targeted movements is disrupted by shifts of visual attention. However, they also demonstrated disruption by smooth pursuit eye movements that appears even when attention is focused on a single location. This suggests that eye movement control as well as shifting visual attention may be linked with memory for movement sequences.

This investigation of the effects of shifts in attention driven by auditory rather than visual cues was extended by Merat (1999; Merat & Groeger, in press) who used sound localization with response via a directional dial rather than by pointing. Her data indicated that sound localization also has an impact on verbal serial recall tasks and tasks involving verbal memory updating, suggesting that localization may have a general attentional load rather than being specific to spatial memory and processing.

Similar data have been gathered by Rudkin (2001) showing that retention and recall of sequences of movements to randomly arranged blocks appear to be prone to disruption from concurrent oral random generation of numbers. This last task involves inhibiting well learned sequences such as 1–2–3–4–5 and keeping track of how frequently particular numbers have been generated. It appears to have the characteristics of a task that might require attentional or executive control as well as oral generation (Baddeley, 1966, 1996; Evans, 1978; Logie et al., 1994; Towse, 1998). Additional experiments by Rudkin involved presenting a sequence of tones selected from nine different locations spread around a semicircle behind and out of sight of the participant. Following a short retention interval, a second sequence of tones was presented, and participants were required to indicate orally if the second sequence was identical to or different from the first sequence. The main task then involved memory for a sequence of spatially distributed locations, but there was no spatial or visual element to the response required.

The auditory spatial sequence memory task was performed on its own and then together with either spatial tapping or random interval generation. The spatial tapping task involved tapping keys in a figure of eight pattern on keys arranged in a 3 by 3 array on a button box. The random interval generation task required the participant to press a single key repeatedly but to vary the time intervals between key presses in as random a fashion as possible, with a maximum interpress interval of 4 seconds. Random interval generation was intended to employ executive control without any spatial, visual, or verbal demands and was derived from a similar task originally developed by Vandierendonck, De Vooght, and Goten, (1998). In this sense it is thought to offer a "purer" measure of executive function without a spatial, visual, or verbal demand. The participant's hand and the key array were covered and out of sight throughout for both secondary tasks.

Summary results from this Experiment are shown in Figure 7. Both figure of eight and random interval tapping resulted in a significant drop in

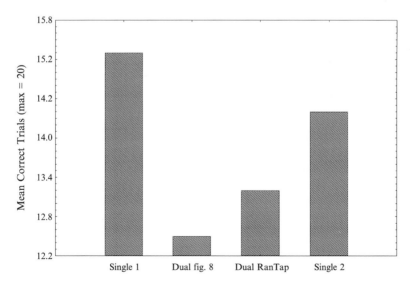

Fig. 7. Mean number of correct responses for recall of location of auditory stimuli on two occasions as a single task, and while performing concurrent figure of eight tapping or concurrent random interval tapping. Data from Rudkin (2001).

memory for the auditory spatial sequences, reinforcing earlier findings that even a nonspatial task thought to require executive control appears to disrupt memory for spatial sequences.

The general idea that spatial immediate memory might involve an attentional as well as a memory load was indicated in a series of experiments reported by Salway and Logie (1995). Their experiments involved contrasting spatial memory with verbal memory using versions of tasks originally employed by Brooks (1967, 1968). The spatial memory task involved asking participants to imagine a four by four square matrix pattern, and then to remember a series of instructions that described a path among the squares of the matrix. The verbal task involved retaining a sequence of verbal instructions relying on verbal codes. The original work by Brooks and subsequent studies by Baddeley and Lieberman (1980) and by Quinn and Ralston (1986) had shown that recall of the imagined path was disrupted by a concurrent visual input or concurrent arm movement, while the verbal task was disrupted by concurrent vocalization. Salway and Logie (1995) demonstrated this pattern of selective disruption of the imagined path recall by concurrent arm movement to a set of four targets, and of the verbal recall task by concurrent articulatory suppression. However, they employed a third task requiring the participant to generate random sequences of numbers aloud. In the Salway and Logie studies, oral random generation had a greater effect on the spatial memory task than it did on the verbal memory task. Given that the same experiments found no effect of articulatory suppression on spatial memory, it seems unlikely that random generation was having its effects because of the oral output required or because of the use of some underlying verbal coding for the spatial task. It appeared then that the spatial task was not as pure a measure of spatial immediate memory as previously had been assumed, but drew heavily on executive control functions that also were required to perform oral random generation.

The overall conclusion from these studies is that immediate memory for static visual patterns appears to be rather different from immediate memory for more dynamic spatial tasks that involve pathways or targeted movement sequences. This kind of evidence led to a proposal that visuospatial working memory might consist of a visually based temporary store for visual patterns and a more dynamic spatial memory system referred to by Logie (1995), respectively, as "the visual cache" and "the inner scribe" (see Figure 2). These were separable components of what had been referred to previously as the visuospatial sketch-pad of working memory (Baddeley & Hitch, 1974). It is clear from the evidence that has accumulated over the past few years that at least one distinctive feature of the inner scribe system is that it may draw heavily on aspects of attentional control, while the visual cache may operate as a more passive visual temporary memory.

IX.   Unilateral Spatial Neglect as a Disorder of Visuospatial
Working Memory

The concept of visuospatial working memory has been useful in understanding the disorders of mental imagery suffered by some brain-damaged individuals, and the dissociations between the selective impairments observed in such individuals has in turn offered evidence for the characteristics of visual and spatial working memory in the healthy brain. In the discussion above, I mentioned several individual case studies of some patients who have particular disorders of imagery and temporary memory for spatial dynamic material, while others have selective impairments of immediate memory for the visual appearance of scenes. Another class of patients who suffer from a disorder referred to as unilateral spatial neglect also has provided insight into the characteristics of visual and spatial working memory, and in particular speak to the possible divorce between perception and visuospatial representation that I have proposed (Logie, 1995) and discussed in the earlier parts of this chapter.

The most widely cited early cases of individuals with unilateral spatial neglect were reported by Bisiach and Luzzatti (1978). These individuals had suffered damage to the right brain hemisphere, and appeared to have deficits both in the processing of perceptual information and in reporting information from a mentally generated image. When asked to describe their immediate environment, they successfully described key elements of the scene in the center and to the right of their body midline, but failed to report details on their left. It was clear that their visual perceptual abilities were intact, so the problem did not arise from some peripheral damage to the visual system. It appeared to be more a deficit of visual attention to one half of their visible environment.

Bisiach and Luzzatti (1978), also tested the ability of these individuals to report details of a familiar scene from memory, in their case the Cathedral Square in Milan, Italy. The participants were asked to describe the scene while imagining themselves facing the Cathedral. They were quite successful in reporting details that would appear on the right of the square from that viewpoint, but mentioned very few details from the left of the square. Later they were asked to describe the square while imagining themselves with their back to the Cathedral, and from that imagined viewpoint they omitted details that were now on their imagined left and that they had previously been able to report from the opposite viewpoint. Conversely, they reported details that they had omitted previously, but that were now on their imagined right. This pattern of report indicated that their difficulty did not arise from a failure of memory for details from one or the other side of the square. Nor did the problem arise simply because there were fewer landmarks on one side of the square and therefore fewer to recall. The neglect seemed to apply to their ability to report details from a remembered image, and was determined by the imagined perspective in their mental representation.

The brain-damaged individuals in this study showed problems in both perception of scenes and in reporting scenes from a visuospatial representation in memory. However, the representational problem could not have arisen from their perceptual problem, because the information about the Cathedral Square was acquired long before these individuals suffered brain damage leading to their cognitive impairments. Bisiach (1993) suggested that the representational problem might reflect damage either to a visuospatial component of working memory, analogous to the left half of some kind of mental screen being torn or distorted, or might reflect an inability to attend to the left half of the mental image of the scene that was otherwise well formed in working memory.

One possible interpretation of the patterns of impairment found in individuals with this form of brain damage might be to suggest that the cognitive systems responsible for perception overlap those that support mental imagery. This would account for the fact that they showed impairments of both perception and of imagery. However, if this were the case, presumably these individuals would have had great difficulty discriminating between real scenes and those that they imagined, yet there was no evidence that they had any such difficulty. Moreover, there have now been many more individuals reported who have the characteristic unilateral bias to their visuospatial deficit, but who show this only in perception, only in representation, or only when dealing with space close to their body or that is distant from their body. In other words, there are several different forms of neglect, not all of which are accompanied by disorders of both perception and imagery within the same individuals (e.g., Beschin, Basso, & Della Sala, 2000; Beschin, Cocchini, Della Sala, & Logie, 1997; Denis, Beschin, Logie, & Della Sala, 2002; Guariglia, Padovani, Pantano, & Pizzamiglio 1993; Halligan & Marshall, 1991, 1993; Marshall & Halligan, 1988).

One particularly interesting dissociation in this domain has come from the observation of individuals who appear to show neglect in their representations but not in their perception. The first such case was reported briefly by Guariglia et al. (1993). However, the first case to be examined using a full range of experimentally and theoretically driven tests, case NL, was reported by Beschin et al. (1997). NL had a lesion in the right parietal lobe. He showed no evidence of the perceptual problems that are associated with perceptual neglect, for example, his scores were within the normal range for reading of horizontal and vertical words, for reading through a mirror, for scoring out items in a visual array, for determining the midpoint of lines of different length, and for removing markers placed at various points on his body ("Fluff Test"). He also performed well within the normal range on several different measures of intellectual function, including short-term and long-term memory, Ravens Matrices, and face recognition. However, he showed very clear deficits in tasks that required access to information about familiar scenes. For example, when asked to describe the main square in his home town from a given imagined vantage point, he reported only details that were on the imagined right hand side of the square. Like the cases of Bisiach and Luzzatti, NL could readily report the omitted details when asked to image the square from the opposite perspective. When asked to draw a familiar country scene from memory, he included a great deal of detail on the right of the drawing, but omitted many details on the left (see Figure 8). In addition, he had great difficulty in the formation and manipulation of new visuospatial representations, although he had no difficulty describing novel scenes that were in view, and showed no evidence of anterograde amnesia or general learning difficulty.

NL showed impairments in his ability to find targets in a tactile maze with his eyes closed, but had no difficulty with his eyes open. Also, he had problems in forming images from verbal instructions. In the latter case, we used the matrix path memory task discussed earlier (Brooks, 1967). NL's score was well below that obtained with age-matched controls. He also had difficulty with a version of the task in which he simply had to detect whether the described path exceeded the boundaries of the four by four square

Fig. 8. Drawing of a familiar country scene by an individual (NL) suffering from representational neglect. Reproduced from Beschin, Cocchini, Della Sala, and Logie (1997).

imagined matrix (e.g., commencing in the square in the second row and second column—go down, go left, go left). His errors were almost exclusively failures to detect paths going off the left of the matrix, while he could readily detect such illegal moves to the right. However, when he was given a diagram of the matrix as an external visual memory aid, his performance improved dramatically. Moreover, his performance on the verbal version of the task was well within the normal range.

The pattern of data from NL demonstrated that representational neglect could occur in the absence of accompanying difficulties in perception, pointing to the clear separation between the perceptual system and the representational system. Moreover, previous studies of representational neglect (with individuals who also had perceptual neglect) had focused primarily on the ability to access prior knowledge about familiar spatial layouts, such as the main square in their home town. More recently Denis et al. (2002) described nine cases of individuals with representational neglect. Many of these individuals also showed perceptual neglect, and one was, like NL, a new case of pure representational neglect. Following a battery of standard neuropsychological tests for general intellectual functions and for the presence of neglect, we presented these individuals with novel layouts of familiar objects. In one condition, they saw pictures of four objects arranged in a two by two array, and the task was simply to report the presented objects and their location. Here, we expected few errors, except perhaps for some of the patients who had perceptual as well as representational neglect. In a second condition, the object array was left in view for a period of 90 seconds, and then removed. The task was again to report the objects and their location, but this time relying on memory for the layout that had just been removed. If representational neglect affects immediate visual memory for novel layouts as well as reports of visual details of familiar scenes, we would expect errors in recall that would appear more frequently for items depicted on the left of the array. In a third condition, the participants were not shown any objects, but instead heard an object layout described, for example, in front, on the right is a banana, to the left of the banana is an orange, behind the orange is a pear, to the right of the pear is a plum. The task, as in the previous two conditions, was to report the objects and their location, but in this case the task was accomplished without any visual perceptual input. If the participants attempted to form a mental representation such as a mental image, despite their imagery impairment, then we might expect that they would have more errors in recall from the left of the described array than from the right. If, however, they rely on their intact verbal memory then there should be no evidence of lateralized bias in their errors. Finally, we tested verbal memory by presenting, aurally, a series of sentences describing arbitrary properties of a series of objects, but with no spatial or locational references, for example, "the sugar is expensive, the coffee is bad, the tea is pleasant, the milk is fresh."

Recall performance in the verbal memory conditions was almost the same for the patients (mean=11.56, max=16) as for the controls (mean=11.60, max=16). A summary of the data from the other three manipulations for both the patient group and the healthy controls is shown in Table I. In the visual perceptual condition, the participants with neglect tended to omit items that were presented on the left, but were at ceiling for items on the right. This would be expected since most of them suffered from perceptual as well as representational neglect. In the memory following visual perception condition, the lateralized bias in the errors appeared again for the groups of patients. There is evidence of some forgetting, with an overall drop in performance compared to the perceptual condition, but this is also present for the controls. It is notable that memory for items presented on the right is almost identical for the two groups of participants.

The observation that the patients show poorer reporting of items on the left than on the right might indicate that they are relying on a damaged representational system. However, it is also possible that this result could have arisen from the fact that perceptual input from the left was impoverished as a result of their additional perceptual neglect, leading to a greater likelihood of forgetting material that had been represented on that side. However, from Table I it is clear that the patients also showed a clear lateralized bias in the aural presentation condition, indicating not only that they were relying on a damaged representational system, but also that the representational neglect observed could not have arisen as a result of any visual perceptual difficulty. For the one case of pure representational neglect, performance in the perceptual condition was at ceiling, and he showed lateralized error patterns only when he had to rely on memory for

TABLE I

NUMBER OF ITEMS REPORTED CORRECTLY FROM THE LEFT OR RIGHT OF AN ARRAY OF FOUR PICTURES OF EVERYDAY OBJECTS[a]

Participants	Perception		Memory following perception		Memory following description	
	Left	Right	Left	Right	Left	Right
Representational neglect ($N = 9$)	5.7	10.0	4.5	8.4	4.6	5.5
Healthy controls ($N = 15$)	10	10	9.1	8.5	7.1	7.5

[a]Maximum score = 10 for each cell.

the previously seen, or previously described arrays. A further two patients showed only perceptual neglect, and their performance for the aurally presented description was no different from the pattern obtained with healthy control participants.

In other words, perception and representation can be damaged independently of one another across different individuals. Moreover, for individuals that are unfortunate enough to suffer from both perceptual and representational neglect, the fact that they show lateralized errors following an auditory verbal description, with no visual perceptual input, demonstrates that their representational problem is largely independent of their perceptual problem. Even more compelling evidence for this independence comes from a case study reported by Beschin et al. (2000). Their patient, Signor Piazza, had the very rare combination of a right hemifield perceptual neglect and a left hemifield representational neglect following bilateral lesions. An example of the problem faced by this patient is shown in Figure 9. The top of the picture shows an object that the patient was asked to draw. The middle picture shows what he produced when copying the picture while it was still in view. Only the left half was copied, indicating a perceptual neglect for material on the right of the depicted object. The bottom picture shows what Signor Piazza produced when drawing from memory, without the original in view. Only the right half of the picture is shown, indicating neglect for the left half of the representation held in memory. However, the fact that he was able to reproduce the left half of the picture when it was visually present clearly demonstrated that the representational problems did not arise from a failure of visual perception.

Some very recent experiments have shown that representational patients can undertake mental rotation of novel layouts or arrays of objects. Logie, Della Sala, Beschin, and Denis (in press) followed the procedure used by Denis et al. (2002) with arrays of objects presented visually or verbally described for later recall. However, in one condition, the patients were asked to recall the layout of the objects as if they had been viewed from the opposite side of the table. This task could be accomplished only if the participants were capable of representing the object layout and then mentally rotating that object layout prior to report. Logie et al. (in press) found that the representational patients could successfully rotate the array, and that their errors arose from those items that were presented on their left or were imagined on their left. The mental transformation itself resulted in no evidence of additional loss of material in their oral reports. It seems reasonable to assume that had the patients been suffering primarily from an attentional deficit that prevented them from attending to the left of their representation, then this deficit would have had an impact on their ability to undertake the mental transformations necessary for mental rotation. These

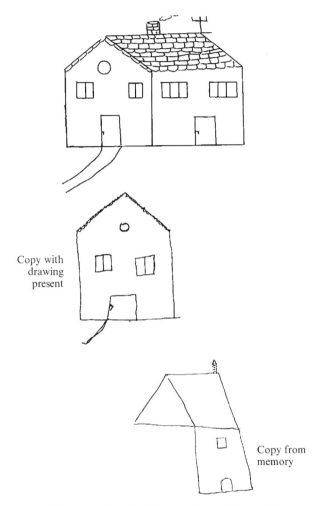

Copy with
drawing
present

Copy from
memory

Fig. 9. Presented picture and copies drawn when in view and from memory by an individual suffering from right perceptual neglect and left representational neglect. Reproduced with permission from Beschin, Basso, and Della Sala (2000, Figure 4, p. 407).

data therefore point to the idea that the neglect in the patients tested by Logie et al. may reflect damage to their "mental screen," that is an impairment of the visual cache or visual temporary memory for static visual arrays discussed in Section VII.

In summary, evidence from studies of patients with representational neglect points toward the suggestion that the visual perceptual system would have grounds for theoretical divorce (by mutual consent) from the cognitive system responsible for maintaining a representation of the visual and spatial properties of objects and scenes. This appears true whether the information arises from knowledge of familiar scenes previously stored in long-term memory, or memory for recently presented, novel arrays of depicted objects. Moreover, there are now some hints as to ways in which impairments of the visual cache of working memory might be distinguished from deficits of the more dynamic spatial component, the inner scribe.

X. Conclusions

I have reviewed a wide range of studies that have explored the phenomena associated with the concept of visuospatial working memory, drawing on evidence from healthy adults as well as children, and from individuals who have selective deficits or selective sparing of visuospatial temporary memory or of visuospatial representations. The cumulative story leads to the idea that the concept of a specialist visuospatial component of working memory might be useful in accounting for this broad range of evidence. Simpler models that suggest working memory might comprise a single, general purpose system for both processing and storage appear increasingly tenuous, as do suggestions that working memory, and in particular, visuospatial working memory, might comprise simply the currently activated elements of long- term memory. Visuospatial working memory deals with the products of those activated elements, whether derived just from stored knowledge or as a result of stimulus input. However, the evidence points to a separate section of the cognitive system, that I have referred to as a mental workspace. This mental workspace comprises elements responsible for temporary storage as well as for manipulation, allowing for memory functions but also allowing for the process of mental discovery and the generation of new knowledge from old.

The compelling notion that our mental visual and spatial world is intimately and directly linked with the external visual and spatial world begins to seem illusory. The mental workspace allows us to represent visual, spatial, and other aspects of the world that we perceive, but that representation incorporates our interpretations, the results of mental manipulations, and additional knowledge from our past experience. In this sense it is very different from perception, and our mental workspace is due for an upgrade from a holding area for recently perceived information to a hub that draws on the products of activating knowledge.

REFERENCES

Anderson, R. E., & Helstrup, T. (1993). Visual discovery on mind and on paper. *Memory and Cognition, 21*, 283–293.

Andrade, J., Kemps, E., Werniers, Y., May, J., & Szmalec, A. (2002). Insensitivity of visual short-term memory to irrelevant visual information. *Quarterly Journal of Experimental Psychology, 55A*, 753–774.

Ashcraft, M. H. (1992). Cognitive arithmetic: A review of data and theory. *Cognition, 44*, 75–106.

Baddeley, A. D. (1966). The capacity for generating information by randomization. *Quarterly Journal of Experimental Psychology, 18*, 119–130.

Baddeley, A. (1996). Exploring the central executive. *Quarterly Journal of Experimental Psychology, 49A*, 5–28.

Baddeley, A. D. (2000). The episodic buffer: A new component of working memory? *Trends in Cognitive Sciences, 4*, 417–423.

Baddeley, A. D., & Andrade, J. (2000). Working memory and vividness of imagery. *Journal of Experimental Psychology: General, 129*, 126–145.

Baddeley, A. D., Emslie, H., & Nimmo-Smith, I. (1994). *The doors and people test*. Bury St Edmunds, Suffolk, UK: Thames Valley Test Company.

Baddeley, A. D., & Hitch, G. J. (1974). Working memory. In G. Bower (Ed.), *The psychology of learning and motivation* (Vol. 8, pp. 47–90). New York: Academic Press.

Baddeley, A. D., Lewis, V. J., & Vallar, G. (1984). Exploring the articulatory loop. *Quarterly Journal of Experimental Psychology, 36*, 233–252.

Baddeley, A. D., & Lieberman, K. (1980). Spatial working memory. In R. S. Nickerson (Ed.), *Attention and Performance* (Vol. 8, pp. 521–539). Hillsdale, NJ: Lawrence Erlbaum.

Baddeley, A. D., & Logie, R. H. (1999). Working memory: The multiple component model. In A. Miyake and P. Shah (Eds.) *Models of working memory* (pp. 28–61). New York: Cambridge University Press.

Baddeley, A., Papagno, C., & Valentine, T. (1991). Phonological short- term memory and foreign-language vocabulary learning. *Journal of Memory and Language, 30*, 331–347.

Baddeley, A. D., Thomson, N., & Buchanan, M. (1975). Word length and the structure of short-term memory. *Journal of Verbal Learning and Verbal Behavior, 14*, 575–589.

Barquero, B., & Logie, R. H. (1999). Imagery constraints on quantitative and qualitative aspects of mental synthesis. *European Journal of Cognitive Psychology, 11*, 315–333.

Basso, A., Spinnler, H., Vallar, G., & Zanobio, E. (1982). Left hemisphere damage and selective impairment of auditory verbal short-term memory: A case study. *Neuropsychologia, 20*, 263–274.

Beschin, N., Basso, A., & Della Sala, S. (2000). Perceiving left and imagining right: Dissociation in neglect. *Cortex, 36*, 401–414.

Beschin, N., Cocchini, G., Della Sala, S., & Logie, R. H. (1997). What the eyes perceive, the brain ignores: A case of pure unilateral representational neglect. *Cortex, 33*, 3–26.

Beyn, E. S., & Knyazeva, G. R. (1962). The problem of protoagnosia. *Journal of Neurology, Neurosurgery and Psychiatry, 25*, 154–158.

Bisiach, E. (1993). Mental representation in unilateral neglect and related disorders. *Quarterly Journal of Experimental Psychology, 46A*, 435–461.

Bisiach, E., & Luzzatti, C. (1978). Unilateral neglect of representational space. *Cortex, 14*, 129–133.

Brandimonte, M., & Gerbino, W. (1993). Mental image reversal and verbal recoding: When ducks become rabbits. *Memory and Cognition, 21*, 23–33.

Brandimonte, M., Hitch, G. J., & Bishop, D. (1992). Influence of short-term memory codes on visual image processing: Evidence from image transformation tasks. *Journal of Experimental Psychology: Learning, Memory, and Cognition, 18*, 157–165.

Brandimonte, M., Hitch, G. J., & Bishop, D. (1992). Verbal recoding of visual stimuli impairs mental image transformations. *Memory and Cognition, 20*, 449–455.

Broadbent, D. E., & Broadbent, M. H. P. (1981). Recency effects in visual memory. *Quarterly Journal of Experimental Psychology, 33A*, 1–15.

Brooks, L. R. (1967). The suppression of visualisation by reading. *Quarterly Journal of Experimental Psychology, 19*, 289–299.

Brooks, L. R. (1968). Spatial and verbal components in the act of recall. *Canadian Journal of Psychology, 22*, 349–368.

Carlesimo, G., Perri, R., Turriziani, P., Tomaiuolo, F., Caltagirone, C., (2001). Remembering what but not where: Independence of spatial and visual working memory. *Cortex, 36*, 519–534.

Chambers, D., & Reisberg, D. (1985). Can mental images be ambiguous? *Journal of Experimental Psychology: Human Perception and Performance, 11*, 317–328.

Chambers, D., & Reisberg, D. (1992). What an image depicts depends on what an image means. *Cognitive Psychology, 24*, 145–174.

Connor, J. M., & Hoyer, R. G. (1976). Auditory and visual similarity effects in recognition and recall. *Memory and Cognition, 4*, 261–264.

Conrad, R., & Hull, A. J. (1964). Information, acoustic confusion and memory span. *British Journal of Psychology, 55*, 429–432.

Cornoldi, C., Logie, R. H., Brandimonte, M. A., Kaufmann, K., & Reisberg, D. (1996). *Stretching the imagination: representation and transformation in mental imagery*. New York: Oxford University Press.

Courtney, S. M., Ungerleider, L. G., Keil, L. G., & Haxby, J. V. (1996). Object and spatial visual working memory activate separate neural systems in human cortex. *Cerebral Cortex, 6*, 39–49.

Cowan, N. (1995). *Attention and memory: An integrated framework*. New York: Oxford University Press.

Cowan, N. (1999). An embedded-processes model of working memory. In A. Miyake and P. Shah (Eds.) *Models of Working Memory* (pp. 62–101). New York: Cambridge University Press.

Daneman, M., & Carpenter, P. A. (1980). Individual differences in working memory and reading. *Journal of Verbal Learning and Verbal Behavior, 19*, 450–466.

Daneman, M., & Carpenter, P. A. (1983). Individual differences in integrating information between and within sentences. *Journal of Experimental Psychology: Learning Memory and Cognition, 9*, 561–584.

Della Sala, S., Gray, C., Baddeley, A., Allamano, N., & Wilson, L. (1999). Pattern span: A tool for unwelding visuo-spatial memory. *Neuropsychologia, 37*, 1189–1199.

Della Sala, S., Gray, C., Baddeley, A., & Wilson, L. (1997). *The visual patterns test: A new test of short-term visual recall*. Bury St Edmunds, Suffolk, UK: Thames Valley Test Company.

Della Sala, S., Logie, R. H., Marchetti, C., & Wynn, V. (1991). Case studies in working memory: A case for single cases? *Cortex, 27*, 169–191.

Denis, M., Beschin, N., Logie, R. H., & Della Sala, S. (2002). Visual perception and verbal descriptions as sources for generating mental representations: Evidence from representational neglect. *Cognitive Neuropsychology, 19*(2), 97–112.

De Renzi, E., Faglioni, P., & Previdi, P. (1977). Spatial memory and hemisphere locus of lesion. *Cortex, 13*, 424–433.

De Renzi, E., & Nichelli, P. (1975). Verbal and non-verbal short-term memory impairment following hemispheric damage. *Cortex, 11*, 341–353.

Duff, S. C., & Logie, R. H. (2001). Processing and storage in working memory span. *Quarterly Journal of Experimental Psychology, 54A*, 31–48.

Engle, R. W., Kane, M. J., & Tuholski, A. W. (1999). Individual differences in working memory capacity and what they tell us about controlled attention, general fluid intelligence, and functions of the prefrontal cortex. In A. Miyake and P. Shah (Eds.) *Models of working memory* (pp. 102–134). New York: Cambridge University Press.

Ericsson, K. A., Chase, W. G., & Falloon, S. (1980). Acquisition of a memory skill. *Science, 208*, 1181–1182.

Ericsson, K. A., & Delaney, P. F. (1999). Long-term working memory as an alternative to capacity models of working memory in everyday skilled performance. In A. Miyake and P. Shah (Eds.) *Models of working memory* (pp. 257–297). New York: Cambridge University Press.

Ericsson, K. A., & Kintsch, W. (1995). Long-term working memory. *Psychological Review, 102*, 211–245.

Evans, F. J. (1978). Monitoring attention deployment by random number generation: An index to measure subjective randomness. *Bulletin of the Psychonomic Society, 12*, 35–38.

Farah, M. J., Hammond, K. M., Levine, D. N., & Calvanio, R. (1988). Visual and spatial mental imagery: Dissociable systems of representation. *Cognitive Psychology, 20*, 439–462.

Farmer, E. W., Berman, J. V. F., & Fletcher, Y. L. (1986). Evidence for a visuo-spatial scratchpad in working memory. *Quarterly Journal of Experimental Psychology, 38A*, 675–688.

Finke, R., & Slayton, K. (1988). Explorations of creative visual synthesis in mental imagery. *Memory and Cognition, 16*, 252–257.

Furst, A. J., & Hitch, G. J. (2000). Separate roles for executive and phonological components of working memory in mental arithmetic. *Memory and Cognition, 28*, 774–782.

Garden, S., Cornoldi, C., & Logie, R. H. (2002). Visuo-spatial working memory in navigation. *Applied Cognitive Psychology, 16*(1), 35–50.

Gathercole, S., & Baddeley, A. D. (1989). Evaluation of the role of phonological STM in the development of vocabulary in children: A longitudinal study. *Journal of Memory and Language, 28*, 200–213.

Gilhooly, K. J., Logie, R. H., Wetherick, N. E., & Wynn, V. (1993). Working memory and strategies in syllogistic reasoning tasks. *Memory and Cognition, 21*, 115–124.

Guariglia, C., Padovani, A., Pantano, P., & Pizzamiglio, L. (1993). Unilateral neglect restricted to visual imagery. *Nature, 364*, 235–237.

Halligan, P. W., & Marshall, J. C. (1991). Left neglect for near but not far space in man. *Nature, 350*, 498–500.

Halligan, P. W., & Marshall, J. C. (1993). Homing in on neglect: A case study of visual search. *Cortex, 29*, 167–174.

Hanley, J. R., & Davies, A. D. M. (1995). Lost in your own house. In R. Campbell and M. A. Conway (Eds.) *Broken memories: Case studies in memory impairment* (pp. 195–208). Oxford, UK: Blackwell Publishers.

Hecker, R., & Mapperson, B. (1997). Dissociation of visual and spatial processing in working memory. *Neuropsychologia, 35*, 599–603.

Hitch, G. J. (1990). Developmental fractionation of working memory. In G. Vallar and T. Shallice (Eds.) *Neuropsychological impairments of short-term memory* (pp. 221–246). Cambridge, UK: Cambridge University Press.

Hitch, G. J., Halliday, M. S., Schaafstal, A. M., & Schraagen, J. M. C. (1988). Visual working memory in young children. *Memory and Cognition, 16*, 120–132.

Hitch, G. J., Woodin, M. E., & Baker, S. (1989). Visual and phonological components of working memory in children. *Memory and Cognition, 17*, 175–185.

Hue, C., & Ericsson, J. R. (1988). Short-term memory for Chinese characters and radicals. *Memory and Cognition, 16*, 196–205.

Hulme, C., Maughan, S., & Brown, G. D. A. (1991). Memory for familiar and unfamiliar words: Evidence for a long-term memory contribution to short-term memory span. *Journal of Memory and Language, 30*, 685–701.

James, W. (1902). *Principles of psychology, Vol. II*, London: Macmillan & Co.

Jones, D. M., Farrand, P., Stuart, G. P., & Morris, N. (1995). Functional equivalence of verbal and spatial information in serial short-term memory. *Journal of Experimental Psychology: Learning, Memory, and Cognition, 21*, 1008–1018.

Jonides, J., Smith, E. E., Koeppe, R. A., Awh, E., Minoshima, S., & Mintun, M. (1993). Spatial working memory in humans as revealed by PET. *Nature, 363*, 623–625.

Just, M., & Carpenter, P. (1992). A capacity theory of comprehension: Individual differences in working memory. *Psychological Review, 99*, 122–149.

Knox, H. A. (1914). A scale, based on the work at Ellis Island, for estimating mental defect. *Journal of the American Medical Association, 62*, 741–747.

Larsen, J. & Baddeley, A. D. (in press). Disruption of verbal STM by irrelevant speech, articulatory suppression and manual tapping: Do they have a common source? *Quarterly Journal of Experimental Psychology..*

Logie, R. H. (1986). Visuo-spatial processing in working memory. *Quarterly Journal of Experimental Psychology, 38A*, 229–247.

Logie, R. H. (1995). *Visuo-spatial working memory*. Hove, UK: Lawrence Erlbaum.

Logie, R. H. (1996). The seven ages of working memory. In J. T. E. Richardson, R. W. Engle, L. Hasher, R. H. Logie, E. R. Stoltzfus, and R. T. Zacks (Eds.) *Working memory and human cognition* (pp. 31–65). New York: Oxford University Press.

Logie, R. H., Della Sala, S. (in press). Disorders of visuo-spatial working memory. In A. Miyake & P. Shah (Eds.), *Handbook of visuospatial thinking*. New York: Cambridge University Press.

Logie, R. H., Della Sala, S., Beschin, N., & Denis, M. (in press). Dissociating mental transformations and visuo-spatial storage in working memory: Evidence from representational neglect. *Memory.*

Logie, R. H., Della Sala, S., Laiacona, M., Chalmers, P., & Wynn, V. (1996). Group aggregates and individual reliability: The case of verbal short-term memory. *Memory and Cognition, 24*(3), 305–321.

Logie, R. H., Della Sala, S., Wynn, V., & Baddeley, A. D. (2000). Visual similarity effects in immediate verbal serial recall. *Quarterly Journal of Experimental Psychology, 53A*, 626–646.

Logie, R. H., Gilhooly, K. J., & Wynn, V. (1994). Counting on working memory in arithmetic problem solving. *Memory and Cognition, 22*, 395–410.

Logie, R. H., & Marchetti, C. (1991). Visuo-spatial working memory: Visual, spatial, or central executive? In R. H. Logie and M. Denis (Eds.) *Mental images in human cognition* (pp. 105–115). Amsterdam: Elsevier Science Publishers BV.

Logie, R. H., & Pearson, D. G. (1997). The inner eye and the inner scribe of visuo-spatial working memory: Evidence from developmental fractionation. *European Journal of Cognitive Psychology, 9*, 241–257.

Luzzatti, C., Vecchi, T., Agazzi, D., Cesa-Bianchi, M., & Vergani, C. (1998). A neurological dissociation between preserved visual and impaired spatial processing in mental imagery. *Cortex, 34*, 461–469.

Macken, W. J., Jones, D. M. (in press). Reification of phonological storage. *Quarterly Journal of Experimental Psychology.*

Manning, S. K. (1977). Ratings of the auditory and visual similarity of consonants: Implications for research. *Behavior Research Methods and Instrumentation, 9*, 495–498.

Marshall, J. C., & Halligan, P. W. (1988). Blindsight and insight in visuo-spatial neglect. *Nature, 336*, 766–767.

McConnell, J., & Quinn, J. G. (2000). Interference in visual working memory. *Quarterly Journal of Experimental Psychology, 53A*, 53–67.

Merat, N. (1999). *The role of working memory in auditory localisation* Unplublished Ph.D. thesis, University of Leeds, UK.

Merat, N., Groeger, J. (in press). Working memory and auditory localization: Demand for central resources impairs performance. *Quarterly Journal of Experimental Psychology.*

Milner, B. (1971). Interhemispheric differences in the localization of psychological processes in man. *British Medical Bulletin, 27*, 272–277.

Miyake, A. (2001). Individual differences in working memory: Introduction to special section. *Journal of Experimental Psychology: General, 130*, 163–168.

Miyake, A., Friedman, N. P., Rettinger, D., Shah, P., & Hegarty, M. (2001). How are visuo-spatial working memory, executive functioning, and spatial abilities related? A latent variable analysis. *Journal of Experimental Psychology: General, 130*, 621–640.

Miyake, A., and Shah, P., (Eds.) *Models of working memory.* New York: Cambridge University Press.

Neath, I. (2000). Modeling the effects of irrelevant speech on memory. *Psychonomic Bulletin and Review, 7*, 403–423.

Neath, I., Farley, L. A., Surprenant, A. (in press). Directly assessing the relationship between irrelevant speech and articulatory suppression. *Quarterly Journal of Experimental Psychology.*

Parks, T. E., Kroll, N.E.A., Salzberg, P. M., & Parkinson, S. R. (1972). Persistence of visual memory as indicated by decision time in a matching task. *Journal of Experimental Psychology, 92*, 437–438.

Pearson, D. G., Logie, R. H., & Gilhooly, K. J. (1999). Verbal representation and spatial manipulation during mental synthesis. *European Journal of Cognitive Psychology, 11*, 295–314.

Pearson, D. G., Sahraie, A. (in press). Oculomotor control and the maintenance of spatially and temporally distributed events in visuo-spatial working memory. *Quarterly Journal of Experimental Psychology.*

Phillips, W. A., & Baddeley, A. D. (1971). Reaction time and short-term visual memory. *Psychonomic Science, 22*, 73–74.

Phillips, W. A., & Christie, D. F. M. (1977a). Components of visual memory. *Quarterly Journal of Experimental Psychology, 29*, 117–133.

Phillips, W. A., & Christie, D. F. M. (1977b). Interference with visualization. *Quarterly Journal of Experimental Psychology, 29*, 637–650.

Pickering, S. J. (2001). Cognitive approaches to the fractionation of visuo-spatial working memory. *Cortex, 37*, 457–473.

Pickering, S. J., Gathercole, S. E., Hall, S., & Lloyd, S. (2001). Development of memory for pattern and path: Further evidence for the fractionation of visual and spatial short-term memory. *Quarterly Journal of Experimental Psychology, 54A*, 397–420.

Posner, M. I., Boies, S. J., Eichelman, W. H., & Taylor, R. L. (1969). Retention of visual and name codes of single letters. *Journal of Experimental Psychology, 79*, 1–16.

Posner, M. I., & Keele, S. W. (1967). Decay of visual information from a single letter. *Science, 158*, 137–139.

Quinn, J. G., & McConnell, J. (1996). Irrelevant pictures in visual working memory. *Quarterly Journal of Experimental Psychology, 49A*, 200–215.

Quinn, J. G., & McConnell, J. (1999). Manipulation of interference in the passive visual store. *European Journal of Cognitive Psychology, 11*, 373–389.

Quinn, J. G., & Ralston, G. E. (1986). Movement and attention in visual working memory. *Quarterly Journal of Experimental Psychology, 38A*, 689–703.

Rudkin, S. (2001). *Executive processes in visual and spatial working memory tasks.* Unpublished Ph.D. thesis, University of Aberdeen, UK.

Saffran, E. M., & Marin, O. S. M. (1975). Immediate memory for word lists and sentences in a patient with deficient auditory short-term memory. *Brain and Language, 2*, 420–433.

Salamé, P., & Baddeley, A. D. (1982). Disruption of short-term memory by unattended speech: Implications for the structure of working memory. *Journal of Verbal Learning and Verbal Behavior, 21*, 150–164.

Salway, A. F. S., & Logie, R. H. (1995). Visuo-spatial working memory, movement control and executive demands. *British Journal of Psychology, 86*, 253–269.

Shah, P., & Miyake, A. (1996). The separability of working memory resources for spatial thinking and language processing: An individual differences approach. *Journal of Experimental Psychology: General, 125*, 4–27.

Shallice, T., & Warrington, E. K. (1970). Independent functioning of verbal memory stores: A neuropsychological study. *Quarterly Journal of Experimental Psychology, 22*, 261–273.

Smyth, M. M. (1996). Interference with rehearsal in spatial working memory in the absence of eye movements. *Quarterly Journal of Experimental Psychology, 49A*, 940–949.

Smyth, M. M., & Scholey, K. A. (1994). Interference in spatial immediate memory. *Memory and Cognition, 22*, 1–13.

Smyth, M. M., & Waller, A. (1998). Movement imagery in rock climbing: Patterns of interference from visual, spatial and kinaesthetic secondary tasks. *Applied Cognitive Psychology, 12*, 145–157.

Towse, J. N. (1998). On random generation and the central executive of working memory. *British Journal of Psychology, 89*, 77–101.

Towse, J., Hitch, G. J., & Hutton, U. (2000). On the interpretation of working memory span in adults. *Memory and Cognition, 28*, 341–348.

Towse, J., Hitch, G. J., & Hutton, U. (2002). On the nature of the relationship between processing activity and item retention in children. *Journal of Experimental Child Psychology, 82*, 156–184.

Tresch, M. C., Sinnamon, H. M., & Seamon, J. G. (1993). Double dissociation of spatial and object visual memory: Evidence from selective interference in intact human subjects. *Neuropsychologia, 31*, 211–219.

Vandierendonck, A., De Vooght, G., & Goten, K. V. (1998). Interfering with the central executive by means of a random interval repetition task. *Quarterly Journal of Experimental Psychology, 51A*, 197–218.

Walker, P., Hitch, G. J., Doyle, A., & Porter, T. (1994). The development of short-term visual memory in young children. *International Journal of Behavioral Development, 17*, 73–89.

Walker, P., Hitch, G. J., & Duroe, A. (1993). The effect of visual similarity on short-term memory for spatial location: Implications for the capacity of visual short-term memory. *Acta Psychologica, 83*, 203–224.

Warrington, E. K., & Rabin, P. (1971). Visual span of apprehension in patients with unilateral cerebral lesions. *Quarterly Journal of Experimental Psychology, 23*, 423–431.

Wetherick, N. E. (1975). The role of semantic information in short-term memory. *Journal of Verbal Learning and Verbal Behavior, 14*, 471–480.

Wilson, B., Baddeley, A. D., & Young, A. W. (1999). LE, a person who lost her 'mind's eye.' *Neurocase, 5*, 119–127.

Wolford, G., & Hollingsworth, S. (1974). Evidence that short-term memory is not the limiting factor in tachistoscopic full-report procedure. *Memory and Cognition, 2*, 796–800.

Yik, W. F. (1978). The effect of visual and acoustic similarity on short-term memory for Chinese words. *Quarterly Journal of Experimental Psychology, 30*, 487–494.

SCENE PERCEPTION AND MEMORY

Marvin M. Chun

I. Introduction

Everywhere we look a visual scene is in view. Scenes embody most of the objects and events that we must locate and identify to guide our thoughts and actions. Thus, it may not be an exaggeration to state that to understand scene processing would be to understand vision.

The ability to perceive one's local visual environment is so important for navigation and other daily activities that it is perhaps not surprising that a region of the brain appears to be specialized for processing scene information. The parahippocampal cortex responds robustly to visual scenes, namely, depictions of visual space (Aguirre, Detre, Alsop, & D'Esposito, 1996; Aguirre, Zarahn, & D'Esposito, 1998; Epstein, Harris, Stanley, & Kanwisher, 1999; Epstein & Kanwisher, 1998). This region has been dubbed the parahippocampal place area (PPA) (Epstein & Kanwisher, 1998), and it can be readily identified within subjects using functional magnetic resonance imaging (fMRI) by localizing the cortical regions that respond significantly stronger to scene stimuli compared to face, object, or scrambled scene stimuli. Figure 1 shows a sampled region of the PPA within medial temporal cortex in a human subject. These data were collected in our laboratory, and the bar graph indicates mean signal strength of the fMRI signal that correlates with neural activity. The results indicate that the PPA region is more active to scenes than to faces or scrambled stimuli.

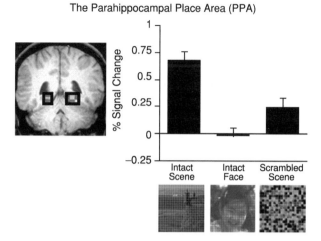

The Parahippocampal Place Area (PPA)

Fig. 1.   The brain image shows a coronal slice of the human parahippocampal place area (PPA), defined as the region (outlined with a black square) with higher activity to scenes than to faces, objects, and scrambled scenes. The bar graph shows the percent signal strength of the fMRI signal, relative to fixation baseline, in the PPA when the subject was viewing scenes, face, scrambled scenes, or scrambled faces. Activity was highest for scenes.

Despite great strides in understanding *where* scenes are perceived in the brain, not enough is known about *how* people perceive scenes and use scene information to guide their actions. Theoretical insights into scene recognition have been hampered by the fundamental question of how to classify and characterize scenes. Unlike faces, which share a similar configuration of commonly shared diagnostic features such as two eyes, a nose, and a mouth, the tremendous variety of scenes we experience do not appear to share much in common, except for the fact that scenes depict a three-dimensional layout containing objects and surfaces. Researchers lack a grammar to describe scenes or even criteria to distinguish different scenes. These limitations pose a fundamental challenge for the study of scene recognition because any scientific investigation requires at least some common language and rules for characterizing what is being studied.

As a step toward understanding scene recognition and memory, this chapter reviews studies from the literature and also identifies my laboratory that describe how visual scenes and scene properties are learned and represented in the brain. This chapter also identifies outstanding issues in scene perception and memory that deserve further research. In Section III.A, a dual-path model of scene representation is shown as one possible framework to guide future work.

The chapter reviews some basic properties of scenes. Despite a lack of consensus on how to operationalize different scenes, visual scenes share a number of properties that are uncontroversial and three of these characteristics are described.

A. SCENES ARE COMPLEX

Most everyday scenes are complex in detail, presenting a rich multitude of objects and surfaces to the observer. In fact, the amount of information in any given scene greatly exceeds what can be handled by the brain at any given time: the well-known problem of information overload (Broadbent, 1958; Chun & Wolfe, 2001; Pashler, 1998). Such complexity leads to dramatic gaps in people's perceptual grasp of the visual world and has led to rather sophisticated attentional selection mechanisms that efficiently locate and detect important information within complex scenes (Chun & Marois, 2002).

Some of the most compelling laboratory demonstrations of limited capacity in scene processing are based on the "change blindness" paradigm (Rensink, 2002; Simons & Levin, 1997). One dramatic example was in a study that demonstrated real-world failures to detect a switch in a person's identify when that switch happened behind a brief occluding event, such as a door passing in between the observer and the switched person (Simons & Levin, 1998). Simpler, though no less compelling, demonstrations of change blindness from the laboratory involved failures to detect a change between two otherwise identical pictures of scenes flickering back and forth with an intervening mask to disrupt visual transients (Rensink, O'Regan, & Clark, 1997). In these "flicker tasks," subjects have trouble detecting salient changes such as a bridge disappearing and reappearing across flicker. Even in situations in which a scene does not flicker, subjects have difficulty detecting changes that are introduced into the scene during eye movements (Irwin, 1991; McConkie & Currie, 1996) or with other visual transients (O'Regan, Rensink, & Clark, 1999).

Such powerful demonstrations of blindness to details in scenes appear to support proposals that very little visual information is retained from one moment to the next (Horowitz & Wolfe, 1998; O'Regan, 1992). Although this view is probably too extreme, in light of recent demonstrations of good memory for objects in scenes (Gibson, Li, Skow, Brown, & Cooke, 2000; Hollingworth & Henderson, 2002; Hollingworth, Williams, & Henderson, 2001; Kristjansson, 2000; Peterson, Kramer, Wang, Irwin, & McCarley, 2001; Shore & Klein, 2000b), there is no doubt that human observers must constantly contend with a burdensome amount of visual information.

What's remarkable is that the visual environment typically does not "feel" so burdensome, because we can usually find and attend to the information we need without much time and effort (Chun, 2000; Rensink, 2000). This highlights the efficiency of powerful attentional mechanisms that direct limited capacity cognitive processing to the most important object or event that is relevant to our current behavioral goals. For example, while driving, we rapidly detect and usually obey traffic signals and stop signs without much second thought. Yet, such important, but seemingly easy tasks daunt the abilities of the many computer chips that control so many other functions within our automobiles these days. Biological perception is more powerful and more intelligent, based on the brain's ability to utilize both bottom-up and top-down cues (Treisman & Sato, 1990; Wolfe, 1994). Bottom-up cues within a scene include abrupt onsets or salient visual features that are unique in the color, size, orientation, motion direction, or other visual primitive (Bravo & Nakayama, 1992; Theeuwes, 1992; Treisman & Gelade, 1980; Yantis & Jonides, 1984). Top-down cues include perceptual set (Egeth, Virzi, & Garbart, 1984; Folk, Remington, & Johnston, 1992), novelty (Johnston, Hawley, Plew, Elliott, & DeWitt, 1990), and scene context (Biederman, Mezzanotte, & Rabinowitz, 1982; Chun & Jiang, 1998, 1999). These factors when combined drive selection in an efficient manner.

The efficiency of bottom-up and top-down cues is studied using visual search tasks, where observers are asked to search for a target appearing among a variable number of distractors. The visual search displays form artificial scenes that are controlled to study the factors that influence attentional selection. For inefficient search tasks, target detection time increases with set size; for efficient search tasks, target detection time is independent of set size. Uniquely colored targets are detected rapidly, and targets that are more similar to distractors take more time to find (Duncan & Humphreys, 1989).

B. Scenes Have Invariant Structure

The visual world is not random, and the statistics of the environment do not change radically over time. Rather, scenes contain "structure," an obvious, but underappreciated feature of everyday scenes that we consider to be extremely important (Chun, 2000; Fiser & Aslin, 2001, 2002; E. J. Gibson, 1969; J. J. Gibson, 1966; Olshausen & Field, 2000; Reber, 1989; Saffran, Aslin, & Newport, 1996). Structure refers to the regularities the visual environment contains, properties that recur over time: cars travel on roads, people walk on sidewalks, windows can be found on buildings, and so on. Even novel scenes resemble those we have experienced in the past, allowing us to drive through new neighborhoods and stroll in new shopping malls. In sum, natural environments tend to be stable over time, and when dynamic features exist, they tend to move about and change in fairly regular, predictable ways.

The invariant structure of scenes is key to understanding scene perception, and this property provides the motivation for much of the work in my laboratory on scene perception and memory. Our basic proposal is that observers are exquisitely sensitive to visual information that is invariant. For example, the configuration of furniture in one's office or the layout of buildings on one's campus tends to be stable. Even local "scenes," such as the instrumentation panel of one's car, do not change from moment to moment or day to day. Encoding such regularities should facilitate one's interactions with these "scenes" on future encounters. Understanding how scene information is processed and used by the brain can be studied as a problem of learning and memory. How does the brain encode invariant visual information, and how does invariant information benefit visual behaviors and action?

One may first approach this problem by first cataloging the different types of structure that scenes contain. Henderson and Hollingworth (1999) defined a visual scene as "a semantically coherent view of a real-world environment comprising background elements and multiple discrete objects arranged in a spatially licensed manner." Thus, we can identify the following key features of everyday scenes. First, scenes contain spatial configuration information about where objects are located relative to each other. Such spatial regularities can be stable, such as buildings in a neighborhood, or approximate, such as paper on a desk or forks on a table. Second, scenes contain object shapes that covary with each other. A kitchen typically contains a sink, a stove, dishes, cups, and so on. A living room one is more likely to have a sofa than an elephant. Thus, regularities exist in the range of objects that tend to cooccur within a scene. Finally, in addition to spatial and object shape information, scenes viewed over time also contain rich temporal structure. Dynamic environments, such as driving or basketball, contain regularities in how objects move about and change over time, allowing us to anticipate what would happen next. Thus, we need to understand how scene information is integrated over time. Studies that illustrate these points are reviewed in Section II.

C. Scenes Provide Contextual Information to Object Recognition

Objects in natural scenes rarely occur in isolation, but are almost always presented within a rich, detailed mosaic of other features, surfaces, objects, and events. These properties form the global visual context that exists for most of our perceptual interactions with the world. As noted earlier, global context is the source of information overload that complicates the task of individual object recognition. However, there are redundancies and regularities in this flux of information (Biederman, 1972). In most natural scenes, objects and events tend to correlate with each other providing a rich, invariant *covariational texture* of information that serves to decrease complexity and increase predictability (E. J. Gibson, 1969). Although presented in a different theoretical framework and level of analysis, both E. J. Gibson (1963, 1966) and J. J. Gibson (1966) spoke about the attunement of perceptual systems to invariant information in the physical world. In short, sensitivity to regularities in the environment is informative and helpful, and perceptual experience educates and optimizes attention. Reber (1989) states that when the stimulus environment is structured, people learn to exploit the structure to coordinate their behavior in a coherent manner.

Such theoretical considerations lead to the simple prediction that global visual context should provide important constraints to visual processing. We propose that one important role of visual context is to guide the deployment of visual attention (Chun, 2000). Attention handles how information is extracted from scenes and how this information can be used to guide behavior. For example, context and scene meaning may guide eye movements toward important regions within scenes that are consistent with the ongoing goals of the observer. Numerous eye movement studies have shown that fixations indeed tend to cluster around regions deemed to be central to the meaning of the scene or relevant to an ongoing task (Loftus & Mackworth, 1978; Mackworth & Morandi, 1967; Shinoda, Hayhoe, & Shrivastava, 2001; Yarbus, 1967).

II. Contextual Cuing

My colleagues and I have developed a number of tasks to study how the invariant nature of complex scenes comprises contextual information that guides visual behavior. We use the term contextual cuing to refer to the process by which scene context information guides visual attention to important locations, objects, and events within scenes. Unlike most prior work in scene recognition that uses real-world scenes or depictions of real scenes, we employ rather impoverished, artificial "scenes." What we lose in realism, we gain in our ability to operationalize and control different components of scenes such as their layout and content. More importantly, by using novel scenes, we can explore how scene information is learned. In relation to this, we aim to elucidate the neural mechanisms involved in representing complex scene information. Note that the principles that benefit performance in our artificial displays have correlates in studies that employ more naturalistic, real-world images (Ryan, Althoff, Whitlow, & Cohen, 2000; Sheinberg & Logothetis, 1998).

A. How Does Spatial Layout Cue Location?

As reviewed above, a primary feature of scenes is that objects are arranged in a "spatially licensed manner" (Chun & Jiang, 1998; Henderson & Hollingworth, 1999). Buildings maintain their configurations over time, as does the furniture in one's office. Certainly variation occurs, but by and large, the positions of most objects in the visual world are fairly stable, especially from one moment to the next. Such regularities are presented to observers in the form of invariant visual context, such that encoding such contextual information is not only critical for navigating around the environment, but also for orienting to objects within scenes.

Our first study on contextual cuing examined how spatial context cues attention (Chun & Jiang, 1998). We required subjects to quickly detect a target, a rotated T, appearing among 11 other rotated L shapes (see Figure 2). This is a difficult search task that requires careful scanning of the display using focused visual attention, and we measured the time it took to locate the target. Such displays can present clearly defined multiple objects in a flexible, but fully controlled manner. But what is "context" for such sparse displays? Our insight was to define context as the spatial layout of the distractor items surrounding the target. To make this scene property "invariant," we repeatedly presented a set of 12 different scenes (search arrays) across blocks throughout the entire session. To make the scene property useful and predictive, for each repeated scene, we had the target

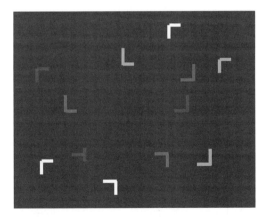

Fig. 2. A sample search trial display from the spatial contextual cuing task (Chun & Jiang, 1998). The task was to search for a T rotated to the right or to the left. The L shapes were also rotated in random directions, and the layout of the distractors forms a "visual context" around the T target. When the distractor configuration was repeated and correlated with a consistent target position, search performance improved in comparison to displays where the distractor configuration was randomly generated.

appear in a consistent location relative to its visual context (global configuration). If observers are sensitive to the invariant spatial configuration surrounding the target, then subjects should be able to detect the target within repeating displays more quickly as they experience more repetitions. Search for targets appearing in the repeated old scenes was compared to that for targets appearing in new contexts, randomly generated in each block to serve as a baseline. Subjects were significantly faster at detecting targets appearing in old displays compared to targets appearing in new displays. We call this the contextual cuing effect because visual context served to cue attention to the target, facilitating search. In addition, subjects were not aware of which displays were old or new, making this task an implicit one, a point that we will return to in Section III.B. Similar results were observed using pseudonaturalistic displays with three-dimensional perspective (Chua & Chun, 2003).

What exactly is contextual information guiding? We had proposed that context guides "attention" based on the assumption that the allocation of attention to a target precedes any action directed toward it. However, we had to infer this based on manual response times. An example of a more direct visual behavior would be eye movements that direct foveal resolution to a target item. Indeed, a recent study that measured eye movements showed that fewer saccades were needed to acquire a target appearing in an old display compared to a new display (Peterson & Kramer, 2001a). Similar results have been observed in monkeys making eye movements to targets embedded in natural scene backgrounds (Sheinberg & Logothetis, 1998). Interestingly, such contextual cuing of eye movements may even override the powerful pull of salient visual events such as abrupt onsets (Peterson & Kramer, 2001a,b).

Although the contextual cuing paradigm was developed to better understand the notion of "context" in visual processing, a number of questions arise from the demonstration of robust, implicit contextual learning. Namely, what is the limit? Any given scene contains a prohibitively large amount of information, all of which need not be encoded. So what counts as context? To begin to address this issue, we raised two questions to examine what counts as context in the artificial displays used in Chun and Jiang's (1998) study.

First, is the entire display of 12 items encoded as global context, or does local context around the target suffice? Olson and Chun (2002) tested this by making only half of each display invariant, while the other half of the display changed randomly from repetition to repetition. The invariant half of the display could either be on the side containing the target or on the opposite side. Thus, for each old scene, half of the display was always invariant and predictive of target location. What varied was whether the target was embedded within the invariant, predictive side or within the random side. Contextual cuing was observed only when the side containing the target was invariant, suggesting that local context is sufficient, and that random local context is not.

Second, Jiang and Chun (2001) explored the role of selective attention in implicit learning of background context information. Jiang and Chun presented displays of rotated L distractors. Half were colored green and the other half were colored red. Each subject had a target color that was red or green, and they were instructed to always attend to that color because the rotated T target never appeared in the unattended color. Thus, for any given display of intermixed red and green items, half of the items was attended and the other half was unattended. Jiang and Chun varied whether the attended context (spatial layout of distractors) was repeated or whether the unattended context was repeated. Only the attended displays produced contextual cuing; unattended items did not, even though they were repeated the same number of times as the attended items, and even though all of the items were interleaved with each other. This finding demonstrates the importance of selective attention in controlling learning, even implicit learning, to items of behavioral relevance. Thus, in the real world, we propose that when contextual information is encoded, such learning is restricted to the subset of items within a complex scene that is most relevant to the ongoing task.

Broadly speaking, contextual cuing illustrates the importance of learning and memory mechanisms in visual perception. The predictive context information was learned as subjects performed the search task. In other words, observers encoded the invariant visual information that benefited target detection. We propose that such learning occurs most of the time that observers are interacting with their visual environment. However, learning is not indiscriminate and it does not have infinite capacity. Thus learning is strongest for local context and especially for attended information. Not all that repeats gets encoded.

B. How Does Shape Context Cue an Object?

Another key feature of scenes is that they contain objects that tend to cooccur with each other. Modern-day classrooms contain desks, chairs, whiteboards, and computer projection systems, and they are unlikely to contain bottles of scotch or ashtrays. Such statistical information provides another form of "structure" that should be useful for the observer. Importantly, covariation information acquired through perceptual experience allows each object within a scene to cue the presence of other related objects.

We studied this in the laboratory using novel shapes (Chun & Jiang, 1999). Subjects searched for a target that was the only shape in the display

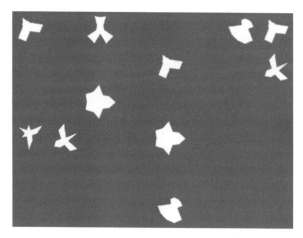

Fig. 3. A sample search trial display from the object shape contextual cuing task (Chun & Jiang, 1999). The task was to search for a vertically symmetric shape. All of the other shapes were symmetric around a nonvertical axis. When the target shape was correlated with the distractor shapes, then search was faster in comparison to a control condition where the target and distractor shapes were repeated but not correlated with each other.

that was symmetric around the vertical axis. The other distractors were novel shapes symmetric around a nonvertical axis (see Figure 3). Thus, we were able to define a target task without specifying or labeling the precise shape of the target, which could be any one of a large number of vertically symmetric shapes. Upon target detection, subjects pressed a key as quickly as possible, and their response time was measured. The display was then replaced with an array of probe letters, each appearing in a location previously occupied by an object. Subjects reported the probe letter that appeared in the same location as the target on the prior search display. The probe task simply allowed us to ensure that the target was properly identified.

We controlled the statistics of this novel visual world by varying whether the target shape was correlated with its distractor shapes (old condition) or whether the target and distractor shapes were not correlated (new condition). In other words, target shapes were consistently mapped to distractors in the old condition, and variably mapped in the new condition (Schneider & Shiffrin, 1977; Shiffrin & Schneider, 1977). If subjects are sensitive to covariation information, they should be faster in the old condition, and indeed, they were. Importantly, the locations of targets and distractors were completely random in this experiment, so that any cuing effects could be attributed to shape association learning alone. Presumably, this type of learning subserves the intraobject priming effects observed with real objects (Henderson, 1992; Henderson, Pollatsek, & Rayner, 1987).

C. How Does Ongoing Temporal Context Cue an Upcoming Event?

Spatial layout and shape association information are prominent features of static scenes, but they fail to encompass the fact that the visual environment is dynamic. Not only do objects move about within scenes, our perception of scenes changes from moment to moment as we navigate around them. Thus, there is rich temporal structure in the environment that may guide our expectations for what will happen in future time steps.

First, let us consider situations with moving objects. A classic example would be a basketball or soccer game where players move about along with the ball. The movements are obviously not random, and moreover, there are regularities not only in how a single player may move, but how the field of players moves relative to the ball. Effective athletes have what is called "field sense," which basically refers to their above-average ability to read the dynamic field of players to predict how key players will move and where the ball will go in the next time step. This ability is not just an index of natural talent but also of perceptual experience, which tunes the player to important regularities in how plays unfold during the game.

We studied this in a dynamic search task, where subjects were asked to quickly detect a T target that was moving about among other moving L distractors (Chun & Jiang, 1999). The movements of all of the items were independent and seemingly random with the constraint that they could not run into each other. However, for half of the displays, the target trajectory was perfectly correlated with its distractor trajectories, such that the dynamic context of moving distractor items cued the target trajectory. For the other half of the displays, the target trajectory was not correlated with the distractor trajectory. Although the displays were seemingly quite arbitrary, subjects were faster to detect targets appearing along trajectories that were correlated with their distractor trajectories. They demonstrated contextual cuing from dynamic displays without awareness of which dynamic display was old and which was new.

Another form of temporal context exists in how visual events change and unfold over time, even in the absence of explicit motion in the display. Namely, an invariant sequence of events forms a temporal context that benefits visual processing for upcoming events. Olson and Chun (2001) presented sequences of letters and varied whether the letter identities appeared in a fixed sequence or randomly. When the onset of the target letter was preceded by a fixed sequence of letter identities, subjects detected the target more quickly. Thus, when visual events unfold in a previously experienced manner, then the sequential information helps observers predict what is forthcoming. Such temporal context learning undoubtedly benefits everyday perception.

How do subjects acquire such temporal associative information? Fiser and Aslin (2002) demonstrated that subjects are tuned to transitional probabilities between successive shapes. In fact, even passive viewing allowed observers to extract temporal correlations from an ongoing stream of different visual shape sequences. Thus, the acquisition of temporal structure may be understood as a problem of statistical learning, important for both the visual and auditory domains (Saffran, Johnson, Aslin, & Newport, 1999).

D. Scene Structure and Contextual Cuing

To sum, our perceptual environment is highly structured, such that knowledge of such structure, presented in the form of visual context, may guide perceptual processes to rapidly orient to a location, identify an object, or prepare for an upcoming event. The meaningful regularities in the environment may be extracted and internalized using powerful statistical learning mechanisms within the brain. Contextual cuing is a paradigm for studying how regularities are learned through perceptual experience, and how such visual knowledge facilitates behaviors such as search. Understanding the neural mechanisms that encode such regularities should provide insights into how the brain stores visual knowledge for everyday perception.

III. Issues for the Study of Scene Recognition and Learning

In the following sections, we will discuss three issues that deserve further research. For each topic, we will summarize outstanding problems, review existing work, and outline directions for future investigation.

A. How Are Scenes Represented?

What is the nature of scene representations in the mind? This seemingly basic question does not have a straightforward answer. We will divide our discussion into two sections. The first concerns whether scenes are more critically defined by the collection of objects they contain or whether the background configuration is important. The second section develops a dual-path model of scene processing that is based on evidence that spatial layout information and object association information may make separable contributions to scene recognition and may have dissociable substrates in the brain.

1. Objects or Background?

Are scenes merely collections of cooccurring objects or is the background structure of a scene important as well? This question has been traditionally asked by studies that probe the effects of scene context on object recognition. In addition, novel insights have recently been obtained from functional neuroimaging.

Consider an office scene. An office contains objects that cooccur in the real world: chairs, computers, telephones, pens, papers, books, etc. In addition to these objects, offices typically contain a certain background structure: four walls, floor, ceiling, windows, and perhaps some built-in bookshelves and desk countertops attached to the wall. This background structure depicts a sense of three-dimensional space within which objects can be arrayed in coherent spatial relations to each other. Of course, in principle, the distinction between object and background is much less clear than described above. However, to start, we wish to follow the convention that objects tend to be things that either move around or can be moved around, while backgrounds depict more stable, fixed entities, thus providing reference points to define the space in which they appear (Boyce, Pollatsek, & Rayner, 1989).

With such a distinction in hand, researchers differ in the relative importance they place on objects versus backgrounds in defining scenes and in understanding scene context effects. Several authors propose that global scene information, formally called "schemas" or "frames," is extracted based on the overall spatial organization of objects appearing within a background context. Such information may be extracted even before individual objects are identified. The schemas serve to facilitate recognition of the embedded objects (Antes & Penland, 1981; Biederman et al., 1982).

Alternatively, scene recognition and scene context effects may be dependent on recognition of the objects that typically comprise a scene (Friedman, 1979; Henderson, 1992; Henderson et al., 1987). Scene context facilitation of object identification would occur by priming from other objects within the scene. Scene recognition itself is largely driven by rapid identification of diagnostic objects within scenes (e.g., an oven to define a kitchen scene, or a car for a garage scene).

Boyce et al. (1989) supported the schema hypothesis to explain scene context effects on target facilitation. Namely, global background infor-mation appeared to be more critical than surrounding objects. They observed that objects were more difficult to identify within a semantically inconsistent background even when related objects were present. Moreover, for their displays, whether simultaneously presented objects were related or unrelated did not matter.

Other studies support an intralevel object-to-object priming account (de Graef, 1992; Henderson et al., 1987). This account is based on facilitation effects observed from related objects that were fixated prior to the target object (Henderson et al., 1987). Even when spatial layout was unstructured, extended viewing of a scene containing statistically correlated objects yielded robust item-to-item priming effects (Chun & Jiang, 1999).

The answer to this debate perhaps lies in between the two accounts (de Graef, 1992). Within the first few hundred milliseconds of analysis of a scene, it is likely that global scene properties, which may include diagnostic color information (Oliva & Schyns, 2000), are rapidly registered and used to guide exploration of the scene (Chun & Jiang, 1998; de Graef, 1992; Henderson, Weeks, & Hollingworth, 1999; Oliva & Schyns, 2000; Schyns & Oliva, 1994). Thus, experimental studies that rely on briefly flashed scenes are more likely to observe global schema effects rather than local object priming effects. As scene viewing progresses across multiple fixations, object-to-object priming is likely to augment how the scene is processed and how component objects are identified. We will develop this idea in further detail below.

2. A Dual-Path Model of Scene Processing

It seems likely that global spatial structure and object shape covariation information make joint contributions to the recognition of scenes as well as objects within scenes. This is reasonable given that scenes contain both spatial layout and object shape information. However, are spatial layout information and shape information stored in an integrated manner or are the internal representations for these somewhat independent? This question immediately brings to mind the popular "what" versus "where" distinction, where spatial information is processed primarily through a dorsal pathway, and object information through a ventral pathway (Ungerleider & Mishkin, 1982). Although the distinction is not absolute, it has proven useful for understanding how spatial or object shape information may make separable contributions to a variety of behavioral tasks. For example, damage to the dorsal pathway impairs the ability to utilize spatial cues in a choice task while damage to the ventral pathway impairs the ability to use shape cues (Pohl, 1973). In working memory, holding spatial locations in mind typically activates the dorsal stream while holding object shape information in mind activates the ventral stream (Kohler, Kapur, Moscovitch, Winocur, & Houle, 1995).

The dorsal versus ventral stream distinction does not map directly on how scenes may be represented in long-term memory, but it is interesting to note that there is some evidence that spatial and object shape information in scenes may be stored in anatomically distinct regions of the medial temporal cortex.

For example, the brain area that is sensitive to scene stimuli appears to care more about spatial structure than component objects. In a seminal neuroimaging study that characterized the parahippocampal place area (PPA), Epstein and Kanwisher (1998) demonstrated that the neural activity in this region was substantially higher for an "empty" room than for a two-dimensional array of multiple related objects (e.g., furniture from a room on a blank background that lacked three-dimensional spatial context). Based on this and other converging evidence, they concluded that the PPA was most sensitive to information that depicted the layout of local space.

Then where are object associations stored? One promising candidate is the perirhinal cortex, which is located at the ventromedial aspect of the primate temporal lobe. It plays an important role in both the perception and memory of objects, especially associations among objects (Gaffan & Parker, 1996; Murray & Bussey, 1999; Murray & Richmond, 2001). Although most work in this cortical region has been conducted in nonhuman primates, our laboratory is currently pursuing a number of hypotheses to establish a role for perirhinal cortex in object association learning.

We believe that the behavioral work and neurophysiological data reviewed here point to a dual-path model of scene recognition. Soon after a scene comes into the eyes, global features of its spatial layout that depict three-dimensional space will activate the parahippocampal place area. This initial "gist" is available within 200 ms (Thorpe, Fize, & Marlot, 1996), even when a mask is present. The global information serves to guide further exploration of the scene (Chun & Jiang, 1998; de Graef, 1992; Henderson et al., 1999; Oliva & Schyns, 2000; Schyns & Oliva, 1994). As interrogation of a scene progresses, multiple eye movements will foveate different objects within a scene. The sequential pattern of these highly detailed object fixations will activate object representations in temporal areas such as perirhinal cortex, where activation will spread on to neuronal representations of other associated objects. These two streams of information should interact with each other, such that global spatial information processed in the PPA may guide the deployment of eye movements and access to associated object shape information in perirhinal cortex. In turn, object shape information may help the PPA to discriminate one local layout from another, as well as cue the presence of other objects within the scene based on associative knowledge stored in perirhinal cortex.

B.   How Do People Learn Environmental Regularities in Scenes?

A very important question that is related to the issue of scene representation is to understand how people encode scenes from perceptual experience. More broadly speaking, how do observers encode important environmental regularities? One thing that we do know about scene memory is that it is exceptionally good. Behavioral studies have revealed that observers can recognize thousands and thousands of scene images that were novel to them prior to a brief study phase (Shepard, 1967; Standing, 1973; Standing, Conezio, & Haber, 1970). Although such memory performance probably relies more on scene gist rather than a detailed engram, it is still remarkable how many scene images can be encoded, sometimes even based on a single trial of exposure. Furthermore, we suspect that remarkable scene memory performance measured in such recognition tasks may actually be a gross underestimate of the brain's capacity to encode and discriminate scene information. We base this conjecture on the hypothesis that conscious recognition memory, measured in these prior studies, has smaller capacity than that of unconscious, implicit recognition memory.

A considerable bulk of memory research is organized around the distinction between explicit and implicit memory (Roediger, 1990; Schacter, 1987; Squire, Knowlton, & Musen, 1993). Explicit (declarative) memory supports the ability to consciously retrieve and declare past facts and events. Implicit (nondeclarative) memory supports improved performance in a variety of perceptual and motor tasks, although observers cannot recall or articulate the learned information. The basic feature of implicit memory is that much information that cannot be consciously retrieved can produce effects on behavior due to prior exposure. In fact, amnesic patients with very little explicit memory show intact implicit memory for a variety of perceptual and motor tasks (Cohen & Squire, 1980; Corkin, 1968). Thus, implicit memory may be more sensitive than explicit memory in revealing traces of past experience. Another related feature of implicit memory is its robustness over time. Information that fades away from explicit retrieval over time may be accessed with implicit memory tasks (Cave, 1997; Cave & Squire, 1992; Jacoby & Dallas, 1981; Tulving, Schacter, & Stark, 1982).

Returning to scene context learning, the work of our own laboratory on contextual cuing also shows that "scene" memory can be remarkably powerful, even for the rather sparse, similar-looking displays. Another interesting key feature of contextual cuing is that it is implicit (Chun & Jiang, 1998, 1999, 2003; Olson & Chun, 2001). Most observers do not consciously notice the predictive relationship between repeating contexts and embedded target locations or identities. In fact, most subjects do not even notice that scene layouts or object shapes were repeating. When probed to explicitly discriminate old displays from new displays, subjects performed at chance. Even when alerted to the fact that displays were repeated and should be noted, subjects did not show more contextual cuing or better performance on the explicit recognition task (Chun & Jiang, 2003). Fiser and Aslin (2001, 2002) have also observed that subjects may implicitly learn important statistical regularities from structured spatial arrays or temporal sequences of visual objects.

Such implicit learning is perhaps essential for visual perception, because as a number of authors have argued (Lewicki, 1986; Reber, 1989), implicit learning allows the learner to extract statistical regularities in a more efficient manner than may be possible through explicit learning. As noted above, a practical feature of implicit learning is that it tends to be more robust and sensitive than explicitly learned information. For example, in the spatial contextual cuing task, it is quite remarkable to observe such a specific contextual cuing effect based on 12 arbitrary artificial scenes that were not discriminable from the other novel scenes with which they appeared. Even more notable is the finding that such implicitly learned artificial scene information may persist for up to an entire week (Chun & Jiang, 2003).

Characterizing contextual scene learning as implicit need not imply that different mechanisms or brain systems should be involved for implicit perceptual learning versus conscious, explicit perceptual learning. Indeed, an amnesic patient study suggested that explicit and implicit learning may share the same neural substrates. Chun and Phelps (1999) examined contextual learning in amnesic patients with damage to the hippocampus, which is a brain structure important for encoding relational, configural information, critical for a variety of memory tasks such as spatial learning, contextual learning, and episodic encoding (Cohen & Eichenbaum, 1993; Hirsh, 1974; McClelland, McNaughton, & O'Reilly, 1995; O'Keefe & Nadel, 1978; Rudy & Sutherland, 1994). However, in humans, the hippocampus and neighboring medial temporal lobe structures are also essential for explicit, declarative memory (Squire, 1992), such that damage to these structures produce profound amnesia. In contrast, implicit memory, as expressed in perceptual priming studies or motor skill learning tasks, relies on other nonhippocampal brain structures. Does this mean that spatial contextual cuing, which requires spatial learning but is also implicit, does not rely on the hippocampus? Interestingly, Chun and Phelps (1999) demonstrated that amnesic patients with hippocampal and neighboring medial temporal lobe damage were impaired in their ability to benefit from repeating spatial layouts. The patients showed no contextual cuing, suggesting that the hippocampus and neighboring structures are important for spatial scene learning, regardless of whether the learning is conscious or unconscious.

The finding of Chun and Phelps (1999) supports views that the hippocampus is important for configural and relational processing. However, further work is needed. One complication is the finding that partial hippocampal damage is not sufficient to observe contextual cuing impairments (Manns & Squire, 2001), suggesting that complete hippocampal damage is necessary to observe a deficit. Given that the hippocampal patients in the Chun and Phelps study had damage that also extended into other medial temporal lobe structures, it is possible that these other areas play a critical role in contextual cuing. However, a recent neuroimaging study has provided further evidence for hippocampal involvement (Preston, Salidis, & Gabrieli, 2001). Thus, the hippocampus is likely to be essential for spatial contextual learning, independent of whether other medial lobe structures also contribute or not.

Another limitation is that the amnesic patients were only tested with the spatial context task. Thus, it is possible that other nonspatial forms of implicit configural learning may not be impaired by hippocampal damage. It would be very useful to test the object shape contextual cuing task in a group of amnesic subjects with hippocampal damage. If the hippocampus is important for any type of contextual, configural learning, then the patients should not show object contextual cuing. However, if the hippocampus is relevant only for configural learning that involves spatial relations, then hippocampal patients should show normal object contextual cuing. Following similar logic, it would be useful to test hippocampal patients in the temporal contextual cuing tasks as well. An advantage of the contextual cuing paradigm is its flexibility to test spatial, object, and temporal factors separately. Thus, further studies with the contextual cuing task promise to yield further insights into how different components of scene memory are represented in long-term memory.

C.   Does Scene Context Facilitate Object Recognition?

As reviewed throughout this chapter, one of the most basic functions of scene context and gist is to drive eye movements and attention toward objects relevant to a scene. Eye fixations tend to cluster around regions of interest within scenes and to objects relevant to an ongoing task (Loftus & Mackworth, 1978; Mackworth & Morandi, 1967; Yarbus, 1967). Detection of changes, which requires attention, within scenes tends to be faster for features that are central to the context of a scene that for features that are less central to the context of a scene (Kelley, Chun, & Chua, 2003; Rensink et al., 1997; Shore & Klein, 2000a). These findings can be extended to hypothesize that context directly facilitates the identification of consistent objects within a scene. Thus, Palmer (1975) demonstrated that the scene context of a kitchen enhanced recognition of an embedded breadbox as opposed to a drum. Biederman et al. (1982) showed that subjects were better at detecting objects appearing in valid locations compared to invalid locations. Even using novel shapes, targets that were consistently paired with their context were detected more rapidly than those that were not. In sum, it would seem a foregone conclusion that scene context facilitates object recognition in an interactive manner.

Unfortunately, despite considerable work on this topic, a fundamental question about this basic hypothesis remains unresolved: Where is the locus of contextual effects on object perception? Does scene context bias an early stage of visual processing by biasing feature extraction? Or does it operate on higher-level representations, at the stage where perceptual representations are matched with stored descriptions of known objects? Or is scene knowledge completely isolated from object identification processes? Although prior work may appear to support the former two possibilities that place scene context effects on object recognition stages or earlier, recent studies have questioned this assumption with evidence showing that scene context effects may reflect response bias or selective encoding, rather than facilitated perception.

A wide variety of paradigms have been used to address this question, but each has specific problems, as reviewed by Henderson and Hollingworth (1999). First, in eye movement paradigms, the dwell time of fixation on an object may be interpreted as one index of object recognition efficiency. Thus, shorter fixations may be predicted for objects consistent with their global scene context. The problem with such measures is that evidence for shorter fixations on scene-consistent objects is not clear, at least not for the first fixation within a scene. A more fundamental problem is that fixation may reflect the contribution of other mental processes beyond perception, such as an increased difficulty of remembering the item for later report or the increased time involved to cognitively assimilate an item that is incongruous with its surrounding context. Thus, eye movement measures, at least as they have been used in the past, may not afford decisive insights into the locus of scene context effects. This problem generalizes to other methods such as naming tasks, which provides response times that reflect other additional cognitive processes beyond perceptual recognition.

Given these problems with eye movement and naming measures, object detection paradigms appear more promising, at least for understanding object facilitation effects. In detection tasks, experimenters measure the accuracy of detecting a target object appearing within a briefly presented scene. A classic study demonstrated that objects appearing within intact scenes were more accurately detected than objects appearing within jumbled scenes (Biederman, 1972). One may also measure response time to objects within scenes. Accordingly, subjects take less time to find a target object within a normal scene than in a jumbled scene (Biederman, Glass, & Stacy, 1973). Although Biederman's early studies demonstrated the importance of coherent scene context, one limitation is that the findings may instead reflect an "incoherent scene disadvantage," given that the jumbled scenes introduced new contours, confounding visual complexity between intact and jumbled scenes.

Such concerns may be addressed by exploring object recognition within coherent scenes only. To manipulate scene context effects, one may vary whether the target object is consistent or inconsistent with the scene (Loftus & Mackworth, 1978; Palmer, 1975). Broadly speaking, inconsistent objects may be incongruous with scene context in their identity (a camel in a restaurant) or in their spatial position (a chair glued to the ceiling in an office scene) or both (a sofa floating in the sky of an outdoor city scene). Using signal detection measures, early studies showed that the advantage for consistent objects (Biederman et al., 1982; Biederman, Teitelbaum, & Mezzanotte, 1983) reflected higher sensitivity, a measure of perceptual discriminability, rather than bias, a measure of postidentification decision processes. However, this finding has been sharply criticized by Hollingworth and Henderson (1998), who demonstrated a problem in the experimental design that affected how perceptual sensitivity was calculated. Using a corrected design, Hollingworth and Henderson not only replicated the results of Biederman et al. using their original uncorrected design, they demonstrated that the advantage of context-consistent objects disappeared when the design was corrected. If anything, Hollingworth and Henderson (2000) have repeatedly observed an inconsistent object advantage, which they attribute to postperceptual selective encoding in memory. Bolstering a postperceptual explanation, Henderson and colleagues (1999) demonstrated that inconsistent objects were fixated longer, but not earlier than consistent objects during scene viewing. In sum, they favor a functional isolation model that posits that scene knowledge and object perception processes are segregated. Evidence for interactions between global scenes and embedded objects may reflect cognitive processes occurring beyond recognition, such as guessing strategies or selective encoding strategies. In sum, current behavioral evidence is very mixed in regards to whether scene context facilitates object recognition or not.

My opinion is that scene context effects occur at both perceptual and postperceptual stages. Different tasks and dependent measures may reveal scene context effects at different levels of perceptual and cognitive processing. Thus, this question should be approached with a variety of methodologies. In particular, cognitive neuroscience methods that look into brain activity may provide novel insights, as I will review below.

To resolve the issue of how scene context influences object recognition, one must consider both anatomical and temporal factors. Anatomically speaking, scene context may influence object recognition at an early or late stage of visual processing. Early stages may include areas in temporal cortex, where object shape information is processed, and they may even include the earliest stages of visual analysis, such as areas V1, V2, and V4, where features are initially extracted from the incoming image. Conversely, scene context may not influence visual processing in the occipital or temporal cortex at all. Instead, one may observe effects of context only in frontal areas that are not specialized for visual analysis, but are more involved in working memory and response selection.

In conjunction with such anatomical factors, one may consider the time course of contextual influences as well. For example, does contextual information modulate stimulus processing as sensory information passes through visual areas, say, within 200 ms of stimulus onset? Or are contextual influences observed at a later latency that may be more consistent with postperceptual processes?

There are a variety of methods to probe the anatomical and temporal characteristics of contextual processing in the brain. We will consider three here. First, single-cell neurophysiology affords insights into contextual influences with very high spatial and temporal resolution. However, such methods are not typically available to study activity in human cerebral cortex. For human studies, there are two noninvasive methodologies that are popularly used. Event-related potentials measure stimulus and task-relevant neuronal activity that can be recorded at the scalp. Although anatomical resolution is poor, temporal resolution is high. Complementary insights may be obtained from functional neuroimaging methods such as positron emission tomography (PET) or functional magnetic resonance imaging (fMRI). These methods measure changes in blood flow that correlate with neural activity. They afford more anatomical precision than event-related potential (ERP) methods, while lacking temporal precision. The anatomical precision can be quite revealing in the case of fMRI.

When one considers the neurophysiological evidence in the literature, it becomes abundantly clear that some form of scene context benefits perceptual processing, at a fairly short latency within the earliest of visual cortical areas: V1. However, the meaning of "scene" becomes critical here, as most work has focused on processing low-level features using stimuli that do not resemble the natural scenes we typically encounter in the world. Nevertheless, if one may (momentarily) allow a collection of discrete items in an array to be called a scene, then one will find that such scene context influences processing of items within it. Consider the neural response of a cell in V1 that is optimally tuned to an oriented line (target) within its receptive field. If the target is the only item within the display, then its orientation will determine the strength of the neural response because V1 neurons are orientation sensitive. Of course, the neuron responds to stimuli only within its receptive field. If the target is presented outside the neuron's receptive field, no response is observed, and no modulation is observed as the target moves around outside the receptive field. However, if the target is in the neuron's receptive field, and there are other items in the context of the target outside of the receptive field, then an interesting result emerges. As the orientation of the items in the context deviates from the target orientation, the neuron's response increases. For example, the neuronal response to a vertical target is maximal when the target is surrounded by a field of horizontal lines, and it is weakened when the surrounding field is also vertical. It is as if the neuron fires to permit "pop-out" rapid segregation of the target feature relative to the background (Knierim & van Essen, 1992). What is remarkable is that such influences are being driven by stimuli outside the target's receptive field. In addition, the latency of such influences is rapid, occurring within 20 ms of stimulus array onset. Such long-range interactions in visual cortex may provide the foundation for psychophysical observations that revealed how thresholds for discriminating faint, oriented visual targets are dependent on interactions with other stimuli that spatially flank the target (Polat, Mizobe, Pettet, Kasamatsu, & Norcia, 1998; Polat & Sagi, 1993, 1994).

Similar observations of contextual influences in V1 have been observed for visual surfaces as well. When the orientation of lines within a target surface patch is different from the texture of lines in the background of the target surface patch, the neural response to the lines within the target surface patch becomes enhanced, supporting the sense of perceptual segregation experienced from such displays (Lamme, 1995; Zipser, Lamme, & Schiller, 1996; but see Rossi, Desimone, & Ungerleider, 2001).

Of course, most people will resist calling these artificial displays scenes. In fact, the mechanisms described above most likely play a role in low-level visual processing, promoting texture segregation and feature pop-out. The point that I wish to draw is that one of the most fundamental stages of visual processing harbors neural mechanisms to support highly interactive processing. No feature is processed in isolation of another, and this fact encourages the search for similar processing principles within higher levels of visual processing.

One attempt to do so employed the contextual cuing paradigm. Olson, Chun, and Allison (2001) had the opportunity to collect electrophysiological recordings directly from the cortical surface of patients who were being monitored for epileptic seizure foci. We trained a group of patients on a set of spatial contexts that predicted the embedded target location. The patients showed a significant contextual cuing effect, faster detection of targets appearing in old contexts compared to targets appearing in new contexts. Because no other visual cues existed to distinguish old from new contexts, the search benefit must have been driven by learned context information. Thus, any difference in neural activity to old scenes versus new scenes must reflect some process that distinguishes the two types of trials, leading to faster detection. Olson et al. observed significant differences in the

N210 component of the ERP waveform to old versus new scenes. Thus, this finding demonstrates that learned context information can influence neural processing within 210 ms of stimulus onset. Moreover, the relatively higher resolution of intracranial recordings permitted Olson et al. to demonstrate that much of this differential activity occurred in early visual areas such as V4, V2, and perhaps even V1. The latency of the N210 is such that it probably does not reflect modulation of activity within the initial volley of visual information through visual cortex, but rather backward feedback from higher-level stages, presumably scene representations in medial temporal cortex. Unfortunately it is not clear what the N210 is revealing: whether it simply reflects the discrimination of old versus new displays or whether it signals the top-down control of spatial attention to the target associated with an old context. Much further work is needed. Nevertheless, this study provides some of the clearest evidence that learned context information can induce changes in neural activity within 210 ms in early visual areas.

At higher stages of visual processing, there is less direct neural evidence for contextual interactions. However, the potential for contextual influence seems high. Consistent with the dual-path model of scene processing, the first step of scene context effects is likely to be rapid recognition of global scene context and configuration information. Behavioral work has shown that scene recognition is very efficient, based on Potter's (1975) finding that the gist of a target scene can be reliably extracted from a rapid ongoing stream of different scenes. Still, behavioral work cannot pinpoint the time course of scene processing because categorization processes progress even after the stimulus is no longer present. ERP measures can provide more direct measures, and it is very interesting that ERP signals begin to distinguish scene categories by 150 ms after stimulus onset (Thorpe et al., 1996). A follow-up of this study used fMRI to reveal that differential activation for target and distractor scenes occurs in high-level visual areas such as the fusiform and parahippocampal gyri (Fize et al., 2000).

Such solid evidence for rapid scene categorization makes it tempting to postulate that scene information develops in parallel with object information in a way that the two streams of information interact throughout the visual pathway. The next step is to establish that such scene information impacts the representations of embedded objects. Such interactions must be based on associative links between objects that tend to appear together such that the presence of one object cues the presence of the other. Toward this goal, one must demonstrate associative learning in temporal cortex, where object knowledge is thought to reside. One of the most classic studies to do so was a neurophysiological study by Miyashita and colleagues (Miyashita, 1988; Sakai & Miyashita, 1991). By training monkeys on novel visual shapes, they first showed that neurons in inferotemporal (IT) cortex become shape-selective with learning. In addition, they demonstrated that these neurons became selective to other temporally associated but geometrically unrelated stimuli. Presumably, this type of associative learning would assist the neuron's ability to link different views of the same object (Logothetis & Pauls, 1995), in addition to linking different objects that typically cooccur with each other. Of further interest is the recent suggestion that visual experience may induce the development of clusters of neurons with similar stimulus preferences (Erickson, Jagadeesh, & Desimone, 2000).

One limitation of these past studies of associative learning in visual cortex is that they were limited to temporal associations. Namely, a cue stimulus was temporally correlated with a stimulus that trailed in time. However, with respect to the dual-path model of scene recognition, temporal cuing may play a central role, as most objects in complex scenes are fixated in a serial manner. Nevertheless, it would be important to extend these insights to understand how simultaneously presented object shapes may influence the neural activity, and corresponding behavioral response, to a target shape. Our laboratory is currently testing fMRI tasks that examine stimuli sets that are temporally associated and/or spatially associated, and we believe that the results will further clarify how scene context facilitates object recognition within visual processing areas in temporal cortex.

IV. Summary Remarks

Scenes are complex, but this complexity provides a rich source of contextual information that constrains visual processing in a useful manner. In particular, scenes contain many regularities in their spatial layout, object shape correlations, and dynamic features. Encoding such statistical regularities allows observers to use ongoing contextual information to constrain their search and identification of visual objects relevant to behavior. Much scene learning appears to occur implicitly such that past experience with scenes and scene properties may influence behavior even when the observer is not consciously aware of having seen them before. We believe that implicit measures of scene memory reveal a prodigious visual memory capacity that is at least as large, if not larger than the rich capacity for distinguishing previously viewed scenes, as measured through explicit recognition measures.

To understand how such environmental regularities are represented in the brain, it is useful to consider both behavioral and neuroscientific data. Past findings appear to converge to support a dual-path model of scene processing, where global spatial configuration information is rapidly registered and used to guide how a scene is interrogated with multiple eye movements. As fixations move from one object to the next, each object serves to define the scene as well as prime expectancies for other objects within a scene. In addition, neuroscience studies suggest that global spatial configuration information may be represented separately from object association information in the brain throughout the medial temporal cortex. A rich theory of visual processing will emerge through understanding how scene knowledge is acquired, how scene knowledge is represented, and how scene knowledge interacts with early perceptual and late response selection mechanisms.

REFERENCES

Aguirre, G. K., Detre, J. A., Alsop, D. C., & D'Esposito, M. (1996). The parahippocampus subserves topographical learning in man. *Cerebral Cortex, 6*(6), 823–829.

Aguirre, G. K., Zarahn, E., & D'Esposito, M. (1998). Neural components of topographical representation. *Proceedings of the National Academy of Sciences of the United States of America, 95*(3), 839–846.

Antes, J. R., & Penland, J. G. (1981). Picture context effects on eye movement patterns. In D. F. Fisher, R. A. Monty, & J. W. Senders (Eds.), *Eye movements: cognition and visual perception.* Hillsdale, NJ: Erlbaum.

Biederman, I. (1972). Perceiving real-world scenes. *Science, 177*(4043), 77–80.

Biederman, I., Glass, A. L., & Stacy, E. W., Jr. (1973). Searching for objects in real-world scences. *Journal of Experimental Psychology, 97*(1), 22–27.

Biederman, I., Mezzanotte, R. J., & Rabinowitz, J. C. (1982). Scene perception: Detecting and judging objects undergoing relational violations. *Cognitive Psychology, 14*(2), 143–177.

Biederman, I., Teitelbaum, R. C., & Mezzanotte, R. J. (1983). Scene perception: A failure to find a benefit from prior expectancy or familiarity. *Journal of Experimental Psychology: Learning, Memory, & Cognition, 9*(3), 411–429.

Boyce, S. J., Pollatsek, A., & Rayner, K. (1989). Effect of background information on object identification. *Journal of Experimental Psychology: Human Perception & Performance, 15,* 556–566.

Bravo, M. J., & Nakayama, K. (1992). The role of attention in different visual-search tasks. *Perception & Psychophysics, 51,* 465–472.

Broadbent, D. E. (1958). *Perception and communication.* London: Pergamon Press.

Cave, C.-B. (1997). Very long-lasting priming in picture naming. *Psychological Science, 8,* 322–325.

Cave, C.-B., & Squire, L. R. (1992). Intact and long-lasting repetition priming in amnesia. *Journal of Experimental Psychology: Learning, Memory, & Cognition, 18*(3), 509–520.

Chua, K.-P., & Chun, M. M. (2003). Implicit spatial learning is viewpoint-dependent. *Perception & Psychophysics.* (in press).

Chun, M. M. (2000). Contextual cueing of visual attention. *Trends in Cognitive Science, 4*(5), 170–178.

Chun, M. M., & Jiang, Y. (1998). Contextual cueing: Implicit learning and memory of visual context guides spatial attention. *Cognitive Psychology, 36,* 28–71.

Chun, M. M., & Jiang, Y. (1999). Top-down attentional guidance based on implicit learning of visual covariation. *Psychological Science, 10,* 360–365.

Chun, M. M., & Jiang, Y. (2003). Implicit, long-term spatial contextual memory. *Journal of Experimental Psychology: Learning, Memory, & Cognition, 29,* (in press).

Chun, M. M., & Marois, R. (2002). The dark side of attention. *Current Opinion in Neurobiology, 12,* 184–189.

Chun, M. M., & Phelps, E. A. (1999). Memory deficits for implicit contextual information in amnesic subjects with hippocampal damage. *Nature Neuroscience, 2*(9), 844–847.

Chun, M. M., & Wolfe, J. M. (2001). Visual attention. In B. Goldstein (Ed.), *Blackwell handbook of perception.* (pp. 272–310). Oxford, UK: Blackwell Publishers.

Cohen, N. J., & Eichenbaum, H. (1993). *Memory, amnesia, and the hippocampal system.* Cambridge, MA: MIT Press.

Cohen, N. J., & Squire, L. R. (1980). Preserved learning and retention of pattern-analyzing skill in amnesia: Dissociation of knowing how and knowing that. *Science, 210*(4466), 207–210.

Corkin, S. (1968). Acquisition of motor skill after bilateral medial temporal-lobe excision. *Neuropsychologia, 6*(3), 255–265.

de Graef, P. (1992). Local and global contextual constraints on the identification of objects in scenes. *Canadian Journal of Psychology, 46,* 489–508.

Duncan, J., & Humphreys, G. W. (1989). Visual search and stimulus similarity. *Psychological Review, 96*(3), 433–458.

Egeth, H. E., Virzi, R. A., & Garbart, H. (1984). Searching for conjunctively defined targets. *Journal of Experimental Psychology: Human Perception & Performance, 10*(1), 32–39.

Epstein, R., Harris, A., Stanley, D., & Kanwisher, N. (1999). The parahippocampal place area: Recognition, navigation, or encoding? *Neuron, 23*(1), 115–125.

Epstein, R., & Kanwisher, N. (1998). A cortical representation of the local visual environment. *Nature, 392,* 598–601.

Erickson, C. A., Jagadeesh, B., & Desimone, R. (2000). Clustering of perirhinal neurons with similar properties following visual experience in adult monkeys. *Nature Neuroscience, 3*(11), 1143–1148.

Fiser, J., & Aslin, R. N. (2001). Unsupervised statistical learning of higher-order spatial structures from visual scenes. *Psychological Science, 12*(6), 499–504.

Fiser, J., & Aslin, R. N. (2002). Statistical learning of higher-order temporal structure from visual shape sequences. *Journal of Experimental Psychology: Learning, Memory, & Cognition, 28*(3), 458–467.

Fize, D., Boulanouar, K., Chatel, Y., Ranjeva, J. P., Fabre-Thorpe, M., & Thorpe, S. (2000). Brain areas involved in rapid categorization of natural images: An event-related fMRI study. *Neuroimage, 11*(6 Pt. 1), 634–643.

Folk, C. L., Remington, R. W., & Johnston, J. C. (1992). Involuntary covert orienting is contingent on attentional control settings. *Journal of Experimental Psychology: Human Perception & Performance, 18*(4), 1030–1044.

Friedman, A. (1979). Framing pictures: The role of knowledge in automatized encoding and memory for gist. *Journal of Experimental Psychology: General, 108,* 316–355.

Gaffan, D., & Parker, A. (1996). Interaction of perirhinal cortex with the fornix-fimbria: Memory for objects and "object-in-place" memory. *Journal of Neuroscience, 16,* 5864–5869.

Gibson, B. S., Li, L., Skow, E., Brown, K., & Cooke, L. (2000). Searching for one or two identical targets: When visual search has a memory. *Psychological Science, 11,* 324–327.

Gibson, E. J. (1963). Perceptual learning. *Annual Review of Psychology, 14,* 29–56.

Gibson, E. J. (1966). *Perceptual development and the reduction of uncertainty.* Moscow: Paper presented at the Proceedings of the 18th International Congress of Psychology.

Gibson, E. J. (1969). *Principles of perceptual learning and development.* New York: Appleton-Century-Crofts.

Gibson, J. J. (1966). *The senses considered as perceptual systems*. Boston: Houghton Mifflin.

Henderson, J. M. (1992). Identifying objects across saccades: Effects of extrafoveal preview and flanker object context. *Journal of Experimental Psychology: Learning, Memory, & Cognition, 18*(3), 521–530.

Henderson, J. M., & Hollingworth, A. (1999). High-level scene perception. *Annual Review of Psychology, 50*, 243–271.

Henderson, J. M., Pollatsek, A., & Rayner, K. (1987). Effects of foveal priming and extrafoveal preview on object identification. *Journal of Experimental Psychology: Human Perception & Performance, 13*(3), 449–463.

Henderson, J. M., Weeks, P. A., Jr., & Hollingworth, A. (1999). The effects of semantic consistency on eye movements during complex scene viewing. *Journal of Experimental Psychology: Human Perception & Performance, 25*, 210–228.

Hirsh, R. (1974). The hippocampus and contextual retrieval of information from memory: A theory. *Behavioral Biology, 12*(4), 421–444.

Hollingworth, A., & Henderson, J. (1998). Does consistent scene context facilitate object perception. *Journal of Experimental Psychology: General, 127*, 398–415.

Hollingworth, A., & Henderson, J. M. (2000). Semantic informativeness mediates the detection of change in natural scenes. *Visual Cognition, 7*, 213–235.

Hollingworth, A., & Henderson, J. M. (2002). Accurate visual memory for previously attended objects in natural scenes. *Journal of Experimental Psychology: Human Perception & Performance, 28*, 113–136.

Hollingworth, A., Williams, C. C., & Henderson, J. M. (2001). To see and remember: Visually specific information is retained in memory from previously attended objects in natural scenes. *Psychonomic Bulletin and Review, 8*(4), 761–768.

Horowitz, T. S., & Wolfe, J. M. (1998). Visual search has no memory. *Nature, 394*, 575–577.

Irwin, D. E. (1991). Information integration across saccadic eye movements. *Cognitive Psychology, 23*(3), 420–456.

Jacoby, L. L., & Dallas, M. (1981). On the relationship between autobiographical memory and perceptual learning. *Journal of Experimental Psychology: General, 110*, 306–340.

Jiang, Y., & Chun, M. M. (2001). Selective attention modulates implicit learning. *Quarterly Journal of Experimental Psychology, A, 54A*, 1105–1124.

Johnston, W. A., Hawley, K. J., Plew, S. H., Elliott, J. M., & DeWitt, M. J. (1990). Attention capture by novel stimuli. *Journal of Experimental Psychology: General, 119*, 397–411.

Kelley, T. A., Chun, M. M.., & Chua, K.-P. (2003). Effects of scene inversion on change detection of targets matched for visual salience. *Journal of Vision*. (in press).

Knierim, J. J., & van Essen, D. C. (1992). Neuronal responses to static texture patterns in area V1 of the alert macaque monkey. *Journal of Neurophysiology, 67*(4), 961–980.

Kohler, S., Kapur, S., Moscovitch, M., Winocur, G., & Houle, S. (1995). Dissociation of pathways for object and spatial vision: A PET study in humans. *Neuroreport, 6*(14), 1865–1868.

Kristjansson, A. (2000). In search of remembrance: Evidence for memory in visual search. *Psychological Science, 11*, 328–332.

Lamme, V. A. (1995). The neurophysiology of figure-ground segregation in primary visual cortex. *Journal of Neuroscience, 15*(2), 1605–1615.

Lewicki, P. (1986). Processing information about covariations that cannot be articulated. *Journal of Experimental Psychology: Learning, Memory, & Cognition, 12*(1), 135–146.

Loftus, G. R., & Mackworth, N. H. (1978). Cognitive determinants of fixation location during picture viewing. *Journal of Experimental Psychology: Human Perception & Performance, 4*, 565–572.

Logothetis, N. K., & Pauls, J. (1995). Psychophysical and physiological evidence for viewer-centered object representations in the primate. *Cerebral Cortex, 3*, 270–288.

Mackworth, N. H., & Morandi, A. J. (1967). The gaze selects informative details within pictures. *Perception & Psychophysics, 2*, 547–552.

Manns, J., & Squire, L. R. (2001). Perceptual learning, awareness, and the hippocampus. *Hippocampus, 11*, 776–782.

McClelland, J. L., McNaughton, B. L., & O'Reilly, R. C. (1995). Why there are complementary learning systems in the hippocampus and neocortex: Insights from the successes and failures of connectionist models of learning and memory. *Psychological Review, 102*(3), 419–457.

McConkie, G. W., & Currie, C. B. (1996). Visual stability across saccades while viewing complex pictures. *Journal of Experimental Psychology: Human Perception & Performance, 22*(3), 563–581.

Miyashita, Y. (1988). Neuronal correlate of visual associative long-term memory in the primate temporal cortex. *Nature, 335*(6193), 817–820.

Murray, E. A., & Bussey, T. J. (1999). Perceptual-mnemonic functions of the perirhinal cortex. *Trends in Cognitive Sciences, 3*, 142–151.

Murray, E. A., & Richmond, B. J. (2001). Role of perihinal cortex in object perception, memory, and associations. *Current Opinion in Neurobiology, 11*(2), 188–193.

O'Keefe, J., & Nadel, L. (1978). *The hippocampus as a cognitive map.* Oxford, UK: Clarendon Press.

O'Regan, J. K. (1992). Solving the "real" mysteries of visual perception: The world as an outside memory. Special Issue: Object perception and scene analysis. *Canadian Journal of Psychology, 46*(3), 461–488.

O'Regan, J. K., Rensink, R. A., & Clark, J. J. (1999). Change-blindness as a result of 'mudsplashes'. *Nature, 398*(6722), 34.

Oliva, A., & Schyns, P. G. (2000). Diagnostic colors mediate scene recognition. *Cognitive Psychology, 41*(2), 176–210.

Olshausen, B. A., & Field, D. J. (2000). Vision and the coding of natural images. *American Scientist, 88*, 238–245.

Olson, I. R., & Chun, M. M. (2001). Temporal contextual cueing of visual attention. *Journal of Experimental Psychology: Learning, Memory & Cognition, 27*, 1299–1313.

Olson, I. R., & Chun, M. M. (2002). Perceptual constraints on implicit learning of spatial context. *Visual Cognition, 9*, 273–302.

Olson, I. R., Chun, M. M., & Allison, T. (2001). Contextual guidance of attention: ERP evidence for an anatomically early, temporally late mechanism. *Brain, 124*, 1417–1425.

Palmer, S. E. (1975). The effects of contextual scenes on the identification of objects. *Memory and Cognition, 3*, 519–526.

Pashler, H. (1998). *The psychology of attention.* Cambridge, MA: MIT Press.

Peterson, M. S., & Kramer, A. F. (2001a). Attentional guidance of the eyes by contextual information and abrupt onsets. *Perception & Psychophysics, 63*(7), 1239–1249.

Peterson, M. S., & Kramer, A. F. (2001b). Contextual cueing reduces interference from task-irrelevant onset distractors. *Visual Cognition, 8*, 843–859.

Peterson, M. S., Kramer, A. F., Wang, R. F., Irwin, D. E., & McCarley, J. S. (2001). Visual search has memory. *Psychological Science, 12*, 287–292.

Pohl, W. (1973). Dissociation of spatial discrimination deficits following frontal and parietal lesions in monkeys. *Journal of Comparative and Physiological Psychology, 82*, 227–239.

Polat, U., Mizobe, K., Pettet, M.W., Kasamatsu, T., & Norcia, A. M. (1998). Collinear stimuli regulate visual responses depending on cell's contrast threshold. *Nature, 391*(6667), 580–584.

Polat, U., & Sagi, D. (1993). Lateral interactions between spatial channels: Suppression and facilitation revealed by lateral masking experiments. *Vision Research, 33*(7), 993–999.

Polat, U., & Sagi, D. (1994). Spatial interactions in human vision: From near to far via experience-dependent cascades of connections [see comments]. *Proceedings of the National Academy of Sciences of the United States of America, 91*(4), 1206–1209.

Potter, M. C. (1975). Meaning in visual search. *Science, 187*(4180), 965–966.

Preston, A. R., Salidis, J., & Gabrieli, J. D. E. (2001). Medial temporal lobe activity during implicit contextual learning. Paper presentation at the Society for Neuroscience 31st Annual Meeting, San Diego, CA.

Reber, A. S. (1989). Implicit learning and tacit knowledge. *Journal of Experimental Psychology: General, 118*, 219–235.

Rensink, R. A. (2000). The dynamic representation of scenes. *Visual Cognition, 7*, 17–42.

Rensink, R. A. (2002). Change detection. *Annual Review of Psychology, 53*, 245–277.

Rensink, R. A., O'Regan, J. K., & Clark, J. J. (1997). To see or not to see: The need for attention to perceive changes in scenes. *Psychological Science, 8*(5), 368–373.

Roediger, H. L., III (1990). Implicit memory: Retention without remembering. *American Psychologist, 45*, 1043–1056.

Rossi, A. F., Desimone, R., & Ungerleider, L. G. (2001). Contextual modulation in primary visual cortex of macaques. *Journal of Neuroscience, 21*(5), 1698–1709.

Rudy, J. W., & Sutherland, R. J. (1994). The memory-coherence problem, configural associations, and the hippocampal system. In D. L. Schacter & E. Tulving (Eds.), *Memory systems.* (pp. 119–146). Cambridge, MA: MIT Press.

Ryan, J. D., Althoff, R. R., Whitlow, S., & Cohen, N. J. (2000). Amnesia is a deficit in relational memory. *Psychological Science, 11*(6), 454–461.

Saffran, J. R., Aslin, R. N., & Newport, E. L. (1996). Statistical learning by 8-month-old infants [see comments]. *Science, 274*(5294), 1926–1928.

Saffran, J. R., Johnson, E. K., Aslin, R. N., & Newport, E. L. (1999). Statistical learning of tone sequences by human infants and adults. *Cognition, 70*(1), 27–52.

Sakai, K., & Miyashita, Y. (1991). Neural organization for the long-term memory of paired associates. *Nature, 354*, 108–109.

Schacter, D. L. (1987). Implicit memory: History and current status. *Journal of Experimental Psychology: Learning, Memory, & Cognition, 13*, 501–518.

Schneider, W., & Shiffrin, R. M. (1977). Controlled and automatic human information processing: I. Detection, search and attention. *Psychological Review, 84*(1), 1–66.

Schyns, P. G., & Oliva, A. (1994). From blobs to boundary edges: Evidence for time and spatial scale dependent scene recognition. *Psychological Science, 5*, 195–200.

Sheinberg, D. L., & Logothetis, N. K. (1998). Implicit memory for scenes guides visual exploration in monkey. *Society for Neuroscience Abstracts, 24*(pt. 2), 1506.

Shepard, R. N. (1967). Recognition memory for words, sentences, and pictures. *Journal of Verbal Learning and Verbal Behavior, 6*, 156–163.

Shiffrin, R. M., & Schneider, W. (1977). Controlled and automatic human information processing: II. Perceptual learning, automatic attending and a general theory. *Psychological Review, 84*(2), 127–190.

Shinoda, H., Hayhoe, M. M., & Shrivastava, A. (2001). What controls attention in natural environments? *Vision Research, 41*(25–26), 3535–3545.

Shore, D. I., & Klein, R. M. (2000a). The effects of scene inversion on change blindness. *Journal of General Psychology, 127*, 27–43.

Shore, D. I., & Klein, R. M. (2000b). On the manifestations of memory in visual search. *Spatial Vision, 14*, 59–75.

Simons, D., & Levin, D. (1997). Change blindness. *Trends in Cognitive Science, 1*, 261–267.

Simons, D. J., & Levin, D. T. (1998). Failure to detect changes to people in a real-world interaction. *Psychonomic Bulletin & Review, 5*, 644–649.

Squire, L. R. (1992). Memory and the hippocampus: A synthesis from findings with rats, monkeys, and humans. *Psychological Review, 99*, 195–231.

Squire, L. R., Knowlton, B., & Musen, G. (1993). The structure and organization of memory. *Annual Review of Psychology, 44*, 453–495.

Standing, L. (1973). Learning 10,000 pictures. *Quarterly Journal of Experimental Psychology, 25*, 207–222.

Standing, L., Conezio, J., & Haber, R. N. (1970). Perception and memory for picture: Single-trial learning of 2500 visual stimuli. *Psychonomic Science, 19*, 73–74.

Theeuwes, J. (1992). Perceptual selectivity for color and form. *Perception & Psychophysics, 51*, 599–606.

Thorpe, S., Fize, D., & Marlot, C. (1996). Speed of processing in the human visual system. *Nature, 381*(6582), 520–522.

Treisman, A. M., & Gelade, G. (1980). A feature-integration theory of attention. *Cognitive Psychology, 12*(1), 97–136.

Treisman, A., & Sato, S. (1990). Conjunction search revisited. *Journal of Experimental Psychology: Human Perception & Performance, 16*(3), 459–478.

Tulving, E., Schacter, D. L., & Stark, H. (1982). Priming effects in word fragment-completion are independent of recognition memory. *Journal of Experimental Psychology: Learning, Memory, & Cognition, 8*, 336–342.

Ungerleider, L. G., & Mishkin, M. (1982). Two cortical visual systems. In D. J. Ingle, M. A. Goodale, & R. J. W. Mansfield (Eds.), *Analysis of visual behaviour.* (pp. 549–586). Cambridge, MA: MIT Press.

Wolfe, J. M. (1994). Guided Search 2.0: A revised model of guided search. *Psychonomic Bulletin & Review, 1*(2), 202–238.

Yantis, S., & Jonides, J. (1984). Abrupt visual onsets and selective attention: Evidence from visual search. *Journal of Experimental Psychology: Human Perception & Performance, 10*(5), 601–621.

Yarbus, A. L. (1967). *Eye movements and vision.* New York: Plenum.

Zipser, K., Lamme, V. A., & Schiller, P. H. (1996). Contextual modulation in primary visual cortex. *Journal of Neuroscience, 16*(22), 7376–7389.

SPATIAL REPRESENTATIONS AND SPATIAL UPDATING

Ranxiao Frances Wang

The nature of spatial representations is a central issue in many areas of cognitive psychology. For example, object recognition depends on how an object's geometric structure is encoded; navigation is determined by the nature of the underlying spatial representation of the environment; spatial inference and reasoning depend on how spatial relationships are represented; and so on. Various models have been proposed on how spatial information is encoded, organized, and processed to guide different tasks. This chapter reviews traditional models of spatial representations on navigation, object and scene recognition, and spatial reasoning recent findings that challenge these models.

The chapter is divided into three sections. Each of the first two sections addresses a central issue on the nature of spatial representations. The first section focuses on the reference frame used for encoding spatial information and reviews evidence arguing for allocentric representations in traditional models of navigation, spatial reasoning, and object recognition, in three subsections, and discusses recent findings supporting an alternative, egocentric updating model. The second section focuses on the structure of spatial representations and discusses the traditional hierarchical models and two recent studies suggesting that spatial representations of nested environments learned through navigation are fragmented by nature, rather than integrated hierarchical networks. The last section summarizes findings on both the reference frame and the structure of spatial representations and discusses the relationship between the two.

THE PSYCHOLOGY OF LEARNING
AND MOTIVATION VOL. 42

I. Spatial Reference Frames

A. THE DEFINITIONS

Reference frames can be defined in various ways. For the purpose of this chapter, a pure allocentric representation contains spatial information that does not involve an observer. For example, a cup is two feet from the telephone; a maple tree is south of the tower; and so on. These representations remain valid no matter where the viewer is, which way the viewer is facing, or how she or he moves. An allocentric representation can be defined relative to an object, an array of objects, or the earth/ground.

A pure egocentric representation encodes the position of other objects relative to the viewer. For example, a cup is 2 feet to my left. In this case, both the origin and the direction are defined by the viewer. When the viewer moves, both the egocentric direction and distance of the object change. Thus, spatial memory of the egocentric position of an object obtained at a given perspective becomes invalid as soon as the observer moves.

There are at least two kinds of mixed representations. The first one encodes an object's position relative to the viewer. However, instead of defining the object's direction according to the orientation of the viewer, as in a pure egocentric representation, one may encode the direction according to another object or the earth. For example, one may encode "a cup is two feet north of me." The second one does the opposite. Although the direction is defined according to the viewer's orientation, the origin is anchored on another object. One may encode "a cup is left of the ball." Both mixed representations share the fundamental feature of a pure egocentric representation: the representation correctly reflects the spatial relationship only when the viewer is at specific locations facing specific orientations.

Studies of spatial language typically emphasize the coding of directions when distinguishing between different reference frames. For example, if the direction of an object relative to some origin (which is often called the "reference object") is defined by the earth (north/south/east/west), then the representation is based on an "absolute reference frame" regardless of whether the origin is the viewer or another object. If the direction is defined by another object (an object that is not symmetrical and therefore has an axis to define orientations), then the representation is referred to as using an "intrinsic reference frame." If that object happens to be the viewer herself, then the reference frame is referred to as the "relative reference frame." The reference object (or the origin) plays no role in the definition of reference frames.[1]

---

[1] Although the definition of reference frames does not involve the reference object, the specific spatial relationships (e.g., above) have been shown to be affected by the shape and the

In contrast, studies of navigation tend to emphasize the origin as well as the direction. For example, the vector representation of an object's position is often referred to as "egocentric" when it originates from the viewer. Mixed representations may be considered egocentric because these relationships change as the viewer moves (e.g., Wang & Spelke, 2000), but most of the time they remain ambiguous. For this discussion, an egocentric representation refers to whenever the viewer is involved in encoding the spatial relationship, either as the reference object (the "origin") or as the direction definer.

A similar distinction has been made in studies of object and scene recognition. A representation of an object is considered to be "viewpoint-specific" if the representation is valid only for specific viewpoints. Thus, according to this definition, a viewpoint-specific representation is by nature egocentric, or at least partly egocentric, because a viewer's position or orientation is reflected in the representation. A viewpoint-specific representation may be two-dimensional (2-D), such as a "snapshot," or more abstract and encode the three-dimensional (3-D) information. In contrast, a representation is viewpoint-invariant if the information contained in the representation does not change as the viewer moves. Thus, by definition a viewpoint-invariant representation is purely allocentric.

B. SPATIAL REPRESENTATIONS FOR NAVIGATION

A true allocentric representation of the environment, which is often referred to as an allocentric cognitive map, is traditionally considered the ultimate form of spatial representation that an animal is capable of acquiring when its cognitive system is sophisticated enough. Simpler organisms, who lack the cognitive capacity to acquire cognitive maps, have to navigate based on more primitive strategies such as beaconing, path integration, and view matching. Thus, to demonstrate that an animal has a "cognitive map," it has to exhibit behavior that cannot be achieved by these simpler mechanisms. First, I'll first discuss properties of the path integration process in various animals including humans.

1. Path Integration

The primary form of oriented navigation is path integration. The basic idea of path integration is continuous updating by vector summation (see Figure 1). The relationship between a significant place (e.g., home) and the animal is represented as a vector **H**. When the animal moves, it assesses its movement

---

functional properties of the reference object (Carlson-Radvansky & Tang, 2000; Regier & Carlson, 2001).

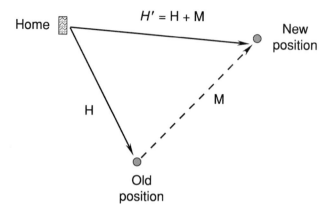

Fig. 1.   An illustration of the path integration process (the allocentric view). The animal's old position relative to home is specified by vector **H**. When the animal moves by **M**, its new position relative to home **H'** is calculated by adding **M** to **H**.

vector **M**. To estimate the new spatial relationship after it moves, the path integration system adds **M** to **H**. The resulting vector **H'** therefore represents the new relationship between home and the animal's new position. Some researchers consider vector **H** as representing the animal's position relative to home (e.g., Collett, Collett, & Wehner, 1999; Etienne, Maurer, Berlie, Reverdin, Rowe, Georgakopoulos, & Séguinot, 1998; Gallistel, 1990). According to this view, path integration is a process that updates one's position in an allocentric map. Alternatively, vector **H** may be interpreted as representing the home location relative to the animal. Thus, vector **H** is an egocentric representation of the home, and this egocentric representation is updated as the animal moves. This distinction will be discussed in detail below. In either case, this process requires accurate assessment of the animal's movements in the form of direction and distance traveled.

There has been ample evidence that path integration is a common navigation process found in almost all species tested, such as insects, birds, rodents, and primates including humans. Wehner and colleagues (Collett, Collett, Bisch, & Wehner, 1998; Wehner & Srinivasan, 1981; Wehner & Lanfranconi, 1981) studied desert ants who leave their nest to forage in a relatively featureless ground, travel on random routes, and may end up in any direction from the nest. Once they find some food, they will carry it and take a direct path back home. This direct-homing behavior might be achieved in three possible ways. First, if there is a landmark at the ant's home site that is visible from a distance, then the ant can just look for the landmark and head toward it directly. This strategy is referred to as *beaconing*. Second, the animal may recognize some landmarks and memorize the homing direction according to the landmarks. Third, the animal may calculate the homing direction by adding up its movement vectors along the journey. This strategy is referred to as *path integration*.

To distinguish between these possibilities, Wehner and Srinivasan (1981) captured the ants after they found the food and were ready to return home, and carried them to a new location and released them. If the ants use beaconing or landmarks to return home, then they will either return home correctly (assuming they can still see the landmarks), or become confused and head in random directions (if the appropriate landmarks are not available). However, Wehner and Srinivasan (1981) showed that neither occurred: the ants headed off in a specific direction and traveled a specific distance, arriving at a site that would have been their nest if they had not been displaced. Thus, the ants appeared to use the path integration strategy instead of beaconing or landmarks. This result also suggests that desert ants are not able to do path integration when they are passively moved, otherwise the ants could have continued the integration process during the displacement and chosen the right direction. Moreover, the ants have a global compass system that is independent of path integration, otherwise they would not have been able to follow the original direction after displacement.

Similar behavior was observed in birds. When geese were carried away from their nest to an unfamiliar site in a cage without cover, they were able to take a direct route back home from the novel releasing point (Saint Paul, 1982). If the cage was covered during part of the journey, they would take off as if the covered part of the trip was erased from their experience. These results suggest that correct homing after a long journey depends on the trip rather than the starting and ending points. Furthermore, it also suggests that without visual cues the geese cease to update, at least not accurately. Rodents are very skillful in path integration, too. O'Keefe and Speakman (1987) showed that after a rat stayed in the central platform of a radial arm maze and located the baited arm, one could turn off the lights and force the rat into an irrelevant arm. After the rat was released from the detour, it could correctly find the food in the now featureless environment. Humans were also tested in the same task. Loomis, Klatzky, Golledge, Cicinelli, Pellegrino, and Fry (1993; Rieser, Ashmead, Talor, & Youngquist, 1990) blindfolded human adults and led them along a path that consisted of several linear segments of different lengths and turns of different angles. At the end of the path, the participants were asked to return to the origin. Because no perceptual cues of the environment were available to the participants, the only way to return to the origin was to calculate the returning direction and distance by integrating their ego-motion during the outward journey. In this path integration task, human adults were able to return to the origin with reasonable accuracy, although systematic errors did occur.

Several features of this remarkable, universal navigation mechanism were examined in detail afterward. Schmidt, Collett, Dillier, and Wehner (1992) asked whether ants continued to update the home vector on their returning journey. They placed a wide barrier on the ants' returning path. The ants turned around the barrier and continued their trip heading toward the correct location regardless of the detour. The authors argued that the homing vector is updated all the time, even during the homeward trip. Ziegler and Wehner (1997) tested the memory span of the direction and distance after path integration in desert ants by capturing the homing ants and placing them in a jar. The ants were then released after various delays. They found that their ability to follow a particular vector course vanished after a few days, suggesting the homing vector may be lost over time.

It is generally believed that the accuracy of path integration is determined by the accuracy of self-motion estimation. Different animals may rely on different perceptual cues for estimating their self-motion, such as optical flow (Ronacher & Wehner, 1995; Srinivasan, Zhang, Lehrer, & Collett, 1996), magnetic fields (Frier, Edwards, Smith, Neale, & Collett, 1996), and internal cues such as energy expenditure (effort to move), efferent copy of the motor command, and vestibular and proprioceptive information (e.g., Berthoz, Israel, Francois, Grasso, & Tsuzuku, 1995; Israel, Bronstein, Kanayama, Faldon, & Gresty, 1996; Kirchner & Braun, 1994; Loomis et al., 1993). Kirchner and Braun (1994) systematically varied the direction and speed of wind in a wind tunnel through which foraging bees had to pass, so that sometimes the bees may fly without moving forward (opposite wind), and sometimes they may fly through it effortlessly (same direction wind). They found that the distance of food source indicated by their dances varied accordingly, suggesting that the distance is encoded en route by estimating the energy expenditure. Ronacher and Wehner (1995) showed that when desert ants walked on a featureless floor, or when they wore eye-covers, distance estimation was still quite accurate, suggesting that they use internal cues. Berthoz et al. (1995) had blindfolded human adults sit in a motor chair that moved along a linear path according to a preprogrammed motion pattern. When the participants were asked to reproduce the distance traveled by actively driving the motor chair, they not only reproduced the distance, the velocity and acceleration over time also matched the original passive motion profile. The authors suggested that people not only record the distance during path integration, but also record the velocity and acceleration profile over time.

Visual cues are powerful and some studies suggest that bees and desert ants rely more on visual cues than their internal senses. Bees flying through a patterned tunnel with wind can correctly estimate the distance traveled, suggesting that optical flow information overrides the energy expenditure measure (Srinivasan et al., 1996). Ronacher and Wehner (1995) trained desert ants to walk along a transparent platform with patterns presented underneath. The patterns were moved at different velocities forward or backward. They found that the manipulation of the patterns' motion, which effectively changed the optical flow on the ants' retina, influenced their homing distance: the desert ants shortened or elongated their trip according to the direction and speed of the pattern motion. These results suggest that ants and bees trust optical flow more than their internal senses.

Despite the multiple sources of information in distance and direction estimation, path integration is always subject to cumulative errors. Thus, it has constraints in its ability to provide accurate guidance for navigation. Some studies suggest that path integration is reset every once in a while. For example, Müller and Wehner (1994) showed that desert ants reset the homing vector to zero when they return to their nest. Collett et al. (1999) showed that path integration can be recalibrated by familiar targets. They trained the ants to a given feeder through an enclosed tunnel, which induced systematic errors in their path integration. Thus, the result of path integration on their return route did not match the result of their outward journey. This discrepancy led to recalibration of the path integration system and biased the ants' navigation both to the feeder and the nest.

Despite its prevalence in different species of navigating animals, path integration is usually not considered "advanced" enough as a cognitive system. The more advanced form of navigation is the allocentric cognitive map. It is often the implicit assumption among researchers of spatial representations that egocentric representations are more primitive and inflexible, and are derived directly from sensory experience. In contrast, allocentric representations require abstraction from egocentric information, are more flexible and thus superior to egocentric representations, and therefore are milestones in both the advancement of evolution and development of individual animals. Thus, one of the goals of research on spatial representations is to search for evidence of allocentric representations in various species and in developing children. Here I discuss three major sets of research that are typically considered as evidence of allocentric cognitive maps.

2. The Landmark Manipulation Test

The first set of evidence comes from landmark manipulation studies. In a typical study, the animal is exposed to a set of objects (landmarks). During testing, the relationship among these objects is altered. If the animal shows exploratory behavior in response to the change, or searches for a goal according to the configuration of the landmarks, then it is concluded that the animal possesses a cognitive map of these objects. For example, Thinus Blanc, Durup, and Poucet (1992) exposed hamsters to a circular open field containing four different objects. The hamsters showed increased exploratory behavior when two of the objects exchanged locations in the test session. Collett and Land (1975) showed that hoverflies identify their station according to a set of surrounding landmarks, and moving the landmarks also moves their station. Rats were shown to locate an escape platform in a Morris water maze according to surrounding visual cues, regardless of where they entered the maze (Morris, 1981). Collett and Cartwright (1983) trained honeybees to find a feeder surrounded by one or more cylinders. During testing, the cylinders either increased size, or the distance between them changed. Honeybees searched at the correct compass direction and at a distance proportional to the size change of a single cylinder, suggesting they encode the location of the feeder in geographic relationship to the landmark. Moreover, when the distance between two cylinders changed, honeybees searched according to the configuration of the two landmarks.

These results have been taken as evidence that the animals encode the spatial relationship among a set of landmarks. The allocentric cognitive map hypothesis can explain all these findings easily. However, alternative explanations based on egocentric representations are also available. For example, an animal's ability to detect a change in the environment can be based on an egocentric representation, either in the form of a 2-D retinal image (snapshots), or in the form of more abstract, egocentric vectors that represent the distance and direction of the objects from a specific viewpoint. Collett and Cartwright (1983) proposed a mechanism of such strategies. They suggested that an animal can approach a specific location defined by a set of landmarks by calculating the difference between the current view of the landmarks to the stored representation acquired from a specific viewpoint, and move in a way that decreases the difference. Thus, simpler mechanisms based on egocentric representations of landmarks relative to a specific viewpoint can also explain these behaviors, suggesting these animals do not necessarily have a true allocentric map.

3. The Novel Shortcut Test

One of the best known tests for cognitive maps is the novel shortcut test. In this paradigm, an animal is led to location A from a home site. Then the animal is led to location B, again from the home site. During testing, the animal is released from A and required to go to B. If the animal goes directly to B instead of returning to home first, then it is taken as evidence that the animal acquired a cognitive map.

Evidence of such novel shortcuts has been demonstrated in various animals including honeybees, rodents, children, and human adults (Gould,

1986; Landau, Spelke, & Gleitman, 1984; Mittelstaedt & Mittelstaedt, 1980; Rieser & Rider, 1991; Tolman, 1948). Tolman (1948) first used this test by training rats through a maze with several turns to retrieve food at a fixed location. During testing, the regular route was blocked and alternative routes pointing at various directions were offered. Instead of following the route closest to the blocked, familiar route, the rats headed directly toward the food site. The ability to take such a novel path, according to Tolman, provides evidence that the rat has an internal representation of the food site relative to its home, which he referred to as a "cognitive map." Gould (1986) used a slightly modified procedure, in which honeybees were trained to forage at feeder A. Then they were trained to feed at feeder B. After the training, honeybees were captured when they left the hive taking off to feeder B, and transported to feeder A. Instead of returning to home, which was a familiar route, the bees took off directly to feeder B. Because the relationship between feeders A and B was never trained, it was thus taken as evidence that bees learned the geometric configuration between the two feeders and their home, which allowed them to navigate flexibly using novel routes.

However, these findings can be explained by a path integration mechanism as well. For example, if the animal starts the path integration from the target feeder B and keeps updating that vector as it travels to home and then to A, then the direction to take from A to B is available when they arrive at A, with no need for a separate representation of the spatial relationship between A and B. The question is, can we distinguish between these two possibilities, one of encoding the spatial relationship among external landmarks and locating oneself within that allocentric cognitive map, and the other of encoding the egocentric vectors of these landmarks and updating them while moving?

If an animal navigates by encoding the location of an object with respect to another object or a set of other objects, or relative to the earth, then it has an allocentric representation (i.e., a cognitive map). The fundamental nature of an allocentric representation is that the spatial relationships specified in an allocentric representation are not affected by the location and orientation of the observer. The allocentric cognitive map may change over time, as new information is acquired, or as a result of forgetting or interference. However, the representation should not change as a result of observer movement. To compute the egocentric direction and distance of any target on the cognitive map, the animal needs to locate its current position and heading on the cognitive map. Moreover, an animal may continuously calculate its position on the cognitive map during navigation by vector summation, or path integration. Once its position and orientation on the map are known, it is straightforward to calculate the course to take to any target on the map.

On the other hand, an animal can encode the locations of other objects or landmarks relative to itself and thus acquire an egocentric representation of the environment. The egocentric relationships change as the animal moves, however. Thus, in order to know where things are after an animal moves, it needs to update these measurements according to its movement vectors. Figure 2 illustrates such a mechanism. Targets A and B's egocentric positions are acquired when the animal is at the old position and represented as vectors **A** and **B**. When the animal makes a movement **M**, the vector **M** is subtracted from both **A** and **B**, yielding two new vectors **A′** and **B′**. **A′** thus corresponds to the new egocentric position of target **A** and **B′** represents the new egocentric position of target B. Although the spatial relationship between targets A and B is never explicitly represented, the animal nonetheless can respond properly relative to both targets from novel positions.

One fundamental difference between an allocentric cognitive map and a dynamic egocentric representation is that the allocentric cognitive map is

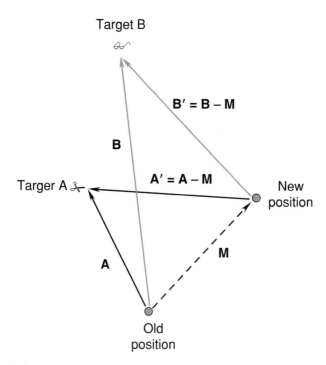

Fig. 2.   An illustration of the egocentric updating model. The positions of targets A and B are represented as egocentric vectors **A** and **B** relative to the animal's old position. When the animal moves by **M**, the new egocentric representation is calculated by subtracting **M** from the old representation: **A′** = **A**−**M** and **B′** = **B**−**M**.

independent of self-motion, while the dynamic egocentric representation relies on the coherence of the updating process. Based on this distinction, Wang and Spelke (2000) made the assumption that an allocentric representation itself is always the same regardless of how the animal moves, whether it reflects the object-to-object distances and angles or measures the object positions individually with respect to an environment-anchored reference frame. What changes over time is the representation of the animal's own position and orientation, which may be calculated continuously from the self-motion estimation. If an animal localizes multiple targets by combining an allocentric map of these targets with an inaccurate estimation of its position and orientation, it will get an inaccurate estimation of all target positions relative to itself, but all targets will be off by the same amount, equal to the error in the self-position estimation. In other words, absolute error will be high, but the configuration of target localization will remain the same.

On the contrary, if the animal localizes multiple targets from novel viewpoints by updating an egocentric representation, then each target's egocentric vector will need to be updated individually. If the estimation of self-motion is inaccurate but the updating process is coherent, then all target vectors will receive the same amount of change and the configuration of multiple targets will remain the same, even though all of them may be off by the same amount (heading error). However, if a certain disturbance impairs the coherence of the updating process, then it will produce random errors or asynchrony among different targets, and disturb the configuration among them. Therefore by investigating the effect of distracting events on the configuration of target localization one may be able to distinguish between these two types of processes: whether one relies on an invariant allocentric map and updates self-position and orientation, or whether one directly represents the egocentric target positions and updates these egocentric vectors based on self-motion.

In a series of experiments Wang and Spelke (2000) tested human adults on object localization after disorientation. The experiments were conducted in a square room, surrounded by six target objects in random positions. Participants learned the target locations and then sat in a swivel chair fixed at the center of the room. After they were blindfolded and pointed to the targets in a random sequence, they were disoriented by turning themselves in the swivel chair for 1 minute. After they stopped, they sat still for 30 seconds to recover from the physical disturbance, and then pointed to the targets as before.

Two types of errors were calculated. One is the *heading error*, which reflects an overall shift that is common to all targets. In case of rotation only, heading error can be estimated by simply averaging the angular errors for all targets. Heading error may stem from inaccuracy in self-motion estimation. That is, if you think you have turned $80°$ but you actually turned $100°$, then there will be a $20°$ heading error. The other kind of error, *configuration error*, measures the coherence of multiple target localization, and can be estimated by taking the standard deviation of the individual target errors. If two configurations are just misaligned, then all targets would be off by the same amount and the individual target errors would be the same, therefore the standard deviation (i.e., configuration error) would be 0. The more variable the individual errors, the larger the difference between the two configurations.

Wang and Spelke (2000) compared the heading errors and configuration errors before and after disorientation. Heading errors were small before disorientation and large and random after disorientation, suggesting that the disorientation procedure was effective. Moreover, participants' configuration errors significantly increased after disorientation, suggesting that the disorientation process impaired the internal consistency of pointing to multiple objects. This is consistent with the egocentric updating hypothesis. However, the increase in configuration error after disorientation may stem from various other factors associated with the procedure, not disorientation per se. For example, participants may be less accurate and consistent simply due to the physical disturbance and fatigue of the spinning; or the representation may be allocentric in nature and independent of self-orientation but the temporal delay between the two conditions caused some memory degradation. If these hypotheses were true, then participants should show increased configuration error whenever they experience the same amount of self-rotation, regardless of whether they lose their sense of orientation or not.

Wang and Spelke (2000) examined these possibilities by introducing a directional cue during the self-rotation period, allowing participants to remain oriented while experiencing the same physical disturbance and temporal delay. They turned off three of the four lights, so that the remaining one would serve as a directional cue. Participants wore a translucent blindfold that allowed them to see the light but not other room features. Again participants pointed to targets before and after the self-rotation. Because the light was on throughout the whole procedure, participants never lost track of their own orientation, although the physical activity and the amount of time elapsed were exactly the same as in the disorientation condition.

Participants showed no increase in configuration error after the rotation. This result suggests that neither the physical rotation and the vestibular stimulation nor the temporal delay can account for the disorientation effect on configuration errors. However, there are still other alternatives. It's possible that object localization by an oriented participant is guided by an allocentric representation, but this representation becomes temporarily inaccessible when one loses one's sense of orientation: Without knowing one's position and orientation, one cannot "look up" the allocentric map to guide the action, even though the map itself may always be accurate and intact. Furthermore, when one's orientation is uncertain, one may constantly vary the guessed heading, producing inconsistency from one pointing response to another.

Both alternative hypotheses predict that the influence of disorientation on configuration errors is associated with the testing condition (namely being tested in a state of disorientation), not the process that produced that state. On the other hand, the egocentric updating hypothesis claims that the damage is done during the disturbance of the process, and not during the testing stage. To distinguish between the egocentric updating hypothesis and the alternatives, Wang and Spelke (2000) followed exactly the same procedure, except that the directional light was turned off during the rotation to induce disorientation, and was turned on again after the participants stopped. In this procedure, the egocentric updating model predicts impairment because of the disorientation, and the alternative hypotheses predict recovery because of the reorientation.

Participants showed small heading errors, suggesting they used the light to correct for the overall error in estimated self-orientation. However, the configuration error increased significantly, and was not reliably different from the disorientation condition. Thus, participants had an intact sense of orientation but not an accurate internal representation. These results suggested that the high configuration error was not due to testing in a state of disorientation. Object localization in humans seems to rely on process-dependent representations (i.e., egocentric representations that are updated as one moves) rather than an invariant allocentric map.

These results also shed light on the nature of the path integration process. Most researchers do not distinguish between the two possible interpretations of path integration. However, it seems more plausible to consider path integration as an egocentric system than an allocentric system, for three reasons. First, the egocentric model of path integration can explain all findings of animal navigation using path integration just as well as the allocentric model of path integration. Therefore there is no a priori reason to assume that path integration is an allocentric system.

Second, path integration based on egocentric representations is a complete navigation system of its own. That is, by representing the egocentric vectors of targets in the environment and updating them by vector summation, the animal can navigate to any one of them directly, without involving any other representations. However, path integration by representing the allocentric position of the animal on a cognitive map is not a complete system by itself. That is, the path integration system is a complementary subsystem of the cognitive map; without a cognitive map, the path integration system cannot stand on its own to guide navigation. Given that path integration is more universal and fundamental in spatial processing, it is more plausible that it is a complete, independent system rather than a component of a more sophisticated system such as an allocentric cognitive map.

Finally, the data on human spatial updating described above are more consistent with the egocentric model, and are difficult to interpret by the allocentric representations. If one believes in the evolutionary continuity in the path integration system of humans and other animals, and therefore believes that they share the same fundamental features, then it would be difficult to imagine that the path integration system in animals is an allocentric system. Instead, path integration is by nature an egocentric system in both humans and other animals.

4.   The Hippocampus as a Cognitive Map

The third set of evidence for cognitive maps, probably the strongest one of all, comes from neurophysiological studies. In particular, a large set of studies has shown that individual neurons in the hippocampus of freely moving rats are active when the rats move through a particular region of the environment (McNaughton, Knierim, & Wilson, 1995; O'Keefe & Nadel, 1978). O'Keefe and Speakman (1987) put rats on a four-arm plus-shaped maze with visible landmark objects around. Rats were trained to go to a "goal arm" that was defined by the landmarks and varied from trial to trial. After they learned the rule, electrodes were inserted into the hippocampus to record the activities of pyramid cells in CA1 and CA3. They found that these cells developed receptive fields (place fields) corresponding to the position of the rat on the maze, regardless of the direction the rat was facing or the direction of the rat's movements. Thus, these cells were named "place cells," indicating that they represent the position of the animal in the environment.

O'Keefe and Speakman (1987) further examined the place cell's behavior in the absence of landmarks. When they removed the landmark objects in the middle of a trial, the place fields still persisted, suggesting that these cells are not merely responding to visual cues. It was also shown that when there were few external cues, such as in the dark without odor marks, texture marks, or sound sources, place fields can maintain at least for a period of time (McNaughton et al., 1996; Quirk, Muller, & Kubie, 1990). The firing also persisted when the rat was carried passively, suggesting that active movements and proprioceptive cues are not necessary for place cell activity.

Moreover, O'Keefe and Speakman (1987) showed that the activity of place cells correlates nicely with the rat's behavior. When the rat made an error and chose the wrong goal arm of the maze, the place cells showed a corresponding error in their place fields. To rule out the possibility that place cells represent certain motor sequences, they introduced a "detour trial" in which the rats were locked on one arm while they detected the goal arm by watching the landmark cues. Then these cues were removed, lights turned off and after a delay the rats were released but forced into a "wrong" arm instead of the goal arm (a detour). From the "detour arm" the rats had to find the goal. In these "detour trials" a completely different, unpredictable motor sequence was involved, but the place fields showed the same correlation with rats' behavioral choices. Thus, it was argued that these place cells not only look and behave like "place" cells, they really function as "place" cells and tell the animal where it is.

A complementary system to the place cells was found in related brain regions, such as postsubiculum, thalamus, and striatum. Taube and colleagues (Goodridge & Taube, 1995; Knierim, Kudrimoti, & McNaughton, 1995; Dudchenko & Taube, 1997; Taube, Muller, & Ranck, 1990a,b) recorded neurons in postsubiculum and found cells that charge whenever the rat's head was pointing at a specific orientation on the horizontal plane. These cells were thus named *head direction* (HD) cells. When both place and HD cells were recorded simultaneously in navigating animals the receptive fields of different place cells and HD cells in the same animal showed internal coherence during cue manipulations (Knierim et al., 1995; Muller & Kubie, 1987). When the visual cues rotated by a certain amount, both place and HD cells rotated their receptive fields by the same amount.

Based on these findings, O'Keefe and colleagues (O'Keefe & Nadel, 1978; O'Keefe & Speakman, 1987) proposed that the hippocampus in rodents serves as an allocentric cognitive map for the rest of the brain and for the animal's spatial navigation. Different place cells have different preferences in space (place fields), therefore the activities of the whole group of place cells can potentially specify exactly where the animal is at each moment (McNaughton et al., 1995, 1996), namely an allocentric map.

However, more recent studies suggest that place cells have more complicated behavior. First, it has been well documented that different place cells in the hippocampus can respond to different sets of cues at the same time when multiple visual landmarks are used. When some of the environment cues moved from trial to trial and some did not, O'Keefe and Speakman (1987) recorded a small set of place cells maintaining their place fields (bound to the stationary cues or the ground) while the majority rotated together with the moving cues from trial to trial, suggesting that each place cell chooses its own reference landmark (Hetherington &

Shapiro, 1997). Thus, the coherence of a group of place cells is not always maintained.

Second, some place cells show a strong directional property (i.e., they fire only when the rat enters their "place fields" from a certain direction) (McNaughton, Barnes, & O'Keefe, 1983; Markus, Qin, Leonard, Skaggs, McNaughton, & Barnes, 1995; O'Keefe & Burgess, 1996; McNaughton, 1996; Gothard, Skaggs, & McNaughton, 1996). This is especially true when the rats are in a radial arm maze or a narrow passage rather than an open field, when the food pellets are clustered (or there's a goal position) rather than scattered (Markus et al., 1995). Some cells even become silent or have completely different place fields when the rat moves in the opposite direction (Gothard et al., 1996).

Third, place cells can change their place fields when the shape of the environment changes. Several kinds of environment changes have been documented. The container can be replaced with a differently shaped one at the same location, with or without the rat's presence, or the entire container may be moved to another location. In both cases the place and HD cells almost completely changed their receptive fields. The entire change of place fields of a group of place cells in hippocampus is named "remapping." When replacing a cylinder with a rectangular or square box at the same location, most place and HD cells unpredictably changed their receptive fields (Muller & Kubie, 1987; Taube et al., 1990b). When the same-shaped box was scaled up, place cells tended to move to the scaled locations (Muller & Kubie, 1987) or stayed at the same distance relative to the near walls (O'Keefe & Burgess, 1996). When one wall of the box was removed to reveal a neighbor box, new place fields quickly developed for that new space but those in the old box area remained the same (Wilson & McNaughton, 1993; Taube & Burton, 1995).

The most perplexing findings come from a set of reorientation studies in both rats and humans. Both place and HD cells show strong correlation with landmarks (cues). In a rectangular or square box with a cue card (i.e., a patch of the wall with different brightness) covering one of the walls, place and HD cells rotated their receptive fields when the cue card switched from one wall to another, even when the rat was present during the rotation (Muller & Kubie, 1987; Taube et al., 1990b). In a cylindrical chamber containing a single cue card, the receptive fields also typically rotated according to the moving cue card (Knierim et al., 1995; Dudchenko & Taube, 1997; McNaughton et al., 1995), and different place cells usually behaved in synchrony with each other and with the HD cells in the same animal during the rotation (O'Keefe & Speakman, 1987; Knierim et al., 1995). Even when the internal signal conflicts with the external landmarks, both place and HD cells tend to follow the familiar landmarks (Dudchenko & Taube, 1997; Goodridge & Taube, 1995; Gothard et al., 1996; O'Keefe & Speakman, 1987), although some studies suggest that the landmarks are more effective when they are familiar and stable (Knierim et al., 1995).

In contrast, behavioral studies of disoriented animals—both rats and children—suggest that these cues are not used to determine where the animal is. Cheng and Gallistel (1984; Cheng, 1986) placed hungry rats in a rectangular box with distinctive visual and olfactory cues as potential landmarks at the four corners. After the rat discovered a half-buried food pellet, it was removed from the box and disoriented in an enclosed box by turning. Then the rat was returned to the test box and allowed to search for the food location. Rats searched with high and equal frequency at the target location and at the geometrically equivalent location at the opposite side of the box, suggesting that they were sensitive to the shape of the box and used this shape as a cue to target localization. Moreover, rats failed to choose the correct corner over the geometrically equivalent opposite corner, suggesting that they did not use the distinctive texture, brightness, and odor cues to locate hidden targets.

The disorientation paradigm was studied in detail in children (Hermer & Spelke, 1994, 1996; Hermer, 1997; Gouteux & Spelke, 2001; Wang, Hermer, & Spelke, 1999). Hermer and Spelke (1994) had 2-year-old children watch a favorite toy being hidden at the corner of a rectangular chamber with a distinctively colored (blue) wall. Then after being disoriented, they were encouraged to search for the toy. Like rats, children searched the target corner and the geometrically equivalent corner (the opposite one) equally frequently, but not the other two corners, suggesting that they were able to use the room shape to locate the hidden object but ignored the distinctively colored wall. Further experiments suggested that children's failure to search the correct location according to the visual patterns was not a memory failure. Instead, it was a specific cognitive constraint on localizing themselves in space after they were disoriented.

Thus, there is a curious discrepancy between the findings of the above two sets of studies. Although disoriented rats and children show striking insensitivity to visual patterns and color cues in behavioral experiments, such information exerts a powerful influence on the firing patterns of place and HD cells in rats. Wang et al. (1999) suggested two procedural differences between these studies that might account for these contrasting findings. First, behavioral studies of rats and children test subjects in environments with a distinctive and informative shape, such as a rectangular room (Cheng, 1986; Hermer & Spelke, 1994). In contrast, neurophysiological studies often use environments with minimal distinctive geometry: an enclosed cylindrical or square chamber (Knierim et al., 1995; Taube et al.,

1990b). Thus, it is possible that children and rats fail to use the visual pattern cues due to the dominance of the informative geometric cues. Second, neurophysiological studies typically test rats over multiple sessions and therefore they became familiar with the environments, while behavioral studies in children tested subjects in novel environments. Thus, it is possible that animals use color/pattern cues only when these cues are familiar and stable.

To test these possibilities, Wang et al. (1999) examined children's object localization after disorientation in a square chamber with a distinctively colored (red) wall. Children again watched a toy hidden and were then disoriented. If children can use visual cues to locate the toy when there are no informative geometric cues present, then they should search at the correct corner when tested in the square room. However, they did not. When asked to search for the toy, children searched with equal probability at all four corners, suggesting they failed to use the red wall to locate the hidden toy. To further test whether familiarity with the environment improves children's ability to use the color cue, children played in the chamber for half an hour before the test was given, or were tested in five sessions with the red wall in a fixed location (Wang et al., 1999). Neither familiarization procedure improved children's ability to use the red wall to locate the toy.

Thus, studies with children failed to resolve the discrepancy between the behavioral findings with disoriented animals and place cell activities by simply attributing the discrepancy to procedural artifacts. However, one might still argue that the difference may be due to species difference, despite the strikingly parallel behavior in rats and children in the reorientation task. Converging evidence was provided by Dudchenko and colleagues (Dudchenko, Goodridge, Seiterle, & Taube, 1997; Dudchenko, Goodridge, & Taube, 1997). They recorded place and HD cell activities in disoriented rats in a cylindrical apparatus with a cue card. They showed that these cells responded reliably to the cue. In contrast, when the same animals were tested in a reorientation task, they failed to use the cue. These studies further suggest that place and HD cell activities can be dissociated from an animal's behavior.

The dissociation between an animal's target localization after disorientation and place/HD cell activities casts doubt on the prevalent belief that the hippocampus serves as an allocentric cognitive map that tells an animal where it is in the environment. Although place cell activity predicts an animal's behavior when the animal is oriented and landmarks are moved around (O'Keefe & Nadel, 1978; O'Keefe & Speakman, 1987), it does not predict an animal's behavior when the animal is disoriented (Dudchenko, Goodridge, Seiterle, & Taube, 1997). In the former case, the target is not located at a fixed location in space. Thus, the animal is learning an arbitrary rule to associate the target with landmarks, rather than locating itself in space in order to go to a particular location. On the contrary, when an animal is disoriented, it needs to reorient itself in space. Thus, if cognitive maps exist, they are more likely to be used by disoriented animals to find out where they are, than by oriented animals learning an arbitrary rule, who already know where they are. That is, if place/HD cells serve as the cognitive map, their activity should predict an animal's searching behavior after disorientation, but not necessarily when it is oriented with landmarks/targets moving around.

According to this logic, the high correlation between place/HD cell activity and the animal's behavioral choices in these landmark manipulation tasks does not provide evidence for the hippocampus as a cognitive map. In fact, the lack of correlation between place/HD cell activity and searching behavior in disoriented animals suggests the opposite: place cells may not be "place" cells; they are more likely to be involved in learning associative rules, rather than representing an animal's sense of position in space. This associative learning hypothesis is consistent with the fact that different neurons are associated with different landmarks (e.g., O'Keefe & Speakman, 1987), and that their receptive fields change when the shape of the surrounding changes (e.g., O'Keefe & Burgess, 1996). This hypothesis is also consistent with findings that hippocampal neurons respond to nonspatial stimuli (e.g., odors) in discrimination tasks, and lesions in hippocampus lead to deficits in associative learning (e.g., Eichenbaum, Otto, & Cohen, 1992).

In short, three major areas of research that have been interpreted as evidence for allocentric representations are questioned by recent findings in navigation. It is suggested that humans, as well as other animals, navigate by representing the egocentric positions of the target objects and updating these representations as they move.

C. SPATIAL REASONING PROBLEMS

It has been a long-established belief that humans' spatial representations undergo a developmental change from simple, inflexible egocentric coding to more flexible allocentric coding. One of the most important tests of egocentric vs. allocentric representations is the spatial reasoning task. The test was first developed by Piaget (1952, 1954). In a typical Piaget spatial reasoning test, children are shown a set of objects on a table. They are asked where an object would be if they were standing at a different place. Children under 9 years of age tend to point to where the object is instead of where the object would be relative to the imagined perspective (an "egocentric error")

(Piaget, 1954; Huttenlocher & Presson, 1979). Piaget argued that these egocentric errors suggest that children encode where things are relative to themselves, which does not allow them to take a perspective different from their actual one.

To examine the nature of the spatial representations underlying perspective change processes, Huttenlocher and Presson (1979) tested children in the spatial reasoning task by either asking them to imagine themselves moving to a different side of the table, or asking them to imagine the table with the object array rotating in front of them. They also used different types of questions. They found that the relative difficulty of imagined self-rotation and imagined object-array rotation depends on the kind of questions asked. For an "item question" (e.g., "which object would be on your left?"), imagined self-rotation is easier than imagined array-rotation, while the opposite happened in a "position question" (e.g., "where would the pencil be?"). The same basic findings were shown with adults (Presson, 1982; Wraga, Creem, & Proffitt, 2000).

Based on these findings, Huttenlocher and Presson (1979) proposed that children develop allocentric spatial representations that encode the spatial relationships between objects and the permanent, stable surrounding (see Figure 3). They argued that if the object locations are encoded relative to the viewer (left panel, Figure 3), then there should be no difference whether children had to mentally rotate themselves or rotate the object array; both

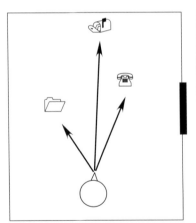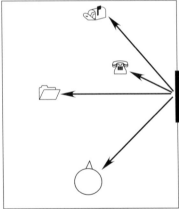

Fig. 3. An illustration of the logic behind Huttenlocher and Presson's (1979) model of environment-centered representations. The left panel illustrates a representation of the object positions relative to the viewer (egocentric representations), and the right panel shows the representation of both the object locations and the viewer position relative to permanent features of the environment.

types of rotations involve the same number of egocentric relationships that needs to be changed. On the other hand, if both the viewer and other objects are encoded relative to the environment (right panel, Figure 3), then moving the viewer involves changing only one relationship, but rotating the object array involves many more relationships that need to be modified. Thus, they argued that children's difficulty in the imagined array-rotation condition supported the model that spatial locations are encoded relative to the environment (allocentric representations).[2]

A different allocentric model was proposed by Rieser (1989). Rieser (1989) tested human adults in a spatial reasoning task. Participants learned an array of target objects around them and were asked to perform two tasks. In the imagined-rotation task, they were asked to "point to where Y would be if you turned to face X." In the imagined-translation task, participants were asked to "point to where Y would be if you were standing at X." Rieser (1989) showed that in the imagined-rotation task, both response time (RT) and pointing errors increased as a function of the angle between the imagined heading and the participant's actual heading (angular disparity effect). In contrast, performance remained constant relative to the location of translation, and was comparable to the no-imagination condition, suggesting that imagined-translation is relatively easy. Rieser (1989) proposed that humans represent the object-to-object relationships rather than the self-to-object relationships (Figure 4). The logic was that a representation of object-to-object relationships directly specifies where other objects are relative to a given object (right panel, Figure 4), thus allowing easy translation to that object but not rotation. In contrast, a representation of the self-to-object relationships (left panel, Figure 4) should be easy to rotate but difficult to translate.

These models rest on an implicit assumption that performance in spatial reasoning tasks reflects the imagination process (i.e., mental rotation and translation of oneself or object arrays). This assumption is intuitively appealing and explains the existing findings reasonably well. The primary support for this assumption is the angular disparity effect. The angular disparity effect is often considered the defining characteristic of mental rotation processes (Cooper & Shepard, 1973, 1975). In addition to the angular disparity effect in imagined self-rotation and array-rotation, Easton and Sholl (1995) showed that in an imagined self-translation task, RT increased as the distance between the imagined location and the actual location increased. Thus, it was interpreted that imagination takes time and

---

[2] In the pointing task, because the object name is given, children need to rotate only one object and therefore the rotate-the-array condition becomes easier (Huttenlocher & Presson, 1979).

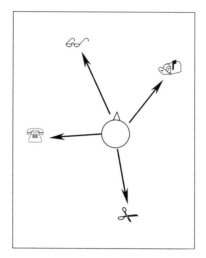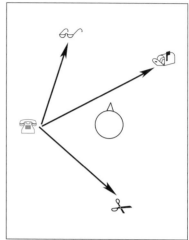

Fig. 4. An illustration of the logic behind Rieser's (1989) model of object-to-object relationships. The left panel shows the spatial representation of object-to-self relationships, and the right panel shows the spatial representation of object-to-object relationships (only shows the objects' relationship relative to one object for clarity).

spatial reasoning processes operate under the same rules as mental rotation of an image or an object.

Wang (in press, 2003a) directly tested this assumption using a paradigm developed by Cooper and Shepard (1973). Cooper and Shepard (1973) showed that RT in determining the handedness of a test letter (i.e., whether the letter is normal or mirror-reversed) presented at a noncanonical orientation increased as their deviation from upright increased (angular disparity effect). They reasoned that if the judgment time reflects a "mental rotation" process, which rotates an upright letter in memory to align with the target letter so that a comparison/judgment can be made, this "mental rotation" process should be independent of the presentation of the test letter. To test this hypothesis, they provided a cue about the orientation of the test letter in advance and gave the participants sufficient time to complete the mental rotation process. Cooper and Shepard (1973) showed that the angular disparity effect disappeared when the cue was provided about 1000 ms in advance. These data suggest that mental rotation can occur without the presentation of the test stimuli as long as one knows what to rotate and to which orientation it should be rotated.

Following the same general logic, Wang (2003a) tested human adults in an imagined self-rotation task. Participants learned five targets in a rectangular room. Then they sat in the middle and were blindfolded and sound masked. Each participant was then tested in two conditions, one with 10-second delay for imagination and one with no delay. The imagination delay (10 seconds) was chosen to allow sufficient time to complete the imagination process. The imagination target was announced first, followed by either a 10-second delay or no delay, before the pointing target was announced and RT timed. If the imagined self-rotation task is primarily a process of mentally rotating onself, then the angular disparity effect should be eliminated, or significantly reduced, in the 10-second delay condition comparing to the no-delay condition.

Participants showed a significant angular disparity effect in both RT and errors. However, there was no significant effect of the delay, nor was there an interaction between delay and angular disparity, suggesting extended time for the imagination process did not affect performance in this task.

One possibility is that the 10-second imagination delay was too long. Participants might have lost the representation of the imagination process by the time the pointing target was announced. To test this possibility, Wang (2003a) asked participants themselves to determine the duration of the imagination delay. This procedure not only provided the appropriate imagination duration for each trial, but also provided a subjective measure of the "imagination" process. Analysis was conducted using only those participants who showed clear angular disparity effect in their self-reported imagination time. The imagination time increased as the angular disparity increased, suggesting that these participants performed the imagination. However, their response latency and angular error failed to show any evidence of improvement in the delay condition. Thus, even when participants themselves determined the duration of the imagination delay and indicated they had completed the "imagination," their performance was not affected in any way by the extra time to perform the "imagination" in advance.

These results again failed to provide any evidence for the traditional view that spatial reasoning tasks reflect the process of mentally rotating oneself. However, one might argue that the participants' self-report does not necessarily prove that they actually completed the imagination process, even though they thought they did. To make sure that the imagination process did occur, Wang (2003a) asked participants to make four pointing responses after a single imagination. The logic is that once the participants made the first response, the imagination process had to be completed. Thus, if completion of imagination improves performance, then multiple responses after a single imagination should show a significant improvement in the later responses comparing to the first response. Contrary to this prediction, however, there was no significant effect of response order, nor was there an interaction between angular disparity and response order. These results provided strong evidence that completion of the "imagination" had little influence on people's performance in an imagined self-rotation task, and thus contradicted the traditional assumption that the spatial reasoning task is akin to a mental rotation process.[3]

One alternative model on the spatial reasoning process was proposed by May (1996; also see Huttenlocher & Presson, 1979; Presson, 1982). It was suggested that the difficulty in the spatial reasoning tasks might reflect the conflict between reality and imagination. For example, the representation of a target's real location can potentially interfere with the representation of its "imagined" location, and make it difficult to respond according to the imagined representation. Evidence supporting the interference hypothesis was provided by May (1996). May (1996) compared performance in an imagined rotation task while participants were oriented and while they were disoriented, and showed that disorientation reduced the angular disparity effect. May (1996) argued that disorientation improved performance because there was less interference from one's representation of the targets' real positions.

Similarly, Brockmole and Wang (2003) asked participants to judge spatial relationships in different environments from different perspectives, and showed that perspective change across environments is much easier than perspective change within an environment. These results are also consistent with the interference hypothesis, because different environments involve different targets and therefore reduced the conflict between two perspectives.

These studies provide evidence against the assumption that performance in spatial reasoning tasks is due to the process of imagined rotation or translation, and thus cast doubt on theories of spatial representations and reference frames based on this assumption (e.g., Huttenlocher & Presson, 1973, 1979; Rieser, 1989; Wraga et al., 2000). For example, Huttenlocher and Presson (1979) showed that children performed better in the self-rotation condition than in the array-rotation condition, and concluded that

---

[3] One might argue that the imagination process cannot begin until the response target is given, therefore extensive imagination delay would not affect performance. Moreover, it could be that the representation generated by the imagination process is short-lived and is lost as soon as the response is made; thus multiple responses after a single imagination would require the imagination process to be repeated for each individual response target. Although these added features of the imagination process can explain these results, it is not clear why mental rotation of oneself should depend on the pointing target. Moreover, they contradict findings in studies of mental rotation. In Cooper and Shepard's study (1973), imagination occurred without the presentation of the test stimuli.

they relied on an environment-centered representation. This theory is called into question because performance in the imagined self-rotation task does not reflect how difficult it is for one to mentally rotate oneself and generate a representation of the new perspective. Furthermore, contrary to the widely accepted belief that children undergo a developmental change in the fundamental nature of their spatial representations, findings by Wang (in press) suggest that the developmental change may instead reflect children's development of inhibition/response selection systems, so that they become more effective in resisting the interference from the representation of their physical perspective when required to respond according to an imagined perspective.

In short, the fundamental assumption underlying traditional models of spatial representations based on spatial reasoning tasks is invalid. Findings in spatial reasoning tasks do no provide evidence for allocentric representations in humans. Instead, the angular disparity effect suggests that the representation is specific to a viewpoint, namely egocentric in nature.

D. Object and Scene Recognition

A similar issue is involved in research on object and scene recognition. It has been an on-going debate whether recognition of an object is based on viewpoint-specific representations, or based on viewpoint-invariant representations. The primary logic is that a viewpoint-invariant representation of an object, such as a description of the spatial relationship among the parts of an object relative to its intrinsic axis, allows the object to be recognized from arbitrary, novel viewpoints as well as from familiar viewpoints at which these relationships are encoded. In contrast, a viewpoint-specific representation encodes the spatial features of an object relative to a specific viewpoint, therefore recognition of the object from novel, unfamiliar viewpoints would be more difficult compared to the familiar viewpoints.

1. Viewpoint-Invariant Models

Biederman and colleagues (Biederman & Cooper, 1991, 1992; Cooper, Biederman, & Hummel, 1992) used a priming paradigm and measured the response latency to name line drawings of familiar objects. In their studies, the amount of priming was unaffected by changes in the retinal size of the object from study to test (scaling invariance). Furthermore, naming latency was also constant relative to the position of the object in the visual field and to the object's orientation in depth. Biederman and Gerhardstein (1993) showed similar orientation invariance when observers were asked to match individual shapes, name familiar objects, and classify unfamiliar objects.

Based on these findings, Biederman (1987) proposed a model of object recognition based on a set of simple, geometric shapes (Geons) and a set of spatial descriptions of the relationships among the Geons. According to Biederman (1987), an object representation system based on Geons and relational descriptions has sufficient power in representing different kinds of objects. Biederman and Gerhardstein (1993) argued that these representations allow viewpoint-invariant object recognition as long as the same parts (Geons) are identifiable from the testing viewpoints as from the study viewpoints, and the structural description of the object is sufficient to distinguish between the target object and the distracters.

2. Viewpoint-Specific Models

Viewpoint-invariant recognition of familiar objects does not necessarily imply viewpoint-independent object representations, however. Due to the lack of control of the learning process, multiple views of the same object could be represented, which can potentially mimic recognition performance based on viewpoint-independent representations. A large number of studies suggest that object recognition of novel, arbitrary shapes is viewpoint-dependent (e.g., Rock, Wheeler, & Tudor, 1989; Shepard & Cooper, 1982; Shepard & Metzler, 1971). Tarr and colleagues (Bülthoff & Edelman, 1992; Tarr, 1995; Tarr, Bülthoff, Zabinski, & Blanz, 1997) used wire-frame or blob-like objects in same–different judgment tasks and found that participants showed fast, accurate recognition for the studied views and impaired performance for novel views. Furthermore, the greater the test view deviated from the studied view, the longer the response latency. These results suggested that object representation is viewpoint-specific and only information from the learned-perspective is represented in memory.

It has been shown that viewpoint-specific representations can approximate viewpoint-invariant performance when multiple views are available. When two or more views of the same object are provided during the studying period, participants showed better recognition performance for intermediate views between two studied views (Bülthoff & Edelman, 1992; Kourtzi & Shiffrar, 1997). Mechanisms for this type of generalization have been proposed. For example, generalization can be accomplished by linear combinations of the 2-D views (Ullman & Basri, 1991) or by view approximation (Poggio & Edelman, 1990; Vetter, Hurlbert, & Poggio, 1995).

Recognition of spatial layouts is also shown to be viewpoint-dependent (Diwadkar & McNamara, 1997; Shelton & McNamara, 1997; Simons & Wang, 1998; Wang & Simons, 1999). For example, Diwadkar and McNamara (1997) had participants study an array of objects on a circular table, and then they judged whether the test image taken from various angles showed the same array of objects or different ones. RT increased as a function of the angular distance between the studied view and the tested views. Furthermore, when more views were presented during study, RT was determined by the angular distance between the test views and the nearest studied view.

Thus, object recognition seems to be viewpoint-invariant in some cases and viewpoint-dependent in others. In general, viewpoint-dependent recognition is often found when the object is novel and relatively complicated. On the other hand, viewpoint-invariant recognition tends to be found when objects are made of distinct parts whose spatial relationship can be coded easily, and when the task does not require precise metric details of the object, such as naming or classification tasks. However, both models, in their traditional form, consider object recognition as a pure visual task, and thus are solely based on the visual information. A series of studies (Simons & Wang, 1998; Simons, Wang, & Roddenberry, 2002; Wang & Simons, 1999) showed that object recognition in the real world is not only affected by what an object looks like, but is also affected by where the viewer is, suggesting that nonvisual processes also play a role in object recognition.

3. Spatial Updating in Object Recognition

To examine the nature of the representations and processes underlying real world scene recognition, Wang and Simons (1999) placed five objects at random locations on a circular table that can be rotated around its center (Figure 5). Participants studied the object array from a specific viewpoint. After the table was occluded and one object was moved during a delay, the participants viewed the array again and decided which object had moved. Participants either were tested at the study position, or walked to a new viewing position. For both groups of participants, the retinal image of the object array during testing was either the same as during studying, or corresponded to the new viewing position (novel view) (see Figure 5).

Accuracy of detecting the moved object was measured in each condition. If real world scene recognition is solely based on visual information, then performance should not be affected by where the observer is, as long as the relative orientation between the observer and the object array is the same. If, like spatial representations for navigation, a viewpoint-specific representation of the object array is updated during observer movement, then performance would show a different pattern depending on where the observer is. The results were consistent with the updating hypothesis. When participants remained in the same location, change of perspective (caused by table rotation) impaired performance, an effect shown in various scene recognition studies (Diwadkar & McNamara, 1997). However, when the

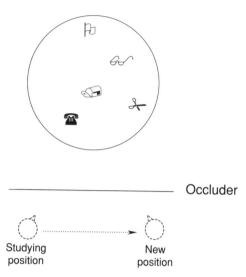

Occluder

Fig. 5. The apparatus used in Simons and Wang (1998). An array of five objects was placed randomly on a circular table, which was occluded from the viewer by a curtain. The participants were tested either at the studying position, or at the new position. In both conditions, the array was presented relative to the viewer either at the orientation corresponding to the studying position (familiar view), or at the orientation corresponding to the new position (novel view).

participants walked to a new observation point, performance was better for the novel view than the familiar, studied view.

One alternative explanation is that participants may have formed a viewpoint-invariant representation of the array, encoding the object positions with respect to the environment. Thus, when the table rotated, the spatial relationship between the objects on the table and the surrounding landmarks changed, and therefore performance was impaired. On the other hand, these relationships remained the same as the viewer walked from one position to another, therefore allowing direct comparison of these spatial relationships during study and test, leading to better performance.

Simons and Wang (1998) tested whether the visual background served as the reference frame for this scene recognition task. They turned off the lights and painted the objects with fluorescent paint. Participants never saw the object array with the background behind the curtain during the whole testing, and they walked in the dark in the observer-movement conditions. Despite the absence of the visual background, participants showed the same pattern in their performance as in normal lighting. These results suggest that visual background is not a necessary component in coding the object arrays.

One might suggest that an allocentric reference frame does not need to be visible. To distinguish between the updating hypothesis and the hypothesis of environment-centered representation based on invisible reference frames, Simons and Wang (1998) employed a disorientation procedure. Participants were seated in a wheeled chair and studied the object array in normal lighting. During the interval they were passively rolled over to the other viewing position while spun around twice with their eyes closed. The table either remained stationary, or rotated with the participant to provide the familiar studied view. If an environment-centered representation is used, disorientation should have no effect and participants should show the same pattern as in the experiment without disorientation. If participants need to update the egocentric representations based on self-motion estimation, then disorientation should disrupt that process and their ability to predict the novel view should be impaired. Participants showed an impairment in their performance as predicted by the egocentric updating hypothesis.

Wang and Simons (1999) further examined whether the poor performance in the table rotation condition was due to the lack of perceptual information of the rotation. When an observer moved, there were both internal and external cues specifying exactly how such movements occurred. When the table rotated, however, participants did not perceive the rotation directly. To test this possibility, Wang and Simons (1999) attached a pole to a circular table. In one condition, the experimenter rotated the table. In the other condition, the participants grabbed the pole and rotated the table themselves. If poor performance in the table rotation condition was primarily due to lack of perceptual information, then performance should improve significantly when the participants rotated the table themselves. However, participants did equally poorly in the two conditions, suggesting that perceptual information of the rotation is not sufficient to account for performance differences between observer movements and table rotations.

One might argue that recognition of object arrays may be different from recognition of single objects. Moreover, a change detection task may also be different from an old/new recognition task. To test whether the same mechanisms apply to single objects, Simons et al. (2002) put an object made of small wooden blocks at the center of a circular table. Participants studied the object from one of the viewing windows. During an interval, the object was either replaced by a similar object, or remained on the table. Participants then viewed the object again from a novel perspective and judged whether the object was the same. The novel view was produced either by the table rotating relative to a stationary observer, or by the observer walking around a stationary table. Similar to findings using an array of objects and a change-detection task, recognition performance was significantly better when the novel view was caused by observer movements than by table rotations. These results suggest that real world recognition of single objects as well as object arrays is based on an egocentric representation that is updated over viewer movement.

E. OTHER ISSUES

The studies discussed above provide evidence for egocentric representations updated over viewer movements and suggested that much of the evidence previously considered to support allocentric spatial representations is either insufficient or misinterpreted. However, the nature of spatial representations also depends on the nature of the environment and the task. Here I discuss qualitative differences in spatial representations for guiding actions vs. for communications, for the geometry of the surrounding space vs. for individual objects, and reference frame use in spatial language.

1. Perception versus Action

Various studies have suggested a dissociation between perception and action systems, showing that a more accurate representation is associated with actions but is not available to the perceptual/knowledge system (e.g., Bridgeman, Kirch, & Sperling, 1981; Bridgeman, Peery, & Anand, 1997; Creem & Proffitt, 1998; Goodale & Milner, 1992; Loomis, Da Silva, Philbeck, & Fukusima, 1996; Proffitt, Bhalla, Gossweiler, & Midgett, 1995). For example, Bridgeman et al. (1997) examined the effect of the induced Roelofs illusion (a target inside an off-center frame appears biased opposite the direction of the frame) on people's target localization. Although perception of the target location was biased by the frame, pointing responses were less affected by the illusion. These results were not due to shifts in participants' perception of the felt straight-ahead position (calibration between visual and motor systems).

Loomis et al. (1996) showed that perception of distances along the line of sight is compressed. They placed two pairs of markers on the floor, one along the viewer's front/back axis and one along the left/right axis. Participants attempted to match the two intervals. The interval along the front/back axis had to be much longer than the interval along the left/right axis in order to be perceived as equal distances. Thus, the perceptual space appears to be compressed remarkably along the front/back axis. In contrast, walking was not affected by this illusion. When participants walked toward the two markers while blindfolded, the distance they walked between the first marker and the second marker was not compressed.

The distinction between perception and action has also been shown in a slope-judgment paradigm by Proffitt and colleagues (Creem & Proffitt,

1998; Proffitt et al., 1995). Participants stood at the foot of a hill and judged the slope either verbally in terms of angles, perceptually by adjusting a representation of the side-view of the slope, or by a motor response, in which they adjusted a tilt-board with their unseen hand to match the slope. Both verbal and perceptual responses showed overestimation of the slope, suggesting that people perceive the slopes as being steeper than they actually are. However, motor responses were not biased, suggesting a dissociation between the perceptual and action systems.

The perceptual and action systems have been shown to interact. Bridgeman et al. (1997) showed that pointing responses were similarly biased as the visual illusion when a delay was introduced between viewing the target and responding. Creem and Proffitt (1998) found a similar delay effect: when participants viewed the slope and after a delay adjusted a tilt-board to indicate the slope, their responses showed similar overestimation as in a perceptual task. Interestingly, motoric estimates differed depending on place of response. With a short delay, motoric responses made in the proximity of the hill did not differ from those evoked without delay. However, when taken away from the hill, participants' motoric responses increased along with the increase in verbal reports. When the delay was long enough, motoric responses also showed overestimation even when participants remained at the site.

These studies suggest that the perceptual and motoric responses are guided by different visual representations of space. However, it is not clear whether representations for perception and action differ only quantitatively in the amount of information contained in these representations. That is, perhaps the action system represents the metric, veridical spatial information, while the perceptual representation is more crude and somewhat degraded/biased.

Using a spatial reasoning paradigm, Wang (in press) examined whether the nature of the spatial representations guiding actions is different from those underlying perception or verbal communications. Participants learned six target locations around them in a square room. Then they were blindfolded, and were asked to imagine facing a different heading and report where the other objects would be from the imagined perspective. In the *pointing* condition, participants reported the target direction by moving their hand in the direction of the target objects. In the *verbal* condition, they reported the target directions by estimating the egocentric angles. That is, straight ahead is $0°$, straight left is $90°$ to the left, straight right is $90°$ to the right, and so on. Participants were instructed to report the angles as precisely as they could.

Response times in the pointing condition were affected by the imagined heading. Participants responded much faster when pointing to the targets from their actual perspective than from the imagined perspective. In contrast, when reporting the target directions in verbal estimation, RT was not affected by the perspective: there was no significant difference whether participants responded according to their actual perspective or responded according to the imagined perspective. A further analysis (Wang, 2003b) compared participants with overall faster RT in the verbal task and those with slower RT in the pointing task. The pattern was essentially the same: the pointing task showed a perspective effect, while the verbal task did not, even when their overall performance was approximately the same.

Based on these findings, Wang (in press; De Vega & Rodrigo, 2001) suggested that representations underlying action and perception/verbal communication differ qualitatively in their fundamental nature, rather than quantitatively in precision or metric details. Although the representation for verbal communication is more flexible, the representation guiding actions is tightly bound to physical reality. Whether the representation for the verbal system is viewpoint-independent, or whether there were multiple representations among which the verbal system can choose freely is still an open question.

2.   The Shape of the Environment

Studies on reorientation (i.e., searching for a target after disorientation) raised an interesting question. Various species, including fish, rodents, and children (Cheng, 1986; Cheng & Gallistel, 1984; Hermer & Spelke, 1994, 1996; Wang et al., 1999) are shown to primarily rely on the geometric shape of the enclosure to locate a target, but ignore other cues such as visual patterns and distinctive odor. Moreover, Gouteux and Spelke (2001) examined whether children can use the geometric configuration of an array of objects to locate a hidden toy. Four large boxes were placed on the floor, forming a rectangular configuration. A toy was hidden inside one of the boxes while the children watched. Then the children were disoriented, and asked to find the toy. Children searched randomly among the four boxes, ignoring the geometric configuration of these boxes.

These studies suggest that the shape of an enclosure is treated differently than a collection of individual objects in fundamental ways. To examine the nature of spatial representations of object arrays and the environment shape, Wang and Spelke (2000) tested participants in a rectangular room (Figure 6). Four individual objects were placed along the side of the rectangular room, forming the same angular configuration as the four corners. Participants were asked to point to either the four corners of the room (corner condition), or the four objects (object condition), both before and after they were disoriented. As discussed above, if the targets (either

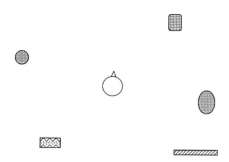

Fig. 6.   The apparatus used in Wang and Spelke (2000, Experiment 6). Four small objects were placed near the walls in a rectangular room so that they formed the same angular configuration as the four corners of the room. Participants sat in the middle of the room and pointed to either the objects or the corners before and after they were disoriented.

individual objects or individual corners) were represented as egocentric vectors, and these vectors were updated according to self-motion, then disorientation should disrupt this updating process and cause an increase in the configuration error among the set of targets. In contrast, if the configuration of the targets were represented independent of the viewer (allocentric cognitive map), and the position of the viewer was updated relative to the targets as a whole, then disorientation should not affect the configuration error.

Although in both corner and object conditions participants were effectively disoriented, they showed a significant increase in configuration error in the object condition, but not in the corner condition. A second study (Wang & Spelke, 2000) used a larger room of irregular shape, and a set of identical objects arranged in the same irregular configuration as the four corners. Participants again showed a significant increase in the configuration errors after disorientation when they pointed to the objects, but not when they pointed to the four corners. Thus, even with the same pointing task, the same disorientation procedure, the same identical targets, and the same learning procedure, corners seem to be represented very differently than individual objects. Although object locations are represented as egocentric vectors and updated individually, the room is coded in a single, coherent representation that contains the shape information, and this representation is independent of spatial updating and thus unaffected by disorientation.

3.   Spatial Language

The distinction between action and verbal communication suggests that language may have a special role in spatial representations. Language is generally very flexible in expressing meanings, and spatial languages often employ multiple reference frames to encode spatial relationships (Carlson & Logan, 2001; Carlson-Radvansky & Irwin, 1993; Levinson, 1996). For example, Carlson-Radvansky and Irwin (1994) showed that multiple reference frames are active when people encounter a scene. When different reference frames are in conflict with each other (e.g., a ball is left of a chair according to the viewer's orientation, but above the chair according to the chair's orientation), people were slower in verifying the spatial relationships than when all reference frames were in agreement. Carlson-Radvansky and Jiang (1998) showed that when multiple reference frames are available, people have to select one reference frame over the others, and selection of one reference frame inhibits other reference frames.

The relationship between spatial language and the representations for perception and action is not clear. Levinson (1996) argued that the nature of spatial language determines the nature of spatial representations for perception and memory based on cross-cultural studies of spatial language and spatial behavior. Brown and Levinson (1993; Levinson, 1992, 1996; Levinson & Haviland, 1994) found that the spatial language in Tzeltal uses an absolute reference frame (e.g., "downhill" for north and "uphill" for south, as the local geography indicates) but not a relative reference frame. To examine the relationship between reference frames present in a language and the speaker's spatial behavior, Brown and Levinson (1993) tested Tzeltal and Dutch in spatial, nonlinguistic tasks. In a "recall memory" task, participants watched a set of objects presented on a table. After a delay, they turned 180° and were asked to reproduce the object array on a second table. In a "recognition memory" test, participants saw a card placed on a table at a particular orientation. Then after a delay they were rotated and asked to select a card most similar to what they saw, among a set of alternatives that either matched the original card according to a geographic reference frame, the relative reference frame, or did not match the original card. Finally, they tested participants in a "transitive inference" task. Participants were shown objects A and B on one table. Then they turned around and were shown objects B and C on another table. Then they were asked to infer the relative position between A and C. In all three tasks, Tzeltal speakers tended to use absolute coding, whereas Dutch speakers tended to use relative coding.

Based on these findings, Levinson (1996) argued that a language-dominant frame is employed consistently in nonverbal memory, inference, imagistic reasoning, and unconscious gesture, suggesting a common frame of reference in their underlying representation. It is clear that spatial language exerts some influence in nonverbal spatial tasks. However, the nature of this influence is not clear. Note that in these studies the task was explained in *language*. Therefore participants may have interpreted the task according to the conventional interpretation in their language. It does not matter whether the task is to reproduce the display or to recognize a new display, the phrase "same as the previous one" is essentially ambiguous: it could mean the display needs to be in the same relationship to the observer, or to the ground. Therefore, the difference between the two groups could be basically linguistic rather than in the underlying representations.

F. Conclusions I

The first main issue on the nature of spatial representations concerns the reference frame used to encode spatial information. In three areas of research (i.e., navigation, object and scene recognition, and spatial reasoning) recent findings suggest that in many tasks that have been traditionally considered to depend on invariant, flexible, allocentric representations, spatial information is in fact encoded relative to the viewer, and these egocentric representations are updated as the viewer moves. In navigation, the primary, universal mechanism, namely path integration, operates as a dynamic egocentric system instead of as a complementary system for an allocentric map, at least in humans. The place cells in the hippocampus, which are often considered the allocentric cognitive map, do not predict a disoriented animal's searching behavior, suggesting they are not "place" cells but responsible for learning associative rules. In real world object and scene recognition, performance depends on where the viewer is, suggesting that representations of objects and scenes are viewpoint specific, and these representations can be updated as the viewer moves. In spatial reasoning, imagined self-rotation does not reflect how one imagines the rotation but depends on how one makes a response, suggesting that the allocentric models based on the spatial reasoning tasks misinterpreted the data. On the contrary, the angular disparity effect itself suggests that pointing responses are guided by an egocentric representation from a specific viewpoint. Thus, many findings previously thought to be evidence for allocentric cognitive maps in both humans and other animals can be explained by spatial updating and egocentric representations.

II. The Structure of Spatial Representations

A. The Traditional Hierarchical Models

1. The Hierarchical Network Model

Humans live in complicated environments. Thus, human spatial memory may involve different scales and different levels of details. For example, people have spatial knowledge of small spaces such as books on a shelf, the arrangement of furniture in a room, as well as larger environments such as rooms in a building, streets in a city, cities in a country, and so on. The dominant view of the organization of human spatial memory is that spatial information is organized into a hierarchical structure (Hirtle & Jonides, 1985; Huttenlocher, Hedges, & Duncan, 1991; McNamara, 1986; McNamara, Hardy, & Hirtle, 1989; Stevens & Coupe, 1978; Taylor & Tversky, 1992; Wilton, 1979). According to the hierarchical network model, humans represent space by dividing it into "chunks." For example, the spatial representation of a house is composed of a tree-like structure. At the top is the house, which has three floors. The arrangement of rooms on each floor is encoded in a lower level and linked to the representation of that floor. Similarly, furniture within each room is further expanded from the "room node" on the floor map. The floor representation encodes the spatial relationship among rooms, with each room treated as a single "object." The house map encodes the spatial relationship among floors, and therefore each floor is one "object." Information about spatial relationships between objects in different rooms is not represented explicitly; instead, it needs to be calculated according to the position of the objects within each room and the relationship between the rooms.[4]

Evidence for the hierarchical organization of environmental representations in memory comes from three major findings. First, people show systematic biases in their spatial judgments about environmental layouts. For example, Stevens and Coupe (1978) found that people make systematic errors in judging spatial relationships between cities in different states. Participants overwhelmingly judged Reno, Nevada to be north*east* of San Diego, California, although Reno is actually north*west*. To account for these distortions, Stevens and Coupe (1978) suggested that the spatial relationship between two locations in separate units needs to be derived by combining within-unit and between-unit information. For example, the biased judgment that Reno is northeast of San Diego can be a result of combining the superordinate knowledge that Nevada is east of California and the subordinate knowledge that San Diego is in southern California and Reno is in northern Nevada.

Similar bias was shown by McNamara (1986) in smaller scale, novel environments. By dividing a room into different regions, he showed that direction estimations between items in the room were influenced by the spatial arrangement of the regions in which the items were located. For example, for items in regions that shared a north–south relationship,

---

[4] Some researchers suggest a partial-hierarchical model, in which cross-unit spatial relationships can be encoded, especially between objects near the border (McNamara, 1986).

direction estimations tended to be biased toward the north–south axis. Thus, McNamara suggested that spatial judgments about items in different regions required the combination of information stored at different levels of a hierarchical system.

The second piece of evidence for hierarchical organization of environmental representations came from studies of spatial memory retrieval. For example, free recall of environments follows an orderly unit-by-unit sequence (Hirtle & Jonides, 1985; McNamara et al., 1989; Taylor & Tversky, 1992). When participants were asked to recall locations in a city, they tended to recall places belonging to the same units together, which can be determined either by explicit borders (McNamara, 1986; Stevens & Coupe, 1978) or subjective boundaries imposed by individual subjects (e.g., Hirtle & Jonides, 1985; McNamara et al., 1989; Taylor & Tversky, 1992). In either case, these divisions are based on factors such as size, spatial arrangement, functional importance, and/or semantic similarity.

Finally, it was shown that judgment about a target facilitates judgment of targets within the same unit (McNamara, 1986), regardless of the Euclidean distance between the target locations. McNamara (1986) showed participants an array of objects in a room divided into four quadrants by transparent or opaque dividers. Then participants were presented with a sequence of objects and judged whether they were present in the room. RT was faster when the target was preceded by a target in the same region than in a different region. McNamara (1986) suggested that objects belonging to the same region were closer to each other in the representation, which is consistent with the hierarchical network model.[5]

2. Prototype Representation

A slightly different model was proposed by Huttenlocher et al. (1991). They presented a dot at a random location inside a circle on a computer monitor. After a delay, participants had to indicate where the dot was. They found that memory of the dot location was systematically biased toward the center of four quadrants (upper left, upper right, lower left, lower right), and errors were greatest for dots presented near the boundaries. Based on this finding,

---

[5] Note that although all these findings are consistent with the hierarchical network models, none of them *requires* a hierarchical network. The unit-by-unit free recall suggests that the semantic information is organized into units, but the spatial information does not have to be arranged in a hierarchical structure. The same is true for facilitation of target recognition within units. The bias of spatial judgments across units is a result of regularization and approximation, not a property of hierarchical structure per se. For example, if one knows precisely where San Diego is in California, where Reno is in Nevada, and where California is relative to Nevada, the judgment will not be biased. Thus, hierarchical models do not necessarily predict biases; the biases are produced by the vagueness of the spatial coding itself.

Huttenlocher et al. (1991) proposed that the location of the dot was represented at two levels. The basic level is a metric representation of the coordinates of the dot in the form of a gradient map: the dot's actual location has the highest activation, and the activation degrades as the distance increases. The second level is a categorical representation of the quadrant the dot is in. When retrieving memory of the dot location, the two representations are combined. For example, the basic activation map is averaged with the prototype representation, which is also a gradient map with the highest activation at the center of the quadrant. The result of this retrieval process is the systematic bias of placing the dots closer to the center of each quadrant than they actually are.

Both hierarchical models have one critical feature. That is, spatial information from adjacent levels of the representation system can be combined. This feature has two consequences. First, different levels of the hierarchical system can be accessed simultaneously. For example, one has to know that Reno is in northern Nevada, San Diego is in southern California, and California is west of Nevada at the same time in order to combine these relationships and infer the direction of Reno from San Diego. Similarly, to integrate the prototype representation and the basic level representation of the dot location, both representations need to be active.

Second, spatial information at different levels needs to be encoded in a common reference frame, at least for the directions, because spatial information encoded in different reference frames cannot be combined directly. For example, *San Diego is in the south of California* and *California is left of Nevada* cannot be combined directly, unless additional information is available to transform them into a common reference frame. If spatial information from adjacent levels of a hierarchical system shares a common reference frame, then the entire system needs to use a single reference frame. Similarly, according to Huttenlocher et al. (1991), the two levels of representations of the dot location need to be coded in identical coordinate systems in order to allow the integration to occur. The implication of the single-reference frame feature is that if you know where you are facing at one level of the hierarchy, you also know where you are at other levels of the representation. In the remainder of this section, I'll discuss studies that examine whether different levels of a hierarchical system can be accessed simultaneously, and whether spatial updating occurs simultaneously for different levels of a hierarchy.

B. ACCESSING ENVIRONMENTAL REPRESENTATIONS AT DIFFERENT LEVELS

Brockmole and Wang (2002) examined whether spatial knowledge of the location of objects inside one environment (e.g., rooms in a building) and places in an environment at the adjacent level (e.g., buildings on campus) can be accessed at the same time. They used a task-set switching paradigm, which required participants to make spatial judgments either about the same environment in successive trials, or about different environments. If people can access both environmental representations at the same time (i.e., spatial information about both environments are available at the same time) then participants should be able to switch between environments freely without a cost in their performance. On the other hand, if only one environmental representation can be accessed at a time, then switching between environments may be associated with a cost. That is, when a switch between the two environments is required, an additional process such as inhibition of the currently active representation and activation of the new representation would be required. For example, when people made a spatial judgment about the building locations on campus following a spatial judgment about room locations in the building, participants would be slower than if the previous trial was also about building locations on campus.

Based on this logic, Brockmole and Wang (2002) asked participants to imagine themselves in the middle of the psychology building and make judgments about the locations of familiar rooms in the building and surrounding buildings on campus. The building targets and the room targets were presented in a random sequence, so that in some trials a switch between environments occurred between successive trials, while in others no switch was required. Contrary to the simultaneous-access hypothesis, participants required additional time to judge spatial relationships immediately following a switch in the probed environment. The direction of switch had no effect on the switch cost; it was equally difficult to switch from a building trial to a campus trial as from a campus trial to a building trial. These results suggest that participants failed to access spatial information about rooms in the building and buildings on campus simultaneously, despite their years of navigation experience within them.

Similar results were found between office and building (Brockmole & Wang, 2002). However, one alternative explanation is that the switch cost was an artifact of switching between semantic categories. To test this hypothesis, Brockmole and Wang (2002) used participants who were unaware that the spatial arrangement of targets represented the layout of real environments. They were told they would learn the identities of two sets of items that contained "things that may be found in a building" and "things that may be found in a personal office" and their arbitrarily assigned positions within a visual display (as far as the participants were concerned). Thus, the same switch between the two semantic categories and the same experimental procedure was used, but no environmental representations were involved. Participants showed no switch costs, suggesting that the cost in switching between real environments was not due to the procedural artifacts or due to switching between semantic categories.

These results are inconsistent with the traditional hierarchical models. As discussed above, the need for combining spatial information across adjacent levels of a hierarchical system implies that these knowledge needs to be accessed simultaneously. Thus, either the spatial knowledge of rooms in a building and buildings on campus is not represented in a hierarchical system, despite participants' familiarity with them, or additional assumptions need to be made about the hierarchical models to allow for integration of spatial information that is not available at the same time.

C. SPATIAL UPDATING IN NESTED ENVIRONMENTS

The second feature of the hierarchical models is that multiple levels of the system are encoded in the same reference frame. This leads to the prediction that if you know your heading at one level of the hierarchy, you also know your heading at other levels. Consequently, if you update your heading relative to one level of the hierarchy, you also know your new heading at other levels.[6] In a series of experiments, Wang and Brockmole (in press, a) investigated this prediction by testing whether spatial updating operates on environments at different levels of a hierarchical system simultaneously.

Participants learned target objects around them in a room and the surrounding campus buildings. Then they were asked to turn either relative to the room targets ("update-room" condition) or relative to the campus buildings ("update-campus" condition). After the turning, they pointed to targets in both environments. Overall performance did not differ between the two conditions before the turning occurred. However, performance differed after the turning. Pointing responses to the campus buildings were significantly impaired when the participants turned relative to the room, both in terms of accuracy and response latency. In contrast, after the participants turned relative to campus, pointing responses to the room targets were not impaired. That is, when people turned relative to the room, they did not update their relationship relative to the campus buildings, but when they turned relative to the campus buildings, they did update their relationship relative to the room targets.

One possible explanation is that these results were due to the relative difficulty of switching between two environments. For example, Brockmole

---

[6] The position may be different. For example, if you know that you are in the kitchen, you would also know that you are at the first floor, and that you are in your house. However, knowing that you are in the house does not specify which floor you are at or which room you are in. That is, locating yourself at a lower level allows you to know your position at higher levels, but not vice versa.

and Wang (2002) showed that switching between environments at different levels of a hierarchy incurs a cost. Although they did not find an effect of the direction of switch, it is still possible that in the current switching from campus to room is easier than switching from room to campus, because a mental image of the "campus" includes the room but not vice versa. Because the update-campus condition required a switch from campus to room and the update-room condition required a switch from room to campus, the poor performance in pointing to campus targets in the update-room condition may reflect the difficulty in mental switching from room to campus.

Wang and Brockmole (in press, b) tested this possibility by requiring participants to switch environments but without spatial updating. Participants followed the same procedure as in the updating experiment, except that turning to face each target was replaced by pointing to each target. When spatial updating was not required, participants showed equal performance whether they switched from room to campus or from campus to room. Thus, the difficulty in pointing to campus buildings after turning relative to the room was not simply a result of mentally switching from room to campus, but rather due to limitations in the spatial updating system per se.

These findings are again inconsistent with predictions of the traditional hierarchical models. Knowing your heading relative to the environment at one level of the hierarchy does not allow you to assess your relationship relative to environments at higher levels. The traditional hierarchical models cannot account for these findings easily. Again, either people do not form hierarchical representations for objects in a room, rooms in a building, and buildings on campus,[7] or the hierarchical representations have important features that are not depicted in the current models.

D. CONCLUSIONS II

The second main issue on the nature of spatial representations concerns the structure, or organization, of spatial knowledge. Human spatial representation has been shown to be organized into units. Traditional models suggest that these units are connected in a hierarchical network, and spatial judgments are made by combining spatial information within and across levels of the hierarchy. However, recent findings suggest that updating of one's heading in one unit does not automatically lead to updating in another unit. Moreover, even after years of navigational experience across

---

[7] The lack of hierarchical representation should not be attributed to the novelty of the environment alone, because McNamara (1986) also used novel environment, although familiarity may play a role in environmental representations.

environments, people fail to access both representations at the same time. These findings suggest that human spatial representations of complex environments learned through navigation are fragmented in nature, rather than integrated, hierarchical networks.

III. Summary

This chapter discusses the basic properties of spatial representations for navigation, spatial reasoning, and object/scene recognition. Contrary to the traditional models of allocentric cognitive maps, recent findings suggest that spatial representations for navigation, real world object and scene recognition, and spatial reasoning are primarily egocentric, and these egocentric representations are updated as the viewer moves. Much of the evidence for allocentric representations, such as the novel shortcut ability, the place and HD cells in rodents, and findings in spatial reasoning tasks, is shown to be either insufficient or based on the wrong assumptions. Moreover, spatial representations of environments at adjacent levels of a "hierarchy" cannot be accessed at the same time, and spatial updating in one environment does not automatically result in updated orientation in another environment, suggesting that representations of these environments are fragmented in nature, rather than integrated hierarchical networks.

The fragmentation of the representations of navigational space is consistent with, and may be a direct consequence of, the egocentric nature of the spatial representations and is difficult to explain by allocentric cognitive maps. According to the egocentric updating model, the amount of computation increases as the number of targets increases. Thus, a direct consequence of such a system is that only a subset of the targets may be updated at a time due to limitations in the capacity of the updating process. Accordingly, one may update targets in one environment but not the others, and people switch the environment they update when they navigate from one environment to another (Wang & Brockmole, in press). In contrast, both a single, comprehensive cognitive map and an interconnected, hierarchical network predict that knowing one's orientation in one environment would also specify one's orientation in another environment, and thus have difficulty explaining these findings.

In summary, recent findings suggest that navigation, spatial reasoning, and object/scene recognition are primarily based on egocentric representations that are updated as the animal moves. The updating process may have limited computational capacity, and does not apply to all environments simultaneously. Thus, spatial representations learned through navigation are fragmented in nature, rather than integrated hierarchical networks.

ACKNOWLEDGMENTS

Thanks to my collaborators Elizabeth Spelke, Daniel Simons, and James Brockmole, and to Steve Pinker, Mary Potter, Nancy Kanwisher, Randy Gallistel, Jack Loomis, John Rieser, Timothy McNamara, Gordon Logan, and David Irwin for inspiration, constructive criticism, and debates on various issues covered in this chapter. Thanks also to Brian Ross and David Irwin for suggestions on an earlier draft of this chapter. Comments should be sent to Frances Wang (francesw@s.psych.uiuc.edu).

REFERENCES

Berthoz, A., Israel, I., Francois, P. G., Grasso, R., & Tsuzuku, T. (1995). Spatial memory of body linear displacement: What is being stored? *Science, 269*, 95–98.

Biederman, I. (1987). Recognition-by-components: A theory of human image understanding. *Psychological Review, 94*, 115–147.

Biederman, I., & Cooper, E. E. (1991). Object recognition and laterality null effects. *Neuropsychologia, 29*, 685–694.

Biederman, I., & Cooper, E. E. (1992). Size in variance in visual object priming. *Journal of Experimental Psychology: Human Perception & Performance, 18*, 121–133.

Biederman, I., & Gerhardstein, P. C. (1993). Recognizing depth-rotated objects: Evidence and conditions for three-dimensional viewpoint invariance. *Journal of Experimental Psychology: Human Perception & Performance, 19*, 1162–1182.

Bridgeman, B., Kirch, M., & Sperling, A. (1981). Segregation of cognitive and motor aspects of visual function using induced motion. *Perception & Psychophysics, 29*, 336–342.

Bridgeman, B., Perry, S., & Anand, S. (1997). Interaction of cognitive and sensorimotor maps of visual space. *Perception & Psychophysics, 59*, 456–469.

Brockmole, J. R., & Wang, R. F. (2002). Switching between environmental representations in memory. *Cognition, 83*, 295–316.

Brockmole, J. R., & Wang, R. F. (2003). Changing perspective within and across environments. *Cognition, 87*, B59–B67.

Brown, P., & Levinson, S. C. (1993). "Uphill" and "downhill" in Tzeltal. *Journal of Linguistic Anthropology, 3*, 46–74.

Bülthoff, H. H., & Edelman, S. (1992). Psychophysical support for a two-dimensional view interpolation theory of object recognition. *Proceedings of the National Academy of Sciences of the United States of America, 89*, 60–64.

Carlson, L. A., & Logan, G. D. (2001). Using spatial terms to select an object. *Memory & Cognition, 29*, 883–892.

Carlson-Radvansky, L. A., & Irwin, D. E. (1993). Frames of reference in vision and language: Where is above? *Cognition, 46*, 223–224.

Carlson-Radvansky, L. A., & Irwin, D. E. (1994). Reference frame activation during spatial term assignment. *Journal of Memory & Language, 33*, 646–671.

Carlson-Radvansky, L. A., & Jiang, Y. (1998). Inhibition accompanies reference-frame selection. *Psychological Science, 9*, 386–391.

Carlson-Radvansky, L. A., & Tang, Z. (2000). Functional influences on orienting a reference frame. *Memory & Cognition, 28*, 812–820.

Cheng, K. (1986). A purely geometric module in the rat's spatial representation. *Cognition, 23*, 149–178.

Cheng, K., & Gallistel, C. R. (1984). Testing the geometric power of an animal's spatial representation. In H. L. Roitblat, T. G. Bever, and H. S. Terrace (Eds.), *Animal cognition.* (pp. 409–423). Hillsdale, NJ: Erlbaum.

Collett, M., Collett, T. S., Bisch, S., & Wehner, R. (1998). Local and global vectors in desert ant navigation. *Nature, 394*, 269–272.

Collett, M., Collett, T. S., & Wehner, R. (1999). Calibration of vector navigation in desert ants. *Current Biology, 9*, 1031–1034.

Collett, T. S., & Cartwright, B. A. (1983). Eidetic images in insects: Their role in navigation. *Trends in Neuroscience, 6*, 101–105.

Collett, T. S., & Land, M. F. (1975). Visual spatial memory in a hoverfly. *Journal of Comparative Physiology, 100*, 59–84.

Cooper, E. E., Biederman, I., & Hummel, J. E. (1992). Metric invariance in object recognition: A review and further evidence. *Canadian Journal of Psychology, 46*, 191–214.

Cooper, L. A., & Shepard, R. N. (1973). The time required to prepare for a rotated stimulus. *Memory & Cognition, 1*, 246–250.

Cooper, L. A., & Shepard, R. N. (1975). Mental transformation in the identification of left and right hands. *Journal of Experimental Psychology: Human Perception & Performance, 1*, 48–56.

Creem, S. H., & Proffitt, D. R. (1998). Two memories for geographical slant: Separation and interdependence of action and awareness. *Psychonomic Bulletin & Review, 5*, 22–36.

De Vega, M., & Rodrigo, M. J. (2001). Updating spatial layouts mediated by pointing and labeling under physical and imaginary rotation. *European Journal of Cognitive Psychology, 13*, 369–393.

Diwadkar, V. A., & McNamara, T. P. (1997). Viewpoint dependence in scene recognition. *Psychological Science, 8*, 302–307.

Dudchenko, P. A., Goodridge, J. P., Seiterle, D. A., & Taube, J. S. (1997). Effects of repeated disorientation on the acquisition of spatial tasks in rats: Dissociation between the appetitive radial arm maze and aversive water maze. *Journal of Experimental Psychology: Animal Behavior Processes, 23*, 194–210.

Dudchenko, P. A., Goodridge, J. P., & Taube, J. S. (1997). The effects of disorientation on visual landmark control of head direction cell orientation. *Experimental Brain Research, 115*, 375–380.

Dudchenko, P. A., & Taube, J. S. (1997). Correlation between head direction cell activity and spatial behavior on a radial arm maze. *Behavioral Neuroscience, 111*, 3–19.

Easton, R. D., & Sholl, M. J. (1995). Object-array structure, frames of reference, and retrieval of spatial knowledge. *Journal of Experimental Psychology: Learning, Memory, and Cognition, 21*, 483–500.

Eichenbaum, H., Otto, T., & Cohen, N. J. (1992). The hippocampus—what does it do? *Behavioral and Neural Biology, 57*, 2–36.

Etienne, A. S., Maurer, R., Berlie, J., Reverdin, B., Rowe, T., Georgakopoulos, J., & Séguinot, V. (1998). Navigation through vector addition. *Nature, 396*, 161–164.

Frier, H. J., Edwards, E., Smith, C., Neale, S., & Collett, T. S. (1996). Magnetic compass cues and visual pattern learning in honeybees. *Journal of Experimental Biology, 199*, 1353–1361.

Gallistel, C. R. (1990). *The organization of learning.* Cambridge, MA: MIT Press.

Goodale, M. A., & Milner, A. D. (1992). Separate visual pathways for perception and action. *Trends in Neurosciences, 15*, 20–25.

Goodridge, J. P., & Taube, J. S. (1995). Preferential use of the landmark navigational system by head direction cells in rats. *Behavioral Neuroscience, 109*, 49–61.

Gothard, K. M., Skaggs, W. E., & McNaughton, B. L. (1996). Dynamics of mismatch correction in the hippocampal ensemble code for space: Interaction between path integration and environmental cues. *The Journal of Neuroscience, 16*, 8027–8040.

Gould, J. L. (1986). The locale map of honey bees: Do insects have cognitive maps? *Science, 232*, 861–863.

Gouteux, S., & Spelke, E. S. (2001). Children's use of geometry and landmarks to reorient in an open space. *Cognition, 81*, 119–148.

Hermer, L. (1997). Internally coherent spatial memories in a mammal. *Neuroreport, 8*, 1743–1747.

Hermer, L., & Spelke, S. S. (1994). A geometric process for spatial reorientation in young children. *Nature, 370*, 57–59.

Hermer, L., & Spelke, S. S. (1996). Modularity and development: The case of spatial reorientation. *Cognition, 61*, 195–232.

Hetherington, P. A., & Shapiro, M. L. (1997). Hippocampal place fields are altered by the removal of single visual cues in a distance-dependent manner. *Behavioral Neuroscience, 111*, 20–34.

Hirtle, S. C., & Jonides, J. (1985). Evidence of hierarchies in cognitive maps. *Memory & Cognition, 13*, 208–217.

Huttenlocher, J., Hedges, L. V., & Duncan, S. (1991). Categories and particulars: Prototype effects in estimating spatial location. *Psychological Review, 98*, 352–376.

Huttenlocher, J., & Presson, C. C. (1973). Mental rotation and the perspective problem. *Cognitive Psychology, 4*, 277–299.

Huttenlocher, J., & Presson, C. C. (1979). The coding and transformation of spatial information. *Cognitive Psychology, 11*, 375–394.

Israel, I., Bronstein, A. M., Kanayama, R., Faldon, M., & Gresty, M. A. (1996). Visual and vestibular factors influencing vestibular "navigation." *Experimental Brain Research, 112*, 411–419.

Kirchner, W. H., & Braun, U. (1994). Dancing honey bees indicate the location of food sources using path integration rather than cognitive maps. *Animal Behaviour, 48*, 1437–1441.

Knierim, J. J., Kudrimoti, H. S., & McNaughton, B. L. (1995). Place cells, head direction cells, and the learning of landmark stability. *Journal of Neuroscience, 15*, 1648–1659.

Kourtzi, Z., & Shiffrar, M. (1997). One-shot view invariance in a moving world. *Psychological Science, 8*, 461–466.

Landau, B., Spelke, E. S., & Gleitman, H. (1984). Spatial knowledge in a young blind child. *Cognition, 16*, 225–260.

Levinson, S. C. (1992). Primer for the field investigation of spatial description and conception. *Pragmatics, 2*, 5–47.

Levinson, S. C. (1996). Frames of reference and Molyneux's question: Crosslinguistic evidence. In P. Bloom et al. (Eds.), *Language & space*. Cambridge, MA: MIT Press.

Levinson, S. C., & Haviland, J. B. (1994). Introduction: Spatial conceptualization in Mayan languages. *Linguistics, 32*, (4–5(332–333)), 613–622.

Loomis, J. M., Da Silva, J. A., Philbeck, J. W., & Fukusima, S. S. (1996). Visual perception of location and distance. *Current Directions in Psychological Science, 5*, 72–77.

Loomis, J. M., Klatzky, R. L., Golledge, R. G., Cicinelli, J. G., Pellegrino, J. W., & Fry, P. A. (1993). Nonvisual navigation by blind and sighted: Assessment of path integration ability. *Journal of Experimental Psychology: General, 122*, 73–91.

Markus, E. J., Qin, Y., Leonard, B. J., Skaggs, W. E., McNaughton, B. L., & Barnes, C. A. (1995). Interactions between location and task affect the spatial and directional firing of hippocampal neurons. *Journal of Neuroscience, 15*, 7079–7094.

May, M. (1996). Cognitive and embodied modes of spatial imagery. *Psychologische Beitraege, 38,* 418–434.

McNamara, T. P. (1986). Mental representations of spatial relations. *Cognitive Psychology, 18,* 87–121.

McNamara, T. P., Hardy, J. K., & Hirtle, S. C. (1989). Subjective hierarchies in spatial memory. *Journal of Experimental Psychology: Learning, Memory, and Cognition, 15,* 211–227.

McNaughton, B. L. (1996). Cognitive cartography. *Nature, 381,* 368–369.

McNaughton, B. L., Barnes, C. A., Gerrard, J. L., Gothard, K., Jung, M. W., Knierim, J. J., Kudrimoti, H., Qin, Y., Skaggs, Q. W., Suster, M., & Weaver, K. L. (1996). Deciphering the hippocampal polyglot: The hippocampus as a path integration system. *The Journal of Experimental Biology, 199,* 173–185.

McNaughton, B. L., Barnes, C. A., & O'Keefe, J. (1983). The contributions of position, direction and velocity to single unit activity in the hippocampus of freely-moving rats. *Experimental Brain Research, 52,* 41–49.

McNaughton, B. L., Knierim, J. J., & Wilson, M. A. (1995). Vector encoding and the vestibular foundations of spatial cognition: Neurophysiological and computational mechanisms. In M. Gazzaniga (Ed.), *The cognitive neurosciences.* (pp. 585–595). Boston: MIT Press.

Mittelstaedt, M. L., & Mittelstaedt, H. (1980). Homing by path integration in a mammal. *Naturwissenschaften, 67,* 566–567.

Morris, R. G. M. (1981). Spatial localization does not require the presence of local cues. *Learning and Motivation, 12,* 239–261.

Müller, M., & Wehner, R. (1994). The hidden spiral: Systematic search and path integration in desert ants, *Cataglyphis fortis. Journal of Comparative Physiology A—Sensory Neural & Behavioral Physiology, 175,* 525–530.

Muller, R. U., & Kubie, J. L. (1987). The effects of changes in the environment on the spatial firing of hippocampal complex-spike cells. *Journal of Neuroscience, 77,* 1951–1968.

O'Keefe, J., & Burgess, N. (1996). Geometric determinants of the place fields of hippocampal neurons. *Nature, 381,* 425–428.

O'Keefe, J., & Nadel, L. (1978). *The hippocampus as a cognitive map.* Oxford, UK: Clarendon.

O'Keefe, J., & Speakman, A. (1987). Single unit activity in the rat hippocampus during a spatial memory task. *Experimental Brain Research, 68,* 1–27.

Piaget, J. (1952). *The origins of intelligence in childhood.* New York: International Universities Press.

Piaget, J. (1954). *The construction of reality in the child.* New York: Basic Books.

Poggio, T., & Edelman, S. (1990). A network that learns to recognize 3D objects. *Nature, 343,* 263–266.

Presson, C. C. (1982). Strategies in spatial reasoning. *Journal of Experimental Psychology: Learning, Memory, and Cognition, 8,* 243–251.

Proffitt, D. R., Bhalla, M., Gossweiler, R., & Midgett, J. (1995). Perceiving geographical slant. *Psychonomic Bulletin & Review, 2,* 409–428.

Quirk, G. J., Muller, R. U., & Kubie, J. L. (1990). The firing of hippocampal place cells in the dark depends on the rat's recent experience. *Journal of Neuroscience, 10,* 2008–2017.

Regier, T., & Carlson, L. A. (2001). Grounding spatial language in perception: An empirical and computational investigation. *Journal of Experimental Psychology: General, 130,* 273–298.

Rieser, J. J. (1989). Access to knowledge of spatial structure at novel points of observation. *Journal of Experimental Psychology: Learning, Memory, and Cognition, 15,* 1157–1165.

Rieser, J. J., Ashmead, D. H., Talor, C. R., & Youngquist, G. A. (1990). Visual perception and the guidance of locomotion without vision to previously seen targets. *Perception, 19,* 675–689.

Rieser, J. J., & Rider, E. A. (1991). Young children's spatial orientation with respect to multiple targets when walking without vision. *Developmental Psychology, 27,* 97–107.

Rock, I., Wheeler, D., & Tudor, L. (1989). Can we imagine how objects look from other viewpoints? *Cognitive Psychology, 21,* 185–210.

Ronacher, B., & Wehner, R. (1995). Desert ants *Cataglyphis fortis* use self-induced optic flow to measure distances travelled. *Journal of Comparative Physiology A—Sensory Neural & Behavioral Physiology, 177,* 21–27.

Saint Paul, U. V. (1982). Do geese use path integration for walking home? In F. Papi and H. G. Wallraff (Eds.), *Avian navigation.* (pp. 298–307). New York: Springer.

Schmidt, I., Collett, T. S., Dillier, F. X., & Wehner, R. (1992). How desert ants cope with enforced detours on their way home. *Journal of Comparative Physiology A—Sensory Neural & Behavioral Physiology, 171,* 285–288.

Shelton, A. L., & McNamara, T. P. (1997). Multiple views of spatial memory. *Psychonomic Bulletin & Review, 4,* 102–106.

Shepard, R. N., & Cooper, L. A. (1982). *Mental images and their transformations.* Cambridge, MA: MIT Press.

Shepard, R. N., & Metzler, J. (1971). Mental rotation of three-dimensional objects. *Science, 171,* 701–703.

Simons, D. J., & Wang, R. F. (1998). Perceiving real-world viewpoint changes. *Psychological Science, 9,* 315–320.

Simons, D. J., Wang, R. F., & Roddenberry, D. (2002). Object recognition is mediated by extra-retinal information. *Perception & Psychophysics, 64,* 521–530.

Srinivasan, M. V., Zhang, S. W., Lehrer, M., & Collett, T. S. (1996). Honeybee navigation en route to the goal: Visual flight control and odometry. *Journal of Experimental Biology, 199,* 237–244.

Stevens, A., & Coupe, P. (1978). Distortions in judged spatial relations. *Cognitive Psychology, 10,* 422–437.

Tarr, M. J. (1995). Rotating objects to recognize them: A case study on the role of viewpoint dependency in the recognition of three-dimensional objects. *Psychonomic Bulletin & Review, 2,* 55–82.

Tarr, M. J., Bülthoff, H. H., Zabinski, M., & Blanz, V. (1997). To what extent do unique parts influence recognition across changes in viewpoint? *Psychological Science, 8,* 282–289.

Taube, J. S., & Burton, H. L. (1995). Head direction cell activity monitored in a novel environment and during a cue conflict situation. *Journal of Neurophysiology, 74,* 1953–1971.

Taube, J. S., Muller, R. U., & Ranck, J. B. (1990a). Head-direction cells recorded from the postsubiculum in freely moving rats: I. Description and quantitative analysis. *The Journal of Neuroscience, 10,* 420–435.

Taube, J. S., Muller, R. U., & Ranck, J. B. (1990b). Head-direction cells recorded from the postsubiculum in freely moving rats: II. Effects of environmental manipulations. *The Journal of Neuroscience, 10,* 436–447.

Taylor, H. A., & Tversky, B. (1992). Descriptions and depictions of environments. *Memory & Cognition, 20,* 483–496.

Thinus Blanc, C., Durup, M., & Poucet, B. (1992). The spatial parameters encoded by hamsters during exploration: A further study. *Behavioural Processes, 26,* 43–57.

Tolman, E. C. (1948). Cognitive maps in rats and men. *Psychological Review, 55,* 189–208.

Ullman, S., & Basri, R. (1991). Recognition by linear-combinations of models. *IEEE Transactions on Pattern Analysis and Machine Intelligence, 13,* 992–1006.

Vetter, T., Hurlbert, A., & Poggio, T. (1995). View-based models of 3D object recognition: Invariance to imaging transformations. *Cerebral Cortex, 5,* 261–269.

Wang, R. F. (in press). Dissociation between verbal and pointing responding in perspective change problems. In L. A. Carlson & E. van der Zee (Eds.), *Functional features in language and space: Insights from perception, categorization and development.* Oxford, UK: Oxford University Press.

Wang, R. F. (2003a). Beyond imagination: Perspective change problems revisited (submitted).

Wang, R. F. (2003b). Action, verbal response and spatial reasoning (submitted).

Wang, R. F., & Brockmole, J. R. (in press, a) Human navigation in nested environments. *Journal of Experimental Psychology: Learning, Memory, and Cognition.*

Wang, R. F., & Brockmole, J. R. (in press, b) Simultaneous spatial updating in nested environments. *Psychonomic Bulletin and Review.*

Wang, R. F., Hermer, L., & Spelke, E. S. (1999). Mechanisms of reorientation and object localization by human children: A comparison with rats. *Behavioral Neuroscience, 113,* 475–485.

Wang, R. F., & Simons, D. J. (1999). Active and passive scene recognition across views. *Cognition, 70,* 191–210.

Wang, R. F., & Spelke, E. S. (2000). Updating egocentric representations in human navigation. *Cognition, 77,* 215–250.

Wehner, R., & Lanfranconi, B. (1981). What do the ants know about the rotation of the sky? *Nature, 293,* 731–733.

Wehner, R., & Srinivasan, M. V. (1981). Searching behavior of desert ants, genus *Cataglyphis* (Formicidae, Hymenoptera). *Journal of Comparative Physiology, 142,* 315–318.

Wilson, M. A., & McNaughton, B. L. (1993). Dynamics of the hippocampal ensemble code for space. *Science, 261,* 1055–1058.

Wilton, R. N. (1979). Knowledge of spatial relations: The specification of information used in inferences. *Quarterly Journal of Experimental Psychology, 31,* 133–146.

Wraga, M., Creem, S. H., & Proffitt, D. R. (2000). Updating displays after imagined object and viewer rotations. *Journal of Experimental Psychology: Learning, Memory, and Cognition, 26,* 151–168.

Ziegler, P. E., & Wehner, R. (1997). Time-courses of memory decay in vector-based and landmark-based systems of navigation in desert ants, *Cataglyphis fortis. Journal of Comparative Physiology A—Sensory Neural & Behavioral Physiology, 181,* 13–20.

SELECTIVE VISUAL ATTENTION AND VISUAL SEARCH: BEHAVIORAL AND NEURAL MECHANISMS

Joy J. Geng and Marlene Behrmann

I. Introduction

Although our visual experiences convey a sense of sensory richness, recent work has demonstrated that our representations of perceptual information are in fact impoverished, relative to the amount of potential information in the distal stimulus (Grimes, 1996; Irwin, Yantis, & Jonides, 1983; Levin & Simons, 1997; Mack & Rock, 1998; O'Regan & Levy-Schoen, 1983; O'Regan, Rensink, & Clark, 1999; Rensink, O'Regan, & Clark, 1997; Simons & Levin, 1998). These studies demonstrate that conscious perceptions are a consequence of myriad social, goal-oriented (e.g., change detection), and stimulus (e.g., exogenous cuing) factors that are subject to neural processing constraints (e.g., attentional blink). How these cognitive and neural factors interact to select certain bits of information and inhibit other bits from further processing is the domain of visual attention.

Visual search is one task domain in which visual attention has been studied extensively. Visual search studies are well-suited as a proxy for real-world attentional requirements as features of the natural environment such as object clutter are captured while a controlled stimulus environment is maintained. In fact, visual search tasks have been used extensively to

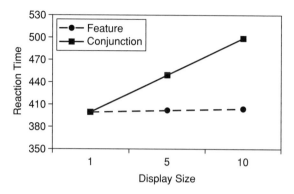

Fig. 1.   Reproduction of typical target-present visual search data.

examine patterns of visual attention over the past several decades (Neisser, 1964; Treisman & Gelade, 1980; Wolfe, 1998). A particularly prolific subset of these studies focuses on the conditions under which the reaction time (RT) and accuracy required to locate the target are affected by distractor set size. Cases in which time to detect a target is largely unaffected by increasing the number of distractors (e.g., 5 ms/distractor item) are labeled as "preattentive," whereas cases in which detection time is significantly slowed by increasing numbers of distractors (e.g., 50 ms/item) are labeled "attentive" (see Figure 1). These different search rates have also been referred to as "parallel" vs. "serial," "disjunctive" vs. "conjunctive," or "simple" vs. "difficult" (although for the suggestion that the preattentive/attentive distinction is orthogonal to the parallel/serial dichotomy see Reddy, VanRullen, & Koch, 2002).

Although all these terms are somewhat imprecise, the phenomena they refer to have been replicated numerous times: visual search for targets distinguished by a single feature is scarcely affected by the number of distractors present whereas targets distinguished by features of conjunctions appear to be affected linearly by the number of distractors present. Despite an abundance of data from behavioral and neural measures, however, the basic mechanisms involved in visual attentive processing as reflected in visual search tasks remain controversial. Specifically, the terms "preattentive" and "attentive" in relation to simple and difficult search have been a point of contentious debate. The source of disagreement surrounds the question of whether mechanisms that underlie visual attention, as seen in visual search tasks, operate in discrete serial stages or as an interactive parallel system. In this chapter we attempt to understand what neuro-psychological and imaging studies contribute to this debate and whether assumptions adopted in various computational models of visual search provide an adequate account of the empirical findings.

II. Basic Concepts

The term "preattentive" was first used by Neisser (1967) as a concept for understanding "focal" attention. His interest in the distinction between preattentive and focal operations was based on the apparent inability of people to simultaneously analyze multiple objects in the visual field. Neisser argued that primary operations such as segmentation of figures from the ground must occur "preattentively" in order for subsequent "focal" analysis of object details to occur:

> Since the processes of focal attention cannot operate on the whole visual field simultaneously, they can come into play only after preliminary operations have already segregated the figural units involved. These preliminary operations are of great interest in their own right. They correspond in part to what the Gestalt psychologists called "autochthonous forces," and they produce what Hebb called "primitive unity." I will call them the *preattentive processes* to emphasize that they produce the objects which later mechanisms are to flesh out and interpret. (Neisser, 1967, p. 89)

Although Neisser used the term "preattentive" to refer to a number of processes that seem to occur "without focal attention," the conceptual characterization of preattentive vs. focal attentional processing has been incorporated into many models of visual search to explain differences in target search times. In these models, the attentional system is characterized as involving a division of labor: processes that occur at a preattentive stage are completed before further processing occurs at an attentive stage. Moreover, the movement of items from one stage to the next occurs serially (Hoffman, 1979). These two-stage cognitive models contrast with interactive models, which claim that multiple levels of processing occur simultaneously and information processing is continuous and bidirectional.

Although there are many such computational models of visual attention, we deal here only with those that explicitly address effects of visual search and issues of preattentive and attentive processing. Although there is much computational and empirical work on space- and object-based effects in visual attention, we do not take up those issues here. Instead, we focus more narrowly on standard visual search paradigms and how they inform us about fundamental attentional processing. Note that in this chapter, we favor the terms "two-staged" and "interactive" over the terms "serial" and "parallel." We find the serial/parallel terminology to be ambiguous and misleading as many models have both parallel and serial components. Furthermore, to make matters worse, the terms "serial" and "parallel" are also used interchangeably with feature and conjunction search. In sum, our goal here is to understand preattentive and attentive processing from the perspective of visual search tasks in computational models, neuropsychological studies, and functional imaging.

III. Theoretical Models of Visual Search

A. TWO-STAGE MODELS

The most prominent two-stage model is feature integration theory (FIT) proposed by Treisman and colleagues (Treisman & Gormican, 1988; Treisman & Gelade, 1980). FIT was developed to provide a mechanistic account of how processing of objects occurs in the nervous system. Developed to contrast with Gestalt ideas of the whole preceding its parts, FIT proposes that the processing of parts must precede that of the whole. The argument is based on the idea that representation of elementary features must logically precede the combination (i.e., binding) of these features. Specifically, features belonging to separable dimensions (Garner, 1988) are processed in discrete preattentive maps in parallel, after which, "focal attention provides the 'glue' that integrates the initially separable features into unitary objects" (Treisman & Gelade, 1980, p. 98). A critical component of FIT involves the serial application of focal attention to specific coordinates within a master map of locations; the "spotlight of attention" allows for the formation of object files within which "free-floating" features from separable dimensions are bound together and to a location.

Modifications of FIT suggest that preattentive and attentive search may reflect a continuum based on the degree to which attention is distributed or narrowly focused on a particular location. Nevertheless, the relationship between the feature maps and later attentive stage at which features are conjoined is necessarily serial. Processing at the "map of locations" acts on completed feature representations passed on from the parallel feature levels. FIT accounts for a variety of phenomena such as illusory conjunctions, search asymmetries, differences between present vs. absent features, set size, and serial feature and rapid conjunction search, among others.

Guided Search 2.0 (Wolfe, 1994) shares some of the same basic assumptions as FIT with additional top-down elements that select task-relevant feature categories. Unlike FIT, input features are first processed through categorical channels that output to space-based feature maps. Activation within these feature maps reflects both bottom-up salience and top-down selection. The strength of the bottom-up component is based on the dissimilarity between an item and its neighbors. Top-down selection occurs for one channel per feature needed to make the discrimination.

Selection is automatic if a unique target category is present, but if no unique feature is present, the channel with the greatest difference between target and distractors is chosen. Similar to FIT, processing in feature maps is preattentive and parallel and output from feature maps projects to an activation map. Limited capacity attentional resources move from peak to peak within the activation map in serial fashion until search is terminated.

Subsequent models from the two-staged processing tradition have moved away from a modular view in which processing of information in one stage must be completed before it is passed to the next stage. Moore and Wolfe (2001) recently put forward a model in which they claim selective attention is both serial and parallel. They use the metaphor of an assembly line to describe how visual search slopes of approximately 20–50 ms/item can be made compatible with studies that find attentional dwell times lasting several hundred milliseconds (Duncan, Ward, & Shapiro, 1994). According to their metaphor, features enter and exit "visual processes" in a serial manner and with a particular rate (i.e., items on a conveyer belt), but many objects can undergo processing at the same time. The idea is captured in the following excerpt:

> The line may be capable of delivering a car every ten minutes, but it does not follow from this that it takes only ten minutes to make a car. Rather, parts are fed into the system at one end. They are bound together in a process that takes an extended period of time, and cars are released at some rate (e.g., one car every ten minutes) at the other end of the system.... Cars enter and emerge from the system in a serial manner.... However, if we ask how many cars are being built at the same time, it becomes clear that this is also a parallel processor. (Moore & Wolfe, 2001, p. 190)

Although this type of model involves cascaded processing, it is still serial in spirit: items enter and exit from the system one at a time. While this model is parallel in the sense that more than one object is processed at a time, processing of a single item is in no way influenced by the concurrent processing of a different item. Processing of individual items appears to occur at a fixed rate. Although this model primarily addresses attentive search processes, it allows for a distinct preattentive stage in which features are processed prior to placement on the assembly line.

One difficulty of two-stage models is the necessity to specify which features or items are processed preattentively and which are not. For example, findings of efficient search slopes for conjunctive stimuli resulted in modification to Guided Search 2.0 to include a limited set of "objects" within the category of stimuli that may be processed preattentively (Wolfe, 1996). This then required the notion of resources to explain why only a limited number of items may be processed preattentively, which then begs the question of how big of a resource there is and how many items of a given complexity might be included within a capacity-limited system.

Results continuously point to objects of greater and greater complexity that can seemingly be processed preattentively (Enns & Rensink, 1990, 1991; Li, VanRullen, Koch, & Perona, 2002; Nakayama & Silverman, 1986; Rousellet, Fabre-Thorpe, & Thorpe, 2002).

Despite some limitations, two-stage models have been successful in classifying limited sets of real world images. Itti and Koch (2001; also Koch & Ullman, 1985) provide a biologically based model of how simple search might occur via preattentive processes using a salience map. Their model is purely driven by bottom-up (feedforward) principles and involves competition derived from relatively long-range inhibitory connections between items within a particular feature map. The result of competition within a feature category is represented within a "conspicuity map," which projects to a salience map. Locations visited by attention are tagged by inhibition of return (IOR) (Klein, 1988), allowing the location with the next greatest activation within the salience map to become the target of attention.

Although this model contains competitive interactions within feature maps, it is stage-like in that the output of preattentive feature maps is passed onto an explicit saliency map, which, in turn, determines the spatial coordinates to which an attentional spotlight is directed. Several other models with similar bottom-up winner-take-all salience maps are also fairly good predictors of search behavior and eye movements (Itti & Koch, 2001; Parkhurst, Law, & Niebur, 2002; Zelinsky & Sheinberg, 1997).

B. INTERACTIVE MODELS

Interactive models, on the other hand, argue that there is no physical distinction between preattentive and attentive processing. There is no discrete preattentive stage or a spotlight of attention that is directed to a spatial coordinate. Instead they rely on the principles of competition and cooperation between features and objects to resolve the constraints of visual attention and to determine the efficiency of attentional selection. Feature search is hypothesized to be fast and accurate because competition is resolved quickly. In contrast, conjunctive search is slower and more prone to error because target–distractor similarity or distractor–distractor heterogeneity produces greater competition between items and therefore takes longer to resolve (Duncan & Humphreys, 1989). By excluding the language of two stages, interactive models circumvent the need to provide a deterministic account for where processing of particular stimulus classes begins and ends.

The biased competition and integrated competition accounts (Desimone & Duncan, 1995; Duncan, Humphreys, & Ward, 1997; Duncan & Humphreys, 1989) argue that attention is an emergent property of competition between representations of stimuli within the nervous system rather than a "spotlight" that is directed at coordinates on a location map. In this view, processing is qualitatively similar regardless of whether a target stimulus in visual search is distinguished from distractors by a single feature or by a conjunction of features. Thus, the implicit debate between two-stage and interactive models involves how stimulus elements interact during processing and not simply how individual features are processed within the visual stream.

The lack of discrete stages within interactive models does not imply the absence of processing order nor does it imply parallelism in the sense that stimuli are necessarily processed to a relatively deep level without attention (e.g., Deutsch & Deutsch, 1963). Rather, interactive models produce graded differences in representational strength between items. The difference is graded because bits of sensory information are, in fact, not "selected" but emerge as "winners." As Hamker (1999) notes, apparent seriality in search behavior may arise from iterations between layers of an interactive network in which degrees of enhancement and suppression are achieved. Neurons coding stimuli that are related by task-set are mutually supportive while unrelated features are mutually suppressive. Attention is an emergent property based on the principles of competition and cooperation at every level of processing and between processing levels (Duncan et al., 1997).

Search via recursive rejection (SERR) is a hierarchical model within a connectionist framework that embodies many of the principles of biased competition (Humphreys & Mueller, 1993). Visual search RTs are simulated through use of grouping principles. The main feature of the model is its ability to build up evidence continuously for the target in a bottom-up fashion, as well as reject distractors, in groups based on similarity, through top-down inhibitory connections. Grouping occurs through excitatory connections between items with similar features in a "match map" and inhibitory connections between unlike features between maps. Activation of a nontarget template results in inhibition of all similar features within a "match" map. Thus, homogeneity between distractors results in rejection of larger groups of distractors, which increases the likelihood of the target being selected next. Heterogeneous distractors require additional iterations of rejections, resulting in slower target detection. The hierarchical structure of the model successfully accounts for parallel processing of simple conjunction features as well as other behavioral effects of simple and difficult visual search (Humphreys & Mueller, 1993).

Hamker (1999) has also implemented a model in which feature maps interact directly with each other. This model contains both salient bottom-up and instructional top-down components. Competition (via inhibitory connections) occurs at multiple levels among feature-sensitive neurons, the integrative neurons that they project to, as well as within the object- and location-sensitive neurons. The higher level location- and object-sensitive neurons project back to lower level feature areas and support units that share receptive field properties. Thus all components of the model are interactive and have either the effect of enhancing or suppressing processing of activated features. The model eventually settles on a winner at the location-sensitive level, which determines where attention is sent via oculo-motor actions (a mechanism that is consistent with much of the empirical data reviewed in the next two sections).

Although the models outlined above are by no means a comprehensive review of visual search models, they represent the two major theoretical perspectives. Other approaches have been successful in accounting for data, but will not be addressed here (e.g., Bundesen, 1999; Cave, 1999; Cohen & Ruppin, 1999; Eckstein, 1998; Eckstein, Thomas, Palmer, & Shimozaki, 2000; Li, 2002). In just considering the models reviewed above, it is apparent that they share superficial traits such as feature maps, but differ quite purposefully in the characterization of (pre)attention. Built into stage-like models are specific maps (location maps or salience maps) at which processing becomes attentive and before which processing is preattentive. Some of these models employ top-down enhancement of target features and others are purely stimulus driven. The major contrast is that interactive models do not explicate a level at which processing becomes attentive. These models use inhibition and excitation within multiple levels to produce faster or slower search RTs.

There are many more models that embody stage-like processing than those that adhere to principles of integrated competition. One reason for this may be that two-stage models provide more transparent descriptions of behavioral data: The bimodal distribution of behavior (near zero vs. positive RT search slopes) is intuitively captured by each of the two stages of processing. The challenge is for the development of interactive models that show how noisy processing at multiple stages can give rise to apparently discrete classes of behaviors such as fast or slow search RTs. We now turn to the empirical data to seek evidence for either stage-like or interactive processing during visual search in humans.

IV. Empirical Data

Visual search tasks have been studied extensively with patient populations and with a number of imaging techniques. We review findings from these methodologies and attempt to draw broad conclusions relevant to the debate on the mechanisms of attentional processing. In this chapter, we review primarily functional magnetic resonance imaging (fMRI) and patient work because there is good correspondence between the spatial resolution of inferred brain area involvement in both methods and the inferences based on the data require similar caution. [For review of event-related potential (ERP) data pertaining to visual search and attention, see Luck & Hillyard, 2000; Mangun, Buonocore, Girelli, & Jha, 1998; Woodman & Luck, 1999, and for review of single-unit recording, see Bichot, Rao, & Schall, 2001; Li, 2002; McPeek & Keller, 2002.]

A. NEUROPSYCHOLOGY

Visual search studies have played an important role in neuropsychological research and hundreds of such studies have been run with patients with various kinds of disorders, including patients with schizophrenia (Lubow, Kaplan, Abramovich, Rudnick, & Laor, 2000), Parkinson's disease (Berry, Nicolson, Foster, Behrmann, & Sagar, 1999), and Alzheimer's disease (Foster, Behrmann, & Stuss, 1999). But perhaps the focus of most neuropsychological work using visual search has been in the domain of hemispatial neglect, a neuropsychological impairment that is thought to reflect an attentional bias that results in a failure to construct an appropriate representation of contralateral space (Duncan et al., 1999; Posner, 1987; Posner, Inhoff, Friedrich, & Cohen, 1987). In this section, we first describe hemispatial neglect and then outline a number of theoretical questions concerning attentional mechanisms that have been addressed using visual search paradigms. Following this, we describe some novel procedures for quantifying the attentional deficit using increasingly precise and systematic measurements.

Hemispatial neglect refers to a deficit in which individuals, after sustaining damage to the brain following a stroke, head injury, or tumor, fail to notice or report information on the side of space opposite the lesion, despite intact sensory and motor systems (Bartolomeo & Chokron, 2001; Bisiach & Vallar, 2000). The disorder usually manifests after a unilateral hemispheric lesion, and does so with greater frequency and severity after right than left hemisphere lesions. Thus, for example, patients with a right hemisphere lesion may fail to copy or even draw from memory features on the contralateral left of a display while incorporating the same features on the ipsilesional right (see Figure 2). The disorder might also manifest in self-care such that these patients may not shave or dress the contralateral side of the face or body and may not eat from the left side of the plate. Interestingly, neglect is not restricted to the visual modality, and auditory (Bellmann, Meuli, & Clarke, 2001; Hugdahl, Wester, & Asbjornsen, 1991), tactile (Moscovitch & Behrmann, 1994), and olfactory (Bellas, Novelly, & Eskenazi, 1989) neglect have all been well documented, although most of the research has investigated visual neglect. Although neglect occurs most often

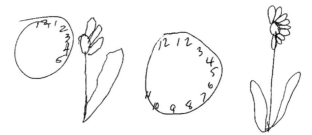

Fig. 2. Examples of copies of a clock and a daisy by two different patients with left-sided neglect following a right-hemisphere lesion.

following lesions to the parietal or temporoparietal cortex, it may also be evident after subcortical lesions (Karnath, Ferber, & Himmelbach, 2001; Karnath, Himmelbach, & Rorden, 2002; Maguire & Ogden, 2002).

1. Is Preattentive Processing Preserved in Hemispatial Neglect?

The standard visual search task, with targets appearing on the contra- or ipsilateral side and distractors appearing on the contra- and/or ipsilateral side, is extremely well designed to examine the mechanisms that underlie hemispatial neglect. For example, one question that comes up repeatedly in the context of two-stage models of attention is whether preattentive processing is intact in neglect. Not only does the answer have implications for neglect but it also has theoretical implications for attentional processing per se: if one could demonstrate intact feature search for contralateral targets in patients with neglect, this would further endorse the claim that that this form of search can be accomplished in the absence of attention. Furthermore, if intact contralateral feature search were observed, this might explain the finding that some patients appear to have access to implicit information about a contralateral stimulus even though they cannot overtly identify or describe the stimulus. For example, some studies have shown that hemispatial neglect patients are primed in their responses to centrally presented probe by a contralateral prime that they cannot overtly report (McGlinchey-Berroth, 1997; McGlinchey-Berroth, Milberg, Verfaellie, Alexander, & Kilduff, 1993). Other studies have documented the ability of the patients to perform various forms of perceptual organization (figure ground segregation, amodal completion, derivation of a principal axis) on the basis of ignored contralateral information (Davis & Driver, 1994; Driver, Baylis, Goodrich, & Rafal, 1994; Driver, Baylis, & Rafal, 1992). The preservation of preattentive processing provides a possible source of information, which might potentially be exploited by the patients in the absence of conscious awareness.

Despite the best of intentions and hosts of studies, we still do not know whether there is intact preattentive processing in neglect. In one recent study, Esterman, McGlinchey-Berroth, and Milberg (2000) reported normal feature search in three neglect patients with cortical lesions and without hemianopia (a visual field defect that affects one visual field). A fourth patient with neglect following a subcortical lesion exhibited a significant effect of array size on search time. All patients were impaired on the difficult search task with contralesional targets, leading the authors to conclude that only effortful search is affected in hemispatial neglect but that the ability to extract low-level featural information across the field in parallel is preserved. Consistent with this conclusion, Aglioti, Smania, Barbieri, and Corbetta (1997) examined the search performance of a very large group of individuals, consisting of 75 left hemisphere-damaged (LHD) and right hemisphere-damaged (RHD) participants with and without neglect. The critical finding was that contralateral errors were disproportionately higher on the difficult tasks as opposed to the feature tasks, indicating that neglect only impaired performance when serial search was required. Finally, Arguin, Joanette, and Cavanagh (1993) investigated LHD participants with and without visual attention deficits on feature detection and conjunction search tasks. Even the patients with attention deficits performed similarly to controls in contralateral hemispace on the feature task, leading the authors to conclude that parallel search was preserved in participants with neglect.

Consistent with this conclusion is the finding of normal search on the contralateral side reported by Riddoch and Humphreys (1987). In this study, the authors presented a series of cards to three patients with left-sided neglect and RTs were recorded manually. The patients were required to search for a target, which was present on half the trials. In the one task in which search was parallel in nonneurological subjects, the target was a red circle among green circle distractors and the patients' RT was unaffected by the number of distractors. Importantly, this was true even when the target appeared on the contralateral side. Although the authors concluded that patients search in parallel on the neglected side, the patients' performance was not completely normal as the error rate for contralateral targets was high. In a second task, which involved detecting an inverted "T" among upright "T" distractors, search was serial for the control subjects and, not surprisingly, target detection (in accuracy and RT) was serial for the patients for targets on both sides.

But for every study showing intact contralateral parallel search in a feature search paradigm, there is a study showing contralateral serial search by neglect patients. For example, Eglin, Robertson, and Knight (1989) had subjects perform two tasks, the first with a red dot as the target among blue and yellow dots (feature search) and the second with a red dot as the target among split blue and intact red dots (conjunction search). In both tasks the array size, distractor number, and location of targets and distractors were varied. The most relevant result was the observed impairment in contralateral feature search in six patients with RHD and in one patient with LHD. Additional studies confirm the presence of contralateral search functions that are consistent with serial rather than parallel search, under conditions when normal subjects show almost no increase in RT with increasing number of distractors (Eglin, Robertson, & Knight, 1991; Eglin, Robertson, Knight, & Brugger, 1994; Pavlovskaya, Ring, Grosswasser, & Hochstein, 2002).

As is evident from the overview of these studies, there is little agreement on whether parallel search for a contralateral feature target is preserved. One obvious explanation for the discrepancies is that the studies vary along several dimensions including the number of subjects tested (with very small numbers in some cases), the lesion size and site of the patients, the severity of the neglect deficit in the patients, the nature of the search task independent of being simple or difficult (color discrimination or cancellation), and the reliance on a single or multiple dependent measures (accuracy and/or RT). But there is one further consideration that is more theoretical in nature and that is that the preattentive/attentive distinction might not hold and that an alternative explanation for the findings should be sought.

One possible alternative explanation, provided by Duncan and colleagues (Desimone & Duncan, 1995; Duncan et al., 1997), is that the outcome of visual search is the reflection of a competitive process between targets and distractors, as well as top-down signals that affect task requirements. According to this view, an important dimension in determining the speed of the search is the similarity or overlap between the target and distractors. This framework may provide a coherent explanation for the existing visual search data and may also account for results where the search task is not easily defined as either feature-based or conjunction-based. For example, with regard to this last point, Hildebrandt, Gieselmann, and Sachsenheimer (1999) compared the performance of patients with neglect following right middle brain artery lesions and without hemianopia with patients with hemianopia following posterior cerebral artery infarctions and patients with right hemisphere lesions but neither neglect nor hemianopia. The task involved detecting the presence of a target, a square with a gap at the top, from distractors, which were squares with gaps in locations other than at the top. This task is neither clearly a feature nor a conjunction task and only the patients with neglect were impaired at detecting contralateral targets, showing a gradual decrease in accuracy with increasingly contralesional targets.

One might also imagine, however, that depending on the severity of the neglect, there would be greater or lesser competition for selection of the target and this might impact search on both the contralesional and ipsilesional sides. This was explored in one recent study, in which performance was investigated in 56 RHD and 48 LHD stroke participants, and 34 controls on simple and difficult search tasks and on a standardized neglect battery (Behrmann, Ebert, & Black, 2003). Compared with RHD patients without neglect, patients with mild left-sided neglect, defined on the standard battery, showed an increase in their search slopes of 32.6 ms and 64.7 ms for contralateral targets in feature and difficult search, respectively, but showed no difference in the slopes for ipsilateral targets. Increased contralateral slopes were also seen in RHD patients with more severe neglect, in comparison with RHD with no neglect, where the slopes were 39.3 ms and 53.7 ms steeper on feature and difficult search, respectively. There is a slight but significant difference for the contralateral feature search for the mild and severe neglect groups but no difference on the contralateral difficult search. There is, however, another interesting difference between the two groups and this concerns search for ipsilesional targets. As might be expected from a model where there is competition between ipsilateral and contralateral items, we might see faster acquisition of ipsilateral targets for the more severe group who have a stronger ipsilateral attentional bias. Indeed, in comparison with RHD patients without neglect, the mild neglect group has a slope that is 8.8 ms/item and 4.5 ms/item steeper for feature and difficult search, respectively, whereas there is a 0.2 ms/item advantage for the severe group in feature search but a 21.2 ms/item advantage for this group in difficult search. Note that the severe group shows a marginally significant 3.6 ms/item advantage for ipsilesional difficult search over the normal nonneurological control subjects. Several important conclusions may be reached: the first is that the severity of neglect, at least in the RHD patients, affects the speed with which they detect a target as a function of the number of distractors compared with brain-damaged individuals without neglect. Second, the differences are apparent in both feature and difficult searches. Interestingly and perhaps counterintuitively, although not without precedent (Behrmann, Barton, Watt, & Black, 1997; D'Erme, Robertson, Bartolomeo, Daniele, & Gainotti, 1992; Làdavas, Petronio, & Umilta, 1990), the severe neglect individuals show faster search on the ipsilesional side compared with both the mild neglect patients and, to some extent, with the brain-damaged nonneglect group. These findings are not easily accommodated in a two-stage model and are perhaps better fit within a framework in which the relationship between simple and difficult search is graded and competitive and the more salient an item, the faster it will be detected.

2. Is the Attentional Deficit in Hemispatial Neglect Lateralized?

Related to the first question is a second question concerning the hemifield differences in hemispatial neglect. Heilman and colleagues (Heilman, Bowers, Valenstein, & Watson, 1987; Heilman, Watson, & Valenstein, 1997) have argued in favor of a hemifield difference as, on their account, the left hemisphere attentional processor can process only right hemifield targets, whereas the right hemisphere attentional processor can process both left and right targets. In contrast, Kinsbourne (1987, 1993) has postulated that search performance is gradually impaired from right to left in both hemifields with no dramatic difference between the two fields. Again, there is no clear solution to this dichotomy. Some visual search studies have found different search patterns in the two fields with response times increasing more markedly to eccentric targets in the contralesional than in the ipsilesional field. Note that some of the same studies also report poorer ipsilesional performance compared with controls (Eglin, Robertson, Knight, & Brugger, 1996; Eglin et al., 1989; Geng & Behrmann, 2002). Other studies, however, have found that the search patterns of neglect patients are equally poor in the contralesional and ipsilesional visual field (Chatterjee, Mennemeier, & Heilman, 1992b; Halligan, Burn, Marshall, & Wade, 1992). The claim that there are no hemifield differences also finds support in studies that do not use visual search; for example, using partial and whole report procedures, Duncan and colleagues document the presence of poor visual processing in both hemifields in neglect patients (Duncan et al., 1999). Note, however, that, as cited above, Behrmann et al. (2003) find an advantage over the nonneglect control subjects for ipsilesional target detection

In addition to comparing the left hemifield with the right hemifield, one can also explore the detection performance of neglect patients when the location of the target is systematically altered across the two fields so that slope can be derived as a function of horizontal target position. In such studies, there is fairly robust evidence for an attentional gradient that crosses the two fields (Behrmann et al., 1997; Chatterjee, Mennemeier, & Heilman, 1992a; Deouell, Sacher, Ben Moshe, & Soroker, 2000; Hildebrandt et al., 1999; Karnath & Nemeier, 2002), with lesser activation the further contralateral the target location (note that there is not clear consensus on where the peak of activation resides on the ipsilesional side). Bolstered by neurobiological evidence concerning the receptive field size and distributional differences in parietal cells in the two hemispheres, a number of recent computational models have also argued in favor of an attentional gradient and have incorporated a smooth, monotonic gradient of attention across both fields into the underlying processing dynamics of the network (Behrmann & Plaut, 2001; Mozer, 2002; Pouget & Driver, 2000).

3. Visual Search for Targets on Left/Right of Space or Objects

One further question that has been addressed by studies of visual search in neglect concerns whether neglect is space- or object-based. Although the neglect syndrome was originally described in terms of a space-based deficit (see Mesulam, 1999, for review), later findings have argued that neglect is also object-centered (Vallar, 1998). Several studies have reported that detection of a target on the relative left of an object is poor, especially if the search is for a conjunction of features, irrespective of the absolute location of the target or object (Arguin & Bub, 1993). For example, Grabowecky, Robertson, and Treisman (1993) had seven neglect patients search for a conjunction target in a diamond-shaped matrix of distractors. Additional grouping stimuli appeared as flanks either to the left, right, or both, of this matrix. When flanks appeared only on the right, a decrement in search performance for the contralateral target was observed, consistent with views of ipsilesional hyperattention and competition between ipsilesional and contralesional stimuli. Most interesting is the return of performance to near baseline levels for contralateral targets when a contralesional flank was included. The addition of the contralesional flank, according to the authors, shifts the frame of reference such that patients are assisted in calculating the center of mass of the object. The patients then use this calculation to determine the spatial distribution of attention.

Consistent with the idea that the boundaries of an object can play a role in determining the distribution of attention (and neglect), more recently, Pavlovskaya et al. (2002) tested several subjects with both left- and right-sided neglect on a search task in which the entire array was placed either centrally or lateralized to the right or left hemifield. The important conclusion is that the patients had great difficulty finding targets located on the contralateral side of the array, irrespective of the absolute placement of the array. These data are taken to reflect the idea that neglect occurs for information on the contralateral side of an object (and not only of space). The same result is also obtained in eye movements; Karnath and Niemeier (2002) had patients search for a target in a large display and then, in a second condition, search again but now the display was presegmented into regions containing particular colors. In this second condition, subjects are prompted to search only, for example, the orange region, which falls on the ipsilateral side of space. When the patients searched the entire surrounding space, the patients neglected the left hemispace and spontaneously attended to the right hemispace. No significant left–right asymmetry was detected in the orange segment. However, in the second condition when visual search was constrained to this segment, all patients completely ignored the left part of this particular segment.

The findings from the studies reviewed here are interesting and, although there is not always convergence, visual search studies have played an important role in the study of hemispatial neglect. There is a clear and obvious need for further definitive studies and more sophisticated and quantitative measures of the attentional deficit in neglect. Some advances have already been made in this direction. Deouell and colleagues (Deouell et al., 2000) have developed a sensitive test known as the Starry Night Test in which a target, a red-filled circle, appears anywhere in a two-dimensional grid (49 virtual cells) accompanied by a dynamically varying array of green distractors. Both reaction time and accuracy (hit, miss) are recorded and a psychophysical function established along horizontal and vertical dimensions. The dynamic nature of the task along with the large sampling of trials and fine-grained measurement has proven sensitive to documenting hemispatial neglect even when standard bedside tests failed to make the diagnosis. Finally, as alluded to previously, Duncan and colleagues have adopted the Theory of Visual Attention Deficits (Bundesen, 1990), in which different components of attentional processing can be measured. Using the assumptions of this model, Duncan et al. (1999) have measured in patients with neglect both sensory effectiveness, indicating how well an element is processed alone, and attentional weight, indicating how strongly a given element competes for attentional selection based both on bottom-up salience and top-down task relevance. These more fine-grained and quantitative measures may complement the standard visual search procedures and provide further insights into the attentional mechanisms involved in hemispatial neglect.

B. FUNCTIONAL IMAGING

Although a more recent development, brain imaging techniques have also been used to examine the neural mechanisms underlying visual attention. In this section we review positron emission tomography (PET) and fMRI studies of visual search that are pertinent to the debate over two-stage vs. interactive models of attentional processing. Similar to the logic from neuropsychology, activation of distinct brain areas during simple and difficult search supports the claim that one task requires attention and the other does not. Activation in the same brain areas during both tasks, on the other hand, supports the notion that a unitary system subserves both tasks. As in the neglect data, however, we find that there is not always convergence between results. We therefore attempt to anchor the data within the larger context of fMRI studies of visual attention. However, as data from other methods such as transcranial magnetic stimulation (TMS) and magnetoencephalography (MEG) are important for disambiguating imaging results, we end this section by drawing upon particular studies from those methods to aid our interpretation of the data.

1. Is There Evidence for Segregation between Preattentive and Attentive Processing?

Perhaps the earliest imaging study to examine the effects of feature vs. conjunction search directly was conducted by Corbetta, Shulman, Miezin, and Peterson (1995) using PET. They asked participants to detect a target stimulus distinguished by color, motion, or the conjunction of color and motion. The behavioral data matched standard search results: search functions were flat in the color and motion tasks and positive with increasing distractors in the conjunction condition. The interesting finding between the feature and conjunction conditions involved activation differences in the superior parietal lobe (SPL). Significant activation occurred in the SPL during the conjunction condition, but not during either feature condition alone. Corbetta et al. (1995) then compared the coordinates of SPL activation with results from a previous study in which participants shifted attention covertly along predictable horizontal locations (Corbetta, Miezin, Shulman, & Petersen, 1993). The coordinates of activity in the two experiments corresponded well, leading the authors to conclude that serial shifts of attention were used to detect the target in the conjunction task, but not in the feature task. Conversely, the lack of activity in the SPL in the feature conditions was interpreted to reflect parallel search that did not require serial shifts of attention.

This conclusion is supported by more recent work demonstrating significant and extensive bilateral activation in the SPL during a luminance detection task. Participants tracked a square stimulus that shifted along a horizontal meridian in 2260-ms intervals, which allowed for the quantification of shift and maintenance phases of a continuous task (Vandenberghe, Gitelman, Parrish, & Mesulam, 2001). They found no significant activation in the SPL in a second experiment that required tonic maintenance of attention at peripheral locations compared to a fixation baseline. The authors conclude that SPL activation is related specifically to spatial shifts of attention.

These results, however, are open to a number of other interpretations as indicated by Corbetta et al. (1995). For example, the functional role of the SPL may involve feature binding, oculomotor preparation, or the resolution of competitive processes through either enhancement or inhibition of early sensory (striate/extrastriate) or later ventral visual stream areas. Furthermore, the lack of activation in feature search and nonshifting attentional conditions may be a product of the chosen baseline task. That is, attentional requirements may differ only incrementally between the baseline and feature search, resulting in statistically nonsignificant activation in the SPL.

To clarify the role of the SPL, Wilkinson, Halligan, Henson, and Dolan (2002) directly compared attentional shifting with feature binding. Similar to Duncan and Humphreys (1989), Wilkinson et al. (2002) manipulated distractor homogeneity. The target was always an upright letter "T" and distractors were rotated "Ts." In the homogeneous distractor condition, all distractors were upside down and in the heterogeneous condition, distractors were randomly oriented. They argue that both conditions require feature binding (as the elementary line features are similar between targets and distractors), but only the heterogeneous condition is difficult. This task is similar to one used to test the SERR model (Humphreys & Mueller, 1993) and consistent with the model, heterogeneous RT was slower than homogeneous RT, although target present trials in both conditions had a slope of 35 ms/item (intercept difference appears to be approximately 30 ms). Target absent search in the two conditions differed considerably (71 ms/item in the heterogeneous condition and 40 ms/item in the homogeneous condition.

The homogeneous – heterogeneous subtraction produced significant activation only in the right temporal-parietal junction (TPJ). The reverse comparison, however, revealed many activated regions bilaterally including the following: motor cortex, cerebellum, SPL including the intraparietal sulcus (IPS), and supplementary motor area (SMA); unilateral right hemisphere activation was found in the pulvinar, superior occipital gyrus, and inferior occipital gyrus. The authors conclude that the TPJ is involved in the preattentive segmentation of the target from grouped distractors and that "parietal and motor" areas are involved in spatial selectivity. However, activation in primary motor areas and the unusual search slope in the homogeneous condition raise some questions of whether the two conditions reflect more general visual search results. It is also difficult to know whether the "parietal and motor" areas involved were participating in the serial distribution of attention as the authors suggest, or the recursive rejection of distractors, as suggested by the SERR model. We return to this issue of excitation vs. inhibition again later in this section.

Another result distinguishing frontoparietal areas from ventral areas was obtained by Patel and Sathian (2000) using a color popout paradigm with PET. The authors manipulated the relationship between a salient color singleton and its status as the target using the following four conditions: *absent* (all items colored gray), *popout* (color singleton always the target), *rare* (singleton rarely the target), and *never* (singleton never the target). In this way, Patel and Sathian (2000) held bottom-up salience constant and manipulated its relevance through top-down instructions. In the first contrast of interest between the *popout* and *absent* conditions, significant activation was found in the right superior temporal gyrus (STG). Interestingly, activation in this area was modulated by top-down search strategies such that activation was reduced in a stepwise fashion based on singleton relevance (*popout* > *rare* > *never*). RTs were significantly faster (and flat across display set size) in the *popout* condition and equally slow in the other three conditions. Thus, although the STG appears to be sensitive to the presence of salient items, activity is muted when the salient object is irrelevant to the task.

In a second contrast of interest between *never* and *popout* conditions, the authors report significant activation in the left parietal operculum/STG area, the parietooccipital fissure, and the precuneus. The patterns of activation in the *absent* and *rare* conditions were less robust, but similar to that of the *never* contrast, suggesting that these regions are involved in attentive search. Although the STG is more anterior than the TPJ location found by Wilkinson et al. (2002), and the precuneus is more medial than the SPL location reported by other studies, the correspondence between dorsal, attentive search and ventral, salience detection is worth noting. An additional finding supporting the dorsal, attentive search result was reported by Donner et al. (2000). Using a conjunction–feature comparison, the authors found consistent activation in the frontal eye field (FEF) bilaterally, ventral precentral sulcus in the left hemisphere, as well as bilateral parietal activation in the postcentral sulcus, anterior and posterior IPS, and at the IPS/transverse occipital sulcus (TOS) junction.

Consistent with results from Patel and Sathian (2000), others have found modulation of activation in early sensory areas based on task relevance. For example, Hopfinger, Buonocore, and Mangun (2000) used event-related fMRI to examine areas involved in responses to an explicit endogeneous cue compared to the presence of a target search display. The time course of the event-related design allows one to examine brain areas activated during the cue and target stages separately. Areas that were activated by the onset of the cue but prior to presentation of the target stimulus included bilateral IPS, SPL, posterior cingulate (PC), FEF, and STS. Interestingly, early visual areas corresponding to the expected target location were activated during the cue phase reflecting expectancy. Onset of the target stimulus activated SMA, ventrolateral prefrontal areas, occipital cortex, and SPL. These results are consistent with findings suggesting that the endogenous orientation of attention involving frontoparietal regions can enhance activation in early visual areas (see also Brefczynski & DeYoe, 1999; Fink, Driver, Rorden, Baldeweg, & Dolan, 2000; Kastner, De Weerd, Desimone, & Ungerleider, 1998; Rosen et al., 1999; Sengpiel & Huebener, 1999; Weidner,

Pollmann, Muller, & von Cramon, 2002). For the purposes of the current discussion, it is most important to note that the SPL was the only location activated by both the cue and target phases of the task. These results are in contrast to those of Vandenberghe et al. (2001) and suggest that the SPL does not simply produce an attentional switch signal, but is involved in the volitional direction of attention (although it is possible that participants were switching attention within the cued visual field during the target display).

The results reviewed thus far fit well with a model of attention that includes a division of labor between areas involved in the volitional distribution of attention (including shifting attention from location to location) and areas involved in salience or popout detection (Corbetta, Kincade, Ollinger, McAvoy, & Shulman, 2000; Corbetta & Shulman, 2002). Although roughly consistent with models of visual search that specify separate preattentive and attentive processing stages, the results are much better fitted by the functional model of Corbetta et al. (2000; Corbetta & Shulman, 2002). They hypothesize that voluntary orienting is driven by activity in the IPS/SPL-frontal network and detection of salient stimuli in unattended locations is signaled by TPJ activity. They further hypothesized that the two systems interact such that the TPJ signal interrupts and redirects the volitional system in response to bottom-up signals, and that sensitivity gain in the TPJ system can be adjusted by top-down signals. Thus, extensive excitatory and inhibitory interactions occur between the volitional system and the "preattentive" detection system. Furthermore, the volitional system is hypothesized to overlap considerably with oculomotor areas, similar to the Hamker (1999) model.

This functional model is bolstered by its correspondence with evidence that neglect patients most often have damage to the TPJ and have difficulty orienting automatically to stimuli in the neglected field, but are capable of voluntarily orienting attention (for discussion of anatomical differences between persisting and acute neglect, see Maguire & Ogden, 2002). Moreover, similar results involving TPJ activity in responses to an exogenous cue and IPS activity to an endogenous cue have been found (Yantis, Schwarzbach, Serences, Carlson, Steinmetz, Pekar, & Courtney, 2002).

2. Is There Evidence for a Unitary System Involved in Both Simple and Difficult Visual Search?

Other studies, however, have not found a straightforward distinction between TPJ involvement in simple search and IPS/SPL in difficult search. They have instead found graded differences in activation between the two visual search conditions in frontal and parietal areas. These studies do not necessarily contradict the previous findings, but suggest that the frontoparietal attentional system may be a system that responds to both simple and difficult search conditions. Differences in activation would therefore reflect quantitative differences in attentional requirement between the two conditions.

Leonards, Sunaert, Van Hecke, and Orban (2000) reported largely overlapping networks involved in feature and conjunctive search. In both search tasks, the target was defined as the unique stimulus, either based on a single feature or a conjunction of features. Although their task is somewhat unconventional, the behavioral data are consistent with traditional search slopes in feature and conjunction search. Comparing each search task with its own control, Leonards et al. (2000) found that both conditions activated large portions of the occipital and parietal lobes but only the conjunction task activated the superior frontal sulcus (SFS). (Based on subsequent studies, the authors conclude that the SFS area is independent of FEF). Occipital regions of overlap included bilateral activity in the collateral sulcus, lateral occipital sulcus, and the transverse occipital sulcus. In the parietal lobe, activation was found bilaterally including dorsal, medial, and ventral IPS. Additional anterior/dorsal portions of the IPS were activated only in the conjunction condition. Importantly, in all regions of overlap, greater activation was found in the conjunction condition than the feature condition.

In a more recent study, Donner et al. (2002) equated search difficulty in feature vs. conjunction search in order to isolate processes involved with the identification of single feature targets vs. conjunctive feature targets. This is the first study that we are aware of that has attempted to equate behavior in feature vs. conjunction search. They do so by use of three tasks: *easy feature* search, *hard feature* search, and *conjunctive* search. In all conditions, stimuli were composed of clusters of vertical/horizontal lines and yellow/blue color. The yellow color was labeled "salient" as its luminance value was greater than blue. In the *easy feature* task participants searched for the salient yellow target (half the stimuli had vertical and the other half had horizontal line orientations). The same stimuli were used in the *hard feature* task, but the target was defined by line orientation rather than color. In the *conjunction* task targets were defined by a combination of features (e.g., vertical-yellow). Behavioral RT increased with increasing display size in the *conjunctive* and *hard feature* tasks (23.8 and 20.1 ms/cluster, respectively) and was flat in the *easy feature* task (−0.7 ms/cluster) (see Figure 3a).

Their imaging results show first that the *hard feature* condition activates substantially more areas than *easy feature* and second, that *hard feature* and *conjunctive* conditions share overlapping, but not identical networks. The *hard feature–easy feature* comparison resulted in activation of large portions of the frontal and parietal lobes. Regions of overlap between *hard feature* and *conjunction* (using easy feature as the baseline) included bilateral FEF, anterior and posterior IPS, and the junction between the IPS and the TOS (i.e., IPTO). Despite similarities, differences in degree of activation were found within all of these areas except posterior IPS [which may correspond to monkey lateral intraparietal (LIP) area, Culham & Kanwisher, 2001]. (For discussion of LIP see Colby, Duhamel, & Goldberg, 1996; Gottlieb, Kusunoki, & Goldberg, 1998; Kusunoki, Gottlieb, & Goldberg, 2000; Platt & Glimcher, 1999.) Specifically, greater activation associated with the *conjunction* task was found in FEF and the IPS/TOS junction, and with the *hard feature* task in anterior IPS. Furthermore, nonoverlapping areas were found in areas adjacent to overlapping areas, suggesting that some segregation of processing occurred between *hard feature* and *conjunctive* search (see Figure 3b).

Despite some inconsistencies between findings, there is good convergence between studies showing the involvement of frontoparietal areas in visual search. The locations of activity overlap considerably with fMRI results of covert and overt shifts of attention as well as general attentional

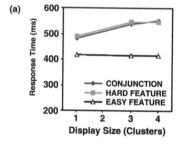

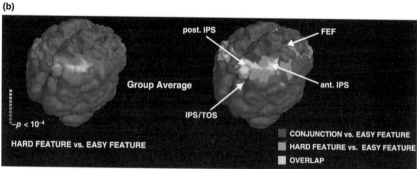

Fig. 3.   Images from Donner et al. (2002). (a) Response time × display size functions for *conjunction*, *hard feature*, and *easy feature* visual search conditions. (b) Group activation maps. Left: activation pattern found in *hard feature–easy feature* comparison. Right: overlaid activation patterns from *conjunction* and *hard feature* conditions (see Color Insert).

mechanisms (Beauchamp, Petit, Ellmore, Ingeholm, & Haxby, 2001; Corbetta, 1998; Corbetta et al., 1998; Luna et al., 1998; Mesulam, 1999; Nobre, Gitelman, Dias, & Mesulam, 2000; Perry & Zeki, 2000; Posner, Cohen, & Rafal, 1982). The involvement of oculomotor areas in attentional shifting is consistent with the premotor theory of attention, which hypothesizes that attentional shifts reflect preparation for motor movements (Rizzolatti, Riggio, Dascola, & Umilta, 1987). It is tempting to conclude from this that the frontoparietal network acts as a generic attentional system that interacts with sensory areas to produce behavior that reflects both bottom-up and top-down effects. The fact that most attentional tasks involve visual processing, however, requires caution in interpretation.

It may be that the great consistency we see across attentional tasks is a by-product of the fact that most visual attention tasks involve eye movements or the inhibition of eye movements. For example, Nobre (2001) suggests that the frontoparietal network may involve egocentric representations appropriate for oculomotor actions, but that other, partially overlapping, networks may be involved in action representations such as reaching and grasping (also see Rizzolatti, Fadiga, Fogassi, & Gallese, 1997). Such findings are consistent with single cell physiology data suggesting that distinct parts of the IPS are involved in different sensorimotor transformations (Colby & Goldberg, 1999). As the spatial resolution of fMRI becomes better, distinctions based on relatively small regions of association areas will become clearer (Culham, in press; Culham & Kanwisher, 2001). The results from this section further complicate interpretation of visual search models in suggesting that a single system may be involved in both tasks, but perhaps in a graded fashion and dependent on which sensorimotor transformation is required for the task.

3. How Do Nonstandard Visual Search and Other Imaging Techniques Influence Interpretation of Functional Imaging Data?

Another way of probing the functional role of the frontoparietal network is to examine attentional effects in nonspatial domains. Unlike all the studies discussed so far, which have focused on the spatial aspect of attentional shifts, Wojciulik and Kanwisher (1999) conducted a study of visual search in the temporal domain. In experiment "1c," participants identified feature or conjunction targets that appeared in rapid serial visual presentation (RSVP). They found robust activation in the SPL and anterior and posterior IPS spreading into the IPL. The authors conducted three different experiments involving difficult vs. easy conditions and found robust bilateral activation in posterior IPS, close to IPTO, and anterior IPS in all three difficult–easy contrasts. Some lateralization involving greater activation was found in the right hemisphere.

Wojciulik and Kanwisher (1999) suggest that these commonalities across tasks may implicate the parietal lobe in suppressing distractors, rather than shifting of attention. This assertion is consistent with biased competition (Desimone & Duncan, 1995) as well as behavioral data indicating that distractor suppression rather than target enhancement occurs under cluttered visual search conditions (e.g., Awh, Matsukura, & Serences, 2002). The suppression of distractors is also consistent with the modulation of activity dependent on the task relevance reviewed earlier. Although these findings are not inconsistent with the functional model of Corbetta and colleagues, they do suggest that the role of the frontoparietal network is more complicated than the volitional movement of spatial attention.

In fact, data from techniques with greater temporal resolution intimate a more complex picture. In a TMS study, Ashbridge, Walsh, and Cowey (1997) show that conjunction and not feature search is disrupted by stimulation to the right posterior parietal lobe. However, they found that conjunction search was disrupted only when TMS was applied 100 ms after stimulus onset for target-present trials and 160 ms for target-absent trials. (Stimulation delays from 0 to 200 ms were used with 20-ms intervals.) They conclude that it is unlikely that TMS disrupted a serial search mechanism as one would not expect selective interference at 100-ms poststimulus onset. Moreover, there was no difference in interference between targets in each visual hemifield (as would be expected based on performance by patients with unilateral damage to the right parietal lobe). Instead, the authors favor the conclusion that the effect of TMS over the right parietal lobe involves spatial focusing: interference occurs for conjunction search because the tuning of the attentional mechanism is disrupted. They also suggest that the interference could be due to an interruption of information transmission between the V4/ temporal lobe areas involved in object recognition and the parietal lobe.

Although we are not reviewing the ERP and MEG data, we raise the results of one MEG study that pertains to the hypothesis of Ashbridge et al. (1997). Hopf et al. (2000) use the resolution of MEG to clarify the origin of the ERP N2-posterior-contralateral (N2pc) component, which has been implicated in attentional tasks including conjunctive vs. feature search (e.g., Luck, Girelli, McDermott, & Ford, 1997; Luck & Hillyard, 1995, 2000; Woodman & Luck, 1999). Hopf et al. (2000) conclude that the N2pc component is actually composed of two spatially and temporally distinct subcomponents: one reflecting neural activity in the parietal lobe at 180–200 ms and the other reflecting activity in the anterior occipital and posterior inferotemporal areas at 220–240 ms. They conclude that the parietal subcomponent reflects attentional shifting and the extrastriate/

inferotemporal component reflects the focusing of attention around a stimulus in response to location selection (consistent with Desimone & Duncan, 1995).

This result suggests an interaction between neural areas that is difficult to see with the poor temporal resolution of fMRI and PET. Moreover, these data are consistent with all three hypotheses that Ashbridge et al. (1997) raise: the parietal lobe could be involved in the spatial shifting of attention, transmit that spatial selectivity to ventral visual areas such as V4 or TPJ (both in terms of inhibition and excitation), which then respond by shrinking their receptive fields around objects of interest. When the stimulus is salient, the selection process need not involve much top-down spatial selection to guide feature detection. This would explain the reduced (or absent) frontoparietal activation and greater TPJ/ventral visual activation in simple search tasks. Just as spatial selectivity may constrain feature processing, information regarding salient or dissimilar stimulus features could also affect activity in parietal areas, possibly producing "feature"-based responses in dorsal stream areas. These reciprocal interactions reflect the strength of goal-oriented direction of attention, stimulus salience, and effector choice.

This interpretation is consistent with the functional model of Corbetta et al. (2000; Corbetta & Shulman, 2002), but includes greater detail regarding the interactive nature within and between areas, which is consistent with biased and integrated competition accounts (Desimone & Duncan, 1995; Duncan et al., 1997; Duncan & Humphreys, 1989) as well as much of the data reviewed here. It will be critical for future work to examine more closely the functional properties of the frontoparietal processing system, particularly in relation to ventral stream areas. Drawing on known anatomical connections between parietal, frontal oculomotor, and ventral areas will be extremely useful in developing theories regarding the interaction between areas involved in producing visual attention (e.g., Paré & Wurtz, 1997; Wurtz, Sommer, Paré, & Ferraina, 2001).

C. COMBINED NEUROPSYCHOLOGY AND FUNCTIONAL IMAGING

Although we have framed this discussion in terms of distinct preattentive and attentive processing stages, perhaps this distinction is misleading. Much like the debate over early vs. late selection, the answer is likely to be that both arguments are at least partially correct. Although there is evidence for attentional modulation of early sensory areas, it is unlikely that we are obligated to attend to the earliest visual processing stages in order to form higher level perceptual units. Furthermore, a system that is insensitive to salient external information would be extremely maladaptive. On the other hand, it is unlikely that there is a specific class of features or objects that is always processed without attention. The lack of clear consensus in both the neuropsychological and fMRI data supports the notion that it is misguided to look for specific preattentive and/or attentive stages in the neural system. Perhaps a better question to ask from a cognitive neuroscience perspective involves how regions of the brain with particular receptive field properties interact to produce discrete perceptual phenomena and behavior. Attention may therefore be the consequence of interactive excitatory connections between areas whose receptive fields mutually support a particular distal visual stimulus. Several studies using functional imaging techniques in patients with extinction using this perspective have produced provocative results (see Rees & Lavie, 2001, for review).

The comparison of interest in these studies involves differences in neural activation between trials in which patients report the presence and absence of stimuli in the left visual field (LVF). Three trial types are of interest: the correct nonreport of LVF stimuli on trials in which only a right visual field (RVF) is present; the incorrect nonreport of a LVF stimulus when bilateral stimuli are present (extinction); and the correct report of a LVF stimulus during bilateral stimulus presentation. In the comparison between extinguished LVF stimulus on bilateral trials vs. right unilateral stimulus, Vuilleumier et al. (2001) found fMRI BOLD responses in right striate cortex and bilaterally in the posteroinferior temporal gyri. Comparing seen LVF stimuli to extinguished LVF stimuli, greater activation was found in striate areas for seen than extinguished stimuli, but the time course for the two trial types was similar. Bilateral fusiform activation occurred only when faces were reported as seen. Interestingly, activity in the following areas was correlated only when LVF face stimuli were reported as seen: left inferior frontal cortex, left inferior and superior parietal cortex, and left anterior temporal cortex. This finding indicates that extinguished stimuli activate early as well as relatively late visual areas, but that the synchrony and strength of activation in larger networks occur only when LVF stimuli are reported as seen. ERP data from the same participant were qualitatively similar (similar responses in seen and extinguished trials in occipital regions, but different responses in central and midline regions).

Similarly, Rees et al. (2000) found striate and extrastriate activation of extinguished stimuli using fMRI with a patient with a right inferior parietal lesion. Interestingly, they used house and face stimuli and found some effect of stimulus category in extinguished trials involving activation in the right fusiform region of interest for extinguished faces, but not extinguished houses. These results suggest that the conscious perception of a visual stimulus is correlated with an interaction of visual areas rather than the static activation of a single perceptual area and are consistent with behavioral findings in neglect patients that show effects of neglected stimuli on subsequent behavior (for review see Driver, 1996). Similarly, studies involving binocular rivalry and interhemispheric competition in normal subjects have shown that modulation of activation related to the perceived stimulus occurs at many stages of the processing stream (Fink et al., 2000; Lumer, 1998; Lumer, Friston, & Rees, 1998; Tong, Nakayama, Vaughan, & Kanwisher, 1998).

V. Relationship between Theoretical Approaches and Empirical Data

We began this chapter with the goal of understanding what neuropsychology and functional imaging contribute to the debate in models of visual search regarding preattentive and attentive processing. We found, however, that the data do not break down simply along those conceptual lines. That is, there are data to support the idea that simple feature-targets are processed without attention, as well as data to support the idea that there is no qualitative difference between the neural systems involved in difficult and easy search conditions.

Taken together, the data reviewed in this chapter implicate a complex, interactive, network of areas with different processing specializations. Although each of the cognitive models reviewed captures some aspect of the complexity and precision involved in the interaction of neural areas related to visual search behavior, none of them seems completely adequate. Nevertheless, we find the neuropsychological and imaging data to be largely consistent with the framework of the integrated competition account of Duncan et al. (1997). The theoretical model cautions neuropsychological and brain imaging work against attributing phenomenological experiences and discrete behaviors to activity in particular damaged or activated brain areas. Rather, it considers dynamic interactions between processing areas to be fundamental. A framework in which competition and cooperation occurs within and between areas of processing is, in our opinion, more likely to capture the conditions within the neural system that give rise to human behavior and experiences. Combinations of methods from cognitive neuroscience including fMRI, neuropsychology, and ERP/MEG appear to be a promising route by which the intricacies of the human attentional system can be probed.

One word of caution in thinking about the relationship between psychological models and empirical data to theorize about levels of processing has been raised by Frith (2001). He notes that the psychological and physiological meanings of bottom-up and top-down processing do not necessarily correspond well. Bottom-up in a psychological sense conveys a notion of preattentive processing and top-down suggests volitional, goal-oriented behavior. Physiologically, bottom-up implies feedforward processing from early visual areas to later ones, and top-down implies feedback modulatory processes. Although the concepts appear to be similar, correspondence between the two can be weak. Thus, preattentive processes in visual search models do not necessarily imply early processing in the brain and vice versa, although more biologically based models may (e.g., Li, 2002). We raise this issue here to comment that there is a distinction between thinking of preattentive processing as an obligatory stage that must occur prior to any effects of attention and preattentive processing as a condition in which visual stimuli are represented within the visual system, but not consciously perceived. Although issues related to consciousness are well beyond the scope of this chapter, we note that we have primarily dealt with the first sense of preattentive processing and not the second.

In sum, there is much work to be done to understand the behavioral and neural mechanisms that underlie visual search processes in particular, and visual attention as a whole. Convergence from multiple methodologies is particularly important as the data will force us to modify existing concepts and seek new formulations for describing functional systems that give rise to human behavior.

REFERENCES

Aglioti, S., Smania, N., Barbieri, C., & Corbetta, M. (1997). Influence of stimulus salience and attentional demands on visual search patterns in hemispatial neglect. *Brain and Cognition, 34*, 388–403.

Arguin, M., & Bub, D. (1993). Evidence for an independent stimulus-centered spatial reference frame from a case of visual hemineglect. *Cortex, 29*, 349–357.

Arguin, M., Joanette, Y., & Cavanagh, P. (1993). Visual search for feature and conjunction targets with an attention deficit. *Journal of Cognitive Neuroscience, 5*(4), 436–452.

Ashbridge, E., Walsh, V., & Cowey, A. (1997). Temporal aspects of visual search studied by transcranial magnetic stimulation. *Neuropsychologia, 35*(8), 1121–1131.

Awh, E., Matsukura, M., & Serences, J. (2002). *Top-down modulation of biased competition during covert spatial orienting.* Paper presented at the Vision Sciences Society, Sarasota, FL.

Bartolomeo, P., & Chokron, S. (2001). Levels of impairment in unilateral neglect. In J. Grafman (Ed.), *Handbook of neuropsychology* (Vol. 4, pp. 67–98). North-Holland, Amsterdam: Elsevier Science.

Beauchamp, M. S., Petit, L., Ellmore, T. M., Ingeholm, J., & Haxby, J. V. (2001). A parametric fMRI study of overt and covert shifts of visuospatial attention. *NeuroImage, 14*(2), 310–321.

Behrmann, M., Barton, J. J. S., Watt, S., & Black, S. E. (1997). Impaired visual search in patients with unilateral neglect: An oculographic analysis. *Neuropsychologia, 35*(11), 1445–1458.

Behrmann, M., Ebert, P., & Black, S. E. (2003). Hemispatial neglect and visual search: A large scale analysis. *Cortex* (in press).

Behrmann, M., & Plaut, D. C. (2001). The interaction of spatial reference frames and hierarchical object representations: Evidence from figure copying in hemispatial neglect. *Cognitive and Affective Behavioral Neuroscience, 1*(4), 307–329.

Bellas, D. N., Novelly, R. A., & Eskenazi, B. (1989). Olfactory lateralization and identification in right hemisphere lesion and control patients. *Neuropsychologia, 27*(9), 1187–1191.

Bellmann, A., Meuli, R., & Clarke, S. (2001). Two types of auditory neglect. *Brain, 124,* 676–687.

Berry, E. L., Nicolson, R. I., Foster, J. K., Behrmann, M., & Sagar, H. J. (1999). Slowing of reaction time in Parkinson's disease: The involvement of the frontal lobes. *Neuropsychologia, 37,* 787–795.

Bichot, N. P., Rao, S. C., & Schall, J. D. (2001). Continuous processing in macaque frontal cortex during visual search. *Neuropsychologia, 39*(9), 972–982.

Bisiach, E., & Vallar, G. (2000). Unilateral neglect in humans. In J. Grafman (Ed.), *Handbook of neuropsychology* (2nd ed., Vol. 1, pp. 459–502). North-Holland, Amsterdam: Elsevier Science.

Brefczynski, J. A., & DeYoe, E. A. (1999). A physiological correlate of the 'spotlight' of visual attention. *Nature Neuroscience, 2*(4), 370–374.

Bundesen, C. (1990). A theory of visual attention. *Psychological Review, 97*(4), 523–547.

Bundesen, C. (1999). A computational theory of visual attention. In G. W. Humphreys and J. Duncan (Eds.), *Attention, space, and action: Studies in cognitive neuroscience* (pp. 54–71). Oxford: Oxford University Press.

Cave, K. R. (1999). The FeatureGate model of visual selection. *Psychological Research, 62*(2–3), 182–194.

Chatterjee, A., Mennemeier, M., & Heilman, K. M. (1992a). Search patterns and neglect: A case study. *Neuropsychologia, 30*(7), 657–672.

Chatterjee, A., Mennemeier, M., & Heilman, K. M. (1992b). A stimulus-response relationship in unilateral neglect: The power function. *Neuropsychologia, 30,* 1101–1108.

Cohen, E., & Ruppin, E. (1999). From parallel to serial processing: A computational study of visual search. *Perception & Psychophysics, 61*(7), 1449–1461.

Colby, C. L., Duhamel, J. R., & Goldberg, M. E. (1996). Visual, presaccadic, and cognitive activation of single neurons in monkey lateral intraparietal area. *Journal of Neurophysiology, 76*(5), 2841–2852.

Colby, C. L., & Goldberg, M. E. (1999). Space and attention in parietal cortex. *Annual Review of Neuroscience, 22,* 319–419.

Corbetta, M. (1998). Frontoparietal cortical networks for directing attention and the eye to visual locations: Identical, independent, or overlapping neural systems? *Proceedings of the National Academy of Sciences of the United States of America, 95*(3), 831–838.

Corbetta, M., Akbudak, E., Conturo, T. E., Snyder, A. Z., Ollinger, J. M., Drury, H. A., Linenweber, M. R., Petersen, S. E., Raichle, M. E., Van Essen, D. C., & Shulman, G. L. (1998). A common network of functional areas for attention and eye movements. *Neuron, 21*(4), 761–773.

Corbetta, M., Kincade, J. M., Ollinger, J. M., McAvoy, M. P., & Shulman, G. L. (2000). Voluntary orienting is dissociated from target detection in human posterior parietal cortex. *Nature Neuroscience, 3*(3), 292–297.

Corbetta, M., Miezin, F. M., Shulman, G. L., & Petersen, S. E. (1993). A PET study of visuospatial attention. *Journal of Neuroscience, 13*(3), 1202–1226.

Corbetta, M., & Shulman, G. L. (2002). Control of goal-directed and stimulus-driven attention in the brain. *Nature Reviews. Neuroscience, 3*(3), 201–215.

Corbetta, M., Shulman, G. L., Miezin, F. M., & Petersen, S. E. (1995). Superior parietal cortex activation during spatial attention shifts and visual feature conjunction. *Science, 270*(5237), 802–805.

Culham, J. C. (in press). *Parietal cortex.* In L. Nadei (Ed.), *Encyclopedia of Cognitive Science* (Vol. 3, pp. 451–457). London: Macmillan.

Culham, J. C., & Kanwisher, N. G. (2001). Neuroimaging of cognitive functions in human parietal cortex. *Current Opinion in Neurobiology, 11*(2), 157–163.

Davis, G., & Driver, J. (1994). Parallel detection of Kanisza figures in the human visual system. *Nature, 371*, 791–793.

Deouell, L. Y., Sacher, Y., Ben Moshe, S., & Soroker, N. (2000). 2D dynamic mapping of attention to visual space following stroke. *Proceedings of the Cognitive Neuroscience meeting*, p. 89.

D'Erme, P., Robertson, I., Bartolomeo, P., Daniele, A., & Gainotti, G. (1992). Early rightwards orienting of attention on simple reaction time performance in patients with left-sided neglect. *Neuropsychologia, 30*(11), 989–1000.

Desimone, R., & Duncan, J. (1995). Neural mechanisms of selective visual attention. *Annual Review of Neuroscience, 18*, 193–222.

Deutsch, J. A., & Deutsch, D. (1963). Attention: Some theoretical considerations. *Psychological Review, 70*(1), 51–61.

Donner, T., Kettermann, A., Diesch, E., Ostendorf, F., Villringer, A., & Brandt, S. A. (2000). Involvement of the human frontal eye field and multiple parietal areas in covert visual selection during conjunction search. *European Journal of Neuroscience, 12*(9), 3407–3414.

Donner, T. H., Kettermann, A., Diesch, E., Ostendorf, F., Villringer, A., & Brandt, S. A. (2002). Visual feature and conjunction searches of equal difficulty engage only partially overlapping frontoparietal networks. *NeuroImage, 15*, 16–25.

Driver, J. (1996). What can visual neglect and extinction reveal about the extent of "preattentive" processing? In A. F. Kramer and M. G. H. Coles (Eds.), *Converging operations in the study of visual selective attention* (pp. 193–223). Washington, DC: American Psychological Association.

Driver, J., Baylis, G. C., Goodrich, S., & Rafal, R. D. (1994). Axis-based neglect of visual shape. *Neuropsychologia, 32*(11), 1353–1365.

Driver, J., Baylis, G. C., & Rafal, R. D. (1992). Preserved figure-ground segregation and symmetry perception in visual neglect. *Nature, 360*, 73–75.

Duncan, J., Bundesen, C., Olson, A., Humphreys, G. W., Chavda, S., & Shibuya, H. (1999). Systematic analysis of deficits in visual attention. *Journal of Experimental Psychology: General, 128*(4), 450–478.

Duncan, J., & Humphreys, G. W. (1989). Visual search and stimulus similarity. *Psychological Review, 96*(3), 433–458.

Duncan, J., Humphreys, G., & Ward, R. (1997). Competitive brain activity in visual attention. *Current Opinion in Neurobiology, 7*(2), 255–261.

Duncan, J., Ward, R., & Shapiro, K. L. (1994). Direct measurement of attentional dwell time in human vision. *Nature, 369*(6478), 313–315.

Eckstein, M. P. (1998). The lower visual search efficiency for conjunctions is due to noise and not serial attentional processing. *Psychological Science, 9*(2), 111–118.

Eckstein, M. P., Thomas, J. P., Palmer, J., & Shimozaki, S. S. (2000). A signal detection model predicts the effects of set size on visual search accuracy for feature, conjunction, triple conjunction, and disjunction displays. *Perception & Psychophysics, 62*(3), 425–451.

Eglin, M., Robertson, L. C., & Knight, R. T. (1989). Visual search performance in the neglect syndrome. *Journal of Cognitive Neuroscience, 1*(4), 372–385.

Eglin, M., Robertson, L. C., & Knight, R. T. (1991). Cortical substrates supporting visual search in humans. *Cerebral Cortex, 1*, 262–272.

Eglin, M., Robertson, L. C., Knight, R. T., & Brugger, P. (1994). Search deficits in neglect patients are dependent on size of the visual scene. *Neuropsychology, 8*(3), 451–463.

Eglin, M., Robertson, L., Knight, R. T., & Brugger, P. (1996). Search deficits in neglect patients are dependent on size of the visual scene. *Neuropsychologia, 8*, 451–463.

Enns, J. T., & Rensink, R. A. (1990). Sensitivity to three-dimensional orientation in visual search. *Psychological Science, 1*(5), 323–326.

Enns, J. T., & Rensink, R. A. (1991). Preattentive recovery of three-dimensional orientation from line drawings. *Psychological Review, 98*(3), 335–351.

Esterman, M., McGlinchey-Berath, R., & Milberg, W. (2000). Preattentive and attentive visual search in individuals with hemispatial neglect. *Neuropsychology, 14*(4), 599–611.

Fink, G. R., Driver, J., Rorden, C., Baldeweg, T., & Dolan, R. J. (2000). Neural consequences of competing stimuli in both visual hemifields: A physiological basis for visual extinction. *Annals of Neurology, 47*(4), 440–446.

Foster, J., Behrmann, M., & Stuss, D. (1999). Attentional dysfunction in Alzheimer's disease. *Neuropsychology, 13*, 1–23.

Frith, C. (2001). A framework for studying the neural basis of attention. *Neuropsychologia, 39*(12), 1367–1371.

Garner, W. R. (1988). Facilitation and interference with a separable redundant dimension in stimulus comparison. *Perception & Psychophysics, 44*(4), 321–330.

Geng, J. J., & Behrmann, M. (2002). Probability cueing of target location facilitates visual search implicitly in normal participants and patients with hemispatial neglect. *Psychological Science, 13*(6), 520–525.

Gottlieb, J. P., Kusunoki, M., & Goldberg, M. E. (1998). The representation of visual salience in monkey parietal cortex. *Nature, 391*(6666), 481–484.

Grabowecky, M., Robertson, L. C., & Treisman, A. (1993). Preattentive processes guide visual search: Evidence from patients with unilateral visual neglect. *Journal of Cognitive Neuroscience, 5*(3), 288–302.

Grimes, J. (1996). On the failure to detect changes in scenes across saccades. In K. A. Akins (Ed.), *Perception* (Vol. 5, pp. 89–110). New York: Oxford University Press.

Halligan, P. W., Burn, J. P., Marshall, J. C., & Wade, D. T. (1992). Visuo-spatial neglect: Qualitative differences and laterality of cerebral lesion. *Journal of Neurology, Neurosurgery and Psychiatry, 55*, 1060–1068.

Hamker, F. (1999). *The role of feedback connections in task-driven visual search.* Paper presented at the Connectionist models in cognitive neuroscience, Proceedings of the 5th Neural Computation and Psychology Workshop, London.

Heilman, K. M., Bowers, D., Valenstein, E., & Watson, R. T. (1987). Hemispace and hemispatial neglect. In M. Jeannerod (Ed.), *Neurophysiological and neuropsychological aspects of spatial neglect* (pp. 115–150). North-Holland, Amsterdam: Elsevier Science B. V.

Heilman, K. M., Watson, R. T., & Valenstein, E. (1997). Neglect: Clinical and anatomical aspects. In M. J. Farah (Ed.), *Behavioral neurology and neuropsychology* (pp. 309–317). New York: McGraw-Hill.

Hildebrandt, H., Gieselmann, H., & Sachsenheimer, W. (1999). Visual search and visual target detection in patients with infarctions of the left or right posterior or the right middle brain artery. *Journal of Clinical and Experimental Neuropsychology, 21*(1), 94–107.

Hoffman, J. E. (1979). A two-stage model of visual search. *Perception & Psychophysics, 25*(4), 319–327.

Hopf, J. M., Luck, S. J., Girelli, M., Hagner, T., Mangun, G. R., Scheich, H., & Heinze, H. J. (2000). Neural sources of focused attention in visual search. *Cerebral Cortex, 10*(12), 1233–1241.

Hopfinger, J. B., Buonocore, M. H., & Mangun, G. R. (2000). The neural mechanisms of top-down attentional control. *Nature Neuroscience, 3*(3), 284–291.

Hugdahl, K., Wester, K., & Asbjornsen, A. (1991). Auditory neglect after right frontal and right pulvinar thalamic lesions. *Brain and Language, 41*, 465–473.

Humphreys, G. W., & Mueller, H. J. (1993). SEarch via Recursive Rejection (SERR): A connectionist model of visual search. *Cognitive Psychology, 25*(1), 43–110.

Irwin, D. E., Yantis, S., & Joindes, J. (1983). Evidence against visual integration across saccadic eye movements. *Perception & Psychophysics, 34*(1), 49–57.

Itti, L., & Koch, C. (2001). Computational modelling of visual attention. *Nature Reviews. Neuroscience, 2*(3), 194–203.

Karnath, H. O., Ferber, S., & Himmelbach, M. (2001). Spatial awareness is a function of the temporal not the posterior parietal lobe. *Nature, 411*(6840), 950–953.

Karnath, H. O., Himmelbach, M., & Rorden, C. (2002). The subcortical anatomy of human spatial neglect: Putamen, caudat nucleus and pulvinar. *Brain, 125*, 350–360.

Karnath, H. O., & Nemeier, M. (2002). Task-dependent differences in the exploratory behaviour of patients with spatial neglect. *Neuropsychologia, 40*(9), 1577–1585.

Kastner, S., De Weerd, P., Desimone, R., & Ungerleider, L. G. (1998). Mechanisms of directed attention in the human extrastriate cortex as revealed by functional MRI. *Science, 282*, 108–111.

Kinsbourne, M. (1987). Mechanisms of unilateral neglect. In M. Jeannerod (Ed.), *Neurophysiological and neuropsychological aspects of spatial neglect* (pp. 69–86). New York: Elsevier Science.

Kinsbourne, M. (1993). Orientational bias model of unilateral neglect: Evidence from attentional gradients within hemispace. In I. H. Robertson and J. C. Marshall (Eds.), *Unilateral neglect: Clinical and experimental studies* (pp. 63–86). Hove, UK: Lawrence Erlbaum.

Klein, R. (1988). Inhibitory tagging system facilitates visual search. *Nature, 334*(6181), 430–431.

Kusunoki, M., Gottlieb, J., & Goldberg, M. E. (2000). The lateral intraparietal area as a salience map: The representation of abrupt onset, stimulus motion, and task relevance. *Vision Research, 40*, 1459–1468.

Làdavas, E., Petronio, A., & Umilta, C. (1990). The deployment of visual attention in the intact field of hemineglect patients. *Cortex, 26*, 307–317.

Leonards, U., Sunaert, S., Van Hecke, P., & Orban, G. A. (2000). Attention mechanisms in visual search: An fMRI study. *Journal of Cognitive Neuroscience, 12*(Suppl 2), 61–75.

Levin, D. T., & Simons, D. J. (1997). Failure to detect changes to attended objects in motion pictures. *Psychonomic Bulletin & Review, 4*(4), 501–506.

Li, F., VanRullen, R., Koch, C., & Perona, P. (2002). *Detection of objects in natural scenes with minimal or no attention.* Paper presented at the Vision Sciences Society, Sarasota, FL.

Li, Z. (2002). A saliency map in primary visual cortex. *Trends in Cognitive Neuroscience, 6*(1), 9–16.

Lubow, R. E., Kaplan, O., Abramovich, P., Rudnick, A., & Laor, N. (2000). Visual search in schizophrenia: Latent inhibition and novel pop-out effects. *Schizophrenia Research, 45*(1–2), 45–56.

Luck, S. J., Girelli, M., McDermott, M. T., & Ford, M. A. (1997). Bridging the gap between monkey neurophysiology and human perception: An ambiguity resolution theory of visual selective attention. *Cognitive Psychology, 33*(1), 64–87.

Luck, S. J., & Hillyard, S. A. (1995). The role of attention in feature detection and conjunction discrimination: An electrophysiological analysis. *International Journal of Neuroscience, 80*, 281–297.

Luck, S. J., & Hillyard, S. A. (2000). The operation of selective attention at multiple stages of processing: Evidence from human and monkey electrophysiology. In M. S. Gazzaniga (Ed.), *The new cognitive neurosciences* (2nd ed., pp. 687–700). Cambridge, MA: MIT Press.

Lumer, E. D. (1998). A neural model of binocular integration and rivalry based on the coordination of action-potential timing in primary visual cortex. *Cerebral Cortex, 8*(6), 553–561.

Lumer, E. D., Friston, K. J., & Rees, G. (1998). Neural correlates of perceptual rivalry in the human brain. *Science, 280*(5371), 1930–1934.

Luna, B., Thulborn, K. R., Strojwas, M. H., McCurtain, B. J., Berman, R. A., Genovese, C. R., & Sweeney, J. A. (1998). Dorsal cortical regions subserving visually guided saccades in humans: An fMRI study. *Cerebral Cortex, 8*(1), 40–47.

Mack, A., & Rock, I. (1998). *Inattentional blindness.* Cambridge, Mass.: MIT Press.

Maguire, A. M., & Ogden, J. A. (2002). MRI brain scan analyses and neuropsychological profiles of nine patients with persisting unilateral neglect. *Neuropsychologia, 40*(7), 879–887.

Mangun, G. R., Buonocore, M. H., Girelli, M., & Jha, A. P. (1998). ERP and fMRI measures of visual spatial selective attention. *Human Brain Mapping, 6*(5–6), 383–389.

McGlinchey-Berroth, R. (1997). Visual information processing in hemispatial neglect. *Trends in Cognitive Sciences, 1*(3), 91–97.

McGlinchey-Berroth, R., Milberg, W. P., Verfaellie, M., Alexander, M., & Kilduff, M. (1993). Semantic processing in the neglected field: Evidence from a lexical decision task. *Cognitive Neuropsychology, 10*(1), 79–108.

McPeek, R. M., & Keller, E. L. (2002). Superior colliculus activity related to concurrent processing of saccade goals in a visual search task. *Journal of Neurophysiology, 87*(4), 1805–1815.

Mesulam, M. M. (1999). Spatial attention and neglect: parietal, frontal and cingulate contributions to the mental representation and attentional targeting of salient extrapersonal events. *Philosophical Transactions of the Royal Society of London, Series B, 354,* 1325–1346.

Moore, C. M., & Wolfe, J. M. (2001). Getting beyond the serial/parallel debate in visual research: A hybrid approach. In K. Shapiro (Ed.), *The limits of attention: Temporal constraints in human information processing* (pp. 178–198). London: Oxford University Press.

Moscovitch, M., & Behrmann, M. (1994). Coding of spatial information in the somatosensory system: Evidence from patients with right parietal lesions. *Journal of Cognitive Neuroscience, 6*(2), 151–155.

Mozer, M. C. (2002). Frames of reference in unilateral neglect and visual perception: A computational perspective. *Psychological Review, 109,* 156–185.

Nakayama, K., & Silverman, G. H. (1986). Serial and parallel processing of visual feature conjunctions. *Nature, 320*(6059), 264–265.

Neisser, U. (1964). Visual search. *Scientific American, 210*(6), 94–102.

Neisser, U. (1967). *Cognitive psychology.* New York: Appleton-Century-Crofts.

Nobre, A. (2001). The attentive homunculus: now you see it, now you don't. *Neuroscience and Behavioral Reviews, 25*(6), 477–496.

Nobre, A. C., Gitelman, D. R., Dias, E. C., & Mesulam, M. M. (2000). Covert visual spatial orienting and saccades: Overlapping neural systems. *NeuroImage, 11*(3), 210–216.

O'Regan, J. K., & Levy-Schoen, A. (1983). Integrating visual information from successive fixations: Does trans-saccadic fusion exist? *Vision Research, 23*(8), 765–768.

O'Regan, J. K., Rensink, R. A., & Clark, J. J. (1999). Change-blindness as a result of "mudsplashes." *Nature, 398*(6722), 34.

Paré, M., & Wurtz, R. H. (1997). Monkey posterior parietal cortex neurons antidromically activated from superior colliculus. *Journal of Neurophysiology, 78*(6), 3493–3497.

Parkhurst, D., Law, K., & Niebur, E. (2002). Modeling the role of salience in the allocation of overt visual attention. *Vision Research, 42*, 107–123.

Patel, G. A., & Sathian, K. (2000). Visual search: Bottom-up or top-down? *Frontiers in Bioscience, 5*, D169–193.

Pavlovskaya, M., Ring, H., Grosswasser, Z., & Hochstein, S. (2002). Searching with unilateral neglect. *Journal of Cognitive Neuroscience, 14*(5), 745–756.

Perry, R. J., & Zeki, S. (2000). The neurology of saccades and covert shifts in spatial attention: An event-related fMRI study. *Brain; A Journal of Neurology, 123*(11), 2273–2288.

Platt, M. L., & Glimcher, P. W. (1999). Neural correlates of decision variables in parietal cortex. *Nature, 400*(6741), 233–238.

Posner, M. I. (1987). Cognitive neuropsychology and the problem of selective attention. In R. J. Ellingson & A. M. Halliday (Eds.), *The London symposium* (EEG Suppl. 39) New York: Elsevier Science.

Posner, M. I., Cohen, Y., & Rafal, R. D. (1982). Neural systems control of spatial orienting. *Philosophical Transactions of the Royal Society of London, Series B, 298*(1089), 187–198.

Posner, M. I., Inhoff, A. W., Friedrich, F. J., & Cohen, A. (1987). Isolating attentional system: A cognitive-anatomical analysis. *Psychobiology, 15*, 107–121.

Pouget, A., & Driver, J. (2000). Relating unilateral neglect to the neural coding of space. *Current Opinion in Neurobiology, 10*, 242–249.

Reddy, L., VanRullen, R., & Koch, C. (2002). *Pop-out and preattentive processing are not equivalent: Taking apart a common assumption about visual attention.* Paper presented at the Vision Sciences Society, Sarasota, FL.

Rees, G., & Lavie, N. (2001). What can functional imaging reveal about the role of attention in visual awareness. *Neuropsychologia, 39*(12), 1343–1353.

Rees, G., Wojciulik, E., Clarke, K., Husain, M., Frith, C., & Driver, J. (2000). Unconscious activation of visual cortex in the damaged right hemisphere of a parietal patient with extinction. *Brain, 123*(8), 1624–1633.

Rensink, R. A., O'Regan, J. K., & Clark, J. J. (1997). To see or not to see: The need for attention to perceive changes in scenes. *Psychological Science, 8*(5), 368–373.

Riddoch, M. J., & Humphreys, G. W. (1987). Perceptual and action systems in unilateral visual neglect. In M. Jeannerod (Ed.), *Neurophysiological and neuropsychological aspects of spatial neglect* (pp. 151–181). New York: Elsevier Science.

Rizzolatti, G., Fadiga, L., Fogassi, L., & Gallese, V. (1997). The space around us. *Science, 277*(5323), 190–191.

Rizzolatti, G., Riggio, L., Dascola, I., & Umilta, C. (1987). Reorienting attention across the horizontal and vertical meridians: Evidence in favor of a premotor theory of attention. *Neuropsychologia, 25*(1-A), 31–40.

Rosen, A. C., Rao, S. M., Caffarra, P., Scaglioni, A., Bobholz, J. A., Woodley, S. J., Hammeke, T. A., Cunningham, J. M., Prieto, T. E., & Binder, J. R. (1999). Neural basis of endogenous and exogenous spatial orienting: A functional MRI study. *Journal of Cognitive Neuroscience, 11*(2), 135–152.

Rousselet, G. A., Fabre-Thorpe, M., & Thorpe, S. J. (2002). Parallel processing in high-level categorization of natural images. *Nature Neuroscience, 5*(7), 629–630.

Sengpiel, F., & Huebener, M. (1999). Spotlight on the primary visual cortex. *Current Biology, 9*(9), R318–R321.

Serences, J. T., Shomstein, S., Leber, A. B., Egeth, H. E., & Yantis, S. (2002). *Neural basis of goal-directed and stimulus-driven attentional control.* Paper presented at the Cognitive Neuroscience Society, San Francisco.

Simons, D. J., & Levin, D. T. (1998). Failure to detect changes to people during a real-world interaction. *Psychonomic Bulletin & Review, 5*(4), 644–649.

Tong, F., Nakayama, K., Vaughan, J. T., & Kanwisher, N. (1998). Binocular rivalry and visual awareness in human extrastriate cortex. *Neuron, 21*(4), 753–759.

Treisman, A. M., & Gelade, G. (1980). A feature-integration theory of attention. *Cognitive Psychology, 12*(1), 97–136.

Treisman, A., & Gormican, S. (1988). Feature analysis in early vision: Evidence from search asymmetries. *Psychological Review, 95*(1), 15–48.

Vallar, G. (1998). Spatial hemineglect in humans. *Trends in Cognitive Sciences, 2*(3), 87–96.

Vandenberghe, R., Gitelman, D. R., Parrish, T. B., & Mesulam, M. M. (2001). Functional specificity of superior parietal mediation of spatial shifting. *NeuroImage, 14*(3), 661–673.

Vuilleumier, P., Sagiv, N., Hazeltine, E., Poldrack, R. A., Swick, D., Rafl, R. D., & Gabrieli, J. D. E. (2001). Neural fate of seen and unseen faces in visuospatial neglect: A combined event-related functional MRI and event-related potential study. *Proceedings of the National Academy of Sciences of the United States of America, 98*(6), 3495–3500.

Weidner, R., Pollmann, S., Muller, H. J., & von Cramon, D. Y. (2002). Top-down controlled visual dimension weighting: An event-related fMRI study. *Cerebral Cortex, 12*(3), 318–328.

Wilkinson, D. T., Halligan, P. W., Henson, R. N., & Dolan, R. J. (2002). The effects of interdistracter similarity on search processes in superior parietal cortex. *NeuroImage, 15*(3), 611–619.

Wojciulik, E., & Kanwisher, N. (1999). The generality of parietal involvement in visual attention. *Neuron, 23*(4), 747–764.

Wolfe, J. M. (1996). Extending guided search: Why guided search needs a preattentive "item map." In A. F. Kramer and M. G. H. Coles (Eds.), *Converging operations in the study of visual selective attention* (pp. 247–270). Washington, DC: American Psychological Society.

Wolfe, J. M. (1998). What can 1 million trials tell us about visual search? *Psychological Science, 9*(1), 33–39.

Woodman, G. F., & Luck, S. J. (1999). Electrophysiological measurement of rapid shifts of attention during visual search. *Nature, 400*(6747), 867–869.

Wurtz, R. H., Sommer, M. A., Paré, M., & Ferraina, S. (2001). Signal transformations from cerebral cortex to superior colliculus for the generation of saccades. *Vision Research, 41*, 3399–3412.

Yantis, S., Schwarzbach, J., Serences, J. T., Carlson, R. L., Steinmetz, M. A., Pekar, J. J., & Courthney, S. M. (2002). Transient neural activity in human parietal cortex during spatial attention shifts. *Nature Neuroscience, 5*(10), 995–1002.

Zelinsky, G. J., & Sheinberg, D. L. (1997). Eye movements during parallel-serial visual search. *Journal of Experimental Psychology: Human Perception & Performance, 23*(1), 244–262.

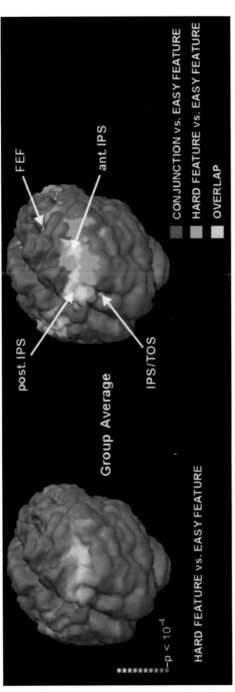

Fig. 3. Images from Donner et al. (2002). Group activation maps. Left: activation pattern found in *hard feature–easy feature* comparison. Right: overlaid activation patterns from *conjunction* and *hard feature* conditions.

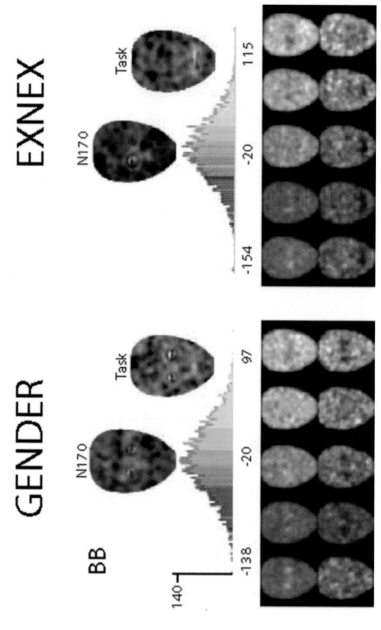

Fig. 11. This figure illustrates the dissociation between diagnostic information for categorization (see Task) and the information to which the N170 responds (see N170) using the bubbles technique (see text for explanations).

CATEGORIZING AND PERCEIVING OBJECTS: EXPLORING A CONTINUUM OF INFORMATION USE

Philippe G. Schyns

I. Introduction

Throughout life, human beings are confronted with a continuous flow of ever-changing stimulation from the physical world. However, stability seems to emerge from these low-level variations and we perceive our environments using a restricted set of labels. For example, the keywords "dark!," "light-switch?," "bathtub, washing basin, mirror," "my face," "oh God!," "tired, unshaven," "running water," "toothpaste," "toothbrush" might evoke a familiar visual scene. The specificity of the scene will differ across individuals, but at some level of abstraction (e.g., that of the example) we appear to have understood each other. The process of categorization is responsible for delivering the abstract labels. Categorization progressively reduces highly variable perceptual inputs to a smaller number of classes of equivalence (called "categories") whose representations (called "concepts") mediate thinking, communication, and adaptive actions.

From the above example, it would appear that categorization deals with the generic issue of "what is this visual input?" To recognize a visual input as your face, a toothbrush, or a bathroom scene is not very different from placing this event in the *my face*, *toothbrush*, or *bathroom* category. The problem is to understand how input information is matched against compatible information stored in memory. This simple idea narrows down the critical research issues to "what is information?" "how is it organized in the visual array?" "how is it organized in memory?" and "how do input and memory information interact to explain behavior?" (Schyns, 1998). The relevant literatures pertaining to these issues are object recognition and categorization.

Despite such profound similarity, research in object categorization and recognition has drifted apart. This could partially stem from differences of focus. Categorization studies have typically sought to explain the abstract rules governing the formation of categories (the idea that the visual features *eyes, mouth, chin, hair* but also the functional attributes *talks, displays emotions* represent a *face*, which is an *animated object*). Recognition researchers have instead focused on the implementation of perceptual attributes underlying the recognition process (e.g., the typical edges, surface properties, aspect ratio, viewpoint, and biological motion attributes that allows the recognition of the face).

However, debates on the possible interactions between object categorization and object perception have suggested that the principles governing the formation of categories should be more tightly coupled with the perceptual aspects of recognition (see Schyns, 1998; Schyns, Goldstone, & Thibaut, 1998, for reviews). In this chapter, I will illustrate that these interactions raise new research issues that could promote the emergence of more integrated theories of visual cognition. One main research question organizes the chapter: "How do input and memory information interact to explain categorization behavior?" I will address this question from within the integrative *diagnostic recognition* framework (Schyns, 1998).

II. The Diagnostic Recognition Framework

Diagnostic recognition starts with the common observation that a single visual event fits into an impressive number of different categories. For example, the same visual input could be recognized as a *Porsche*, a *car*, a *vehicle*, a *man-made object*, a *fast object*. On other occasions, it could be called a *public nuisance*, a *danger*, a *noisy toy*, and so forth. There is little doubt that categorization is flexible and that individuals can place the same input into many different categories, depending on factors such as goals and actions to more generic environmental contingencies (Barsalou, 1983).

A. Task Constraints

Categorization is flexible in part because people have many categories available in memory, and in part because they can selectively attend to the outside world information that is required to place a given input into one (or several) of these categories. For example, we can categorize the same face as

John, a male, who is about 50 years old, with a happy expression in part because knowledge about these categories is stored in memory. That is, in the absence of a visual input, we can readily evoke John, a male of about 50 years of age, who would like to be 20, but nevertheless smiles. Henceforth, task *constraints* will refer to this memory information that would be required for categorizing the visual input. Categorization researchers have been mainly dealing with task constraints (see Murphy, 2002, for a review), not so much recognition researchers. However, task constraints form an inevitable factor of any recognition task.

B. RECOGNITION INFORMATION

The second factor is the difficulty in specifying recognition information. Visual categories are formed because visual events form equivalence classes—i.e., visual events "look alike," or they "are used for similar things," and so forth. For example, objects will share the same parts (e.g., faces typically have only one nose, two eyes, and one mouth), cars will have a typical silhouette (at least when compared with other vehicles), or have similar surface characteristics (e.g., smooth vs. discontinuous, or symmetric). Information shared between category members forms the basis of equivalence classes, and distinctive information contrasts equivalence classes.

When developing theories of visual categorization a real difficulty arises because we simply do not know the basis of critical information defining the perception of similarities and contrasts between objects. Our visual system is designed to extract information along the three main dimensions of luminance, color, and motion variations, but how this basic information is organized to enable multiple categorizations of the same input remains to be explained. To illustrate the difficulty of the problem, consider the simple situation in which a visual array would consist of a 256×256 matrix of intensity capturing receptors (e.g., 256 gray levels per pixel). Gray-level "pictures in the head" would implement task constraints, against which input pictures would be matched. The best match of this correlation could indicate category membership. This template matching approach and its derivatives have well-known limitations (e.g., Palmer, 1999), but they nonetheless represent a useful starting point to illustrate the hurdle of specifying recognition information. The matching process compares each individual pixel of the input matrix, with the corresponding pixels of the images stored in memory. Recognition information is expressed only as gray-level differences between individual pixels. Some would contend that recognition information is much more complex, involving higher-order pixel combinations. Examples of recognition information would include the texture gradients allowing the parsing of a complex scene into distinct objects, the object edges from which vertices and object parts can be derived (e.g., Biederman, 1987), or the shading information from which object surfaces are computed. Information of this sort would enable constant recognition under varying conditions of lighting, scale, object translation, rotation, occlusion, and so forth. Perceptually minded recognition researchers have traditionally been more aware of the issue of recognition information and its availability. However, to the extent that visual categorization is framed as a matching process between compatible input and memorized information, it is clear that it will be difficult to study categories in memory without paying attention to the visual information defining these categories. Recognition information is specifies the information of different recognition tasks.

C. INTERACTIONS BETWEEN TASK CONSTRAINTS AND RECOGNITION INFORMATION

Diagnostic Recognition frames categorization as an interaction between the information required to categorize the event and the information available in the visual array to accomplish this categorization. When a match is established between the information required and that available in the input, the latter acquires an important status: it becomes diagnostic for the task at hand. It should be clear that diagnostic information is essentially dependent on categorization tasks. Diagnostic information is also an essential element of categorization performance. To perform categorization, diagnostic information must be extracted from the visual array, and perceptual constraints on this extraction process will affect performance. Thus, the diagnosticity of information and its availability in the visual array will be the main determinants of categorization performance.

We should be careful and point out that the concepts of information diagnosticity and information availability are not new concepts. For example, information diagnosticity is a core property of models of categorization (Anderson, 1991; Estes, 1986; Gluck, & Bower, 1988; Gosselin & Schyns 2001b; Kruschke, 1992; Lamberts, 2000; Nosofsky, 1984, 1986; and many others). However, these models often place few constraints on what may count as perceptually plausible object information and they tend to neglect perceptual constraints on information availability in their explanations of performance (Schyns, 1998; Schyns et al., 1998, though see Lamberts, 2000). Recognition researchers are aware of the constraints imposed by information availability. Biederman (1987) suggested that the visual system extracts specific edges from the visual array to reconstruct descriptions of the input in terms of simple geometric primitives (called "geons") to match against geon-based representations of objects in memory. However, this tends to overlook the more comprehensive role of information diagnosticity. What happens if the recognition task does not require the use of geometric primitives for object recognition?

This brief discussion justifies the need to bridge between cognition and perception. A complete theory of object categorization will need to integrate the factors affecting the diagnosticity of object cues and the perceptual constraints on their availability. In addition, new issues could arise from a closer look at these interactions. For example, a general issue is the relationship existing between flexible visual categorizations (i.e., the diagnostic use of visual information) and the perception of the stimulus itself. Are they independent, with categorization operating late, on an already perceived input, or are they intertwined, with the act of categorization influencing the early perception of the stimulus itself (Schyns & Rodet, 1997; Schyns & Oliva, 1999)? A related issue is that of the mechanisms underlying the extraction of information. Categorization would not succeed if its diagnostic information was not perceived. Does attention to diagnostic information enhance this aspect of the signal (e.g., in terms of a gain in contrast perception, a diminution of internal noise, or both, e.g., Dosher & Lu, 1998; Gold, Bennett, & Sekuler, 1999; Yeshurun & Carrasco, 1998)? What happens to the nondiagnostic aspects of the signal? Are they nevertheless implicitly processed? Bridging between categorization and perception inevitably raises new issues in attention, because the active search for the diagnostic information specified in the constraints of a categorization task determines which image information to attend and perceive.

The remainder of the chapter is organized as follows. We will first turn to object categories, and the features defining these categories; and the ways in which categories and their features interact to determine object perception. We will then examine the nature of task constraints, and particularly present methods recently developed to study them more rigorously. Finally, we will examine possible links between task constraints and stimulus perception.

III. The Nature of Object Information

A. THE ONTOGENY OF FEATURES IN OBJECT CATEGORIES

In a typical categorization experiment, object information is given, there is no ambiguity as to which features characterize which objects. For example, observers are instructed to learn the rules to categorize simple objects along the color and shape dimensions (see, e.g., Bruner, Goodnow, & Austin, 1956; Bourne, 1982; Shepard, Hovland, & Jenkins, 1961); they could learn that the feature combination "red and circle" defined the objects of a category. Category learning models still adhere to a similar approach: They specify a number of dimensions along which the stimuli can vary, and these form the basis of the similarity comparisons that underlie category learning (see, among many others, Anderson, 1991; Estes, 1986; Gluck & Bower, 1988; Kruschke, 1992; Nosofsky, Gluck, Palmeri, McKinley, & Glauthier, 1994).

Categorization models often adopt a stance of "You tell me what the object information is, and I will tell you how it is integrated to perform the object categorization" (Schyns et al., 1998). The idea that categorization processes operate on such a "preperceived" input has led researchers to concentrate comparatively more on the ways in which object information can be combined to represent categories than on the origin of the object information itself. However, it is legitimate to question whether the features of recognition are fixed and independent of the categorization being performed, or whether they can flexibly tune to the perceptual characteristics of the object categories they must differentiate. In other words, is the object information for categorization a fixed or a flexible basis?

As stated earlier, one important function of the basis of object features is to create the space within which perceptual differences and commonalities between categories are represented. Reasoning backward from this property, Schyns and Murphy (1994) suggested that the requirement to distinguish categories that initially "look alike" could prompt the creation of new object features that change the perception of the stimuli. The *Functionality Principle* summarizes this view (Schyns & Murphy, 1994, p. 310): "If a fragment of a stimulus categorizes objects (distinguishes members from nonmembers), the fragment is instantiated as a unit in the representational code of object concepts." Briefly stated, new object information can be synthesized to implement new categorizations.

Schyns and Rodet (1997) tested one implication of the Functionality Principle: that orthogonal categorizations of the same stimulus could arise from its perceptual organization using different object cues. They reasoned that a different history of categorization of unfamiliar objects could change the cues people learn to perceptually organize the visual input. Their experiments involved categories of unfamiliar objects called "Martian cells" (examples of cells are presented in Figure 1). Not only were these objects unfamiliar to subjects, but their defining cues were also unfamiliar. Learning to categorize the cells involved as much learning which cues go with which category as learning the cues themselves.

Categories were defined by specific blobs common to all members to which irrelevant blobs were added (to simulate various cell bodies). X cells shared the x cue, Y exemplars shared y, and the components x and y were always adjacent to one another in XY cells. (Figure 1 shows, from left to right, an XY, an X, and a Y exemplar. It also shows their defining xy, x, and y cues.). A difference in categorization history simply resulted from one

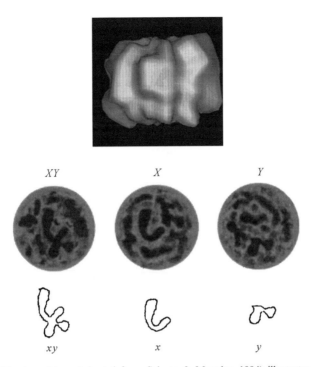

Fig. 1. The top picture (adapted from Schyns & Murphy, 1994) illustrates a "Martian Rock" exemplar used to study the Functionality Principle. The middle pictures illustrate exemplars of "Martian cells" (from left to right, examples of category XY, X, and Y). The bottom pictures isolate the features defining the corresponding categories. Note that the xy feature is the conjunction of x and y. In Schyns and Rodet's (1997) Experiment 2, one observer group ($XY \rightarrow X \rightarrow Y$) learned XY before X before Y, while the other group ($X \rightarrow Y \rightarrow XY$) learned the same categories, but in a different order. Whereas $XY \rightarrow X \rightarrow Y$ observers encoded the xy feature as one holistic unit z, $X \rightarrow Y \rightarrow XY$ encoded the same cell element as the $x \& y$ conjunction. This occurred because the second group already knew the features x and y enabling a conjunctive representation of xy when they experienced the XY category, whereas the other group did not know these features before seeing XY.

group learning X before Y before XY ($X \rightarrow Y \rightarrow XY$) while the other group learned the same three categories, but in a different order ($XY \rightarrow X \rightarrow Y$). The idea was that this simple difference in learning history would elicit orthogonal perceptions and representations of the identical XY Martian cells.

Results revealed that $X \rightarrow Y \rightarrow XY$ subjects initially created the cues x and y when they learned their X and Y categories, respectively. The incoming XY category was then perceived and represented as a conjunction of the acquired x and y cues. Cue creation was different in the group initially exposed to the XY category. Unlike the other group, when $XY \rightarrow X \rightarrow Y$

subjects initially learned XY, they did not possess the x and y components that allowed a conjunctive analysis. Instead, subjects learned to perceive and represent XY with a configural cue (that we call xy, but whose perceptual status is really more like an independent z unit) without even noticing the x&y conjunction that the other group perceived.

This example illustrates that one cannot simply assume the cues on which classification processes operate. A simple change in the history of categorization of unfamiliar materials changed the cues that were learned, the perceptual analyses, perceptions, and representations of identical objects. Because object cues form the basis of the similarity judgments that determine category learning, complete explanations of categorization behavior will need to integrate cue availability.

If object cues form the psychological basis of similarity judgments, a general question is whether the functional features proposed should *really* be the minimal units of a theory of object categorization, a theory that predicts the nature of the perceptual differences between the categories. This question is difficult in part because a good principle of theory construction recommends that the analysis of the goals and purposes of a recognition task (here, the task constraints) precedes the study of its representations and algorithms (Marr, 1982). Thus, the categorizations a feature vocabulary must resolve will determine (at least in part) the nature of the primitives entering this vocabulary. For example, in an influential model of letter recognition (Fisher, 1986), the identification of three primitives (two diagonal bars and one horizontal bar) precedes the categorization of the input as a capital "A." These features were chosen with the task of categorization of capital letters in mind. Similarly, Biederman's (1987) geons were derived for the task of categorizing man-made objects. The same features could hardly solve the task of categorizing types of shoes.

In componential conceptions of recognition, object information is the interface between perception and higher-level cognition. Combination of features represents object categories in memory and so categorization systems seek to match these against input features. At some level of perceptual organization, a version of these functional features must discretize the input for subsequent matching. However, one could argue that functional features are much higher-level, cognitive constructs, and that the "real" features that discretize the input are lower-level, physiological constructs. In one sense, this is trivially true: Rods and cones in the retina provide the original analysis of the visual signal. However, these rods and cones represent the input with the same limitations for recognition as the 256×256 matrix of intensity receptors discussed earlier. Effective recognition systems need low-dimensional invariant recodings of the high-dimensional variable inputs. We are suggesting here that the requirement to distinguish between categories can constrain the recodings of high-dimensional inputs into low-dimensional object information—the categorization features. However, it remains an important issue to determine how perception implements this dimensionality reduction, and whether the dimensionality reduction is affected by the task at hand.

B. Blindness to Category-Defining Features

The example with Martian cells provided an "existence proof" that the differential availability of categorization cues could have dramatic effects on the perception and categorization of identical stimuli. Similar effects can be observed using more naturalistic stimuli and categorizations. In Archambault, O'Donnell, and Schyns (1999), we explored the hypothesis that people could differentially attend to and perceive the visual properties of identical mugs and computers inserted in a natural office scene (see Figure 2)

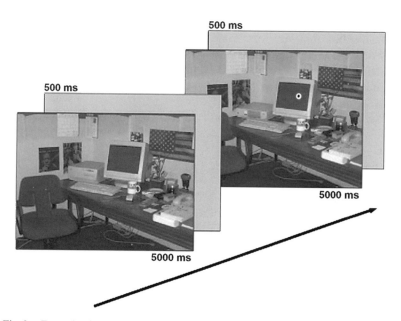

Fig. 2.   Example of a trial in the change blindness experiment of Archambault et al. (1999). Each frame of a two-frame sequence was presented for 5 s, separated by a 500 ms blank to prevent transient motion signals. The sequence was repeated until observer perceived the change (here, the computer). The number of repetitions was used as an independent measure of blindness to object information. When observers knew one of these computers at the subordinate level (e.g., IBM PC), they would detect the change much faster than if they only knew the computers at the basic level (e.g., simply as computer). This occurred even when the same observer knew only a subset of the possible computers at the subordinate level.

depending on their history of categorization. In a first experiment, one group (*MUG-computer*) learned the mugs at a general level and the computers at a specific level, whereas the other group (*mug-COMPUTER*) learned the opposite assignment of category level to objects: mugs as specific and computers as general. This ensured that observers learned an identical set of objects at two levels of categorization. It was expected that the nature of the categorization learned (general and specific) would modify the perceived properties of identical distal objects.

A change detection task (Simons & Levin, 1997) tested the visual encoding of the objects. Mugs and computers were inserted in a complex office scene (see Figure 2). In a trial, two office photographs were successively presented, each for 5 s, separated by a 500 ms blank. Between the two frames, a mug could change (be replaced by a different mug) or disappear, a computer could change or disappear, or other office objects could disappear. All subjects (i.e., MUG-computer and COMPUTER-mug) were exposed to the same object changes and disappearances. Their task was to identify the difference between the two frames. It is important to emphasize that observers were *explicitly* instructed that each trial comprised only one change and that their task was (1) to notice it and (2) to indicate what the change was. The trial was repeated until these two conditions were met and the number of trial repetitions served as the independent measure of change perception.

Observers were "cognitively blind" (i.e., took longer to perceive) changes that involved objects learned at a general level, compared to objects that were learned at a specific level. However, these different perceptions did not simply arise because observers were biased to attend to the office location of the objects learned at a specific level because all observers perceived equally fast the disappearances of all objects—i.e. those learned at a general and a specific level. Thus, the orthogonal perceptions of these identical object changes when disappearances were detected equally fast isolated the effect of category learning modifying the object cues that observers perceived and used.

This categorization-dependent cognitive blindness was repeated in a within-subjects design to rule out the possible objection that observers preferentially attended to the office location where subordinate changes appeared. The design of Experiment 1 orthogonally assigned the categories *mug* and *computer* to general and specific levels across experimental groups. In the second experiment, observers learned to categorize the two categories (*mug* and *computer*) at *both* the general *and* the specific level. Specifically, each observer learned a different subset of *mug* and a subset of *computer* at the specific level, and the remaining objects of each category at the general level. A result of this learning was that the relevant image locations for *mug* and *computer* in the office scene now embodied a general- and a specific-level change, relative to the observers. Thus, attention to a specific-level change implied attention to a general-level change occurring at the same image location. In these conditions, a differential blindness to general- and specific-level changes confirmed that categorization does not affect selective attention to spatial locations, but the selective encoding of the objects present in these locations.

One important commonality between this example with naturalistic objects in scenes and the example with Martian cells is that learning new categorizations (subordinate categorizations of computers and mugs and categorizations of new cells) changed the basis of object features that was used. This information, differentially available across observers, induced different perceptions of identical stimuli. Unfortunately, the reported differences in perception are difficult to relate to established processes of lower-level perception, a drawback addressed in the final example.

C. CATEGORIZATION-DEPENDENT SCALE PERCEPTION

As a third, and final example of categorization modifying the availability of object cues, we will turn to the Experiment 1 of Schyns and Oliva (1999). People can readily categorize the top picture of Figure 3, in the *face, female, neutral,* or *Mary* category, if this was the identity of the face. The pictures of Figure 3 (called "hybrid stimuli") were used in several recognition experiments (Oliva & Schyns, 1997; Schyns & Oliva, 1994, 1999) to examine whether a categorization task can modify the perceptual availability of scale cues (here, the Low and High Spatial Frequencies, henceforth LSF and HSF of an image). To illustrate, consider Figure 3 where fine scale cues (HSF) represent a neutral woman in the top picture and a study in the bottom picture. Coarse scale information (LSF) represents opposite interpretations of the same pictures—i.e., a smiling man in the top picture and a road in the bottom picture. If you blink, squint, or move away from Figure 3 your perception should change, because HSF cues become less available.

Coarse and fine scale cues can represent different information about faces, objects, and scenes. For example, the encoding of detailed edges portraying the contours of a nose, eyelashes, the precise shape of the mouth and eyes, and so forth, can be traced to HSF. In contrast, LSF could encode pigmentation and shading information from the face at a coarser resolution. LSF cues are often thought to provide a useful skeleton of the image from which fine scale details can be fleshed out (Schyns & Oliva, 1994). Turning to psychophysics there is substantial evidence that the visual input is initially processed at multiple spatial scales, functionally described by about four to six spatial frequency channels (Ginsburg, 1986; Wilson & Bergen, 1979). Hence, spatial filters provide an excellent candidate for the building blocks

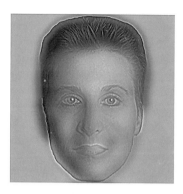

Fig. 3. The top pictures illustrate the stimuli used in the hybrid experiments of Schyns and Oliva (1999). If you squint, blink, or move away from the face picture your initial perception of a neutral woman (based on the high spatial frequencies of the image) should change to a smiling man (based on the low spatial frequencies of the image). The bottom picture illustrates the scene hybrids used in Schyns and Oliva (1994) and Oliva and Schyns (1997). Again, changing the viewing distance should modify the perception of the scene from an office to a road.

of visual perception that might determine visual categorizations (see Morrisson & Schyns, 2001, for a review).

In Schyns and Oliva's (1999) Experiment 1 hybrid faces as described above were presented for 50 ms, and the nature of the categorization was found to moderate the use of LSF and HSF cues, and the perception of the hybrids themselves. For example, when asked if the face was expressive or not, observers tended to perceive and report the fine scale face, whereas there was no bias for a gender decision and there was a coarse scale bias when asked to specify the expression as happy, angry, or neutral. Interestingly, observers were unaware of the presence of two faces in any one image, a result reported with many experiments with hybrids (Oliva & Schyns, 1997; Schyns & Oliva, 1994). Thus, the perception of identical hybrids was determined by the categorization task, suggesting that categorization processes tune into diagnostic information at specific scales.

This and other studies with hybrids (e.g., Oliva & Schyns, 1997) suggest that attention can exert a top-down selective control on low-level vision (i.e., on the processing characteristics of spatial filters). Sowden, Ozgen, and Schyns (2002) recently explored these mechanisms. A first experiment used plaids composed of a left-oriented grating overlapped with a right-oriented grating at a different spatial frequency. With auditory cuing, the attention of observers was directed to either a high- or a low-frequency plaid component. When the components were well-separated in scale space (e.g., by four octaves), observers could report the orientation of the cued component (either LSF or HSF). When the components were less separated (e.g., by 0.5 octaves), no such bias was observed. These results suggest that observers can selectively attend to the cued spatial frequency processing channel, revealing an expectancy effect. The absence of bias arises when the components are less separated (e.g., by 0.5 octaves) because the same spatial frequency channels process both. In another experiment, Sowden et al. (2002) found that the spatial frequency tuning of expectancy effects was restricted to a narrow band around the cued frequency. These findings support the idea that attention can act top-down to modulate spatial frequency at early stages of visual processing, suggesting a mechanism for the effect of a categorization task on the availability and the perception of recognition information at different spatial scales.

D. Summary

We have reviewed three research projects dealing with the availability of object information in different categorization tasks. The Martian cells illustrated how new features could be created as a result of learning new categorizations. The change blindness research showed how learning realistic object categories at a general and a specific level could modify the features that are used to perceptually encode the same stimuli. Finally, the hybrid experiments demonstrated that different categorization tasks tap into different scale cues of the same face stimuli.

These examples share the general idea that a categorization task specifies the input information that is diagnostic, and the encoding of this information for categorization can in turn modify the perception of the input. The examples differ on several critical dimensions. In the Martian cells and the change blindness experiments, new categorizations (i.e., distinguishing similar Martian cells, or specifying precise object categories) forced observers to create new features that augmented the repertoire of object information available to the observer. The hybrid experiments and their subsequent psychophysical testing illustrate another way of modulating the availability of recognition information: attentional modulation. The constraints of a task (i.e., the expectancy of finding information at a given scale) can differentially weigh the processing of spatial frequency channels, and thereby modify the perception of information differentially represented at these scales. Here, I want to suggest that feature creation mechanisms can flexibly modify the basis of available features that form the basis for similarity judgments subtending categorization. Attending to task-relevant information modulates the information that is available to categorization processes.

IV. The Nature of Task Constraints

So far, we have seen that the categorization task can modify the cues that are used to categorize the input. We have also seen that attending to these cues to resolve categorization tasks could critically modify stimulus perception. Thus, complete theories of face, object, and scene categorization will first need to specify which information is required to place the input in this or that category. In the Diagnostic Recognition Framework, this information forms the constraints, or the information requirements of different categorization tasks.

There are basically two approaches to the problem of specifying task constraints. The first approach (that we will call *a priori*) assumes a feature basis to represent objects in memory (e.g., Biederman's 1987 famous set of 36 geometric elements, called geons). Combinations of these *a priori* features are endowed with (1) specifying equivalence classes (objects composed of the same geons will fall in the same category) and (2) contrast classes (objects composed of different geons will fall in different categories). The information constraints of a given categorization task are to locate geons in the input array (from the nonaccidental contours forming these geons) to match them against memory representations.

Another approach closer in spirit to Gibson (1979) does not start with an assumed basis for memory representations and the associated task constraints, but instead takes a closer look at the stimulus. If task constraints specify the stimulus information to be used, then one could attempt to determine the critical aspects of the stimulus (the *effective* stimulus) that the observer uses in a categorization task. Task constraints would then become a "diagnostic filtering function" that specifies how information is extracted from the stimulus in the task. This is the approach recently developed in Gosselin and Schyns (2001a) and Schyns, Bonnar, and Gosselin (2002).

A. BUBBLES TO DERIVE A POSTERIORI A DIAGNOSTIC FILTERING FUNCTION

To derive the diagnostic filtering function of categorization tasks, we developed a new method called "*Bubbles*" (Gosselin & Schyns, 2001a). To illustrate the technique, consider the three face categorization tasks studied in Schyns et al. (2002). In a between-subjects design, a different group of observers resolved one of three possible categorization tasks (*identity, gender, expressive or not*) on the same set of 10 faces split between five males and five females, each displaying two possible expressions (neutral vs. happy). To determine the information diagnostic of each categorization, *Bubbles* samples an input space (to be discussed later) and presents as stimuli sparse versions of the original faces. Observers then categorize these stimuli while the *Bubbles* algorithm keeps track of the samples of face information that lead to a correct vs. incorrect categorization response. Following the experiment, using this performance information, an analysis can reveal the regions of the input space that were particularly useful to resolve the task. The selection of this information from the input space is what we mean by a diagnostic filtering function. To depict the effect of the task constraints on the stimulus, we can use the diagnostic filtering function to derive an *effective stimulus* from the original stimulus (see Figure 4).

In Schyns et al. (2002), the stimulus space comprised the two-dimensional (2-D) image decomposed into six independent SF bandwidths of one octave each represented on a third dimension (see Figure 5, see Gosselin & Schyns, 2001a, for examples with a 2-D input space). The coarsest band served as a constant stimulus background. The face information represented at each band (see Figure 5) was revealed by a number of randomly located bubbles that captured the corresponding face information (see Figure 5). We reconstructed a sparse face stimulus by literally adding together the information revealed within each bandwidth (see Figure 5). It is important to note that the sparse stimulus reveals a subset of the total information present in the original stimulus, where the information sampled is dictated by the bubbles present at each SF bandwidth. It is also important to add that the total number of bubbles was adjusted on-line to maintain the observer's categorization performance at 75% correct.

To derive the diagnostic filtering function of each categorization task depicted in Figure 4, we perform a series of simple computations. First, we analyze the use of information independently within each SF bandwidth. Taking the finest SF bandwidth as an example, we first add together the bubbles that sample fine scale information on each trial of the experiment,

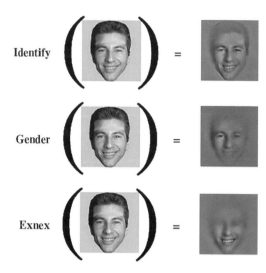

Fig. 4. This figure illustrates the concept of the diagnostic function, as extracted by *Bubbles*. The diagnostic function formalizes how the categorization task constrains the extraction of information from the stimulus. Here, the categorization tasks applied to the same face are Identity, Gender, and Expressive or not. For each categorization, the application of the diagnostic function on a face reveals the effective stimulus of the task considered. This effective stimulus, because it reflects the object information required for the task, is a depiction of the task constraints.

to derive a frequency of information sampling (which should be uniform after many trials given that the bubbles are randomly positioned). Whenever the observer is correct, we add separately the bubbles leading to correct responses, to derive a frequency of diagnostic samples. We then divide the frequency of diagnostic samples by the sampling frequency and obtain a set of proportions. These proportions reveal how accurately each region of the fine SF bandwidth was used to categorize the faces. With a performance threshold of 75%, if the observer was able to use *all* the fine SF bandwidth, the proportions should be uniform, each equal to .75. However, some regions of the face will be better used than others, and observers will be more efficient when they categorize sparse faces displaying this information. Operationally, the proportions for these regions will be significantly higher than .75. We then mark with a white (versus black) dot each proportion that is significantly above (versus below) .75. The outcome of this analysis, performed independently for each SF bandwidth is the diagnostic filtering function of a categorization task. It will formally specify the diagnostic information that the task requires to categorize faces at a 75% correct level.

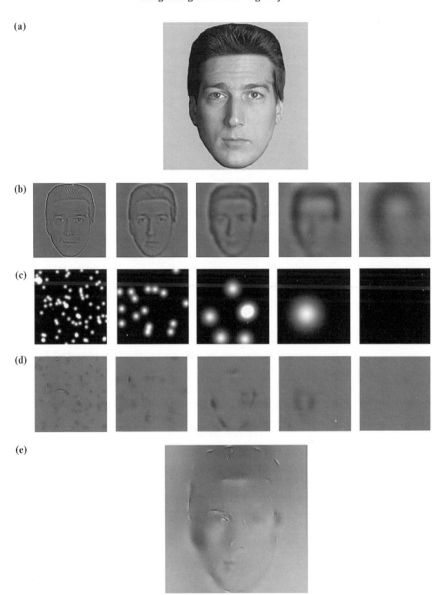

Fig. 5.   This figure illustrates the synthesis of a sparse stimulus (e) from an original face picture
(a). In (b) the original picture is decomposed into a number of nonoverlapping spatial frequency
bandwidth. In (c), Gaussian bubbles are sprinkled to reveal the face information presented in (d).
The partial information from (d) is added together to form the sparse stimulus in (e).

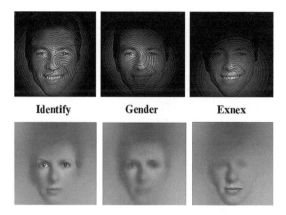

Fig. 6. This figure adapted from Schyns et al. (2002) illustrates two of the computations that can be extracted from the diagnostic filtering function of categorization tasks. For Identity, Gender, and Expressive or not, the top pictures reveal the gradient of attention of the function. The bottom picture reveals the face information that discriminates between fast vs. slow response times in the tasks. It should be clear that this information is well correlated with that of the effective face.

The diagnostic filtering functions derived for Identity, Gender, and Expressive or not from the same set of faces can then be applied to the original face stimuli, to reveal the *effective stimulus* of this particular task (see Figure 6). Whereas the mouth is well defined in Identity and Expressive or not, it is neglected at the finest scales in Gender (compare also the use of the eyes, the nose, and the chin across effective stimuli). The diagnostic filtering function offers rich information about task constraints. From it, we can, for example, compute the biases of each task for different scales by computing the proportion of diagnostic pixels at each scale against the total number of pixels. This is a measure of the probability to find diagnostic information at each scale. If we used this probability as a linear weight, for each pixel, we add across SF bandwidths the probability of finding diagnostic information. This is summarized in a gradient of attention that could be used to predict, for example, eye movements. Many other computations can be derived from the *Bubbles* technique (e.g., an analysis of the information leading to fast vs. slow reaction times, see Figure 6, an analysis of the conjunctions of bubbles driving performance, and so forth; see Schyns et al., 2002).

B. The Diagnostic Filtering Function of Basic and Subordinate Categorization

Observers can categorize the pictures in Figure 7 effortlessly as a whale at the basic level, a sperm whale at the subordinate level, and a mammal at the

Fig. 7. This figure illustrates the relationship existing between spatial frequencies (the large pictures) and the information content of the same object as it might project on the retina with increasing viewing distances (the increasingly smaller pictures). Specifically, starting from the original top left picture of the whale, if we decrease its size by two, this is equivalent to filtering the original image with a low-pass filter that removes all the highest spatial frequencies of the image. As the size is further decreased more and more high-spatial frequencies are removed. To illustrate the natural constraints on the availability of object information for basic and subordinate categorizations, try to categorize the picture as whale and sperm whale at each information level. It should become considerably more difficult to determine the subordinate categorization with low-resolution (small) pictures.

superordinate level (Rosch, Mervis, Gray, Johnson, & Boyes-Braem, 1976). The hierarchical organization of categories in memory is a fundamental principle of organization of task constraints. Of the hierarchical levels, one has a privileged status: observers asked to spontaneously name pictures of common objects tend to use their basic-level name (Brown, 1958; Rosch et al., 1976; Tanaka & Taylor, 1991; Wisniewski & Murphy, 1989), are faster to name objects at this level (Jolicoeur, Gluck, & Kosslyn, 1984; Murphy, 1991; Murphy & Smith, 1982; Rosch et al., 1976), and list many more shape features at this level (Rosch et al., 1976; Tversky & Hemenway, 1984). In addition, throughout development basic names are learned before those of other categorization levels (Brown, 1958; Rosch et al., 1976; Horton & Markman, 1980; Mervis & Crisafi, 1982), and basic names tend to be shorter (Brown, 1958; Rosch et al., 1976). Together, these findings suggested that the initial point of contact between the physical input and memory occurs at the basic level, also known in object recognition as *primal access* (Biederman, 1987), or *entry point* (Jolicoeur et al., 1984).

It is an interesting problem to determine whether the primal access and the entry point identified in the object recognition correspond to the basic level of the categorization literature. However, we would first need to precisely characterize the three concepts before being able to compare them. In Gosselin and Schyns (2001b), we derived a functional theory of what constitutes a basic level category in memory. A basic category simultaneously comprises many redundant features (from each one of which the category can be independently attained) and few features that overlap between categories. This theory was implemented in a model (called "SLIP") that predicted most of the published results on the basic level. In agreement with this model, we will here refer to the basic level as the level of category organization that maximizes feature redundancy and minimizes feature overlap (an implementation of the differentiation model of Rosch et al., 1976).

In Schyns and Gosselin (2002), we sought to derive the diagnostic information underlying basic-level categorizations. In Archambault, Gosselin, and Schyns (2000), we showed that the bias for basic categorizations could naturally arise from ecological constraints on the perceptual availability of basic and subordinate cues. Specifically, basic categorizations were more resilient to changes of scale than subordinate categorizations. At different viewing distances, the information content of an image corresponds to that of different spatial frequencies with a fixed viewing distance. We can then search spatial frequency space for the scale-specific biases of subordinate and basic categorizations.

We adapted *Bubbles* to search the phase space of a Fourier transform. A Fourier transform decomposes a signal into a set of imaginary numbers called the Fourier coefficients. The location of the Fourier coefficients in the Fourier transform represents the spatial frequency (from 1 to 128 cycles per image, for a 256 × 256 pixels image) and an orientation (from 0 to 179° in the image plane). Each Fourier coefficient transformed into polar coordinates represents two important pieces of information about each spatial frequency making up the stimulus: a magnitude (indicating the contrast energy of this particular frequency in the image) and a phase angle.

Fourier coefficients

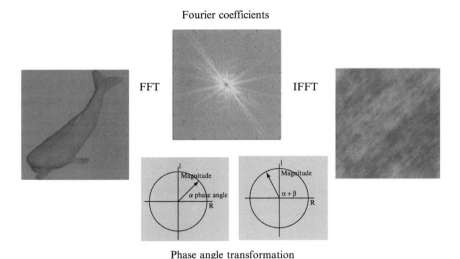

Phase angle transformation

Fig. 8. This figures illustrates the computational steps of transforming the phase information in the Fourier transform (FFT) of an image. The Fourier transform computes the Fourier coefficients. These express the magnitude and phase angle of each spatial frequency composing the original image. Transforming the phase angle while leaving the magnitude of the Fourier coefficients untouched will remove all shape information of the original image, while leaving intact its average contrast energy.

Together, the phase angles of the different Fourier coefficients provide the information necessary to reconstruct a global shape from individual spatial frequencies. For example, in Figure 8, the left picture is the equivalent of the right picture in which all frequencies have been made out of phase and so shape information is lost.

From this observation, we can reconstruct stimuli that comprise information in phase from selected frequencies in the Fourier transform (e.g., the LSF or the HSF marked with a white circle in Figure 9) and information out of phase from the complement frequencies. To "bubble the phase information" one simply needs to randomly select a number of spatial frequencies (each corresponding to a ring in the Fourier transform, see Figure 9), reconstruct a stimulus with the complement frequency out of phase, and probe basic vs. subordinate categorization responses. If the number of frequencies in phase (i.e., rings) is adjusted to ensure 75% correct categorizations independently at the basic and subordinate levels, then the effective stimulus for these categorizations can be reconstructed in a manner analogous to the effective faces presented earlier.

Interestingly, for the same object, the basic-level effective stimulus comprises less high spatial frequencies than the subordinate-level effective

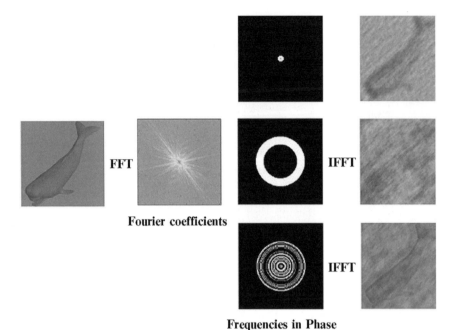

FFT   IFFT

Fourier coefficients

IFFT

Frequencies in Phase

Fig. 9. This figure illustrates the "Bubble the Phase" procedure. An original stimulus is decomposed into its Fourier coefficients with the Fourier transform. Each ring of Fourier coefficients indicates all the orientations (from 0 to 179° of orientation, and symmetrically from 180 to 359° of orientation) of one spatial frequency (from 1 to 127 cycles per image in the application considered). For example, the top ring captures the low spatial frequencies between 1 and 9 cycles per image, while the middle ring captures the higher frequencies between 32 and 64 cycles per image. If the phase angle information of the frequencies within the ring is preserved when the phase angles of the frequencies outside the ring are randomly transformed, versions of the left whale picture are obtained that reveal only the selected information. The bottom ring picture reflects a random selection of spatial frequencies to maintain in phase. Observers were asked to resolve basic and subordinate categorizations of the same object when the phase information was randomly preserved.

stimulus. As the information associated with high spatial frequencies vanishes quickly when a stimulus decreases in size, the subordinate level is effectively more dependent on scale than the basic level. As people tend to categorize objects from a wide range of viewing distances, one determinant for a bias to the basic level could arise from the fact that its cues are available over a wider range of viewing distances than subordinate cues. This difference in cue availability might not reduce the basic level, but it is one of the factors to consider in explaining its phenomenology.

C. SUMMARY

This section started with the observation that the categorization task could modify the input information that is used. We reasoned that this occurs because different categorization tasks require different diagnostic information to categorize the input. We referred to this as the information constraints of a categorization task. The problem with information constraints is that before *Bubbles* there was really no way to precisely assess what these constraints were, and researchers were left with using an *a priori* approach of imaging plausible task constraints and then seek to confirm or refute them.

Here, we started with an *a posteriori* approach that attempts, using *Bubbles*, to determine task constraints from the way a categorization uses stimulus information. The hybrid method presented earlier is as a precursor to *Bubbles* because it searches a one-dimensional input space made of only two SF bandwidths (LSF vs. HSF). However, *Bubbles* is much more generic, as it can be applied to *any* parametric space. That is, it is not restricted to the image but can be applied to any space that can generate a stimulus (i.e., visual, auditory, tactile, and so forth).

V. Back to Perception

Remember that one aim of diagnostic recognition is to offer a framework that bridges between categorization and perception. We would contend that diagnostic information very much erects this bridge between two traditionally independent disciplines. Diagnostic information has a dual role. For categorization, it specifies the information required from memory to categorize the stimulus. For low-level vision, diagnostic information specifies the information that must be particularly well extracted from the visual array to perform a task. Thus, once diagnostic information is sufficiently clearly specified, one can turn to perception to better understand the processes that will extract this information.

To illustrate, consider Salvatore Dali's painting *Slave Market with the Disappearing Bust of Voltaire* (1940), a famous bistable image. The heads of two nuns within a busy market scene also constitute the eyes of the Bust of Voltaire. An observer viewing this painting will typically experience a switch between one and the other perceptual interpretations. Can we apply the *Bubbles* method delineated earlier to specify the information driving each interpretation of the painting, to better understand how attention to information can modify the perception of the stimulus? There is a direct link between this question and the hybrid experiments discussed earlier. Even though we are not here studying typical face, object, or scene categorizations, we are nevertheless studying the information underlying two categorizations (*nuns* vs. *bust of Voltaire*) of an identical stimulus. Thus, the knowledge that we would gain from this situation could be applied to more typical recognition studies.

Bonnar et al. (2002) applied a version of the *Bubbles* technique discussed earlier in which the center of the Dali painting was filtered into nonoverlapping SF bandwidths, sampled using a number of randomly located Gaussian bubbles. Observers saw sparse versions of the painting (see Figure 10) and had to judge whether they looked more like the nuns, like the bust of Voltaire, or whether they could not decide. The number of bubbles was then adjusted to keep "don't know" responses to a 25% rate.

Following the experiment, an analysis was performed to determine which information was most diagnostic of each perception. As Figure 10 illustrates, the Bust of Voltaire encompassed information at lower SFs than the nuns interpretation. It also had a wider spatial extent. With this information circumscribed, we now turn to early vision to better understand the perceptual switching. In the context of the hybrid experiments presented earlier, we pointed out that the visual system is known to analyze the input into a number of SF channels. One possible explanation for the perceptual switching between Voltaire and the nuns is that perceptual mechanisms switch between different SF channels to encode the information that they represent (i.e., the nuns and the bust of Voltaire).

Bonnar et al. (2002) tested this hypothesis using the frequency-specific adaptation technique (e.g., Blakemore & Campbell, 1969). The rationale behind frequency-specific adaptation is that an adaptation to pattern X changes the appearance or sensitivity to X, but not the appearance or sensitivity to pattern Y, thus indicating that the underlying structures simultaneously process independent aspects of the patterns. The results of *Bubbles* applied to the Dali painting provide a complete description of the spatial frequencies that must be adapted to selectively affect the perception of the nuns or Voltaire. However, we could not adapt the observers to the patterns of the nuns and Voltaire themselves. We wanted to adapt the specific frequency channels underlying the percepts, not the percept themselves. To this end, observers adapted to high-contrast dynamic noise created in one group (LSF-adapt) from the LSF driving the perception of Voltaire, and in the other group (HSF-adapt) from the HSF underlying the perception of the nuns. In a transfer phase both groups saw the same low-contrast version of an ambiguous hybrid image composed of the information of both the nuns and Voltaire. We observed that LSF-adapted observers preferentially saw the nuns in this hybrid when the HSF-adapted group saw Voltaire. Such orthogonal perceptions following SF channel

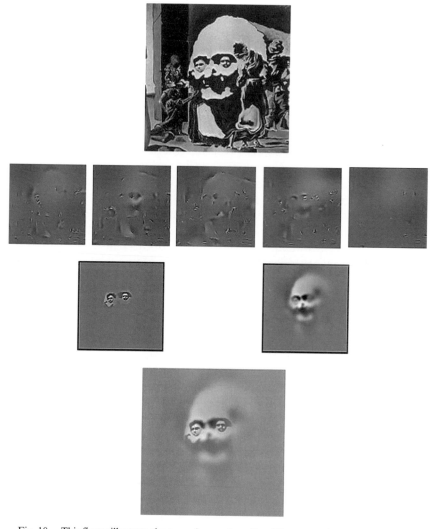

Fig. 10.   This figure illustrate the procedure and results of Bonnar et al. (2002). From top to bottom, a black and white version of the ambiguous portion of the Dali painting. Examplars of the stimuli presented to observers (who had to decide whether they saw Voltaire, or the nuns). The *Bubbles* solution of the information required to perceive the nuns and Voltaire. A depiction of the ambiguous gist of the Dali painting.

adaptation provide a direct link between stimulus interpretation and a fundamental mechanism of early vision, SF processing. Studies are currently generalizing this approach to the face categorizations of Schyns et al. (2002). The idea is to reconstruct a sophisticated hybrid in which, for example, a male face is projected in the diagnostic subspace of gender, and a female face is projected in the nondiagnostic subspace. Using then a frequency-specific adaptation paradigm similar to the one just described, we should obtain orthogonal categorizations of identical, low-contrast hybrid faces.

VI. Brain Signals and Categorization Behavior

We have seen that *Bubbles* can be applied to understand the information making up the task constraints of visual categorization tasks leading to specific perceptions of the input. It is only recently that researchers have attempted to address similar issues in terms of brain processes. For example, Sigala and Logothetis (2002) recording the behavior of cell assemblies in the infratemporal (IT) cortex of monkeys to isolate those that were sensitize to diagnostic information in a face, and a fish categorization task. Recently, Schyns, Jentzsch, Schweinberger, Johnson, and Gosselin (2002) examined whether the event-related potential N170 (a negativity of EEG activity occuring roughly 170 ms after stimulus onset) could also be related to attention to diagnostic information. There is agreement in the literature that the N170 is related to face processing, but there is still considerable debate about whether its response is characteristic of a structural encoder for faces, a feature (e.g., eye) detector, or something else.

When dealing with complex stimuli, how can a brain response be attributed to a specific category (e.g., a face), a specific feature (e.g., the eye), or a specific function (e.g., attending to diagnostic information)? This is still one of the greatest methodological challenge in the burgeoning field of the cognitive neuroscience of recognition. The absence of a principled method forces researchers to ascertain the specificity of response (e.g., to the face) by contrast with responses from other categories (e.g., cars, furniture, hands, and so forth), and to test informal hypotheses. Unfortunately, this approach minimizes the rich structure of visual inputs. Typically, there is a dense correlative structure in the low-level visual properties of category members (e.g., luminance energy, main directions of orientation, spatial frequency composition, and so forth). Only a small subset of these properties is controlled with a finite number of contrast categories. Consequently, the specificity of the brain response might be attributable to incidental input statistics, not to the category, per se.

Bubbles was designed to resolve such issues of credit assignment. The technique uses the stimulus (not other stimuli) as its own control for amplitude of brain response. Schyns et al. (2002) applied *Bubbles* in two separate tasks (GENDER and expressive or not, EXNEX) and compared the information determining the N170 and categorization behavior. Stimuli

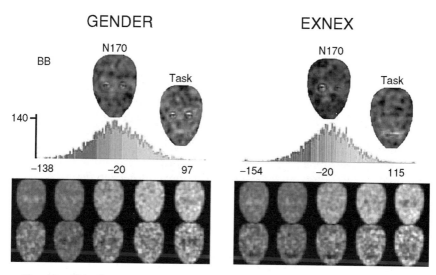

Fig. 11. This figure illustrates the dissociation between diagnostic information for categorization (see Task) and the information to which the N170 responds (see N170) using the bubbles technique (see text for explanations) (see Color Insert).

consisted of 4000 sparse faces (five males, five females, each displaying a happy and a neutral expression) revealed in each task by 14 randomly located Gaussian apertures. Observers resolved the two tasks in two separate experimental sessions while we recorded both their categorization accuracies (Task) and N170 brain response (N170).

The analysis compared the information responsible for explicit categorization behavior and the N170 brain response in GENDER and EXNEX. On each trial of a categorization task, the 14 randomly located Gaussian apertures make up a two-dimensional mask that reveals a sparse face. We measured the N170 in response to this sparse face. Following each task, we divided the N170 distribution into five bins. Each bin determined an N170 amplitude interval within which we added, for each trial, the aperture mask eliciting these amplitudes (see Figure 11). The two rows of pictures below each distribution in Figure 11 represent the average face information samples that elicited the corresponding ranges of amplitudes for correct (top) and incorrect (bottom) trials. We determined the diagnostic categorization information (the pictures labeled "Task" in Figure 11) and the information driving the N170 (the pictures labeled "N170" in Figure 11) from different arithmetic manipulations of the same rows of pictures. For the N170, we summed the average face information sample of the last two bins (the yellow and white bins in Figure 11) and subtracted this from the sum of the first two bins (the red and orange bins in Figure 11)—that is, discrimination image = (bin1+bin2) − (bin4+bin5), collapsing across correct and incorrect responses. For each discrimination image, we computed Z-scores, marked in red the regions of statistically significant discrimination ($p < .01$, in red in each image), and revealed the corresponding face features that discriminate between low and high N170 amplitudes. In GENDER, this computation reveals that the eyes discriminate between high vs. low N170 amplitudes.

To determine the information diagnostic of the categorization task, we performed the following computation—that is, discrimination image = (bin1+bin2+bin4+bin5), only for correct responses/(bin1+bin2+bin4+bin5), collapsed over correct and incorrect responses. For each discrimination image, we computed Z-scores, marked in red the regions of statistically significant discrimination ($p < .01$, in red in each image), and revealed the corresponding face features that were diagnostic of the task. In GENDER, we found that the eyes were diagnostic of GENDER. In GENDER, the information leading to correct categorizations and high N170 amplitudes were correlated. From this correlation, one could infer that the N170 reflects the encoding of the diagnostic features (in this case, the eyes) that observers require to correctly categorize the gender of faces. This conclusion is warranted only if, using the same faces in a categorization task that requires different diagnostic face features, the N170 also responds to this other information. Analysis of behavior in the expression task revealed that correct categorization required the diagnostic use of the mouth (see Figure 11, EXNEX the "Task" pictures). In contrast, the presence of information from the eyes still discriminated between small and large N170 amplitudes, when the mouth did not (see Figure 11, EXNEX, the "N170" pictures). Here, the information leading to correct categorizations and high N170 amplitudes was decorrelated. Thus, the N170 signature does not reflect a use of diagnostic information.

The status of the N170 is therefore not a response to diagnostic features, but instead an automatic response to the eyes. This approach, illustrated with the N170 and face categorization, could be generalized to other event-related potential (ERP) components, to functional magnetic resonance imaging (fMRI) amplitude reponses, or to the firing rates of individual cells or cell assemblies, to gain insight in the brain mechanisms subtending object categorization and recognition.

VII. Conclusions

This chapter developed the Diagnostic Recognition Framework, an approach seeking to explain categorization performance in terms of interactions between the information constraints of categorization tasks and the information available in the input. One explicit goal of Diagnostic Recognition is to bridge between cognition and perception, to develop more powerful theories of categorization.

Starting with the example of Martin cells, we saw how the constraints of discriminating between new categories could create new features that changed the availability of object information and modified the perception of identical objects. In a related vein, the acquisition of subordinate-level expertise with realistic computers and mugs modified the availability of their information and the perception of object changes in a change blindness experiment. Experiments with hybrids also revealed that the constraints of a categorization task modulate the availability and the perception of scale-specific information, a phenomenon related to the monitoring of spatial frequency channels in psychophysics.

These examples suggest that the categorization of the stimulus modifies the availability of visual information, which in turn influences the perception of the input. Thus, a better understanding of the information constraints of categorization tasks would better predict the allocation of attention to object information, and the ensuing perception of the stimulus. To this end, I developed the concept of a diagnostic filtering function. The diagnostic filtering function specifies the information extraction process associated with a categorization task. Using *Bubbles*, we approximated the diagnostic filtering function of three face categorization tasks: Identity, Gender, and Expressive or not. From this account of information use, we could predict the allocation of attention over the face stimulus, scale preferences, and spatial filtering. The implications of spatial filtering were successfully tested with the perception of the ambiguous Salvatore Dali painting. Studies are currently underway to examine the spatial filtering that occurs when observers diagnostically use scale information in face, object, and scene categorization tasks.

One considerable interest of *Bubbles* is that the technique can be used to unravel the information that determines categorization behavior, but also the information that determines brain and other physiological responses. Turning to the N170 as a possible "wave of diagnostic information," we found a decorrelation between the diagnostic information for behavior, which was dependent on the task, and that of the N170, which responded only to the eyes, irrespective of the task.

As discussed earlier, the diagnostic function opens promising new research avenues at the interface between categorization, attention, and stimulus perception. To the extent that the information for categorization is specified, and that this information must be attended and perceived to categorize the stimulus, it becomes possible to better understand how categorization tasks modulate the signal via well-studied mechanisms of spatial frequency processing, contrast modulation, and noise reduction. However, this approach has one main limitation: it focuses on the treatment of the stimulus, not on the representation of object categories per se. This deemphasis of representations stems from methodological and theoretical constraints. Methodologically, we now have tools to better understand what is an effective stimulus, and how this information is coded, but we are still missing the tools to study representations. Theoretically, good hygiene of theory construction recommends that we start thinking from the computational goals of an organism (e.g., recognizing the parts of an object) before considering specific representational schemes (e.g., geons). However, this approach could overrepresent the task constraints in the proposed representational scheme. For example, if we discovered that the information requirements of an object categorization task were X (e.g., recognizing the parts of an object), it would be tempting to assume that X (e.g., parts) effectively represents the object in memory. But then, how would we distinguish a representation of the constraints of a task from the representation of the object itself. By this, I mean that an object representation should encompass many tasks, not just the task under study (see Schyns, 1998, for discussions).

This chapter started with the generic question: "How do input and memory information interact to explain categorization behavior?" I presented Diagnostic Recognition, a framework that expresses recognition and categorization phenomena as interactions between the information demands of categorization tasks and the perceptual availability of object information. This framework raises new issues that could shed some light on the nature of the interactions among categorization, attention, and perception.

ACKNOWLEDGMENTS

I am indebted to Lizann Bonnar, Frederic Gosselin, Ines Jentzsch, Aude Oliva, and Luc Rodet for their invaluable contributions to the research described here. One should not be left with the impression that the research owes more to me than to them. Many of the ideas and experiments described resulted from genuine and often exciting collaborations. This research was funded by ESRC.

REFERENCES

Anderson, J. R. (1991). The adaptive nature of human categorization. *Psychological Review, 98*, 409–429.
Archambault, A., O'Donnell, C., & Schyns, P. G. (1999). Blind to object changes: When learning the same object at different levels of categorization modifies its perception. *Psychological Science, 10*, 249–255.
Barsalou, L. W. (1983). Ad hoc categories. *Memory & Cognition, 11*, 211–227.

Biederman, I. (1987). Recognition-by-components: A theory of human image understanding. *Psychological Review, 94*, 115–147.

Blakemore, C., & Campbell, F. W. (1969). On the existence of neurones in the human visual system selectively sensitive to the orientation and size of retinal images. *Journal of Physiology, 203*, 237–260.

Bonnar, L., Gosselin, F., & Schyns, P. G. (2002). Understanding Dali's *Slave Market with the Disappearing Bust of Voltaire*: A case study in the scale information driving perception. *Perception, 31*, 683–691.

Bourne, L. E., Jr. (1982). Typicality effects in logically defined categories. *Memory & Cognition, 10*, 3–9.

Brown, R. (1958). How shall a thing be called? *Psychological Review, 65*, 14–21.

Bruner, J. S., Goodnow, J., & Austin, G. A. (1956). *A study of thinking*. New York: Wiley.

Dosher, B. A., & Lu, Z. (1998). Perceptual learning reflects internal noise filtering and internal noise reduction through channel reweighting. *Proceedings of the National Academy of Sciences of the United States of America, 95*, 13988–13993.

Estes, W. K. (1986). Array models of category learning. *Cognitive Psychology, 18*, 500–549.

Fisher, D. L. (1986). *Hierarchical models of visual search: Serial and parallel processing*. Paper presented at the meeting of the Society for Mathematical Psychology, Cambridge, MA.

Gibson, J. J. (1979). *The ecological approach to visual perception*. Boston: Houghton Mifflin.

Ginsburg, A. P. (1986). Spatial filtering and visual form perception. In K. R. Boff, L. Kaufman, & J. P. Thomas (Eds.), *Handbook of perception and human performance, II: Cognitive processes and performance*. New York: Wiley.

Gluck, M. A., & Bower, G. H. (1988). Evaluating an adaptive network model of human learning. *Journal of Memory and Language, 27*, 166–195.

Gold, J., Bennett, P., & Sekuler, A. (1999). Signal but not noise changes with perceptual learning. *Nature, 402*, 176–178.

Gosselin, F., & Schyns, P. G. (2001a). Bubbles: A new technique to reveal the use of visual information in recognition tasks. *Vision Research, 41*, 2261–2271.

Gosselin, F., & Schyns, P. G. (2001b). Why do we SLIP to the basic-level? Computational constraints and their implementation. *Psychological Review, 108*, 735–758.

Horton, M. S., & Markman, E. M. (1980). Developmental differences in the acquisition of basic and superordinate categories. *Child Development, 51*, 708–719.

Jolicoeur, P., Gluck, M., & Kosslyn, S. M. (1984). Pictures and names: Making the connection. *Cognitive Psychology, 19*, 31–53.

Kruschke, J. K. (1992). ALCOVE: An exemplar-based connectionist model of category learning. *Psychological Review, 99*, 22–44.

Lamberts, K. (2000). Information-accumulation theory of speeded categorization. *Psychological Review, 107*, 227–260.

Marr, D. (1982). *Vision*. San Francisco: Freeman.

Mervis, C. B., & Crisafi, M. A. (1982). Order of acquisition of subordinate-, basic-, and superordinate-level categories. *Child Development, 53*, 258–266.

Morrisson, D., & Schyns, P. G. (2001). Usage of spatial scales for the categorization of faces, object and scenes. *Psychonomic Bulletin and Review, 8*, 454–469.

Murphy, G. L. (1991). Parts in objects concepts: Experiments with artificial categories. *Memory & Cognition, 19*, 423–438.

Murphy, G. L. (2002). *The big book of concepts*. Cambridge, MA: MIT Press.

Murphy, G. L., & Smith, E. E. (1982). Basic level superiority in picture categorization. *Journal of Verbal Learning and Verbal Behavior, 21*, 1–20.

Nosofsky, R. M. (1984). Choice, similarity, and the context of categorization. *Journal of Experimental Psychology: Learning, Memory, and Cognition, 10*, 104–114.

Nosofsky, R. M. (1986). Attention, similarity, and the identification-categorization relationship. *Journal of Experimental Psychology: General, 115*, 39–57.

Nosofsky, R. M., Gluck, M. A., Palmeri, T. J., McKinley, S. C., & Glauthier, P. (1994). Comparing models of rule-based classification learning: A replication and an extension of Shepard, Hovland, and Jenkins (1961). *Memory & Cognition, 22*, 352–369.

Oliva, A., & Schyns, P. G. (1997). Coarse blobs and fine edges? Evidence that information diagnosticity changes the perception of complex visual stimuli. *Cognitive Psychology, 34*, 72–107.

Palmer, S. E. (1999). *Vision science: Photons to phenomenology*. Cambridge, MA: MIT Press.

Rosch, E., Mervis, C. B., Gray, W. D., Johnson, D. M., & Boyes-Braem, P. (1976). Basic objects in natural categories. *Cognitive Psychology, 8*, 382–439.

Schyns, P. G. (1998). Diagnostic recognition: Task constraints, object information and their interactions. *Cognition, 67*, 147–179.

Schyns, P. G., Bonnar, L., & Gosselin, F. (2002). Show me the features. Understanding recognition from the use of visual information. *Psychological Science, 13*, 402–409.

Schyns, P. G., Goldstone, R. L., & Thibaut, J. P. (1998). The development of features in object concepts. *Behavioral and Brain Sciences, 21*, 17–41.

Schyns, P. G., Jentzsch, I., Johnson, M., Schweinberger, S. R., & Gosselin, F. (2002). A principles method for determining the functionality of ERP components. Submitted.

Schyns, P. G., & Gosselin, F. (2002). A natural bias for basic-level object categorizations. *Journal of Vision, 2*, 7.

Schyns, P. G., & Murphy, G. L. (1994). The ontogeny of part representation in object concepts. In D. L. Medin (Ed.), *The psychology of learning and motivation* (Vol. 31, pp. 301–349). San Diego, CA: Academic Press.

Schyns, P. G., & Oliva, A. (1994). From blobs to boundary edges: Evidence for time-and spatial-scale-dependent scene recognition. *Psychological Science, 5*, 195–200.

Schyns, P. G., & Oliva, A. (1999). Dr. Angry and Mr. Smile: When categorization flexibly modifies the perception of faces in rapid visual presentations. *Cognition, 69*, 243–265.

Schyns, P. G., & Rodet, L. (1997). Categorization creates functional features. *Journal of Experimental Psychology: Learning Memory and Cognition, 23*, 681–696.

Shepard, R. N., Hovland, C. I., & Jenkins, H. M. (1961). Learning and memorization of classifications. *Psychological Monographs, 75*.

Sigala, N., & Logothetis, N. K. (2002). Visual categorization shapes feature selectivity in the primate temporal cortex. *Nature, 415*, 318–320.

Simons, D. J., & Levin, D. T. (1997). Change blindness. *Trends in Cognitive Sciences, 1*, 261–267.

Sowden, P. T., Ozgen, E., & Schyns, P. G. (2002). Expectancy effects on spatial frequency processing. Submitted.

Tanaka, J. W., & Taylor, M. (1991). Object categories and expertise: Is the basic level in the eye of the beholder? *Cognitive Psychology, 23*, 457–482.

Tversky, B., & Hemenway, K. (1984). Objects, parts and categories. *Journal of Experimental Psychology: General, 113*, 169–191.

Wilson, H. R., & Bergen, J. R. (1979). A four mechanism model for spatial vision. *Vision Research, 19*, 1177–1190.

Wisniewski, E. J., & Murphy, G. L. (1989). Superordinate and basic category names in discourse: A textual analysis. *Discourse Processing, 12*, 245–261.

Yeshurun, Y., & Carrasco, M. (1998). Attention improves or impairs visual performance by enhancing spatial resolution. *Nature, 396*, 72–75.

FROM VISION TO ACTION AND ACTION TO VISION: A CONVERGENT ROUTE APPROACH TO VISION, ACTION, AND ATTENTION

Glyn W. Humphreys and M. Jane Riddoch

I. Introduction

Mutual interactions between vision and action determine both what we see and what behaviors are selected to stimuli. Experimental, neuropsychological, computational, and functional imaging studies indicate that vision can directly lead to the activation of categorical actions to objects, not mediated by conceptual/semantic knowledge. Experimental and neuro-psychological evidence indicates that action also affects vision by (1) "weighting" action-related properties of stimuli and by (2) binding together separate objects that are in appropriate relations for action. Vision and action are coupled through processes of selective attention, and, in particular, through the interaction between perceptual selection and selection of the response to a stimulus. This interactive framework provides a means of understanding normal behavior and a wide spectrum of neuropsychological disorders.

II. From Vision to Action

Consider the object illustrated in Figure 1. Judged by a coarse test carried out with our own students, this object is highly unfamiliar for a large

Fig. 1.   An example of an unfamiliar object (an "olive-pitter") to which participants
nevertheless make a consistent action (pushing down the top section).

proportion of the UK undergraduate population, who report that they have
never seen it before. Nevertheless, when asked how they might use the object
there is considerable consensus—most students reply that they would push
the top "arm" of the object down so that the attached vertical part plunges
through the circle beneath it. This action happens to be correct, for the
object is designed to take stones out of olives. However, the interesting point
is that participants can make accurate judgments about how an object such
as this can be used even if they have never encountered the object before and
have no "learned concept" about the stimulus. The visual properties of this
object can be used to infer a possible action, and this can take place
independently of our conceptual knowledge about the object. There can be a
direct link between vision and action, not mediated by conceptual knowledge.
    This article examines whether, beyond our coarse sampling of students,
there is evidence for a direct route between action and vision. In addition,
we ask whether information about action itself interacts with vision in a
direct way, influencing what we see. We consider evidence from a range of
sources (experimental, neuropsychological, brain imaging, and computational modeling) that supports the existence of a route from vision to
action and that tells us about its nature. We ask, is the route set up "on the
fly" by inferential reasoning and problem solving, or does it operate
automatically, even when a task does not demand it? If a direct link
operates automatically, then on what kinds of information does it depend?
For example, does it depend on stored perceptual representations, and are
these stored perceptual representations coded for possible action-based
relations between the parts of objects? Are directly evoked actions sensitive
to the perceptual relations between multiple objects? We present an
argument for a direct route from vision to action that is sensitive to stored
perceptual knowledge about single objects and to learned "procedural"
relations between objects. We suggest that this route normally works
cooperatively with information derived from other sources (including
conceptual knowledge about objects) to constrain actions, and we show
how such a "convergent route" model can simulate data from both normal

and pathological performance (e.g., in patients with brain lesions). In the next section, we go on to show how this is not a one-way process: action influences vision as well as vision action. We propose that there are reciprocal links from action to vision, so that what we see can be influenced both by what we do and by "action relations" between objects in the world. Action is intrinsic to the way we see the world.

A. FROM PREHENSILE ACTION TO CATEGORICAL ACTIONS

Over the past 10 years, there has been mounting evidence (albeit some of it controversial) that the perceptual information used for action can be distinguished from the perceptual information used for simple prehensile actions, such as reaching to and grasping an implement. Perhaps the strongest argument for this comes from the neuropsychological dissociation between visual agnosia and optic ataxia. Visual agnosic patients fail to recognize objects (see Riddoch & Humphreys, 1987a), and, in some cases, they may fail even on simple perceptual judgments about the orientation or size of stimuli. Despite poor perceptual judgments, such patients can reach appropriately to stimuli. For example, Milner et al. (1991) documented patient DF who was severely impaired at judging the orientation of a slot in a surface, yet could reach accurately to post a letter through the slot, orienting her hand correctly in the process. In contrast to this, optic ataxic patients can make accurate perceptual judgments (about line orientation) but be impaired at placing their fingers in the correct relative orientations to guide their hand through a slit (Perenin & Vighetto, 1988). From this double dissociation, Milner and Goodale (1995) argued that the visual information used for action was independent of the visual information used both for conscious perceptual judgments and for object recognition. In addition they linked vision for action to a dorsal (occipitoparietal) pathway damaged in optic ataxia, and vision for perceptual judgments and recognition to a ventral (occipitotemporal) pathway damaged in agnosia. Other evidence supporting the distinction between vision for action and vision for perceptual judgments/recognition comes from contrasts between immediate and delayed action (only immediate action appearing to be guided by the dorsal system; see Milner, Paulignan, Dijkerman, Michel, & Jeannerod, 1999), from differences in the effects of location and color changes during reaching actions (Pisella et al., 2000), and from differential effects of illusions on reaching and grasping and perceptual judgments (Aglioti, DeSouza, & Goodale, 1995; Bridgeman, 2002; Haffenden & Goodale, 1998; though see Franz, Gegenfurtner, Bülthoff, & Fahle, 2000; Pavani, Boscagli, Benvenuti, Ratbuffetti, & Farne, 1999, for contrary arguments; see Rossetti & Pisella, 2002, for an overview).

There is certainly evidence in this literature that visual information may be used directly, and independent of object recognition processes, to control prehensile actions. Our concern, however, is not with the guidance of immediate, prehensile actions to objects, but with the processes leading to what we might term a "categorical action" to an object—for example, to drink rather than pour into a cup. This requires not only reaching and grasping, but also the selection of an appropriate class of action to the stimulus. Our question is whether this kind of categorical action is accessed directly from vision, without being mediated by conceptual knowledge about the object—where, by conceptual knowledge, we mean abstracted knowledge about (1) the function of an object that can be applied in different contexts and about (2) its associative relationship with other objects. We begin by again taking neuropsychological evidence, this time based on the distinction between disorders such as optic aphasia and semantic dementia, on the one hand, and visual apraxia on the other. We propose that the double dissociation between these disorders supports the idea of a direct route from vision to the selection of categorical action. We then consider experimental evidence for the direct route from normal participants.

B. Neuropsychological Evidence for a Direct Route to Action

1. Optic Aphasia

Optic aphasia, as the name indicates, refers to a modality-specific naming disorder, where a patient is impaired at naming visually presented stimuli. The problem was first described by Freund in 1889, and has been documented in a number of subsequent cases (e.g., Beauvois, 1982; Coslett & Saffran, 1992; Hillis & Caramazza, 1995; Lhermitte & Beauvois, 1973; Manning & Campbell, 1992; Riddoch & Humphreys, 1987b). The cardinal symptoms of optic aphasia are that a patient has problems in naming visually presented objects, but is much better at generating the same names when given a verbal definition for the stimuli. In addition, such patients are typically able to make relatively good gestures to the items that they cannot name. Such good gestures have often been taken to indicate that the patients gain full access to conceptual knowledge about objects, but then fail at a name retrieval stage (Lhermitte & Beauvois, 1973). However, in two cases in which the investigators tested detailed conceptual knowledge about the stimuli using matching tasks, the patients showed a modality-specific deficit in performance. In our study (Riddoch & Humphreys, 1987b) the patient, JB, was presented with three objects from the same category (e.g., hammer, nail, spanner) and he was required to pick the two that would be used together (hammer and nail, in this example). Though JB was above-chance at this task, he was nevertheless impaired relative to when he was given the names and performed the task verbally. Thus he did have conceptual knowledge about which objects were associated together, but he was impaired at accessing this knowledge from vision. Despite this, JB made many precise gestures to objects, some of which were even hand-specific (responding with his right hand to a knife but his left hand to a fork). In fact, on many of the occasions where JB named the object from vision, he seemed to do so on the basis of the gestures that he had made beforehand. Quite similar results were reported by Hillis and Caramazza (1995).

How are patients such as JB able to make precise gestures to visually presented objects if they are unable to access detailed conceptual representations? To account for this, we proposed that JB gestured using a direct route from stored perceptual knowledge about the stimulus to associated actions, which by-passed stored conceptual knowledge (Riddoch & Humphreys, 1987b). This pathway is outlined in Figure 2. Consistent with this proposal, we also found that JB had intact access to stored perceptual knowledge about objects, for example, he performed well on difficult object decision tasks requiring discrimination between real objects and nonobjects created by combining the parts of different, real objects. Alternatively, optic aphasic patients may be able to gesture based on partial access to conceptual knowledge (as shown by above-chance performance on associative matching tests) along with inferences concerning action derived from the shape of the

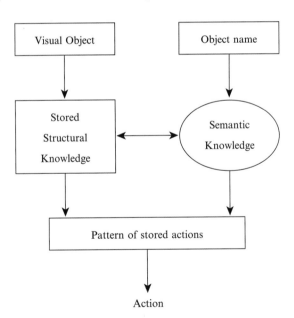

Fig. 2.   A dual-route model of action selection (adapted from Riddoch et al., 1989).

object (Hillis & Caramazza, 1995). The evidence indicates that actions can be formed even when conceptual knowledge accessed from stimuli is deficient.

2. Semantic Dementia

Other neuropsychological evidence indicating that actions can be relatively preserved when access to conceptual knowledge is impaired comes from semantic dementia. The term semantic dementia is applied to patients with progressive, degenerative loss of tissue, initially in the medial and anterior temporal lobes, which is histologically distinct from Alzheimer's disease (Garrard, Lambon Ralph, & Hodges, 2002). The syndrome is characterized by the gradual degeneration of knowledge about facts, objects, and the meanings of words. In contrast to Alzheimer's disease, short-term (working) memory and episodic memory can be good; in addition, spatial processing and nonverbal problem solving can be spared (Snowden, Goulding, & Neary, 1989). Patients with semantic dementia are typically impaired on tasks assessing their conceptual knowledge about objects. They may be unable to define what objects are, they can be impaired at assigning objects to their categories, and they may find it difficult to match associatively related objects. Does this mean that such patients are also impaired at object use?

In a group study of semantic dementia patients, Hodges, Bozeat, Lambon Ralph, Patterson, and Spatt (2000) reported both that the patients were generally impaired at using objects and also that the degree of impairment on tests of conceptual knowledge correlated with the ability of the patients to use objects appropriately. This result suggests that object use is dependent on conceptual knowledge. On the other hand, this does not mean that intact conceptual knowledge is necessary for objects to be used correctly. Patients in whom the dementia has progressed may well have a range of problems that may affect a direct visual route to action in addition to effects on conceptual knowledge. Correlations across a group of patients are not particularly informative about whether, on an individual basis, patients remain able to use objects when conceptual knowledge is impaired. It is interesting in this respect to note single cases reported by Hodges, Spatt, and Patterson (1999) who were able to make judgments about how novel objects might be used, despite demonstrating poor conceptual knowledge on formal testing.

In other instances, patients with semantic dementia have been documented where the ability not only to use single objects but also to employ them in multistep tasks has been preserved. Lauro-Grotto, Piccini, and Shallice (1997), for example, described a patient RM with poor object naming and who was impaired at making semantic judgments with words. Nevertheless, RM remained able to shop and to cook complex meals, presumably using the utensils appropriately. Lauro-Grotto et al. also noted that RM was better at semantic matching tasks with pictures than words, and suggested that she was still able to access conceptual knowledge from objects. It is possible that, in this case, at least residual support from a conceptual/semantic memory system helped actions to be performed correctly. A yet more striking dissociation, though, was reported by Riddoch, Humphreys, Heslop, and Castermans (2002). They compared patient MC to a group of "control" dementia patients. Relative to this control group, MC was reliably worse at categorizing and providing definitions to pictures relative to words. In this case, there was evidence of impairment of visual access to conceptual knowledge about objects. However, like RM (Lauro-Grotto et al., 1997), MC performed well when asked to carry out everyday life tasks with the objects (e.g., make a cup of tea using a kettle, a teapot, a cup, a spoon, milk, and sugar), and in fact she tended to be better than not only the dementia controls but also the non-brain-damaged controls at generating correct actions in the correct sequences when performing the tasks. She also made more correct sequential actions when using the objects than when she was asked to sequence cards in which the action steps were written (though she was able to read the words aloud). Thus, when using the objects, MC showed the opposite pattern (with objects being better than words) than she did on tests of conceptual knowledge from single items (when words were better than objects). This evidence indicates that patients may still use objects appropriately even when access to conceptual knowledge is impaired. The result is consistent with the everyday tasks being supported by a direct visual route to action, which is relatively preserved in such cases. Note that this evidence for relatively preserved use of objects together, in everyday, multistep tasks, suggests that direct links between vision and action can be sensitive to learned "procedural" knowledge of how one object is used in connection with another.

3. Visual Apraxia

Visual apraxia presents a picture opposite to optic aphasia and semantic dementia, in that visual apraxic patients can be impaired at using visually presented objects even though they have intact access to conceptual knowledge. Patients are labeled as apraxic if they have difficulty in performing skilled, learned movements that cannot be explained in terms of a pure motor deficit, general intellectual deterioration, or defective comprehension (Liepmann, 1905; Rothi & Heilman, 1997). In visual apraxia, the problem in action is worse when stimuli are presented visually than when they are presented verbally (as written or spoken words). Visual apraxia was first documented by De Renzi, Faglioni, and Sorgato (1982), who noted this pattern of performance in a subset of a group of patients; more detailed case studies have been reported by Pilgrim and Humphreys (1991) and by Riddoch, Humphreys, and Price (1989). The detailed case studies demonstrate that visual apraxic patients can have intact visual access to conceptual knowledge, judged from semantic matching tasks, and they may even be able to name the object presented to them. Despite this, the patients are impaired at gesturing the appropriate action. Thus there is the opposite profile of performance to optic aphasic and semantic dementia patients. Optic aphasics and semantic dementia cases can show good object use when access to conceptual knowledge is impaired; visual apraxic patients can have good access to conceptual knowledge but are deficient at making actions to visually presented objects.

One other striking result in visual apraxia is that the patients can gesture the action when just given the object's name, without the object being shown. In such patients, actions can be made on the basis of conceptual knowledge from verbal input, but actions seemed to be blocked when objects are present. To account for this pattern, Riddoch et al. (1989) proposed that there was damage to a visual route to action, and that this interfered with the retrieval of actions from conceptual knowledge. Interestingly, this disruptive effect of vision on action retrieval suggests that any direct link between vision and categorical action is not based just on inference and visual problem solving, but rather it operates in a more automatic fashion, even when it is disruptive to task performance (in patients with visual apraxia). In the section on formal modeling, we return to consider the implications of this result on visual blocking for understanding action retrieval from vision.

C. Evidence from Normal Participants

1. Action Errors

Although neuropsychological cases can provide clear dissociations between the ability to make actions and the ability to access conceptual knowledge, converging evidence can be derived from normal participants under particular conditions. Diary studies of action slips, for example, reveal that we all make occasional errors in using objects, especially under conditions in which we are distracted (see Reason, 1984). Sometimes, these action slips suggest that actions may be based on the visual properties of objects without our having gained full access to conceptual knowledge about the individual stimuli—an example might be using a can of shaving foam as hair spray (which, we presume, would arise when the shaving foam has not been recognized!). However, it is difficult to ascertain from such examples whether errors reflect activation within a direct visual route to action or whether they reflect misrecognition of the objects in the first place (e.g., perhaps under difficult viewing conditions). If there is misrecognition, then actions would be based on conceptual information (rather than on direct activation of actions from vision), but the conceptual information would simply be incorrect in this instance.

Rumiati and Humphreys (1998) developed an experimental analogue of the everyday action errors that was useful for at least two reasons. One is that it generated increased numbers of errors, so that we could begin to assess more systematically the conditions under which action errors occur. A second is that access to conceptual knowledge could be assessed alongside the retrieval of actions to objects. From this we may judge whether "visual action errors" (e.g., shaving foam used as hair spray) reflect misrecognitions or early activation of actions based on visual rather than semantic properties of objects. To generate action errors, Rumiati and Humphreys had normal participants make gestures to objects under response deadline conditions (they had to respond faster than normal, to "beat" a timed "beep"). Error rates were raised under these conditions. When pictures of objects were shown, participants made a relatively high number of "visual" gesture errors, in which the response was related to the visual rather than the semantic properties of a target (e.g., making a shaving gesture to a hammer—this was termed a visual error because the hammer looked like a razor rather than the two stimuli sharing common conceptual features). Other errors tended to be both visually and semantically related to target objects (e.g., making a drinking action to a jug, as if the target was a cup; in this case the jug shares perceptual features with the cup and it is semantically related). In contrast, when gesturing to deadline was examined to word targets, the errors were either both visually and semantically related or just semantically related to the targets (e.g., making a drinking gesture for a cup to the word saucer). This last result suggests that gestures to words were based on semantic/conceptual knowledge, and that "visually related" gesture errors to pictures did not occur simply because these gestures were frequently made to the particular items involved. The visual errors in gesturing to objects also contrasted with the naming errors that arose under deadline conditions, which were predominantly either semantically related or both visually and semantically related to the targets. The increase in visual gesture relative to visual naming errors indicates that visual gesture errors did not arise solely due to visual misrecognition of stimuli. Instead, the data suggest that proportionately high numbers of visual gesture errors occur due to activation of actions along a direct visual route. Under deadline conditions, actions may be initiated before full processing is completed along both a direct visual route to action and a route mediated by access to conceptual knowledge (see Figure 2); the result is errors based on the shared visual properties of stimuli as well as on shared visual and conceptual properties.

2. Action and Semantic (Context) Decisions to Words and Pictures

The tendency for high numbers of visual errors to occur when gestures are made to a deadline (Rumiati & Humphreys, 1998) provides some indication that direct visual access to action may take place in a relatively rapid fashion. It follows that visually derived activation then sometimes affects action selection prior to activation mediated by conceptual/semantic knowledge. Other evidence for fast direct activation of action from vision comes from comparisons between the time taken by normal participants to make action vs. associative (semantic) decisions about stimuli. Chainay and Humphreys (2002a) had normal participants make either an action decision to a stimulus (would you use this to make a twisting or a pouring action?) or a decision about the context in which a stimulus would typically be found (would you use this object indoors or outdoors?). The stimuli were presented as either pictures or words. Previously, Potter and Faulconer (1975) had shown that semantic categorization decisions could be made faster to pictures than to words, and this has provided some of the primary support for the idea that there is privileged access to semantic/conceptual knowledge from objects relative to words (e.g., Caramazza, Hillis, Rapp, & Romani, 1990). However, is there privileged access to all types of knowledge or is the difference between pictures and words most pronounced for tasks mediated by the retrieval of action knowledge, which may be rapidly activated by pictures through a direct route to action? Chainay and Humphreys (2002a) found that pictures were advantaged relative to words for the action decision compared with the semantic decision, about where an object would be used. This was not due to simple object features being correlated with the action decision, since care was taken not to have a common feature (e.g., the presence of a thread or a lip on a container) across the items assigning to the "twisting" and "pouring" categories. In addition, action decisions were faster to objects than to nonobjects, chosen to share critical features with objects. Hence it appears that there is privileged access to actions from objects relative to words, over and above any differences in access to more abstract functional and contextual knowledge (e.g., that serves as the basis of deciding whether an object is used indoors or out of doors). This is consistent with a direct route to action existing for objects but not for words. The fact that action decisions were faster to objects than nonobjects also suggests that this direct route is sensitive to stored knowledge about object–action relations.

3. *Affordance Effects with Normal Participants*

Further evidence that visual properties of objects affect action selection in a rather direct way comes from studies of "affordances" on normal performance. The term affordance was first introduced by Gibson (1979) to describe intrinsic perceptual properties of objects that provide the potential for action. For example, the handle of a cup can be said to afford grasping, the sharp edge of a knife may afford cutting, and so forth. Although this term has been employed in the context of theories of direct perception, where it is assumed that we do not need to posit intervening representational processes to explain behavior, we use it outside of this context and indeed we assume that activation of actions, based on affordances (action-related perceptual properties of objects), is contingent on access to perceptual representations about object parts or even whole objects.

Tucker and Ellis (1998, 2001; Ellis & Tucker, 2000) had normal participants make decisions about whether objects were depicted in an upright or an inverted orientation, with the response signalled by a right- or left-hand button press. The objects had handles turned to the left or right. Tucker and Ellis found a compatibility effect between the orientation of the object's handle and the hand used for the response, even though the orientation of the handle was irrelevant to the task. Right-hand responses were speeded when the handles faced to the right and left-hand responses when the handles faced left. Tucker and Ellis interpreted the result as indicating a potential action to an object (linked to the orientation of the handle) was automatically invoked even when observers made a decision as to whether objects were upright or inverted. The affordance of the object (e.g., for a grasping response to the handle) potentiates a motor response with the affected hand. This may reflect a form of spatial compatibility effect, in this case contingent on the spatial relations between a part of an object used for action and the hand used for response.

However, other researchers have queried whether the compatibility effects observed by Tucker and Ellis reflect direct object–action relations, or whether they are caused by compatibility between more abstract spatial codes sensitive to both the hand for action and the orientation of the object (see Hommel, 2000, for a discussion of the role of abstract codes in other spatial compatibility effects). Phillips and Ward (2002) presented a picture of an object with its handle oriented either left or right (the prime), followed by an imperative (target) stimulus to which a left- or right-hand button-press was made. Like Tucker and Ellis, Phillips and Ward also found a compatibility effect on performance; responses were speeded when the orientation of the prime matched the hand used to respond to the target. To test whether the compatibility effect resulted from a response by a specific hand being potentiated by the prime, Phillips and Ward had participants cross their hands so that a left-hand response was now made to the right imperative stimulus, and vice versa for the left imperative stimulus. They again found a compatibility effect, but this was based on the side of response, not the hand used. When the handle of the prime was on the right, a response on the right side was speeded, even though this was now made with the left hand. Phillips and Ward suggest that the compatibility effects here reflect the overlap in spatial codes between stimuli and responses, not the automatic activation of a hand for a response. Indeed, these investigators also found a compatibility effect between the side of the handle and whether a right or left foot-press response was made; it is difficult to account for this result in terms of an affordance potentiating the specific effector used in the task.

Nevertheless, other results in the literature are less easy to attribute to effects of spatial compatibility rather than compatibility between the action-related parts of objects and the associated action. For example, Tucker and Ellis (2001) have extended their results beyond the orientation of the handle of an object to reveal effects of the compatibility of the grip required for the response. A power-grip response is facilitated if the object requires a power grip, whereas a fine-grip response is speeded to objects that take a fine grip. Pavese and Buxbaum (2002) have also demonstrated interference effects from distractors depending upon whether they require the same or a different response to a target object. Two objects were presented on a trial, at any of four locations, and the target was defined by its color. Rather than making a simple button-press response, participants either grasped the target or they reached and pressed a button on the target's surface. The contrasting responses were made in different blocks of trials. The time to initiate the response to a button-press target was slowed when the distractor also required a button-press relative to when a grasp response would be made to it. The opposite result occurred when a grasp response had to be made to the target. In these last studies, responses are in all cases made with the same effector and so cannot be attributed to spatial overlap between different effectors and response-related properties of stimuli. The results do, however, fit with the idea that specific responses are cued by response-related properties of objects (affordances). The evidence on interference effects, when distractors "afford" the response that should be made to the target, further indicates that such effects can arise in a relatively automatic way. There are some constraints, however. One is that the interference is specific to when the response-related visual properties of distractors are relevant to the required response (grasping vs. pressing, in Pavese & Buxbaum, 2002). Objects afford action, but this is governed by the task set. This proposal is also supported by neuropsychological evidence on the "anarchic hand syndrome" discussed below.

D. THE NATURE OF THE DIRECT ROUTE

If there is a direct route from vision to action that can operate in a relatively automatic manner (but governed by task set), what is its nature? Is the route sensitive to learned relations between objects and action, or would nonobjects with the appropriate parts invoke actions as strongly as familiar objects? If the route is sensitive to stored representations, what form do these representations take? Again neuropsychological studies have been helpful in suggesting answers to these questions.

1. Anarchic Hand Syndrome and "Utilization Behavior" after Frontal Lobe Damage

"Anarchic hand" behavior, often linked to the syndrome of corticobasal degeneration (affecting connections into frontal cortex, plus also the corpus callosum), is used to describe instances in which a patient's hand moves in a manner that the patient does not intentionally control (e.g., Della Sala, Marchetti, & Spinnler, 1991). Although usually described anecdotally, Riddoch et al. (1998) and Riddoch, Humphreys, and Edwards (2000a,b) were able to assess experimentally the factors that determined behavior by the affected hand. In their study, the patient was required to reach to and grasp a cup placed either on the left or right side of a table using the hand aligned with the cup (using the right hand to reach to a cup on the right and the left hand to reach a cup on the left). The handle of the cup could be oriented to the right or left, but this was not relevant to the task. Although their patient, ES, was able to understand the instructions, she nevertheless made many errors by reaching to a cup with the wrong hand, and this was affected by the orientation of the cup's handle. Many errors were made by reaching automatically with the right hand to a cup on the left whose handle was oriented to the right (see Figure 3). Such errors are consistent with the right-oriented cup invoking a right-handed grasp response, which ES was unable to inhibit. There were several other aspects to the case. One is that these involuntary responses were controlled by the task set. When the task was to point to rather than grasp the cups, far fewer errors occurred. Apparently the affordance of the handle for grasping was effective primarily when grasping was the required response. In addition, the likelihood of incorrect reaches varied according to the properties of the stimulus. If the cup was turned upside down, incorrect

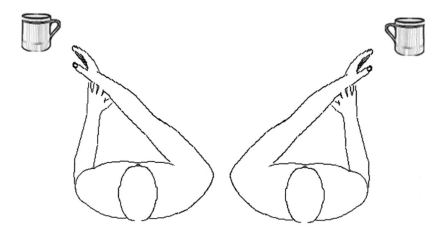

Fig. 3. Illustration of the paradigm used to elicit anarchic hand and utilization errors experimentally. The task was to reach to the cup using the hand on the side where the object was placed (after Riddoch et al., 1998). The examples illustrate error trials.

reaches decreased[1]; if a nonobject with a main container and a handle was substituted for the cup, the incorrect reaching errors again decreased. These last results are important since they indicate a role for stored knowledge in the automatic activation of actions by objects. If the object is unfamiliar (a nonobject) or a familiar object in an unfamiliar orientation (an inverted cup), the associated response is less likely to be invoked. Nevertheless, some incorrect reaches were made even in these last cases, indicating that actions may be activated to some degree even by parts of objects, when the parts relate to the goal of the task. A final point to raise here is that we found similar effects with ES, but this time on automatic leg and foot movements when she had to place her feet in shoes placed on the right or left of her body (using either right or left shoes; Riddoch, Humphreys, & Edwards, 2001). Thus, in this instance, there was a generalized problem of motor control, contingent on whether the stimuli afforded the action within the task. However, foot movements were not made to cups and hand movements were not made to shoes—incorrect actions were confined to the associated effector.

---

[1] Note that this meant that ES reached with her left hand to grasp an inverted cup on the left whose handle was oriented to the right, even though the final lifting response was somewhat awkward and at least as awkward as that involved when picking up an upright cup with its handle on the right with the left hand. The awkwardness of the final lifting response was not a critical factor here.

Although we first investigated stimulus-cued automatic actions in the context of corticobasal degeneration, we have replicated the results in a patient with medial frontal lobe damage (Riddoch et al., 2000b, patient FK). Patients with frontal lobe damage have been described as showing "utilization behavior" in which they respond directly to stimuli in the environment in a manner that appears unconstrained by the task instructions. Lhermitte (1983), for example, described examples in which the experimenter repeatedly put a pair of glasses on a table and found that a patient picked up each pair and placed them on his nose, even if there were already pairs there! Again it seems that these behaviors reflect the strength of the learned response to a visual stimulus, with patients finding it difficult to select the task-appropriate response when another, overlearned action is invoked. When patient FK was asked to carry out the same reach-and-grasp task as ES (reach with your left hand to a cup on the left and with your right hand to a cup on your right), he made many errors by reaching with his right hand to a cup on his left whose handle faced right. This is consistent with affordances being sensitive of the orientation of the objects with respect to the effector. We also noticed one other interesting result, relevant to the work on "affordance effects" with normal subjects (particularly Phillips & Ward, 2002). We had FK perform a second task in which he had to respond directly with an "afforded action" (Humphreys & Riddoch, 2000; Riddoch et al., 2000b). In this second task, FK had to grasp a target cup at the center of the table in front of him, using his right hand if the cup's handle was on the right, and his left hand if its handle was on the left. We then placed another distractor cup along the reach trajectory of either his right or left hand to the target cup (see Figure 4). FK typically responded with the hand cued by the orientation of the target cup, indicating that he was able to select the target for action (a point we return to at the end of the chapter, when we discuss the relations between action and attention). However, if the distractor cup lay in the reach trajectory of the hand to the target, then FK often made errors by picking up the distractor rather than the target. It appeared that the distractor along the reach trajectory captured the response activated initially by the target. In a further manipulation (Humphreys & Riddoch, 2000) FK started from a position with crossed hands (Figure 4, right). FK again made errors by picking up the distractor, and again this occurred when the distractor fell in the reach trajectory for the hand cued by the orientation of the target—for example, if the target cup was oriented to the right, he would pick up a distractor in the reach trajectory from the right hand to the target, even though this was on the left side of his body (as in Figure 4, right). Here the effect was specific to the hand cued by the target being captured by the distractor used and it cannot be attributed to effects of spatial compatibility (unlike the findings

Fig. 4.   Illustration of the paradigm used to elicit "distractor capture" errors in action, in a patient with medial frontal lobe damage (after Humphreys & Riddoch, 2000). The task here would be to pick up the black cup using the hand cued by the handle (the right hand). On the left, a trial that was likely to elicit a distractor capture error with uncrossed hands; on the right, a trial likely to elicit a distractor capture error with crossed hands.

of Phillips & Ward, 2002). The result is similar to data on distractor interference in normal participants reported by Tipper and colleagues (Meegan & Tipper, 1999; Tipper, Howard, & Jackson, 1997). These researchers have demonstrated that interference in a task requiring a pointing response to a target is most pronounced when the distractor is close to the hand used for reaching. Interestingly, Tipper, Howard, and Houghton (1998) reported that distractors interfere less when covered by a transparent surface, because their visual properties no longer provide such a strong response signal (see Tipper, Meegan, & Howard, 2002). In addition, the pattern of interference effects changed when a verbal rather than a reaching response was made to the target. These data are again consistent with a response being directly activated by the visual properties of the environment, when a particular motor task is performed.

Humphreys and Riddoch (2000) also showed that distractor "capture" effects, in their frontal lobe patient FK, were influenced by learned relations between stimuli. When the target was a cup and the distractor a jug (used to pour into the cup), then distractor capture errors occurred. FK frequently picked up the jug en route to the cup. However, when the items were reversed (target = jug, distractor = cup), fewer errors arose—he tended not to pick up the cup en route to the jug. The likelihood of the distractor taking over the response cued by the target was increased when the distractor was frequently used in relation to the target (the jug, used to pour into the cup, but not vice versa). Again it seems that any direct visual activation of a response was influenced by past learning (and interobject action associations).

2. Perceptual Knowledge Sensitive to Action: Evidence from a Case of Semantic Impairment

If direct visual access to action is sensitive to past learning, we can also ask about the nature of the representations involved. For example, if actions are evoked most strongly by known objects (Riddoch et al., 1998), this presumably means that the activation of actions is contingent on access to stored perceptual representations of stimuli. If these stored perceptual representations are part of a direct route, then they too should be independent of semantic knowledge.

We have recently derived evidence on this from a case study of a patient with access to stored perceptual knowledge, despite having impaired semantic knowledge. The patient, JP, suffered a stroke that affected the left inferior and medial frontal cortex. Subsequently, she had minimal spoken and written output, but could match some pictures to words. JP's ability to match words to pictures was particularly poor for tools and body parts, compared to objects from other categories. For the categories of animals, fruits, vegetables, musical instruments, clothing, and furniture she scored about 70% correct when required to match a word to one of six pictures; for tools and body parts she scored at chance. This was not simply a problem with words, since she also scored at chance when matching a picture of one tool to other tools with which it would be used (e.g., matching a nail to a hammer rather than to other tools). For the other categories, associative picture matching was around the 60% level. The poor picture–word matching for tools and body parts was also most pronounced when the distractors belonged to similar categories, and matching performance improved when the distractors were drawn from different categories. This is consistent with JP having a deficit in accessing semantic knowledge for tools and body parts, so that she derives only coarse semantic information about the items.

Despite this, JP scored well on some tasks requiring her to discriminate between photographs of real objects and of nonobjects created by moving the parts of the real objects (see Figure 5a). In this case her "object decision" performance (deciding which was a real object and which was not) was close to controls. In contrast, she was greatly impaired when we created

(a)

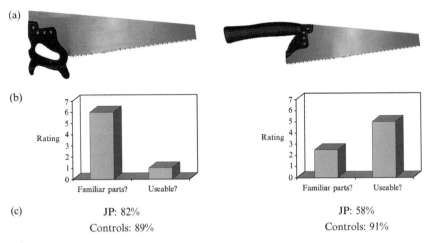

(b)

(c)   JP: 82%   JP: 58%
              Controls: 89%   Controls: 91%

Fig. 5.   (a) Example of the nonobjects used in an object decision task with patient JP (with a
semantic deficit for tools) and controls. On the left, the nonobject is created by moving the parts
of a familiar object; on the right, the nonobject is created by substituting a part of one object
with the equivalent part from a different object (the handle of the saw is replaced with the
handle of a hammer). (b) Ratings from independent participants. The task was to rate whether
the parts of the nonobjects were familiar together, and whether the nonobject was usable
(1=low, 7=high). (c) The percentage correct responses in object decision by JP and by age-
matched controls. The familiar objects were always the same but the two types of nonobjects
were blocked.

nonobjects by interchanging the parts of objects to create stimuli that could
plausibly be used for action (Figure 5b—note that chance was 50% in this
task). We verified the difference between these two types of nonobject by
having normal participants rate (1) how familiar the parts were together and
(2) whether the stimulus was usable. Nonobjects of the type shown in
Figure 5a (left) were judged as having familiar parts but were nonusable.
Nonobjects of the type shown in Figure 5a (right) were judged as usable but
also as having parts that were not familiar together. JP was unable to
discriminate real objects and nonobjects when the nonobjects appeared to
be usable. We suggest that this indicates that despite her severely impaired
semantic knowledge, she could still access perceptual knowledge that was
sensitive to whether an object was usable. By extension we may speculate
that our perceptual knowledge codes the parts of objects in relation to the
actions that may be performed on them. This knowledge may be preserved
even when general associative and contextual knowledge about the world
is lost. It is also interesting that JP was able to make plausible actions to
about 90% of the tools with which she was presented, despite her evident
semantic problem. This again provides evidence for a direct route from

vision to action, operating independently on conceptual/semantic knowledge about objects.

3. Actions to Parts and Wholes: Evidence from Apraxia

In addition to being sensitive to what we might term the action-based relations between object parts, there is also neuropsychological evidence for particular parts linking to action. Evidence for this comes from apraxia. As we have noted, apraxic patients are selectively impaired at making actions to objects. Chainay and Humphreys (2002b) tested three apraxic patients with nonobjects similar to those depicted in Figure 5b, asking each patient to make a gesture appropriate to either part of the nonobject ("make the action for the object that has this part of the nonobject," where the experimenter points to the critical part[2]). They found that the patients were relatively good at acting to what we will label the "action part" of the nonobject—that is, the part that would come into contact when other objects were acted upon [in the example in Figure 5a (right), they may make a sawing gesture when the experimenter pointed to the blade of the saw]. However, the patients were poor at gesturing the appropriate response to the "nonaction" part of the stimulus (e.g., the handle), even when they could name the object from which that part came. For example, in Figure 5a (right), the patients might be able to identify that the handle came from a hammer, but they were impaired at making an action appropriate to this object from the part depicted. The differential gesturing to the "action" and "nonaction" parts of nonobjects, even when the parent objects for the parts are named, indicates that actions can be made directly to parts, as well as to more wholistic representations in which the spatial relations between the parts are coded.

In sum, the neuropsychological data suggest that the direct route from vision to categorical action is (1) sensitive to the familiarity of objects, as well as to factors such as viewpoint (whether or not a handle is turned toward an effector), (2) supported by perceptual representations that code parts in relation to action, but also (3) actions can be invoked directly from "action parts," in addition to effects supported by more holistic perceptual codes.

E. THE CONVERGENT ROUTE MODEL

1. Simulating Normal and Pathological Performance

We have discussed both neuropsychological and experimental data from normal participants that are consistent with there being a direct

---

[2] Unlike visual apraxic patients such as CD (Riddoch et al., 1989), these patients were impaired when tested in all modalities.

(nonsemantic) as well as a conceptual/semantic route to categorical action from vision. What is the relationship between these routes? Over the past 25 years, cognitive psychology has seen several "dual-route" accounts of particular tasks—the most prominent probably being the dual-route model of reading (e.g., Coltheart, 1978). Characteristic of these accounts is the idea that there is a "horse race" between the two routes, with performance being dependent on the route that generates its output first. Given some overlap in output times from the two routes, reaction times will be faster for tasks that can be accomplished via either route than for tasks that depend on one output alone, since in a horse-race model performance depends simply on which horse/route finishes first. This could explain the faster action decision times for objects than for words reported by Chainay and Humphreys (2002a) since action decisions to objects could be based on either the direct or the conceptual/semantic route, whereas those to words depend solely on the conceptual/semantic route. However, on such an account it is difficult to explain a disorder such as visual apraxia. For example, such patients can be shown to have a relatively preserved conceptual/semantic route to action (e.g., when tested verbally), and yet they fail when presented with objects visually (Riddoch et al., 1989). This suggests a standard horse-race model is not correct.

Rather than a horse-race model of action retrieval, Yoon, Heinke, and Humphreys (2002) proposed a "convergent route" account. According to their account, activation from the direct and indirect (conceptual/semantic) routes to action normally cooperates to facilitate selection of the appropriate action to an object—the selection process then being influenced by both the visual properties of objects *and* by more abstract functional and contextual knowledge about the object. They suggest that cooperative interactions between these routes pushes activation within an action selection system into a stable state that represents the memory for particular categorical actions ("raise the cup to the lips," "pour from the cup," even "throw the cup across the room"!). The convergent route account can explain the faster action decisions to objects than to words because, uniquely for objects, there is consistent activation then being accrued from several inputs. The cost of this convergent route approach is that when processing is disturbed along one route (e.g., by a brain lesion), it can affect how well outputs from the other route are used in action selection. For example, due to damage to a visual route, activation within the action selection system may be "pushed away" from the appropriate stable state, so that either no or an incorrect action is selected. This enables the account to explain disorders such as visual apraxia, where damage to a visual route seems to disrupt the use of the conceptual/semantic route, when an object is presented visually.

Yoon et al. (2002) created a formal model of this convergent route account, termed NAM (for Naming and Action Model). Objects activated a "structural description system" sensitive to the presence of component parts in the appropriate spatial locations relative to one another, whereas words activated a visual lexicon sensitive to the presence of letter strokes in the correct relative positions. Activation in each of these input systems was transmitted through a conceptual/semantic system in which processing units corresponded to particular objects and to their superordinate categories. Conceptual/semantic knowledge in this model can be thought to serve as a form of "convergence zone," pulling together activation from different input system and relaying it onto different output systems (see Damasio, 1990, for a discussion of conceptual/semantic knowledge in terms of convergence zones). In NAM two output systems were simulated—one for action selection and one for name selection (again including names for superordinate terms). Within each output system a "winner takes all" competitive process was implemented, so that one action or name was eventually selected. Activation into the name selection system was fed from both the visual lexicon and the conceptual/semantic system. Activation was fed into the action selection system from the structural description system and from the conceptual/semantic system. The architecture of the system is illustrated in Figure 6.

Yoon et al. (2002) showed that NAM could explain the main results that we have summarized here. For example, the advantage for action decisions to objects relative to words (Chainay & Humphreys, 2002a) came about because convergent inputs from the structural description and semantic systems pushed activation in the action selection system rapidly into a stable basin of attraction. This speeded performance relative to when there was only input into action selection from the conceptual/semantic system (for words). Action errors under deadline conditions were simulated by taking an early response threshold, prior to winner-take-all selection being completed. For objects, relatively high proportions of visual errors occurred because activation transmitted from the structural description system was sensitive to overlap in the parts between different objects, and, furthermore, the direct visual route provided faster initial access into the action selection system. When an early response deadline was set, activation in the action selection system could be shared between several visual "neighbors," so creating visual errors. In contrast to this, naming errors were sensitive to both visual and semantic similarity. For objects, input to name selection was mediated by conceptual/semantic knowledge. Though overlap at a structural description level would initially create a set of visual neighbors within the semantic system, this would then be moderated by semantic knowledge, spreading activation between items that were both visually and semantically related to targets (see also Vitkovitch & Humphreys, 1991, for additional evidence on naming errors

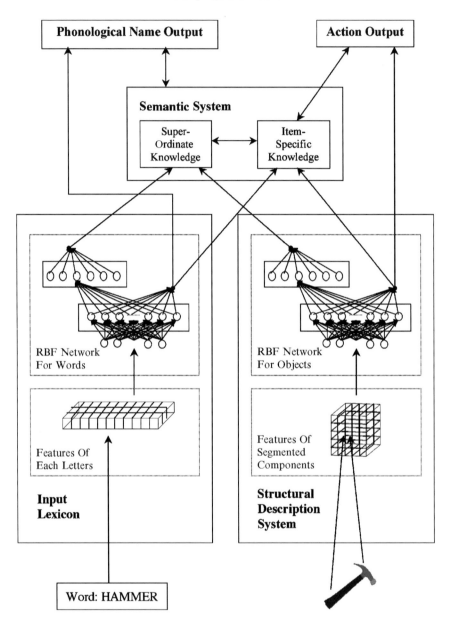

Fig. 6. Framework for NAM (Naming and Action Model), after Yoon et al. (2002). RBF is radial basis function network, which represented the model's stored knowledge of individual words (a visual lexicon) and objects (a structural description system). See the text for details.

under deadline conditions). A different error profile would result in gesturing and naming objects to deadline (see Rumiati & Humphreys, 1998, for empirical evidence).

NAM was "lesioned" by adding noise to the activation at different levels of the model. For example, visual apraxia was simulated by the addition of noise to the route connecting the structural description system to the action selection system. As a consequence, noisy activation from visually presented objects tended to push action selection away from stable basins of attraction, disrupting performance relative to when there was no input to action selection from the structural description system (with words). Optic aphasia was mimicked by adding noise to the inputs to the conceptual/semantic system from the structural description system. This disrupted access to name retrieval more than to action selection, because action selection was still supported to some degree by direct activation from the structural description system. Interestingly, there was still some mild impairment in action retrieval (due to noisy input from the conceptual/semantic system), so that, depending on the degree of naming impairment, NAM predicts that there will tend to be a mild problem in action retrieval in optic aphasia and that, in any case, action selection should be slowed. The speed of action retrieval in optic aphasia has not yet been examined systematically, so this prediction remains unverified.

2. The Convergent Route Account and Cross-Modal Input in Apraxia

As well as the specific disorder of visual apraxia, there are cases in which the action disorder is cross-modal and seems to represent a more central disturbance in accessing an action system from conceptual/semantic knowledge (Rothi & Heilman, 1997). In many such cases, gesturing ability is better when objects are physically present, relative to when patients have to gesture to just the object's name (the opposite pattern to visual apraxia; De Renzi et al., 1982). This pattern follows naturally from the convergent route approach, since performance with visually presented objects will be supported by the (spared) visual route even when conceptual/semantic input into action selection is faulty (see Yoon et al., 2002). In addition, the inputs into the action selection system may come not only from vision and conceptual/semantic knowledge, but also from other sensory modalities, such as touch. The appropriate tactile contact with an object can help "push" activation into a stable state. This generates a further prediction, namely that even if conceptual/semantic input to action selection is impaired, performance may be improved when objects are held and used (due to support from a direct tactile input route into action selection). This too has been commonly observed in apraxic patients (Geschwind, 1965). Chainay and Humphreys (2002b) found the improvement from holding as well as seeing the objects even when patients could name the stimuli from vision alone, so the improvement cannot be attributed to improved object recognition (access to conceptual/ semantic knowledge) from tactile input. In contrast, the benefit can be accounted for in terms of the direct, convergent contribution of tactile/ proprioceptive input to the action selection process.

F.   NEURAL SUBSTRATES OF THE DIFFERENT ROUTES TO ACTION

If there are indeed separate routes to action, a direct route from vision and a route mediated by access to conceptual/semantic knowledge, then we might expect to see some evidence for this at a neural as well as at a functional level of analysis. The neuropsychological data are not particularly helpful on this point. Optic aphasia is associated with damage to the posterior left hemisphere (left occipitotemporal cortex; e.g., Coslett & Saffran, 1992; Hillis & Caramazza, 1995), though it can be found after left occipitoparietal damage (Riddoch & Humphreys, 1987b). Semantic dementia is associated with degenerative changes in the anterior, inferior temporal cortices, usually bilaterally (Garrard, Lambon Ralph, & Hodges, 2002). The localization of damage in such cases is consistent with the ventral (occipitaltemporal) cortex supporting access to conceptual/semantic information from vision (Ungerleider & Mishkin, 1982). Unfortunately, this does not localize a direct visual route to action. In one potential source of evidence, visual apraxia, the data on lesion localization are relatively unclear, with the disorder being reported following left parietal damage (Riddoch et al., 1989) but also after damage to the (right) frontotemporal cortex (Pilgrim & Humphreys, 1991). Nevertheless, it is tempting to link the proposed direct visual route to a dorsal visual stream, passing from the occipital to parietal and then frontal cortex. This would fit with the argument for a dorsal stream concerned with knowledge of "how" to use objects (cf. Milner & Goodale, 1995). Arbib (1997) has also made a similar suggestion, arguing that the parietal cortex responds in situations in which particular motor behaviors are possible—akin to the idea of the parietal cortex responding to affordances. Unfortunately, there is currently little direct evidence from converging sources, such as functional brain imaging, for localizing a direct visual route to dorsal cortex.

For a dual-route account of action selection, the most crucial contrast is that between actions made/retrieved to objects and actions made/retrieved to words, since the direct route should be engaged only when objects are presented. Most imaging studies have not made this contrast, but instead have examined action (typical verb) retrieval in response to object names

(Petersen, Fox, Posner, Mintun, & Raichle, 1988; Warburton, Wise, & Price, 1996) or to pictures (Grabowski, Damasio, & Damasio, 1998; Grafton, Fadiga, Arbib, & Rizzolatti, 1997; Grèzes, Costes, & Decety, 1999). Martin, Haxby, Lalonde, Wiggs, and Ungeleider (1995) did examine verb retrieval to both pictures and words, but the two modalities were not contrasted in the same experiment. Typically these studies examine performance with a particular class of object that has strong action associations, namely tools.

The work on action retrieval from pictures of tools reveals activation in areas that frequently overlap those found in naming (e.g., activation in left inferior and middle frontal gyri; see Grabowski et al., 1998; Grafton et al., 1997; and in the middle temporal and fusiform gyri in the left hemisphere; Grèzes & Decety, 2002), compared with lower-level baseline conditions (e.g., viewing unknown faces in Grabowski et al., 1998; viewing abstract shapes in Grèzes et al., 1999). At least some of these areas seem associated with the retrieval of information about how objects are used/manipulated. For example, Phillips, Noppeney, Humphreys, and Price (in press) presented participants with pictures of tools and fruit and had them make decisions either about the real-life size of the objects (is the tool longer than a paintbrush? Is the fruit larger than a kiwi?) or about object use/manipulation (do you use a twisting motion to manipulate this tool? Can you peel this fruit by hand?). They found that the action decisions increased activation in the left posterior middle temporal cortex, the right posterior medial cerebellum, and the left ventral inferior frontal cortex, compared with perceptual size decisions. Tools, relative to fruit, increased activation in the left posterior middle temporal cortex across the tasks. This suggests that, even in tasks not requiring explicit action decisions (e.g., when making real-life size decisions), tools draw upon brain areas that mediate the retrieval of action knowledge. However, this could reflect activation within a conceptual/semantic system representing abstract functional knowledge about items, rather than some direct visual route to action. The retrieval of abstract functional knowledge may be more important for the identification of tools than for the identification of other classes of object (e.g. Warrington & Shallice, 1984).

Some evidence for more dorsal activation mediating the processing of tools comes from Grèzes et al. (1999) who included "motor imagery" tasks (imaging grasping and using the object) as well as tasks requiring judgments about whether objects were upright, silent verb generation, and silent naming. Across these tasks, there was activation in the left inferior parietal lobe, the left inferior frontal gyrus, and the supplementary motor area (among other regions). But here it is not clear whether the activations reflect simulated production of manual actions rather than, say, affordances offered by the visual properties of stimuli. Inferior parietal activation has also been observed when manual relative to whole body gestures are observed (Bonda, Petrides, Ostrey, & Evans, 1996), when manual gestures are observed with an intention to imitate or memorize for future recognition (Decety et al., 1994, 1997; Grèzes, Costes, & Decety, 1998), and when reaching and grasping responses are observed relative to a nonprehensile gesture in response to an object (Passingham, Toni, Schluter, & Rushworth, 1998). These activations may be part of a system for the production of manual actions, rather than reflecting processes involved in retrieving and selecting between actions associated with whole objects and object parts.

One attempt to address differences in action retrieval between objects and words has been made by Phillips, Humphreys, Noppeney, and Price (2002). They had participants make action or "image size" decisions to pictures of objects, nonobjects, and words.[3] Relative to the "image size" baseline, the action tasks activated the left inferior frontal, the left posterior middle temporal, and the left anterior temporal cortices—areas also found to be activated in previous action retrieval tasks (Grabowski et al., 1998; Grafton et al., 1997; Grèzes & Decety, 2002; Martin et al., 1995). Relative to when pictorial images were presented, words generated more widespread activation, particularly in the left anterior temporal and anterior fusiform gyri. This probably reflects the increased difficulty in accessing knowledge about action from words, even within the conceptual/semantic system; note that the effects of increased task difficulty for words may to some extent mask effects specific to objects. For nonobjects, relative to words, there were, however, some increased activations in the left occipitotemporal cortex and in the left anterior medial fusiform gyrus, for action decisions compared with image size decisions. These last areas are close to the so-called visual motion region (V5), and to the lateral occipital region (LO), which seems to mediate the processing of object-like perceptual structures (Malach et al., 1995). These results suggest that action decisions may lead to more detailed processing of the perceptual structure of objects, and perhaps associated motions of objects, which may in turn lessen the need for semantically based retrieval processes. Note, though, that there was no evidence for actions to either objects or nonobjects being mediated by a dorsal route to action. It may be that dorsal activation more directly mediates processes linked to action production rather than the visual activation of categories of action, but more work is needed on this question.

---

[3] In the "image size" decision participants decided whether the picture or word was small or large; this provided a low-level baseline task performed on the same stimuli used in the action decisions, so taking away differences in perceptual processing between the stimuli.

III.   From Action to Vision

So far we have discussed results from neuropsychology, experimental psychology, computational modeling, and functional brain imaging that are consistent with visual information being used directly to constrain how we select a categorical action to an object. However, this need not be a one-way process. For example, it may well be that an intention for action "configures" the object processing system so that certain perceptual properties, relevant to the action, are assigned a strong "weight" in perceptual processing (see Bundesen, 1990, for a formal discussion of how perceptual weights may be assigned to stimuli). Having the intention to act may thus influence visual perception.

We have already discussed some evidence that suggests this. For example, the finding that the effectiveness of visual affordances in "driving" action may depend on the goal-set (e.g., for grasping rather than pointing, Riddoch et al., 1998) is at least consistent with the goal-set for action modulating the processing of perceptual information from the stimulus. We will now proceed to discuss further evidence that suggests that action can influence perception. We propose that effects of action on perception can arise through at least two distinct processes. One is by action directing attention to the relevant properties of the environment—the location of an action or the features of stimuli that accord with the goals of the action. The second is by action relations between objects providing the "glue" that enables attention to select the objects together. We conclude by discussing the implications of the data for understanding the relations between perceptual selection of stimuli and response selection of the appropriate actions to stimuli.

A.   ATTENTION TO ACTION-RELATED PROPERTIES

1.   Reaching and Looking at a Location

Evidence for action directing attention to the location where the action is made comes from studies by Deubel, Schneider, and colleagues (Deubel & Schneider, 1996; Deubel, Schneider, & Paprotta, 1998; Schneider & Deubel, 2002, though see Bonfiglioli, Duncan, Rorden, & Kennett, 2002, for some contrary evidence). These investigators had participants make either a saccade or a pointing response to a particular location, and they presented a visual stimulus either at that location or at other locations close by, as the response was being prepared. Discrimination of the visual stimulus was enhanced at the location at which the response was programmed, even when it was unlikely that the target would appear there. Deubel and Schneider suggest that there is an obligatory coupling among action, attention, and perception. Attention is drawn to the location at which the action is programmed, and this enhances the perception of stimuli that appear there.

2. Action-Related Attention to Object Orientation

Bekkering and Neggers (2002) required participants to search for a rectangular block target, defined by its color and orientation, relative to other rectangular block distractors. The distractors could be at either the same or a different orientation to the target (45 or 135 degrees). There were two tasks: (1) look at and point to the target or (2) look at and grasp the target. They measured eye movements as well as reaching responses to targets. They found that fewer saccades were made to distractors in the wrong orientation relative to targets when a grasp response had to be made, compared with when a pointing response was made. The intended action here affected how visual attention was guided to the target. Presumably, when a grasping response is made, the goal for the action "weights" information about the expected orientation of the target more strongly than when a pointing response is made. The orientation information, thus weighted, may then provide a strong input to the perceptual selection process guiding eye movements. Action-related properties become salient for attentional selection.

3. Action-Related Frames of Reference

Tipper, Lortie, and Baylis (1992) had normal participants make a pointing response to a light that appeared on a board. To do this, participants had to move their hand forward from just in front of their body to where the target was. Simultaneous with the onset of the target, a distractor light (in a different color) also came on. The distractor could lie in front of or behind the target light. Tipper et al. found that a distractor appearing in front of the target interfered with reaction times to targets. However, if participants began each trial with their hand at the far side of the board and then moved their hand toward their body to respond, then a distractor appearing on the far side of the target (but closer to the responding hand) interfered with performance. Tipper et al. suggested that when pointing responses are made, attention follows a hand-centered frame of reference in which distractors close to the hand are potent competitors for any response. Again it appears that the action determines the deployment of attention, determining which stimuli are highly salient and which less salient for selection.

These examples of action influencing perception through attention either to the effector or to attributes relevant to the action are mirrored by findings in the neuropsychological literature—particularly within the syndrome of visual neglect. In this disorder, patients can fail to respond to stimuli presented on the side of space contralateral to their lesion. The problem can be attributed to a failure either to represent stimuli on the affected side, to direct attention to them, or some combination of both poor representation and attention (see Heinke & Humphreys, 2003). In some instances, such patients can be helped by using action to influence visual attention.

4. Action Templates in Visual Neglect

We were working with one patient with neglect after right hemisphere damage, MP, when he noted that although he often experienced difficulties finding things on his left, he felt he sometimes did better if he tried to think of an item in terms of what he'd do with it instead of thinking of its name (e.g., find the thing to hit the nail, rather than find the hammer). We (Humphreys & Riddoch, 2001) tested this formally. We had MP perform a visual search for a target presented with other objects on a table. The target was defined in terms of its name, its color, or the action that would be done with it. MP was strikingly better at finding a target defined by its action rather than the same item defined by its name or color—even though he could name both objects and colors. In particular, given a "template" based on action,[4] MP showed far fewer neglect errors, as if having this template helped him register the presence of a matching target. Cuing search by action was not effective when we used words instead of objects (e.g., when he was given a set of cards each with the name of an object on it). Also, it was not effective when the objects were rotated so that their handles faced away from MP. The loss of the benefit from cuing by action seemed not to be due to poor recognition of rotated stimuli, since searching by name was equally good with rotated and nonrotated versions—the viewpoint effect was specific to when an action template was used. This suggests that action-related properties of the objects needed to be present to match the template for MP to detect the stimulus. Again we can think here of an action template "weighting" the properties of objects relevant to action, so that objects turned in the correct orientation for action generate more activation than objects turned the wrong way. In a patient such as MP, it appears that a memory template based on the name of the object was less effective in directing attention into an impaired field than one based on action.

5. Attention to (Extended) Effectors

Cases of visual neglect also provide evidence for attention being linked to effectors, when actions are made (cf. Tipper et al., 1992). Ackroyd, Riddoch, Humphreys, Nightingale, and Town (2002) examined a patient, HB, with

---

[4] We use the term template here to describe the memory representation for the target that can guide visual search (see Duncan & Humphreys, 1989, for discussion of this, and Chelazzi et al., 1993, for physiological evidence).

poor detection of stimuli presented away from a particular area near to and on the right of his body. Interestingly, when asked to hold a stick out in front of him with his right hand, HB became able to detect targets further away from his body (though typically on the right again). In contrast, when asked to hold the stick at a horizontal perpendicular angle (holding the right-hand end of the stick, so that it protruded to the left), he became able to detect stimuli on his left (but not in far right locations). There are various ways to conceptualize this intriguing finding. One is that when the patient held the stick, there was some form of "remapping" of the spatial representation of his body, so that it extended to the area including the stick. If the patient had an impaired representation of space both on his left and beyond his body (for "far right" locations), then extending his body space, by holding the stick, would enable him to perceive stimuli that would otherwise be neglected. Other investigators (e.g., Berti & Frassinetti, 2000) have reported opposite cases in which a patient with neglect of "near" but not "far" left space showed neglect of far space when holding a tool. In this instance there may be remapping of an impaired part of space, generating neglect in more distal spatial regions. Iriki, Tanaka, and Iwamura (1996) have reported physiological evidence consistent with this idea of remapping personal space when monkeys gain experience in holding a tool. A related account, however, would link the effect reported by Ackroyd et al. (2002) to attention being linked to the "extended" effector, as the patient held the stick either out in front or pointing to the left. HB typically tried to make pointing responses to stimuli. If attention is tied to the position of the (extended) effector during such responses, then items in far right and near left space may become attended (depending on how the stick is held). Future work needs to tease apart the idea that use of a stick helps to recover an impaired spatial representation from the idea that it provides an action- related cue to attention.

B.   Action as Attentional Glue

Recently we have explored a second way that action can influence visual perception, which is by helping separate stimuli to be attended together. There is much evidence to indicate that, very often, our attention is drawn to single objects. For example, in one classic study, Duncan (1984) presented two visual targets briefly to normal participants and showed that discrimination of both targets was worse when they appeared simultaneously relative to when they appeared successively across a short interval. This apparent attentional limitation in report held when the targets were features from independent objects. However, the limitation was reduced when the targets were features from a single object. Duncan suggested that we attended to a single object, but then select all its features together. In contrast, our intuition was that we might be able attend to two separate objects if they act upon one another. For example, in a game of soccer it would be useful to attend both to the opponent and the ball when making a tackle, so that contact is made with the ball but not the opponent (especially in one's own penalty area!). That is, our attention systems may be sensitive to whether independent objects combine into a joint action (the opponent, running with the ball). In a sense, action may provide a form of glue for our attention, enabling us to select together separate objects in an action relationship.

We have again examined this issue using neuropsychological data, this time with patients who shows "visual extinction" (Karnath, 1988). The term extinction is employed to describe patients who can detect and often identify a single stimulus presented in their impaired visual field (usually contra-lateral to the site of lesion), but who fail to detect/identify the same stimulus (presented for the same duration) when another item appears simulta-neously in the good (ipsilesional) field. Often the symptom is attributed to a spatial bias in visual selection, induced by the lesion, so that ipsilesional stimuli are assigned a greater "weight" in the competition as to which item is attended (e.g., Duncan, 1996; Heinke & Humphreys, 2003). Previously it has been demonstrated that extinction can be modulated by grouping between elements, including grouping by bottom-up Gestalt factors (such as collinearity and common shape, see Humphreys, 1998; Mattingley, Davis, & Driver, 1997) and by activating stored object representations (e.g., as when two letters form a word; Kumada & Humphreys, 2003). Grouping between the contra- and ipsilesional stimuli allows them to cooperate rather than compete for visual selection, since they are then part of a single perceptual object (see Heinke & Humphreys, 2003, for a formal account). We (Riddoch, Humphreys, Edwards, Baker, & Willson, 2003) examined whether action relationships between visual stimuli might also lead to a reduction in visual extinction. To test this, we presented stimuli that would commonly be used together (e.g., a corkscrew and a wine bottle), and placed them either in locations where they could be used together for action or in inverted locations, where they would not combine in a common action. An example is provided in Figure 7. Identification performance was examined in a group of five patients, all of whom had sustained damage to the parietal cortex and all of whom were subject to visual extinction. We found clear evidence that extinction was reduced when objects were in the appropriate locations for action relative to when they were in inappropriate locations (see Figure 8). This result was not due to some objects being particularly difficult to identify in some locations. We also incorporated trials in which single objects were presented and there was then no effect of whether objects

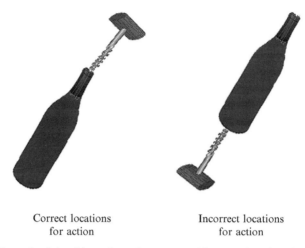

Correct locations   Incorrect locations
for action   for action

Fig. 7.   Example of the objects shown in correct and incorrect locations for action. From Riddoch et al. (2003).

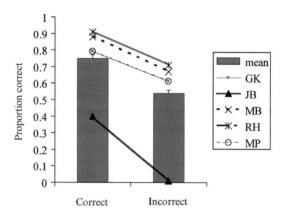

Fig. 8.   The data from the individual patients (bars), and the mean results across patients (histograms), for reporting both objects on two-object trials, as a function of whether the objects are in the correct or incorrect action relations. GK, JB, MB, RH, and MP are the initials of the patients.

fell in the positions they occupied on the correct and incorrect location trials with two items.

   In a further study we contrasted identification performance with pictures of items in the correct spatial locations for action (e.g., mallet + nail, sardine tin + tin opener) with performance when the objects were associatively related but not typically related together (e.g., mallet + hammer, a sardine tin + can). Would the target item, common to these conditions, be less affected by extinction when the objects were in an action relationship? This is what we found. There was less extinction for the action-relation items (mallet + nail, sardine tin + tin opener), relative to a condition in which the same objects were used but occurred in unrelated pairs (mallet + tin opener; sardine tin + nail). In contrast, there was no benefit for the associatively related objects (mallet + hammer; sardine tin + can) compared with a re-paired control condition (mallet + can; sardine tin + hammer). Independent observers also rated the action pairs as no more familiar together than the associate pairs, so the effect cannot be attributed to greater visual familiarity of the action-related objects as pairs. The reduction in extinction was specific to an action relation between the objects acting as a strong cue for them to be selected together. Here action affects perception by providing a form of "binding" for attention. It may be, for instance, that a direct visual route to action is tuned to objects being in the correct relative locations for action. Feedback from this route to early visual processing could then "push" visual attention to include both objects in an action relationship.

IV. Vision, Action, and Attention

We have argued that (1) visual information from objects can activate associated actions in a relatively direct manner, independent of access to conceptual/semantic knowledge, and (2) action also influences vision by selectively "weighting" action-relevant features (stimulus locations, particular properties) and by binding together stimuli so that they are selected together. In this respect, we propose that vision and action are mutually interactive, and are coupled through attention. Action-relevant properties of objects can bias perceptual selection to a target (Bekkering & Neggers, 2002; Humphreys & Riddoch, 2001), whereas visual affordances from objects can bias the selection of a particular response (e.g., Riddoch et al., 2000a,b; Tucker & Ellis, 2001). This does not mean that perceptual selection of an object and response selection of one of several actions are one and the same process. Indeed there is evidence that perceptual selection and response selection can be dissociated. Consider the evidence on utilization errors and anarchic hand behavior provoked by tasks such as that illustrated in Figure 3. As well as using single object trials, Riddoch et al. (2000a,b) also examined trials with two objects in which the task was to respond to a target defined by its color. The patients tested never made an error by responding to the distractor cup (with the wrong color), indicating good perceptual selection of the target. Nevertheless, they still made many action errors by using the effector cued by the affordance rather than the effector consistent with the task rule (e.g., picking up a right-facing cup on the left of the table with their right hand, though the rule was to pick up the cup using the hand on the side where the cup was placed). There was a clear deficit in action selection. The idea that perceptual selection can be dissociated from action selection fits with neuroanatomical accounts of selective attention. For example, Posner and Petersen (1990) distinguish between a posterior attentional system, concerned with perceptual selection, and an anterior system, concerned with response selection. In some patients we witness a disorder in the response selection system with the perceptual selection system relatively spared.

Nevertheless, we have also proposed that processes concerned with response selection, such as setting a certain goal for action, can influence perceptual selection. Thus our view is that the perceptual and response selection systems are interactive rather than being serial processes (first perceptual selection and then response selection). Boutsen and Humphreys (2002) provide evidence for this from utilization errors in patient FK, who had suffered bilateral damage to his medial frontal and temporal lobes. They had FK always reach with his right hand (minimizing competition for selection of the effector for action) to a target cup defined by its color (a distractor cup was present, but in a different color). Unlike the study of Riddoch et al. (2000a) the target color was cued at the start of each trial, so that sometimes the target had the color of the distractor on the previous trial and the distractor had the color of the previous target. Boutsen and Humphreys found that FK sometimes misreached to the distractor when the colors of the target and distractor changed across trials. Presumably, any template specifying the target color for perceptual selection on trial *n* was then placed in competition with a template specifying the target color on the

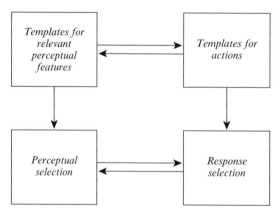

Fig. 9. A framework for how the systems governing perceptual selection and action selection may interact.

previous trial $n-1$. Interestingly, the likelihood of this error in perceptual selection increased when the target had a weak affordance for the action (e.g., its handle was facing left) and the distractor had a strong affordance (its handle was facing right). Thus the strength of perceptual selection was also determined to some degree by factors influencing response selection (the strength of an affordance). This is consistent with activation in the response selection system feeding-forward to influence perceptual selection, particularly under conditions in which there is not a strong "set" determining perceptual selection. We illustrate this idea in the framework in Figure 9. We propose that vision and action mutually determine both what is perceived and what behaviors are evoked by stimuli, and that they do so by selectively biasing the systems that govern perceptual selection on the one hand and response selection on the other.

ACKNOWLEDGMENTS

This work was supported by grants from the Medical Research Council, the Wellcome Trust, and the Stroke Association, UK.

REFERENCES

Ackroyd, K., Riddoch, M. J., Humphreys, G. W., Nightingale, S., & Townsend, S. (2002). Widening the sphere of influence. Using a tool to extend extrapersonal visual space in a patient with severe neglect. *Neurocase, 8,* 1–12.

Aglioti, S., DeSouza, J. F. X., & Goodale, M. A. (1995). Size contrast illusions deceive the eye but not the hand. *Current Biology, 5,* 679–685.

Arbib, M. A. (1997). Modelling visuomotor transformations. In M. Jeannerod & J. Grafman (Eds.), *Handbook of neuropsychology: Action and cognition* (Vol. II, pp. 65–90). Amsterdam: Elsevier Science.

Beauvois, M.-F. (1982). Optic aphasia: A process of interaction between vision and language. *Philosophical Transactions of the Royal Society of London, Series B, 289,* 35–47.

Bekkering, H., & Neggers, S. F. W. (2002). Visual search is modulated by action-intention. *Psychological Science, 13,* 370–374.

Berti, A., & Frassinetti, F. (2000). When far becomes near: Remapping of space by tool use. *Journal of Cognitive Neuroscience, 12,* 415–420.

Bonda, E., Petrides, M., Ostrey, D., & Evans, A. (1996). Specific involvement of human parietal systems and the amygdala in the perception of biological motion. *Journal of Neuroscience, 16,* 3737–3744.

Bonfiglioli, C., Duncan, J., Rorden, C., & Kennett, S. (2002). Action and perception: Evidence against converging selection processes. *Visual Cognition, 9,* 458–476.

Boutsen, L., & Humphreys, G. W. (2002). On the interaction between perceptual and response selection: Evidence from a patient with frontal lobe damage. *Neuropsychologia.*

Bridgeman, B. (2002). Attention and visually guided behaviour in distinct systems. In W. Printz & B. Hommel (Eds.), *Attention and performance XIX: Common mechanisms in perception and action* (pp. 120–135). Oxford, UK: Oxford University Press.

Bundesen, C. (1990). A theory of visual attention. *Psychological Review, 49*, 113–121.

Caramazza, A., Hillis, A. E., Rapp, B. C., & Romani, C. (1990). Multiple semantics or multiple confusions? *Cognitive Neuropsychology, 7*, 161–168.

Chainay, H., & Humphreys, G. W. (2002a). Privileged access to action from objects relative to words. *Psychological Bulletin and Review, 9*, 348–355.

Chainay, H., & Humphreys, G. W. (2002b). Neuropsychological evidence for a convergent route model for action. *Cognitive Neuropsychology, 19*, 67–93.

Chelazzi, L., Miller, E. K., Duncan, J., & Desimone, R. (1993). A neural basis for visual search in inferior temporal cortex. *Nature, 363*, 345–347.

Coltheart, M. (1978). Lexical access in simple reading tasks. In G. Underwood (Ed.), *Strategies of information processing* (pp. 151–216). London: Academic Press.

Coslett, H. M., & Saffran, E. M. (1992). Optic aphasia and the right hemisphere: A replication and extension. *Brain and Language, 43*, 148–161.

Damasio, A. R. (1990). Category-related recognition defects as a clue to the neural substrates of knowledge. *Trends in the Neurosciences, 13*(3), 95–98.

Decety, J., Grèzes, J., Costes, N., Perani, D., Jeannerod, M., Procyk, E., Grassi, F., & Fazio, F. (1997). Brain activity during observation of actions: Influence of action content and subject's strategy. *Brain, 120*, 1763–1777.

Decety, J., Perani, D., Jeannerod, M., Bettinardi, V., Tadary, B., Woods, R., Mazziotta, J. C., & Fazio, F. (1994). Mapping motor representations with PET. *Nature, 371*, 600–602.

Della Sala, S., Marchetti, C., & Spinnler, H. (1991). Right-sided anarchic (alien) hand: A longitudinal study. *Neuropsychologia, 29*, 1113–1127.

De Renzi, E., Faglioni, P., & Sorgato, P. (1982). Modality-specific and supramodal mechanisms of apraxia. *Brain, 105*, 301–312.

Deubel, H., & Schneider, W. X. (1996). Saccade target selection and object recognition: Evidence for a common attentional mechanism. *Vision Research, 36*, 1827–1837.

Deubel, H., Schneider, W. X., & Paprotta, I. (1998). Selective dorsal and visual processing: Evidence for a common attentional mechanism. *Visual Cognition, 5*, 1827–1837.

Duncan, J. (1984). Selective attention and the organisation of visual information. *Journal of Experimental Psychology: General, 10*, 501–517.

Duncan, J. (1996). Cooperating brain systems in selective perception and action. In T. Inui & J. L. McClelland (Eds.), *Attention and performance XVI* (pp. 549–578). Cambridge, MA: MIT Press.

Duncan, J., & Humphreys, G. W. (1989). Visual search and stimulus similarity. *Psychological Review, 96*, 433–458.

Ellis, R., & Tucker, M. (2000). Micro-affordance: The potentiation of components of action by seen objects. *British Journal of Psychology, 91*, 451–471.

Franz, V. H., Gegenfurtner, K. R., Bülthoff, H. H., & Fahle, M. (2000). Grasping visual illusions: No evidence for a dissociation between perception and action. *Psychological Science, 11*, 20–25.

Freund, C. S. (1889). Über optische aphasie and seelenblindheit. *Archiv für Psychiatrie und Nervenkrankheiten, 20*, 371–416.

Garrard, P., Lambon Ralph, M., & Hodges, J. R. (2002). Semantic dementia: A category-specific paradox. In E. M. E. Forde & G. W. Humphreys (Eds.), *Category specificity in brain and mind* (pp. 149–180). Hove, UK: Psychology Press.

Geschwind, N. (1965). Disconnection syndromes in animals and man. *Brain, 88*, 237–294, 585–644.

Gibson, J. J. (1979). *The ecological approach to visual perception*. Boston: Houghton Mifflin.

Grabowski, T. J., Damasio, H., & Damasio, A. R. (1998). Premotor and prefrontal correlates of category-related lexical retrieval. *Neuroimage, 7*, 232–243.

Grafton, S. T., Fadiga, L., Arbib, M. A., & Rizzolatti, G. (1997). Premotor cortex activation during observation and naming of familiar tools. *Neuroimage, 6*, 231–236.

Grèzes, J., Costes, N., & Decety, J. (1998). Top-down effects of strategy on the perception of human biological motion: A PET investigation. *Cognitive Neuropsychology, 15*, 553–582.

Grèzes, J., Costes, N., & Decety, J. (1999). The effects of learning and intention on the neural network involved in the perception of meaningless actions. *Brain, 122*, 1875–1887.

Grèzes, J., & Decety, J. (2002). Does visual perception of object afford action? Evidence from a neuroimaging study. *Neuropsychologia, 40*, 212–222.

Haffenden, A. M., & Goodale, M. A. (1998). The effect of pictorial illusion on prehension and perception. *Journal of Cognitive Neuroscience, 10*, 122–136.

Heinke, D., & Humphreys, G. W. (2003). Attention, spatial representation and visual neglect. *Psychological Review, 110*, 29–87.

Hillis, A. E., & Caramazza, A. (1995). Cognitive and neural mechanisms underlying visual and semantic processing: Implications from "optic aphasia." *Journal of Cognitive Neuroscience, 7*, 457–478.

Hodges, J. R., Bozeat, S., Lambon Ralph, M. A., Patterson, K., & Spatt, J. (2000). The role of conceptual knowledge in object use: Evidence from semantic dementia. *Brain, 123*, 1913–1925.

Hodges, J. R., Spatt, J., & Patterson, K. (1999). 'What' and 'how': Evidence for the dissociation of object knowledge and mechanical problem solving skills in the human brain. *Proceedings of the National Academy of Sciences of the United States of America, 96*, 9444–9448.

Hommel, B. (2000). The prepared reflex: Automaticity and control in stimulus-response translation. In S. Monsell & J. Drive (Eds.), *Control of cognitive processes: Attention and performance XVIII* (pp. 247–274). London: Academic Press.

Humphreys, G. W. (1998). Neural representation of objects in space. *Philosophical Transactions of the Royal Society of London, Series B, 353*(1373), 1341–1351.

Humphreys, G. W., & Riddoch, M. J. (2000). One more cup of coffee for the road: Object-action assemblies, response blocking and response capture after frontal lobe damage. *Experimental Brain Research, 133*, 81–93.

Humphreys, G. W., & Riddoch, M. J. (2001). Detection by action: Neuropsychological evidence for action-defined templates in visual search. *Nature Neuroscience, 4*, 84–88.

Iriki, A., Tanaka, M., & Iwamura, Y. (1996). Coding of modified body schema during tool use by macaque postcentral neurones. *NeuroReport, 7*, 2325–2330.

Karnath, H.-O. (1988). Deficits of attention in acute and recovered visual hemi-neglect. *Neuropsychologia, 26*, 27–43.

Kumada, T., & Humphreys, G. W. (2001). Lexical recovery from extinction: Interactions between visual form and stored knowledge modulate visual selection. *Cognitive Neuropsychology, 18*, 465–478.

Lauro-Grotto, R., Piccini, C., & Shallice, T. (1997). Modality-specific operations in semantic dementia. *Cortex, 33*, 593–622.

Lhermitte, F. (1983). 'Utilisation' behaviour and its relations to lesions of the frontal lobes. *Brain, 106*, 237–255.

Lhermitte, F., & Beauvois, M. F. (1973). A visual-speech disconnection syndrome. Report of a case with optic aphasia. *Brain, 96*, 695–714.

Liepmann, H. (1905). Die linke hemisphaere und das handeln. *Muenchner Medizinische Wochenschrift, 49*, 2322–2326.

Malach, R., Reppas, J. B., Benson, R. R., Kwong, K. K., Jiang, H., & Kennedy, W. A. (1995). Object-related activity revealed by functional magnetic resonance imaging in human occipital cortex. *Proceedings of the National Academy of Sciences of the United States of America, 92,* 8135–8139.

Manning, L., & Campbell, R. (1992). Optic aphasia with spared action naming: A description and possible loci of impairment. *Neuropsychologia, 30,* 587–592.

Martin, A., Haxby, J. V., Lalonde, F. M., Wiggs, C. L., & Ungeleider, L. G. (1995). Discrete cortical regions associated with knowledge of colour and knowledge of action. *Science, 270,* 102–105.

Mattingley, J. B., Davis, G., & Driver, J. (1997). Pre-attentive filling in of visual surfaces in parietal extinction. *Science, 275,* 671–674.

Meegan, D. V., & Tipper, S. P. (1999). Visual search and target-directed action. *Journal of Experimental Psychology: Human Perception and Performance, 25,* 1347–1362.

Milner, A. D., & Goodale, M. A. (1995). *The visual brain in action.* Oxford, UK: Oxford University Press.

Milner, A. D., Paulignan, Y., Dijkerman, H. C., Michel, F., & Jeannerod, M. (1999). A paradoxical improvement of misreaching in optic ataxia: Evidence for two separate neural systems for visual localisation. *Proceedings of the Royal Society of London, Series B, 266,* 2225–2229.

Milner, A. D., Perrett, D. I., Johnston, R. S., Benson, P. J., Jordan, T. R., Heeley, D. W., Bettucci, D., Mortara, F., Mutani, R., Terazzi, E., & Davidson, D. L. W. (1991). Perception and action in 'visual form agnosia.' *Brain, 114,* 405–428.

Passingham, R. E., Toni, I., Schluter, N., & Rushworth, M. F. (1998). How do visual instructions influence the motor system? *Novartis Foundation Symposium, 218,* 129–141.

Pavani, F., Boscagli, I., Benvenuti, F., Ratbuffetti, M., & Farne, A. (1999). Are perception and action affected differently by the Titchener circle illusion? *Experimental Brain Research, 127,* 95–101.

Pavese, A., & Buxbaum, L. J. (2002). Action matters: The role of action plans and object affordances in selection for action. *Visual Cognition, 9,* 559–590.

Perenin, M.-T., & Vighetto, A. (1988). Optic ataxia: A specific disruption in visuomotor mechanisms. 1. Different aspects of the deficit in reaching for objects. *Brain, 111,* 643–674.

Petersen, S. E., Fox, P. T., Posner, M. I., Mintun, M., & Raichle, M. E. (1988). Positron emission tomographic studies of the cortical anatomy of single word processing. *Nature, 331,* 585–589.

Phillips, J. A., Humphreys, G. W., Noppeney, U., & Price, C. J. (2002). The neural substrates of action retrieval: An examination of semantic and visual routes to action. *Visual Cognition, 9,* 662–684.

Phillips, J. A., Noppeney, U., Humphreys, G. W., & Price, C. J. (in press). To what extent can category-specific deficits be explained by a differentiated semantic system? A PET study. *Brain.*

Phillips, J. C., & Ward, R. (2002). S-R correspondence effects of irrelevant visual affordance: Time course and specificity of response activation. *Visual Cognition, 9,* 540–558.

Pilgrim, E., & Humphreys, G. W. (1991). Impairment of action to visual objects in a case of ideomotor apraxia. *Cognitive Neuropsychology, 8,* 459–473.

Pisella, L., Grea, H., Tilikete, C., Vighetto, A., Desmurget, M., Rode, G., Boisson, D., & Rossetti, Y. (2000). An "automatic pilot" for the hand in posterior parietal cortex. Toward reinterpreting optic ataxia. *Nature Neuroscience, 3,* 729–736.

Posner, M. I., & Peterson, S. E. (1990). The attention system of the human brain. *Annual Review of Neuroscience, 13,* 25–42.

Potter, M. C., & Faulconer, B. A. (1975). Time to understand pictures and words. *Nature, 253,* 437–438.

Reason, J. T. (1984). Lapses of attention. In R. Parasuraman, R. Davies, & J. Beaty (Eds.), *Varieties of attention.* Orlando, FL: Academic Press.

Riddoch, M. J., Edwards, M. G., Humphreys, G. W., West, R., & Heafield, T. (1998). An experimental study of anarchic hand syndrome: Evidence that visual affordances direct action. *Cognitive Neuropsychology, 15*, 645–683.

Riddoch, M. J., & Humphreys, G. W. (1987a). A case of integrative agnosia. *Brain, 110*, 1431–1462.

Riddoch, M. J., & Humphreys, G. W. (1987b). Visual object processing in optic aphasia: A case of semantic access agnosia. *Cognitive Neuropsychology, 4*, 131–185.

Riddoch, M. J., & Humphreys, G. W. (2000). The Neuropsychology of object recognition. In B. Rapp (Ed.), *The handbook of cognitive neuropsychology* (pp. 45–74). Hove, UK: Psychology Press.

Riddoch, M. J., Humphreys, G. W., & Edwards, M. G. (2000a). Neuropsychological evidence distinguishing object selection from action (effector) selection. *Cognitive Neuropsychology, 17*, 547–562.

Riddoch, M. J., Humphreys, G. W., & Edwards, M. G. (2000b). Visual affordances and object selection. In S. Monsell & J. Driver (Eds.), *Attention and performance XVIII* (pp. 603–626). Cambridge, MA: MIT Press.

Riddoch, M. J., Humphreys, G. W., & Edwards, M. G. (2001). An experimental analysis of anarchic lower limb action. *Neuropsychologia, 39*, 574–579.

Riddoch, M. J., Humphreys, G. W., Edwards, S., Baker, T., & Willson, K. (2003). Seeing the action: Neuropsychologial evidence for action-based effects on object selection. *Nature Neuroscience, 6*, 82–89.

Riddoch, M. J., Humphreys, G. W., Heslop, J., & Castermans, E. (2002). Dissociations between object knowledge and everyday action. *Neurocase, 8*, 100–110.

Riddoch, M. J., Humphreys, G. W., & Price, C. J. (1989). Routes to action: Evidence from apraxia. *Cognitive Neuropsychology, 6*, 437–454.

Rossetti, Y., & Pisella, L. (2002). Several different "vision for action" systems: A guide to dissociating and integrating dorsal and ventral functions. In W. Printz & B. Hommel (Eds.), *Attention and performance XIX: Common mechanisms in perception and action* (pp. 62–119). Oxford, UK: Oxford University Press.

Rothi, L. G. G., & Heilman, K. M. (1997). *Apraxia: The neuropsychology of action.* Hove, UK: Psychology Press.

Rumiati, R. I., & Humphreys, G. W. (1998). Recognition by action: Dissociating visual and semantic routes to action in normal observers. *Journal of Experimental Psychology: Human Perception and Performance, 24*, 631–647.

Schneider, W. X., & Deubel, H. (2002). Selection-or-perception and selection-for-spatial-motor-action are coupled by visual attention: A review of recent findings and new evidence from stimulus-driven saccade control. In W. Prinz & B. Hommel (Eds.), *Attention and performance XIX: Common mechanisms in perception and action* (pp. 609–627). Oxford, UK: Oxford University Press.

Snowden, J. S., Goulding, P. J., & Neary, D. (1989). Semantic dementia: A form of circumscribed cerebral atrophy. *Behavioural Neurology, 2*, 167–182.

Tipper, S. P., Howard, L. A., & Houghton, G. (1998). Action based mechanisms of attention. *Philosophical Transactions of the Royal Society of London, Series B, 353*, 1385–1393.

Tipper, S. P., Howard, L. A., & Jackson, S. R. (1997). Selective reaching to grasp: Evidence for distractor interference effects. *Visual Cognition, 4*, 1–38.

Tipper, S. P., Lorti, C., & Baylis, G. C. (1992). Selective reaching: Evidence for action-entered attention. *Journal of Experimental Psychology: Human Perception and Performance, 18*, 891–905.

Tipper, S. P., Meegan, D., & Howard, L. A. (2002). Action-centred negative priming. *Visual Cognition, 9*, 591–614.

Tucker, M., & Ellis, R. (1998). On the relations between seen objects and components of potential actions. *Journal of Experimental Psychology: Human Perception and Performance, 24*, 830–846.

Tucker, M., & Ellis, R. (2001). The potentiation of grasp types during visual object categorisation. *Visual Cognition, 8*, 769–800.

Ungerleider, L. G., & Mishkin, M. (1982). Two cortical visual systems. In J. Ingle, M. A. Goodale, & R. J. W. Mansfield (Eds.), *Analysis of visual behavior* (pp. 549–586). Cambridge, MA: MIT Press.

Vitkovitch, M., & Humphreys, G. W. (1991). Perseverant responding in speeded picture naming: Its in the links. *Journal of Experimental Psychology: Learning, Memory and Cognition, 17*, 664–680.

Warburton, E., Wise, R. J., & Price, C. J. (1996). Noun and verb retrieval by normal subjects. *Brain, 119*, 159–179.

Warrington, E. K., & Shallice, T. (1984). Category-specific semantic impairments. *Brain, 107*, 829–854.

Yoon, E. Y., Heinke, D., & Humphreys, G. W. (2002). Modelling direct perceptual constraints on action selection: The Naming and Action Model (NAM). *Visual Cognition, 9*, 615–660.

EYE MOVEMENTS AND VISUAL COGNITIVE SUPPRESSION

David E. Irwin

I. Introduction

The visual world contains more information than we can perceive in a single glance; because of this, eye movements play an important role in many aspects of visual cognition (for reviews see Rayner, 1978, 1998). A single eye fixation provides a view of the world that is approximately 200° of visual angle wide and 130° high (Harrington, 1981), encompassing an area of about 20,000° square. Our ability to resolve fine spatial detail in this vast area is restricted to a region very much smaller region than this, however. The highest spatial resolution (i.e., best visual acuity) is provided by foveal vision, corresponding to the center of our gaze; the fovea is very small, however, subtending only approximately 3° square. Visual acuity drops rapidly as distance increases from the fovea, being reduced by 50% at 5° from the fovea and by 90% at 40° from the fovea (Hochberg, 1978). Because of these acuity limitations, the eyes must move from point to point in space for fine details to be resolved. Thus, eye movements are required for us to do things like identify words while reading and to identify objects that are present in peripheral vision.

Although eye movements are essential for the efficient execution of cognitive tasks, certain costs are associated with making eye movements. For example, little visual information is retained from one eye fixation to the next (see Irwin, 1996, for a review). The costs of eye movements are not restricted to difficulty in retaining visual information, however; this chapter reviews recent evidence that indicates that eye movements can actually interfere with cognitive processing, especially high-level visual processing.

II. Eye Movements and Saccadic Suppression

A. Visual Suppression

People make rapid eye movements called *saccades* about three or four times each second when they read, view pictures, or explore the world around them. Eyes are relatively still during the fixations that separate successive saccades. The average fixation is approximately 250–300 ms in duration, while saccade duration depends on saccade distance. Saccade duration increases as saccade distance increases, but the average saccade duration during reading and picture viewing is approximately 30–50 ms (Rayner, 1978, 1998). Put another way, the eyes move about three times each second, 180 times each minute, 10,800 times each hour, and 172,800 times each 16 hour waking day. If one assumes an average saccade duration of 30 ms, this means that the eyes are in motion about 90 minutes each day.

Visual saccadic suppression refers to the fact that visual sensitivity is reduced during saccades, so that the acquisition of visual information from the environment is restricted largely to fixations (Matin, 1974; Volkmann, 1986; Zuber & Stark, 1966). The reduction in visual sensitivity during saccades appears to be caused primarily by visual masking (Campbell & Wurtz, 1978); the brief, smeared image present on the retina during a saccade is masked by the clear, bright, long-duration fixations that precede and follow it. Central inhibitory mechanisms appear to contribute (Riggs, Merton, & Morton, 1974), however, because a small amount of visual suppression occurs even when a very faint stimulus is viewed in total darkness. The magnitude of saccadic suppression varies with viewing conditions (such as target and background luminance) but under some circumstances subjects are completely unable to detect a stimulus presented briefly during a saccade (e.g., Volkmann, Schick, & Riggs, 1968). Because of saccadic suppression, intake of visual information from the environment is largely restricted to periods of time when the eyes are still. Thus, 90 minutes during the day when we think we are seeing, we actually are not.

B. Cognitive Suppression

Recently several investigators have proposed that at least some cognitive processes may also be suppressed during saccadic eye movements. This raises the possibility that 90 minutes during the day when we think we are thinking, we actually are not. The hypothesis that cognitive processing is suppressed during saccadic eye movements may seem very implausible, because people are not aware of pauses in mental activity during eye movements. Saccade durations are typically very brief, however, so any disruptions that might occur might not be especially salient; we rarely notice the disruptions in visual input that accompany saccades and eyeblinks, for example, so brief cognitive "blackouts" might also go unnoticed. The remainder of this chapter reviews the evidence that indicates that saccades do indeed interfere with some cognitive processes and speculates about the mechanisms that might underlie this phenomenon.

III. Early Investigations of Cognitive Suppression during Saccades

Whereas visual saccadic suppression has been studied for over a century (e.g., Erdmann & Dodge, 1898), investigators recently have begun to examine whether cognitive processing might be suppressed as well. Russo (1978) was the first to raise the possibility, pointing out that logically saccades and cognitive processes could occur either in strict serial alternation or in parallel, perhaps with interference occurring when attentional resources were limited. He concluded that it would be most efficient if saccades and cognitive processing could occur in parallel, but that there were no data to settle the issue.

The first empirical investigation of cognitive suppression during saccades was conducted by Sanders and Houtmans (1985). Subjects performed a same/different matching task in which two stimuli to be compared were presented in separate eye fixations. Subjects viewed one stimulus (a digit) while they were fixating the left side of a visual display, and then they executed a 45° saccade (which took about 95 ms) to the right side of the display to fixate the second stimulus (another digit, either equal to or different in value from the first digit). The visual quality of the first digit was varied across experimental blocks, so that it was either normal or degraded with a dot pattern. The second digit was always undegraded. Sanders and Houtmans found that the effects of stimulus degradation were fully reflected in fixation time on the first digit, as shown by comparison with a no-saccade control condition in which the first digit was presented alone (either degraded or undegraded) and required only a two-choice reaction. This result indicates that in the saccade condition subjects did not execute their saccade until the first digit had been identified. Sanders and Houtmans (and Sanders & Rath, 1991) showed that if subjects were forced to move their eyes before the first stimulus had been identified, then the effects of degradation on the first stimulus were apparent in fixation time on the second stimulus—that is, no stimulus "clean-up" occurred during the 95 ms that the eyes were in motion. They concluded that stimulus encoding must be suspended during saccadic eye movements.

Matin, Shao, and Boff (1993) found a cost in information processing time when subjects had to execute saccades to acquire information from a display. In this study, subjects were presented with three data frames, each containing a single digit. The three frames appeared either in the same spatial location (requiring no saccades to be seen), or distributed across two locations that were separated by 11° (requiring two saccades to be seen; that is, subjects viewed the first frame in one fixation, moved their eyes 11° to view the second frame, then moved their eyes back 11° to view the third frame). The subjects' task was to count the number of odd digits that were presented. Matin et al. measured the frame duration required for subjects to perform this task with 85% accuracy under these two conditions, and they found that total presentation time had to be increased by almost 200 ms when saccades were required compared to when no saccades were required; in other words, there was a "cost" of about 100 ms per saccade. The duration of 11° saccades is approximately 40–45 ms, so this cost cannot be attributed solely to the time required for the eyes to travel from one location to another. The authors concluded instead that saccadic eye movements actively interfere with cognitive processing, perhaps by drawing on a common resource pool. Because this experiment relied on a comparison between saccade and no-saccade conditions, however, it is unclear whether the interference that was observed was due to suppression of cognitive processing during the saccade or to some other consequence of saccade execution, such as motor planning or inaccurate fixation on the target.

Several attempts have been made to determine whether memory comparison processes are suppressed during saccades, but the results have been difficult to interpret. Boer and Van der Weijgert (1988) used the Sternberg (1969) short-term memory scanning procedure to address this question. In their experiments, subjects memorized a memory set containing one, two, or four items, then fixated a letter on the left side of a visual display. The letter either was or was not a member of the memory set. After identifying the letter, subjects executed a 100° saccade (which took about 230 ms) to the right side of the display where they saw a response box that showed the mapping of "yes" (the letter was in the memory set) and "no" (the letter was not in the memory set) responses onto response keys; this mapping varied from trial to trial. Subjects also completed a no-saccade version of the memory scanning task in which response assignment was held constant (i.e., "yes" was always assigned to the left response key). Boer and Van der Weijgert found that the effect of memory set size (i.e., a reaction time increase with increasing set size) was smaller under saccade than under no-saccade conditions. Thus, they concluded that memory search can take place during a saccade. It is important to note that the effect of set size was not completely eliminated, however. Sternberg (1969) found that comparison in short-term memory takes less than 40 ms per item, so no set size effect should have been found in the saccade condition if subjects had completed the memory scanning process (which they had time to do, given a maximum set size of four items) during the 230 ms that the eyes were in motion. Thus, these results leave open the possibility that memory scanning is suppressed during saccades.

van Duren (1993) attempted to replicate the results of Boer and Van der Weijgert (1988) in two experiments. In the first she found that the effect of memory set size was identical under saccade and no-saccade conditions, indicating that memory scanning was completely suspended during the saccade. In the second (using more practiced subjects), she replicated the finding of smaller set-size effects under saccade than under no-saccade conditions. The set-size effect was not eliminated in the saccade condition, however, again leaving open the possibility that memory search is suppressed (but not completely) during saccades.

One problem with the studies of van Duren (1993) and Boer and Van der Weijgert (1988) is that they, like Matin et al. (1993), relied on comparisons between saccade and no-saccade conditions that differed in several respects in order to assess whether suppression occurred during saccades. Thus, the question of whether memory scanning is suppressed during saccades was examined again by van Duren and Sanders (1995) in an experiment that compared performance across saccades of different lengths (and thus of different durations). This had the advantage of controlling for factors such as motor planning and for adverse perceptual consequences that might accompany saccades. As in the previous studies, van Duren and Sanders used a memory-scanning procedure in which subjects memorized a memory set and then viewed a target letter on the left side of a display. Subjects then executed a saccade to the right side of the display to view the response box mapping responses onto response keys. The key procedural difference was that subjects executed either an 8° saccade (whose average duration was 34 ms) or a 100° saccade (whose average duration was 205 ms). The logic of this manipulation was that the effect of memory set size should be smaller after long than after short saccades if memory search occurs while the eyes are in motion. van Duren and Sanders (1995) found that the effect of memory set size was reduced when a long rather than a short saccade was executed, indicating that subjects did engage in some memory scanning during the saccade. However, once again the effect of memory-set size was not eliminated, even though 205 ms should have been ample time for subjects to complete the memory scanning process. Thus, it seems likely that memory search is suppressed somewhat during saccades (even though the authors concluded the opposite).

van Duren and Sanders (1995) also investigated whether response selection is suppressed during saccades. Subjects were presented a digit from the set 1, 2, 3, 4 on the left side of a display, and then they executed either an 8° or a 100° saccade to a point on the right side of the display. Then they pressed a response key corresponding to the digit that they had seen on the left. In one condition the order in which the digits were assigned to the response keys was, from left to right, 1, 2, 3, 4 (compatible responses), while in another condition the order of assignment was 2, 1, 4, 3 (incompatible responses). A 34 ms effect of response compatibility was found when subjects executed 8° saccades, but this effect was a nonsignificant 4 ms following 100° saccades. Because the effect was smaller after a long as opposed to a short saccade, van Duren and Sanders (1995) concluded that processes related to response selection must take place while the eyes are in motion. Although this conclusion is probably correct, it is still possible that response selection was suppressed to some extent, but was not apparent because of a floor effect.

In sum, as of 1995 only a few studies had examined whether saccadic eye movements interfere with cognitive processing. These early investigations provided some support for the hypothesis that at least some cognitive processes are suppressed during saccades. The evidence was less than overwhelming, however, and the results shed little light on the possible mechanisms underlying cognitive saccadic suppression. In the next Section I describe several studies conducted more recently in my laboratory that have examined this question in a systematic fashion.

IV. A Programmatic Investigation of Cognitive Suppression during Saccades

I became interested in the question of whether cognitive processing is suppressed during saccades during a sabbatical leave in 1991–1992 at the Free University in Amsterdam where I worked with Andries Sanders (whose work is featured above). Based in part on his findings, I hypothesized that cognitive suppression during saccades might occur as a result of dual-task interference; that is, suppression would occur only if a cognitive task required the same processes or structures that are active during saccade programming and execution. This hypothesis formed the basis for several experiments that are described below. To overview, two major findings have resulted from this research, and they are both consistent with the dual-task interference hypothesis: Visuospatial processes are suppressed during saccades, but stimulus recognition and stimulus identification processes are not.

A. VISUOSPATIAL PROCESSING IS SUPPRESSED DURING SACCADES

Eye movements involve visuospatial processing. A position in space must be selected as the target of the eye movement, and the spatial positions of at least some of the objects in the world appear to be updated across eye movements (e.g., Andersen, Batista, Snyder, Buneo, & Cohen, 2000; Currie, McConkie, Carlson-Radvansky, & Irwin, 2000; Dassonville, Schlag, & Schlag-Rey, 1993; Duhamel, Colby, & Goldberg, 1992). The generation of saccadic eye movements relies on a complex network of brain structures, but the key cortical areas appear to be the frontal and supplementary eye fields and the posterior parietal cortex (Schall, 1995). Numerous studies have shown that the posterior parietal cortex is also heavily involved in visuospatial processing (see Cabeza & Nyberg, 2000, for a review); thus, the dual-task interference hypothesis predicts that cognitive operations that require visuospatial processing should be suppressed during saccades. This prediction was examined in four major studies.

1. Mental Rotation during Saccades

Mental rotation (imagining the rotation of an object or of oneself in the environment) is a visuospatial process used for activities such as reading a map, packing a box, parking a car, deciding whether a book will fit in a crowded bookshelf, wending one's way through a crowded sidewalk, and perhaps even object and scene recognition. Irwin and Carlson-Radvansky (1996) found evidence that mental rotation is suppressed during saccadic eye movements. Our procedure was based on one used by Cooper and Shepard (1973). Cooper and Shepard had subjects judge the handedness of a stimulus—that is, whether the stimulus was a normal or mirror-image version of itself. They reported that reaction time to make this decision increased as the stimulus was tilted away from the upright, with the maximum reaction time occurring to a stimulus rotated 180° from upright. However, they also showed that performance was improved if subjects were given advance information about the stimulus, such as its identity and the orientation at which it would appear. Moreover, the more time subjects had to process this preview information, the less they were affected by stimulus orientation. Given a sufficiently long preview, even stimuli rotated 180° from the upright were classified just as quickly as upright stimuli. This improvement in performance was attributed to the cognitive process of mental rotation: If the subject knew the identity and the orientation of the target stimulus, the subject could imagine it rotating in the mind; given

Identity Prime (2000 ms):

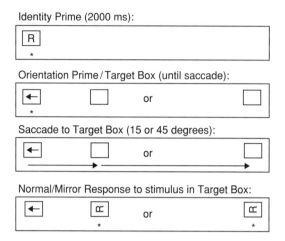

Orientation Prime / Target Box (until saccade):

Saccade to Target Box (15 or 45 degrees):

Normal/Mirror Response to stimulus in Target Box:

Fig. 1.   Schematic illustration of the Irwin and Carlson-Radvansky (1996) procedure.

enough time, the mental rotation could be completed before the target was presented, thereby eliminating any effects of target orientation.

We modified the Cooper and Shepard (1973) procedure by presenting the preview information (i.e., information about the identity and the orientation of the target character) while subjects fixated a leftward fixation mark, then presenting the target character after the subject executed a 15° or a 45° saccade to a rightward fixation mark. The target character was presented at the rightward point, and the subject's reaction time and accuracy to make the normal/mirror judgment were recorded. Of interest was whether the prime information presented before the saccade would be more beneficial when a 45° saccade (which lasts about 110 ms) rather than a 15° saccade (which lasts about 40 ms) was executed to the target character.

The procedure for the *prime* version of the experiment is shown in Figure 1. A subject began each trial by fixating each of four points that were separated by 16° of visual angle on a display. The subject's eye position was monitored with a scleral-reflectance eyetracker during this procedure, which served to calibrate the output of the eyetracker against spatial position. Following calibration, a fixation point appeared on the left side of the display. The subject fixated this point, and then an identity prime was presented for 2 seconds. This prime was always upright and in normal orientation; it informed the subject as to the identity of the target that would be presented later in the trial. Next an orientation prime, an arrow, was presented in the fixation box, and this prime informed the subject about the orientation of the target character, which could be 0, 90, 180, or 270° from vertical. The primes were perfect predictors of the identity and the orientation of the character that the subject would see at the opposite side of the display. Whether the target would be normal or mirror-reversed was not specified. Simultaneous with the presentation of the orientation prime, a saccade target box appeared on the right of the display. In separate blocks of trials, the saccade target box appeared either 15° or 45° away from the left-hand fixation point, and the subject was instructed to initiate a saccade to the box when it appeared. The target character was presented in the target box during the subject's saccade, and it remained there until the subject responded as to whether the stimulus was normal or mirror-reversed.

In addition to the prime condition shown in Figure 1, each subject also completed a *no-prime* version of this task, conducted to determine whether any performance differences might arise merely as a result of making a long as opposed to a short saccade. For example, visual suppression is sometimes greater for long than for short saccades (Volkmann, 1986), so it might take longer for subjects to acquire visual information about the target after a 45° saccade than after a 15° saccade, thereby covering up any effect of mental rotation that might have occurred during the saccade. The no-prime procedure was similar to that shown in Figure 1, except that instead of presenting subjects with an identity prime at the leftmost fixation point, an empty box was presented for 2 seconds; then, an uninformative orientation prime, a plus sign, was presented instead of an arrow prime above the fixation point and the saccade target box appeared on the right of the display. The subject initiated a saccade to this box, and the target character was presented during the saccade and remained present until the subject responded whether the character was normal or mirror-reversed. All other procedural details were the same as in the prime version of the experiment.

Following the completion of a block of trials, the eye movement record for each subject was analyzed and three measures of interest were calculated: TL, *time left*, the time spent fixating the orientation cue before the saccade was initiated to the target box; TM, *time moving*, the duration of the saccade; and TR, *time right*, the time that elapsed between the subject's eye landing on or near the target letter and the subject's response (note that this time might include more than one fixation). Only trials in which the subject's initial saccade landed within 3° of the target letter were analyzed, for the following reason. When the eye landed short of the target, a fixation of some duration took place before a corrective saccade moved the eye the rest of the way to the target. Because additional processing of the prime might take place during this extra fixation, determination of whether mental rotation takes place during eye movements per se might be compromised. Preliminary testing showed that subjects could determine the handedness of the target letter at least 3° away from the center of fixation, so that determined the size of the acceptance window for the

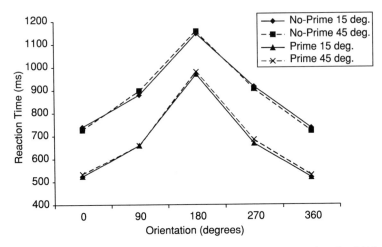

Fig. 2.   Results for the saccade conditions of Irwin and Carlson-Radvansky (1996).

landing site of the initial saccade (a reanalysis of the data using all trials, regardless of landing position, produced exactly the same pattern of results discussed below, with only minor variations among the means reported by Irwin & Carlson-Radvansky, 1996).

Mean fixation time on the left (TL) was significantly longer under prime (378 ms) than under no-prime (318 ms) conditions, suggesting that subjects took time to interpret the informative prime when it appeared. Saccade length had no significant effect on TL, nor did it interact with any other factor. As expected, mean saccade duration (TM) was longer when the eyes had to move 45° (111 ms) rather than 15° (44 ms). The main question of interest was whether subjects would be able to use this additional time, which took place while the eyes were in motion, to mentally rotate the prime. If so, then target classification judgments (TR) should be faster, and orientation effects should be weaker, after 45° saccades than after 15° saccades.

They were not. Figure 2 shows mean TR times in the prime and no-prime versions of this task as a function of target orientation for 15° and 45° saccades. These times represent the sum of all fixations made on the target stimulus; saccade durations are not included (including the increased mean RT by about 30 ms, but did not change the pattern of results). The standard effects of target orientation were observed, but there was no difference in response time or in the effect of orientation between the 15° and 45° movement conditions in either version of the task. The accuracy data were consistent with the response time data.

The results of the no-prime version indicate that there was no cost in target processing time (TR) associated with making a long as opposed to a short saccade; target reaction time was the same in the 15° and 45° movement conditions. Additional analyses of the eye movement data showed that the number of fixations made on the target increased as target orientation increased from 0° (2.28) to 90° (2.51) to 180° (2.94) away from upright, but this did not interact with saccade distance. Saccades made in the 15° condition were more accurate (overshooting the target by 0.03° on the average) than in the 45° condition (undershooting the target by 0.87°). There were significantly more fixations made on the target stimulus following 45° saccades (2.87) than following 15° saccades (2.25). Neither of these effects interacted with prime type, however. Because the small differences in landing position and number of fixations between the two movement conditions did not affect reaction time in the no-prime version, there is no reason to expect that they affected reaction time in the prime version either.

Response times were faster in the prime version of the task than in the no-prime version, indicating that subjects did make use of the informative prime, presumably before and/or after they moved their eyes; for example, mental rotation of the target after the saccade could begin more quickly if its identity and orientation were known as opposed to unknown. Most importantly, the results of the prime version show that target classification judgments were no faster after 45° saccades than after 15° saccades, despite the extra 67 ms of potential processing time allowed by the longer saccade. This result indicates that subjects cannot, or at least do not, perform mental rotation during saccadic eye movements. But, is 67 ms sufficiently long for appreciable mental rotation to occur?

To examine this question, each of the subjects completed a no-eye-movement version of the prime condition of the experiment. In this control, subjects maintained fixation on a central point, and the prime and the target information were presented at that point. The identity of the target was presented for 2 seconds, as in the eye movement version of the experiment, and then the orientation prime was presented for a duration determined by each subject's individual TL time. Then, to mimic what might happen during different TM times, the orientation prime was presented for an additional 0, 50, or 100 ms before the target character was presented, and the subject's reaction time to determine whether the target was normal or mirror-reversed was measured. In essence, the no-eye-movement control was a partial replication of Cooper and Shepard (1973), using the prime durations experienced by our subjects in the eye-movement experiment.

The results of the no-eye-movement control were consistent with those of Cooper and Shepard (1973). As the prime-to-target interval increased by 0 to 50 to 100 ms, mean reaction time decreased from 778 to 733 to 695 ms. The halfwidth of the 95% confidence interval for the difference between two means was 8 ms, so all pairwise differences were significant. In addition, the interaction between prime-to-target interval and target orientation was significant, reflecting the fact that target orientation had a smaller effect as prime processing time increased from 0 to 50 ms. The difference in response time to targets rotated by 180° vs. 0° decreased from 671 ms (1210 ms vs. 539 ms) to 547 ms (1093 ms vs. 546 ms) as the prime-to-target interval increased by 0 to 50 (there was no difference between prime-to-target intervals of 50 and 100 ms, however). These results demonstrate that even 50 ms is sufficiently long for enough mental rotation to occur to produce a detectable difference in target classification time. Thus, if subjects had been performing mental rotation while they were moving their eyes, response time in the eye movement experiment should have been faster in the 45° movement condition than in the 15° movement condition. It was not. In sum, subjects can and do perform mental rotation when their eyes are still, but not when their eyes are moving, demonstrating that at least one kind of cognitive activity, mental rotation, is suppressed during saccadic eye movements.

2. Mental Rotation during Saccades, Revisited

A limitation of the Irwin and Carlson-Radvansky (1996) study is that the conclusion that mental rotation is suppressed during saccades relies on accepting a null hypothesis (i.e., no difference in performance between the 15° and 45° eye movement conditions). It was very important to demonstrate conclusively that mental rotation is suppressed during saccades; thus, we conducted another study in which suppression during saccades would be manifested by significant differences among conditions, rather than by a null effect (Irwin & Brockmole, 2000).

The procedure is shown in Figure 3. Following a routine to calibrate the output of the eyetracker against spatial position (panel 1), a fixation box appeared on the left side of the display. The subject fixated this box for 1500 ms (panel 2), and then a single character (presented either 0, 90, 180, or 270° rotated from the upright, either in its normal or mirror-reversed configuration) was presented within it (panel 3). After 300 ms, a saccade target box was presented on the right side of the display, or the fixation box remained on the left side of the display (for no-saccade control trials). Distributed randomly across trials, the fixation box remained on the left, or the saccade target box appeared either 7.5° or 40° away from the leftward fixation box (panel 4). In all conditions, the subject made a normal/mirror-reversed decision about the single letter on the left. On no-saccade trials the subject made the normal/mirror-reversed decision by pressing one of two response buttons as soon as possible while maintaining fixation on the fixation box; on saccade trials the subject was instructed to press one of two response buttons to indicate whether the character was normal or mirror-reversed

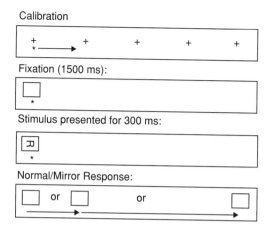

Fig. 3.   Schematic illustration of the Irwin and Brockmole (2000) procedure.

while making a saccade to the target box. Reaction time (measured from character onset) and accuracy were recorded. We reasoned that if mental rotation is suppressed during saccades, then RT should be longer when subjects have to execute a 40° saccade (which takes about 93 ms) as opposed to a 7.5° saccade (which takes about 28 ms). In fact, if suppression is complete, RT should be 65 ms longer in the 40° condition than in the 7.5° condition, because this is the difference in saccade duration (93 − 28).

Reaction time (measured from stimulus onset) as a function of saccade distance and stimulus orientation was the main dependent measure. The results are shown in Figure 4. As noted earlier, it is difficult to compare the no-saccade condition against the saccade conditions because of the differences in processing demands; thus, comparison of the long-saccade condition with the short-saccade condition is of most interest. Response times were significantly longer in the 40° saccade condition ($M = 946$ ms) than in the 7.5° saccade condition ($M = 873$ ms). The main effect of orientation was also significant, but the interaction between saccade distance and orientation was not. All subjects showed the same pattern of results. The error rate was higher in the 40° saccade condition than in the 7.5° saccade condition, as well (13.2% vs. 10.8%). These results show clearly that processing is suppressed during the saccade; the difference between the 40° and 7.5° saccade conditions was 73 ms, suggesting that mental rotation was suppressed completely while the eyes were moving.

To verify that it was mental rotation and not some other aspect of stimulus processing that was suppressed, subjects also completed a no-rotation control condition in which the procedure was the same as described above but the stimuli were always upright and thus never required rotation.

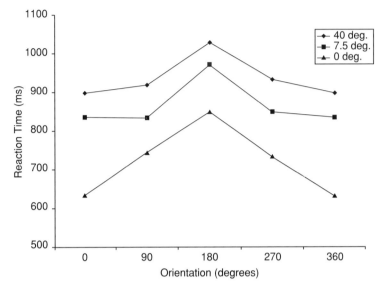

Fig. 4. Results for Irwin and Brockmole (2000).

In this version of the experiment RT and errors were identical in the 40° and 7.5° saccade conditions. Thus, suppression during the saccade was found only when mental rotation was required.

In sum, mental rotation is suppressed during saccadic eye movements. The next two studies examined whether other kinds of visuospatial processing are also suppressed during saccades.

3. Direction Judgments during Saccades

Irwin and Brockmole (2001) conducted an experiment that used a procedure similar to that shown in Figure 3, but in which the stimuli were pictures of individual objects that always appeared in an upright orientation. The subject had to respond whether the object (e.g., a bird, a chair, or a bicycle) faced to the left or faced to the right while executing either a short or a long saccade. Making this judgment requires subjects to identify the stimulus and to impose a spatial frame of reference upon it to identify the front of the stimulus and which direction it is facing. This is a visuospatial operation, hence we expected that saccades would interfere with this process. The predictions were identical to those of Irwin and Brockmole (2000) described above. The results were also identical: RT to make the left/right judgment was 60 ms longer in the long-saccade condition than in the short-saccade condition, as would be expected if visuospatial processing is suppressed completely during saccades.

4. Spatial Scaling during Saccades

Brockmole, Carlson, and Irwin (2002) examined whether people can execute changes in the scale of visual attention during saccades. The experimental procedure was similar to that of Irwin and Carlson-Radvansky (1996) described above. On each trial subjects saw a pair of objects made up of smaller objects (e.g., a large square made out of smaller squares, a large rectangle made out of smaller squares, a large square made out of smaller rectangles, or a large rectangle made out of smaller rectangles). During one fixation they made a judgment about one of the objects at one level of spatial scale (e.g., the local or small-object level) and then they executed a saccade to the other object in the pair and made a judgment about it at the other level of spatial scale (e.g., the global or large-object level in this case). Of interest was whether people could change from a local to global level of analysis (and vice versa) while their eyes were moving. The results indicated that they could not; RT was prolonged by the duration of the saccade, indicating that people cannot execute changes in the scale of visual attention while their eyes are moving. This provides additional support for the hypothesis that visuospatial processes are suppressed during saccades.

B. Stimulus Recognition and Identification Processes Are Not Suppressed During Saccades

As noted earlier, the frontal and supplementary eye fields and the posterior parietal cortex are the main cortical areas involved in the generation of saccadic eye movements. The posterior parietal cortex is also heavily involved in visuospatial processing, so the results of the studies reported in Section IV.A are consistent with the hypothesis that cognitive tasks that require the same brain structures that are active during saccade generation and execution are suppressed during saccades. Stimulus recognition and stimulus identification do not rely on the parietal cortex, however, but rather on more ventral areas of the brain such as the inferotemporal cortex (Mishkin, Ungerleider, & Macko, 1983). Thus, the dual-task interference hypothesis predicts that saccades should not interfere with stimulus recognition and stimulus identification tasks. This was examined in several studies, described next.

1. Identity Priming during Saccades

Irwin, Carlson-Radvansky, and Andrews (1995) used the the Posner and Snyder (1975) primed letter-matching task to investigate whether identity priming is suppressed during saccades. In the Posner and Snyder (1975) experiment most relevant to our study, subjects had to judge whether two *target* letters were identical or different. Subjects' reaction time and accuracy to make this judgment were recorded. Presentation of the two target letters was preceded by a *prime* stimulus. On some trials the prime was a neutral warning signal (a + sign), but on other trials it was a letter that either matched or mismatched the target letters. When the prime was a letter, it was much more likely to match the target letters than to mismatch them (by a 4:1 ratio). Posner and Snyder (1975) found that RT on *same* trials (i.e., trials in which the target letters were identical to each other) was faster when the prime matched the target letters than when the prime mismatched the target letters, even though the prime was irrelevant to the subjects' task (i.e., only the congruence of the target letters was relevant to the response). Furthermore, the difference in RT between match and mismatch prime conditions increased as the stimulus onset asynchrony (SOA) between the prime and the targets increased from 10 to 300 ms. Posner and Snyder (1975) argued that the difference in RT between match and mismatch prime conditions consisted of two components: *facilitation* (assessed by subtracting RT on prime-match trials from RT on neutral prime trials) and *inhibition* (assessed by subtracting RT on neutral prime trials from RT on prime-mismatch trials). They found that the amount of facilitation rose quickly as SOA increased, whereas inhibition did not occur until the SOA exceeded 150 ms, at which point it increased rapidly. Posner and Snyder (1975) attributed these effects to two processes: a rapid, automatic activation of the processing pathway and identity code shared by the prime and the targets, and a slower, attentional expectancy based on the highly predictive nature of the prime.

To determine whether either (or both) of these processes operate during saccades, we modified the Posner and Snyder (1975) procedure by presenting the prime while subjects fixated a leftward fixation mark, then presenting the target letters at a rightward fixation mark after subjects initiated either a 7.5° saccade or a 40° saccade to that location. Of interest was whether the prime would have more effect during a long as opposed to a short saccade, as would be the case if the processes set into motion by the prime continue to operate while the eyes are moving.

The procedure is shown in Figure 5. Following a calibration routine in which the subject fixated each of five points which were separated by 12° of visual angle on the display (not shown), a fixation box appeared on the left side of the display. The subject fixated the point centered within this box, and then a saccade target box was presented on the right side of the display. In separate blocks of trials, the saccade target box appeared either 7.5° or 40° away from the leftward fixation point. The subject was instructed to initiate a saccade to the point centered within the saccade target box as soon as it appeared. Of course, the eyes do not move instantaneously; typically,

Fixation (1500 ms):

Saccade Target Box (Headstart ms):

Prime (until saccade):

Saccade Target Box (7.5 or 40 degrees):

Response

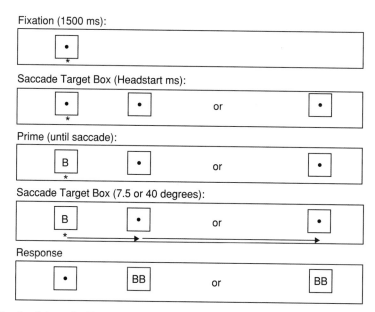

Fig. 5. Schematic illustration of the Irwin, Carlson-Radvansky, and Andrews (1995) procedure.

saccade latencies are between 250 and 300 ms. The prime was presented within the leftward fixation box before the eyes moved. We wanted subjects to view the prime for only 100 ms before they moved their eyes, however, because Posner and Snyder (1975) found that most of the growth in facilitation and inhibition in their task occurred at SOAs between 100 and 300 ms. To achieve a prime duration of 100 ms, the fixation box and the saccade target box were presented alone for some period of time (labeled headstart ms in Figure 5), and then the prime was presented in the center of the fixation box until the eyes began to move toward the saccade target box. For example, suppose that we knew that a subject's saccade latency was always 250 ms; to achieve a prime duration of 100 ms, we would present the empty fixation box and the saccade target box for 150 ms (i.e., headstart in Figure 5 would be set equal to 150 ms) before presenting the prime. Of course, saccade latency varies across subjects and across trials within a subject, so we could not adopt a fixed headstart value like 150 ms. Instead, we monitored each subject's saccade latency continuously during the experiment, and we adjusted the headstart value on each trial to track a 100 ms mean exposure time for the prime. If the prime was viewed for less than 100 ms on trial n (because the saccade occurred earlier than expected), the headstart value was decreased by 14 ms (the refresh rate of the monitor) on trial $n + 1$; in contrast, if the prime was viewed for longer than 100 ms on trial n (because the saccade occurred later than expected), the headstart value was increased by 14 ms on trial $n + 1$. This tracking procedure not only ensured that the prime would be viewed for approximately 100 ms, but it also served to equate the mean prime exposure duration across experimental conditions.

On one-third of the trials the prime consisted of a plus sign. On the remaining trials the prime consisted of an uppercase letter drawn randomly from the set of consonants, excluding Q, W, and Y. The target letters (also uppercase consonants excluding Q, W, and Y) were presented in the saccade target box during the subject's saccade, and they remained there until the subject made the *same/different* response. On half of the trials the two target letters were (physically) identical to each other, and on half they were different. On 54% of the *same* trials the prime letter was identical to the two target letters, whereas on 13% of the *same* trials the prime letter was different from the two target letters (recall that on 33% of the *same* trials the prime consisted of a neutral + sign). Thus, the prime was highly predictive of target identity. On 54% of the *different* trials the prime letter was identical to one of the two target letters, whereas on 13% of the *different* trials all three letters (prime and targets) were different from each other.

Following the completion of a block of trials, the eye movement record for each subject was analyzed to calculate TL, *time left*, the time spent fixating the prime before the saccade was initiated to the target box; TM, *time moving*, the duration of the saccade; and TR, *time right*, the time that elapsed between the subject's eye landing on or near the target letters and the subject's response. Only trials in which the subject's initial saccade landed within 3° of the target letters were analyzed (a reanalysis of the data using all trials, regardless of landing position, produced exactly the same pattern of results discussed below, with only minor variations among the means reported by Irwin et al., 1995). In addition to the landing site criterion, only trials in which the prime was viewed for between 10 and 300 ms were accepted for analysis (i.e., we eliminated trials in which the prime might not have been viewed clearly or in which it was processed for an extended period of time before the eyes moved).

The results on *same* trials are of most importance in this experiment, so only those findings will be discussed. The mean exposure duration of the prime (TL) did not vary as a function of prime type or saccade distance, indicating that the tracking procedure was successful ($M = 113$ ms). As expected, saccade duration (TM) was significantly longer for 40° saccades (89 ms) than for 7.5° saccades (29 ms). Saccade duration did not vary with prime type, nor did prime type interact with saccade distance.

Reaction time (which corresponds to TR in this case) did not vary with saccade distance, but the main effect of prime type and the interaction between saccade distance and prime type were significant. Examination of this interaction was of major interest in this experiment. The error term of the interaction was used to calculate 95% confidence intervals for the difference between two means (± 11.6 ms) and for the interaction between pairs of means (± 16.3 ms). Based on these values, we concluded that there was significant facilitation and inhibition at both saccade distances, but significantly more facilitation when the eyes moved 40° (48 ms) than when the eyes moved 7.5° (23 ms). Inhibition increased slightly with saccade distance (40 ms vs. 44 ms), but this increase was not significant. The increase in total prime effect (facilitation + inhibition) as saccade distance increased (63 ms vs. 92 ms) was significant, however. These results support the conclusion that the prime continued to be processed during the saccade. Analysis of the error rates was consistent with the reaction time analysis.

Additional analyses of the eye movement data showed that saccades made in the 7.5° condition were more accurate (undershooting the target by 0.07° on average) than in the 40° condition (undershooting the target by 0.39°). There were also significantly more fixations made on the target stimuli following 40° saccades (1.46) than following 7.5° saccades (1.09). There was no difference in reaction time to neutral (unprimed) stimuli in the 40° condition ($M = 725$ ms) compared to the 7.5° condition ($M = 734$ ms), however, so it would seem that these small differences in eye position and number of fixations did not affect target processing time. In particular, the increase in priming with increasing saccade distance cannot be attributed to differences in target visibility resulting from differences in the landing position of the eye.

In sum, in this study we found that a prime did have a larger effect following a long as opposed to a short saccade. There was a significant increase in the amount of facilitation generated by the prime, but no evidence for increased inhibition. Viewed within the context of the Posner and Snyder (1975) two-process theory of attention, this pattern of results suggests that only the automatic process of identity node or pathway priming was in operation during the saccade; if subjects had been generating an attention-requiring expectation based on the highly predictive nature of the prime, then inhibition also should have increased with saccade duration.

2. Word Recognition during Saccades

Irwin (1998) investigated whether processes involved in word recognition are suppressed during saccades. The procedure was similar to that of Irwin and Brockmole (2000) shown in Figure 3. The subject fixated a box on the left side of the display, and then a letter string was presented within it. The string was always four letters long; on half the trials it formed a word (e.g., land) and on half the trials it formed a pronounceable nonword (e.g., mafe). A saccade target box was presented on the right side of the display at the same time as the letter string was presented on the left side of the display. The saccade target box appeared either $7.5°$ or $40°$ away from the letter string. The subject was instructed to press one of two response buttons to indicate whether the letter string was a word or a nonword while making a saccade to the target box. A no-saccade control condition during which letter strings were presented at central fixation was also conducted. Reaction time (measured from letter string onset) and accuracy were measured. If processing (word recognition in this case) is suppressed during saccades, then RT should have been longer when subjects had to execute a $40°$ saccade vs. a $7.5°$ saccade because of the difference in saccade duration.

Stimulus type (word versus nonword) did not interact with any other factor, so the results reported next are averaged over all stimuli. Reaction time was 522 ms in the no-saccade condition, 571 ms in the $7.5°$ saccade condition, and 573 ms in the $40°$ saccade condition. The error data were consistent with the RT data. Thus, the results showed that saccades interfered with stimulus processing, but short saccades were just as interfering as long saccades. Most importantly, RT was identical in the two saccade conditions, indicating that lexical processing was not suppressed *during* the saccade itself. Rather, subjects continued to process the stimulus while the eyes were moving.

To examine this more closely, the eye movement records were used to divide total RT into three component parts, TL, TM, and TR, as described earlier. Averaging over stimulus type, subjects spent 287 ms fixating the stimulus (TL) in the $7.5°$ saccade condition, 28 ms moving their eyes from the fixation box to the saccade target box (TM), and then an additional 256 ms before making their response (TR). In the $40°$ saccade condition, subjects spent 268 ms fixating the stimulus (TL), 93 ms moving their eyes from the fixation box to the saccade target box (TM), and then an additional 212 ms before making their response (TR). ANOVAs confirmed that TL and TR were significantly faster in the $40°$ condition than in the $7.5°$ condition, while TM was significantly slower. Thus, in the $40°$ condition subjects were able to use the extra time during the longer saccade to reduce the time needed for stimulus processing in the pre- and postsaccadic fixation periods. In sum, the results show that word recognition was not suppressed during the saccade, but rather subjects continued to process the stimulus while the eyes were moving.

These results were confirmed in a second experiment using the "head-start" procedure developed by Irwin et al. (1995) and illustrated in Figure 5. In this version of the experiment, the saccade target box was presented for some period of time before the letter string was presented, so that saccade programming could begin and the letter string could be presented for a brief time before the eyes moved. Again we found that RT was identical in the two saccade conditions and that TR was shorter in the 40° saccade condition than in the 7.5° saccade condition, indicating that lexical processing continued while the eyes were moving. Thus, this experiment also showed that word recognition is not suppressed during saccades.

3. Word Identification during Saccades

To obtain additional information about lexical processing during saccades, Irwin (1998) also investigated whether word identification (rather than word recognition) is suppressed during saccades. The "headstart" procedure was used again to limit the amount of time that subjects viewed the stimulus before moving their eyes. Subjects fixated a fixation box on the left side of the display. Then the empty saccade target box was presented on the right side of the display, either 7.5° or 30° away. The subject was instructed to initiate a saccade to the saccade target box as soon as it appeared. Shortly before the eyes moved, the word to be identified (five to eight letters long) was presented within the leftward fixation box. When saccade onset was detected, the word was erased from the fixation box and a visual pattern mask was presented in the saccade target box. The subject's task was to identify the word.

Except at extreme exposure durations, identification accuracy was higher when the eyes moved 30° (which took 73 ms) before landing on the pattern mask than when the eyes moved 7.5° (which took 30 ms). In other words, the extra time provided by the longer eye movement led to an improvement in word identification accuracy. These results show that subjects continued to process the word while their eyes were in motion. These results thus indicate that word identification, like word recognition, is not suppressed during saccades.

4. Object Recognition during Saccades

Irwin and Brockmole (2001) investigated the effect of a saccadic eye movement on object recognition. The object recognition task that was employed was based on one used by Kroll and Potter (1984) that required subjects to distinguish pictures of objects from pictures of nonobjects. The experimental procedure was very similar to that of Irwin and Brockmole (2000) described above. The subject fixated a box on the left side of the display, and then a stimulus picture was presented within it. At the same time a saccade target box was presented on the right side of the display, either 10° or 40° away. The subject was instructed to saccade to the saccade target box and to decide whether the stimulus was an object or a nonobject while moving their eyes. They pressed one of two response buttons to indicate their response and their response time and accuracy were measured. Irwin and Brockmole (2001) found that saccade distance had no effect on reaction time or accuracy. Subjects performed the object decision task just as quickly and just as accurately during long saccades as during short saccades. Thus, object processing must not have been suspended while the eyes were in motion.

C. SUMMARY

The results of the studies conducted in my laboratory demonstrate that some cognitive processes are suppressed during saccades whereas others are not. In particular, visuospatial operations such as mental rotation and attentional scaling are suppressed, whereas nonspatial processes such as word identification and object recognition are not. These results are consistent with the notion that cognitive saccadic suppression arises from some kind of dual-task interference. Actually, there seem to be at least two kinds of dual-task interference at work. One kind is demonstrated by the finding that subjects are not always able to use the time during longer saccades to process a stimulus viewed before the saccade (e.g., Irwin & Brockmole, 2000, 2001; Irwin & Carlson-Radvansky, 1996; Irwin et al. 1995), which indicates that processing is slowed or suspended *while the eyes are moving*. But another kind of dual-task interference is demonstrated by the finding that the saccade conditions are sometimes more difficult than corresponding no-saccade control conditions even when the saccade conditions do not differ from each other (e.g., Irwin, 1998). This is probably not surprising since in the no-saccade conditions subjects have only to perform the cognitive task, whereas in the saccade conditions subjects have to perform the cognitive task and a second task—moving their eyes. In the next section I speculate about the mechanisms that might underlie both kinds of dual-task interference.

V. Why Do Saccades Interfere with Some Cognitive Processes?

Given what is known about the human information processing system, why might cognitive saccadic suppression occur? It is well known that people are not always able to do two things at the same time; thus, as I discussed above, cognitive suppression during saccades might occur as a result of dual-task interference. Although eye movements occur very frequently and we are not always aware of them, it is nonetheless the case that whenever we are engaged in some task and moving our eyes we are in a dual-task situation. In dual-task situations, sometimes interference occurs and sometimes it does not. Viewed from the perspective of dual-task performance, suppression of cognitive processing during saccades might be expected to occur only when shared processing structures or resources are called upon. This hypothesis is consistent with the research summarized above, but it is somewhat nonspecific; that is, the precise nature of the interference is unclear and so are the mechanisms responsible for the interference. At least four specific versions of the general dual-task hypothesis seem viable at the present time; these are described next.

One way of conceptualizing the hypothesis that cognitive saccadic suppression arises from dual-task interference is in terms of the functional neuroanatomy of cognitive functions. That is, suppression of cognitive processing during saccades may occur only when some cognitive task must use the same brain areas that are active during saccade programming and execution; this hypothesis follows from Kinsbourne's (1980) functional cerebral distance account of dual-task interference. I will call this the *neural interference* hypothesis. This hypothesis is consistent with the results of the research summarized above. As noted earlier, the frontal and supplementary eye fields and the posterior parietal cortex are the primary cortical areas involved in saccade programming and execution (Schall, 1995). Thus, the neural interference hypothesis predicts that cognitive tasks that require these same brain areas will be suppressed during saccades. Mental rotation is one such task (e.g., Alivisatos & Petrides, 1997; Kosslyn, DiGirolamo, Thompson, & Alpert, 1998; Peronnet & Farah, 1989). In contrast, tasks such as word recognition/identification and response selection do not rely on parietal cortex (Posner & McCandliss, 1993; Requin, Richle, & Seal, 1988), so according to the neural interference hypothesis these tasks should not be suppressed during saccades and indeed they are not (Irwin, 1998; van Duren & Sanders, 1995).

At least three other versions of the dual-task interference hypothesis seem possible, however. These three hypotheses are more functional in nature and they propose more specific sources of dual-task interference. The *spatial interference* hypothesis proposes that the spatial updating that occurs in the brain (especially in parietal cortex) when the eyes move causes dual-task interference, so only visuospatial tasks will be suppressed during saccades. There is considerable physiological evidence for the reorganization and remapping of neuronal representations of space (e.g., Dassonville et al., 1993; Duhamel et al., 1992) during saccades, so it is conceivable that these activities might interfere with cognitive processes that also require visuospatial processing. This hypothesis is also consistent with most of the existing data, since visuospatial tasks are suppressed during saccades, whereas mental operations, such as response selection, pathway priming, and word and object recognition, are not.

Another possibility, however, is that it is not spatial updating that causes interference during saccades, but rather the shift of spatial selective attention that obligatorily precedes a saccadic eye movement to some location. That is, there is considerable evidence (e.g., Deubel & Schneider, 1996; Hoffman & Subramaniam, 1995; Irwin & Gordon, 1998; Kowler, Anderson, Dosher, & Blaser, 1995; Rayner, McConkie, & Ehrlich, 1978; Shepherd, Findlay, & Hockey, 1986) that prior to the onset of a saccade, spatial selective attention is allocated to the to-be-fixated location in an obligatory and involuntary fashion. According to the *attentional interference* hypothesis, when spatial selective attention is bound to the saccade target location during saccade programming and execution it is unavailable for use by other cognitive tasks. This hypothesis predicts that only cognitive tasks that also require spatial selective attention will be suppressed during saccades. This hypothesis, too, appears to be consistent with the results of prior research.

Finally, consider a fourth hypothesis, the *executive interference* hypothesis. Executing a saccade while a cognitive task is being performed requires coordination between the cognitive and motor systems. The timing and organization of component operations must be planned and sequenced for the efficient performance of both tasks and this presumably relies on resource-demanding executive control processes (Monsell & Driver, 2000). The fact that performance in saccade conditions is often worse than performance in a matching no-saccade control condition (e.g., Irwin, 1998) is likely due to the fact that the saccade conditions (which involve a cognitive task plus an eye movement) require more executive processing than the no-saccade condition (which involves only the cognitive task). Executive control processes appear to rely on prefrontal areas of the brain (e.g., Petrides, Alivisatos, Evans, & Meyer, 1993; Petrides, 2000); since the frontal eye fields play a critical role in saccade programming it seems possible that interference between saccade programming and other executive control processes might occur.

Obviously the four hypotheses described above are not mutually exclusive in all respects; spatial updating and shifts of selective attention both accompany saccades, for example, and both activities rely on the same brain areas. Furthermore, different hypotheses may be required to explain different aspects of performance [e.g., the executive interference hypothesis may explain why saccade conditions are more difficult than no-saccade conditions while the attentional interference hypothesis (say) may explain why processing is suspended during saccades per se]. Nonetheless it seems possible (at least to some extent) to discriminate among these hypotheses and that is currently the focus of much research in my laboratory.

VI. Significance

As noted above, saccadic eye movements occur over 150,000 times each day, making them one of the most frequent behaviors that people perform. If cognitive activity is suppressed during saccades then that is something we really should know, and discovering the reasons for this suppression is of fundamental importance to our understanding of human cognition. Understanding cognitive saccadic suppression is also important from a methodological standpoint vis-à-vis the interpretation of reaction time data, one of the most commonly used dependent variables in cognitive research. Specifically, if cognitive processing is suppressed during saccades, then "reaction time" will overestimate the duration of cognitive processing per se when eye movements occur during task performance. In such cases, it would be inappropriate to measure reaction time without monitoring eye position as well. The phenomenon of cognitive saccadic suppression has important implications for the design of visual displays and control panels as well—if cognitive processing is suppressed during eye movements, then requiring a user to make saccades to acquire information from a display should be eliminated whenever possible.

With respect to this latter point, there are several intriguing findings in the literature that suggest that people may (voluntarily or involuntarily) suppress eye movements during the performance of some cognitive tasks. For example, Barlow (1952) found that performing mental arithmetic reduced the frequency and amplitude of microsaccades made during fixation of a small light. Mental arithmetic appears to rely on parietal cortex (e.g., Dehaene, 1997), so this finding is consistent with the dual-task interference hypothesis. In a more complex domain, it has been reported that airplane pilots make almost no eye movements during the last few seconds of landing an aircraft, but rather keep their eyes fixated on the expected landing point (Gerathewohl & Strughold, 1954; Thomas, 1963). Perhaps relatedly, Recarte and Nunes (2000) found that automobile drivers made fewer fixations and searched a more restricted region of the visual environment when they were asked to perform a spatial imagery task during driving compared to when they performed no secondary task or a verbal secondary task. These behaviors could conceivably arise as a result of subjects attempting to minimize the dual-task costs associated with eye movements, though other explanations are possible.

The existing research on cognitive suppression during saccades has focussed exclusively on the effects of saccades on cognitive processing, with very little investigation of whether cognitive processing might affect saccadic behavior. If cognitive saccadic suppression is really due to dual-task conflict, however, then one might expect to find effects of cognition on saccadic behavior as well as effects of saccades on cognitive processing. Such evidence has been provided by Pashler, Carrier, and Hoffman (1993) in the psychological refractory period paradigm. They had subjects make manual responses to a tone and a saccade to a location that was specified by a visual stimulus. They found that the manual response to the tone slowed saccade latency only when the visual stimulus required interpretation (i.e., cognitive processing). There is also some evidence that cognitive processing interferes not only with eye movements, but with other motor movements as well; in particular, Pellecchia and Turvey (2001) found that synchronized arm movements were destabilized when subjects counted backward by three compared to a no-counting control condition. Thus, interference between cognitive processing and motor processing may be a fairly general phenomenon with much theoretical and practical significance.

VII. Conclusion

Eye movements are one of the most frequent behaviors that people perform and they are essential for the successful completion of many perceptual and cognitive activities. The evidence reviewed above demonstrates that in some cases eye movements actually interfere with cognitive processing, however. In particular, saccadic eye movements suppress visuospatial processes but appear to have little or no effect on nonspatial operations. Future research will elucidate the mechanisms underlying the suppressive effects of saccades and will examine further the interplay between cognition and movements of the eyes.

ACKNOWLEDGMENTS

Preparation of this chapter was supported by NSF Grant BCS 01-32272 to the author. I thank Laura Carlson and James Brockmole for collaborating with me on much of the research that is described here and Andries Sanders for stimulating my interest in the question of cognitive suppression during saccades.

REFERENCES

Alivisatos, B., & Petrides, M. (1997). Functional activation of the human brain during mental rotation. *Neuropsychologia, 35,* 111–118.
Andersen, R. A., Batista, A. P., Snyder, L. H., Buneo, C. A., & Cohen, Y. E. (2000). Programming to look and reach in the posterior parietal cortex. In M. S. Gazzaniga (Ed.), *The new cognitive neurosciences* (2nd ed., pp. 515–524). Cambridge, MA: MIT Press.
Barlow, H. B. (1952). Eye movements during fixation. *Journal of Physiology, 116,* 290–306.

Boer, L. C., & Van der Weijgert, E. C. M. (1988). Eye movements and stages of processing. *Acta Psychologica, 67*, 3–17.

Brockmole, J. R., Carlson, L. A., & Irwin, D. E. (2002). Inhibition of attended processing during saccadic eye movements. *Perception and Psychophysics, 64*, 867–881.

Cabeza, R., & Nyberg, L. (2000). Imaging cognition II: An empirical review of 275 PET and fMRI studies. *Journal of Cognitive Neuroscience, 12*, 1–47.

Campbell, F. W., & Wurtz, R. H. (1978). Saccadic omission: Why we do not see a grey-out during a saccadic eye movement. *Vision Research, 18*, 1297–1303.

Cooper, L. A., & Shepard, R. N. (1973). Chronometric studies of the rotation of mental images. In W. G. Chase (Ed.), *Visual information processing* (pp. 76–176). New York: Academic Press.

Currie, C., McConkie, G. W., Carlson-Radvansky, L. A., & Irwin, D. E. (2000). The role of the saccade target object in the perception of a visually stable world. *Perception and Psychophysics, 62*, 673–683.

Dassonville, P., Schlag, J., & Schlag-Rey, M. (1993). Direction constancy in the oculomotor system. *Current Directions in Psychological Science, 2*, 143–147.

Dehaene, S. (1997). *The number sense*. New York: Oxford University Press.

Deubel, H., & Schneider, W. X. (1996). Saccade target selection and object recognition: Evidence for a common attentional mechanism. *Vision Research, 36*, 1993–1997.

Duhamel, J.-R., Colby, C., & Goldberg, M. (1992). The updating of the representation of visual space in parietal cortex by intended eye movements. *Science, 255*, 90–92.

Erdmann, B., & Dodge, R. (1898). *Psychologische untersuchungen uber das lesen*. Halle: Niemeyer.

Gerathewohl, S. J., & Strughold, H. (1954). Time consumption of eye movements and high-speed flying. *Aviation Medicine, 3*, 38–45.

Harrington, D. (1981). *The visual fields: A textbook and atlas of clinical perimetry*. St. Louis, MO: Mosby.

Hochberg, J. (1978). *Perception*. Englewood Cliffs, NJ: Prentice-Hall.

Hoffman, J. E., & Subramanian, B. (1995). The role of visual attention in saccadic eye movements. *Perception and Psychophysics, 57*, 787–795.

Irwin, D. E. (1996). Integrating information across saccadic eye movements. *Current Directions in Psychological Science, 5*, 94–100.

Irwin, D. E. (1998). Lexical processing during saccadic eye movements. *Cognitive Psychology, 36*, 1–27.

Irwin, D. E., & Brockmole, J. R. (2000). Mental rotation is suppressed during saccadic eye movements. *Psychonomic Bulletin and Review, 7*, 654–661.

Irwin, D. E., & Brockmole, J. R. (2001). *Suppressing where but not what: The effect of saccades on dorsal- and ventral-stream visual processing*. Paper presented at the 42nd Annual Meeting of the Psychonomic Society, Orlando, FL.

Irwin, D. E., & Carlson-Radvansky, L. A. (1996). Suppression of cognitive activity during saccadic eye movements. *Psychological Science, 7*, 83–88.

Irwin, D. E., Carlson-Radvansky, L. A., & Andrews, R. V. (1995). Information processing during saccadic eye movements. *Acta Psychologica, 90*, 261–273.

Irwin, D. E., & Gordon, R. D. (1998). Eye movements, attention, and transsaccadic memory. *Visual Cognition, 5*, 127–155.

Kinsbourne, M. (1980). Mapping a behavioral cerebral space. *International Journal of Neuroscience, 11*, 45–50.

Kosslyn, S. M., DiGirolamo, G. J., Thompson, W. L., & Alpert, N. M. (1998). Mental rotation of objects versus hands: Neural mechanisms revealed by positron emission tomography. *Psychophysiology, 35*, 151–161.

Kowler, E., Anderson, E., Dosher, B., & Blaser, E. (1995). The role of attention in the programming of saccades. *Vision Research, 35*, 1897–1916.

Kroll, J. F., & Potter M.C. (1984). Recognizing words, pictures, and concepts: A comparison of lexical, object, and reality decisions. *Journal of Verbal Learning and Verbal Behaviour, 23*, 39–66.

Matin, E. (1974). Saccadic suppression: A review and an analysis. *Psychological Bulletin, 81*, 899–917.

Matin, E., Shao, K., & Boff, K. (1993). Saccadic overhead: Information-processing time with and without saccades. *Perception and Psychophysics, 53*, 372–380.

Mishkin, M., Ungerleider, L. G., & Macko, K. A. (1983). Object vision and spatial vision: Two cortical pathways. *Trends in Neuroscience, 6*, 414–417.

Monsell, S., & Driver, J. (2000). *Control of cognitive processes: Attention and performance XVIII*. Cambridge, MA: MIT Press.

Pashler, H., Carrier, M., & Hoffman, J. (1993). Saccadic eye movements and dual-task interference. *Quarterly Journal of Experimental Psychology, 46A*51–82.

Pellecchia, G., & Turvey, M. T. (2001). Cognitive activity shifts the attractors of bimanual rhythmic coordination. *Journal of Motor Behavior, 33*, 9–15.

Peronnet, F., & Farah, M. J. (1989). Mental rotation: An event-related potential study with a validated mental rotation task. *Brain and Cognition, 9*, 279–288.

Petrides, M. (2000). Mapping prefrontal cortical systems for the control of cognition. In A. Toga & J. Mazziotta (Eds.), *Brain mapping: The systems* (pp. 159–176). San Diego, CA: Academic Press.

Petrides, M., Alivisatos, B., Evans, A., & Meyer, E. (1993). Dissociation of human mid-dorsolateral from posterior dorsolateral frontal cortex in memory processing. *Proceedings of the National Academy of Sciences of the United States of America, 90*, 873–877.

Posner, M., & McCandliss, B. (1993). Converging methods for investigating lexical access. *Psychological Science, 4*, 305–309.

Posner, M., & Snyder, C. (1975). Facilitation and inhibition in the processing of signals. In P. M. A. Rabbitt & S. Dornic (Eds.), *Attention and performance V* (pp. 669–682). New York: Academic Press.

Rayner, K. (1978). Eye movements in reading and information processing. *Psychological Bulletin, 85*, 618–660.

Rayner, K. (1998). Eye movements in reading and information processing: Twenty years of research. *Psychological Bulletin, 124*, 372–422.

Rayner, K., McConkie, G., & Ehrlich, S. (1978). Eye movements and integrating information across fixations. *Journal of Experimental Psychology: Human Perception and Performance, 4*, 529–544.

Recarte, M. A., & Nunes, L. M. (2000). Effects of verbal and spatial-imagery tasks on eye fixations while driving. *Journal of Experimental Psychology: Applied, 6*, 31–43.

Requin, J., Riehle, A., & Seal, J. (1988). Neuronal activity and information processing in motor control: From stages to continuous flow. *Biological Psychology, 26*, 179–198.

Riggs, L. A., Merton, P. A., & Morton, H. B. (1974). Suppression of visual phosphenes during saccadic eye movements. *Vision Research, 14*, 997–1010.

Russo, J. E. (1978). Adaptation of cognitive processes to the eye movement system. In J. W. Senders, D. F. Fisher, & R. A. Monty (Eds.), *Eye movements and the higher psychological functions* (pp. 89–112). Hillsdale, NJ: Erlbaum.

Sanders, A. F., & Houtmans, M. J. M. (1985). There is no central stimulus encoding during saccadic eye shifts: A case against general parallel processing notions. *Acta Psychologica, 60*, 323–338.

Sanders, A. F., & Rath, A. M. (1991). Perceptual processing and speed-accuracy trade-off. *Acta Psychologica, 77,* 275–291.

Schall, J. D. (1995). Neural basis of saccade target selection. *Reviews in the Neurosciences, 6,* 63–85.

Shepherd, M., Findlay, J., & Hockey, R. (1986). The relationship between eye movements and spatial attention. *Quarterly Journal of Experimental Psychology, 38A,* 475–491.

Sternberg, S. (1969). The discovery of processing stages: Extensions of Donders' method. *Acta Psychologica, 30,* 276–315.

Thomas, E. L. (1963). The eye movements of a pilot during aircraft landing. *Aerospace Medicine, 34,* 424–426.

van Duren, L. (1993). Central stimulus processing during saccadic eye movements. In G. d'Ydewalle & J. Van Rensbergen (Eds.), *Perception and cognition: Advances in eye-movement research* (pp. 23–35). Amsterdam: North-Holland.

van Duren, L., & Sanders, A. F. (1995). Signal processing during and across saccades. *Acta Psychologica, 89,* 121–147.

Volkmann, F. C. (1986). Human visual suppression. *Vision Research, 26,* 1401–1416.

Volkmann, F. C., Schick, A. M. L., & Riggs, L. A. (1968). Time course of visual inhibition during voluntary saccades. *Journal of the Optical Society of America, 58,* 562–569.

Zuber, B. L., & Stark, L. (1966). Saccadic suppression: Elevation of visual threshold associated with saccadic eye movements. *Experimental Neurology, 16,* 65–79.

WHAT MAKES CHANGE BLINDNESS INTERESTING?

Daniel J. Simons and Daniel T. Levin

I. Overview

The methods of change detection and the phenomenon of change blindness have received noticeably more attention over the past 10 years. Change blindness is the finding that observers often fail to notice large changes to objects or scenes when the change coincides with a brief visual disruption (Simons & Levin, 1997). For example, observers often fail to notice changes that occur during a brief flash on a computer display (e.g., Hochberg, 1968; Pashler, 1988; Phillips, 1974; Rensink, O'Regan, & Clark, 1997; Simons, 1996), a cut from one view to another in a motion picture (Levin & Simons, 1997), an eye movement (Grimes, 1996; Henderson & Hollingworth, 1999b; McConkie & Currie, 1996), a blink (O'Regan, Deubel, Clark, & Rensink, 2000), or even a real-world disruption (Simons & Levin, 1998). Although change blindness has become more central to the field of visual cognition in recent years (for a recent review, see Rensink, 2002), the phenomenon was described in the empirical literature over 30 years ago (e.g., Hochberg, 1968), and theoretical inferences consistent with change blindness were drawn as early as the 1950s (e.g., Stroud, 1955). In fact, William James (1950/1891) commented on the problem of difference detection in his *Principles of Psychology.* Outside of psychology, the idea of change blindness has been discussed for decades. For example, filmmakers discovered the existence of change blindness shortly after they began

THE PSYCHOLOGY OF LEARNING
AND MOTIVATION VOL. 42

introducing editing into motion pictures (Kuleshov, 1987/1920). Why, then, has there been such a sudden surge of interest in the failure to detect changes? What makes recent findings of change blindness interesting and novel? To fully understand the impact of recent evidence for change blindness, we must situate these findings into the broader historical context, linking them to earlier evidence for change blindness. This chapter reviews historical evidence for change blindness emphasizing both the historical precursors and the innovations of more recent approaches.

II. Introduction

For almost any surprising empirical result, a thorough search of the historical literature reveals an empirical precedent or a consistent theoretical idea; new findings do not occur in a vacuum. However, some findings seem more interesting or surprising than others. The fact that a finding is surprising suggests that, at some level, it was not entirely predictable or obvious from the existing knowledge base, perhaps because some assumptions inherent in the earlier claims or some aspect of the findings deviate from expectations. Historical reviews of literature often seek to identify predecessors and precedents for current claims and findings that would challenge their novelty or originality. That is not our goal. Criticizing the novelty of a new result on the basis of older evidence often relies on the acuity of hindsight: predicting the outcome of a study on the basis of prior knowledge is more challenging than "postdicting" it. Postdiction allows unrestricted filtering of the earlier results, leaving only those that happened to be consistent while purging those that predicted other outcomes. This chapter notes how earlier work was consistent with evidence for change blindness and ways in which earlier findings and theories did not necessarily predict current ones. Our goal is to emphasize how current findings of change blindness are novel and why they are surprising in light of the historical precedents. We argue that recent findings were not entirely predictable from historical precedents, although with the benefit of hindsight, they are consistent.

III. An Early Consideration of Change Detection and Difference Detection

Over the past century or so, change detection research has focused on two distinct questions: What are the mechanisms underlying difference perception and how do we notice changes that occurred some time ago? Our visual system detects changes quite well, provided that the change occurs instantaneously, with one object immediately replacing another. Such changes produce a transient signal, involuntarily and unavoidably bringing the change to awareness (e.g., Reichardt, 1961). The detection of such instantaneous changes has been studied extensively in the motion perception literature. In contrast, relatively few studies, historically, have explored the detection of changes in the absence of such signals. For example, how do you notice when a co-worker changes hair styles or starts wearing glasses? In these cases, the pre- and postchange state of the object are separated by a temporal gap, eliminating the transient signal that would be produced by an instantaneous change. Detecting such changes seems to require an explicit comparison of the pre- and postchange states, inferring that a change occurred.

This distinction, between change detection via a sensory transient and change detection via *inference*, was noted eloquently by William James (1950/1891): "With such direct perceptions of difference as this [a motion transient], we must not confound those entirely unlike cases in which we infer that two things must differ because we know enough about each of them taken by itself to warrant our classing them under distinct heads. It often happens, when the interval is long between two experiences, that our judgments are guided, not so much by a positive image or copy of the earlier one, as by our recollections of certain facts about it" (pp. 496–497, brackets added). I detect my co-worker's haircut not by perceiving the change, but by recollecting the original hair style, comparing what I know about it to the current hair style, and inferring that a change occurred. Change detection via inference does not require a veridical representation; the representation of your co-worker's hair style need not be an exact, image-like replica of that hair style. Rather, the representation can take the form of knowledge about the hair style—a simple verbal description (e.g., "short, parted hair") would suffice for change detection. William James (pp. 499–501) rails against the belief that such inference-based change detection requires exact replicas of the world to be stored internally, instead arguing that knowledge of a thing can take the place of an internal replica of that thing.

Perhaps you have seen the comic strip game of "spot the difference" in which two images are presented side by side and the goal is to detect all of the differences between the images. This task, as James notes, requires detection via inference. The change does not bring attention to itself. Rather observers must actively compare their knowledge of the two images. Detecting the difference between successively presented images can be much easier than detecting the difference between simultaneously presented images because they can produce a transient: "The reason why successive impression so much favors the result seems to be that there is a real sensation of difference, aroused by the shock of transition from one perception to another which is unlike the first" (p. 495). Successively presented images, in the absence of a temporal or spatial gap, produce a change signal or transient. In contrast, simultaneously presented images require a shift of attention from one image to the other. There is no sensation of difference, and no involuntary discrimination. Instead, observers must compare what they know about one image to what they see in the other.

James also notes that the mechanisms operating with simultaneously presented images might also operate when changes are presented successively, provided that the change is small or that the delay between images is long: "where the objective difference is less, discrimination need not so inevitably occur, and may even require considerable effort of attention to be performed at all" (p. 494) and "the longer the interval of time between the sensations, the more uncertain is their discrimination" (p. 496). In these two passages, James anticipates findings of change blindness: provided the change does not produce a motion signal (the delay is long enough), change detection requires an effortful comparison of the representations. In the absence of such a comparison, observers will miss the change.

IV. Early Empirical Evidence for Change Blindness

The recent focus on change blindness comes against a backdrop of decades of empirical research on change detection, priming, and saccadic integration. Perhaps the earliest empirical suggestion of change blindness comes from a series of studies looking at Michotte's tunnel effect (Burke, 1952). In the tunnel effect, a moving object disappears behind a boundary and reappears on the other side. Despite the brief occlusion, observers typically perceive a single, spatiotemporally coherent object because the motion would be consistent with a single object moving at a constant rate and in a constant direction (see Spelke, 1990 for a discussion of this principle). Burke (1952) used a standard tunnel display, but changed the object's appearance during the occlusion event. Although his observers were aware of the change and were required only to judge how continuous the motion appeared, one observer claimed to notice "the changes only at the beginning of each experiment. After a short time the differences became unimportant and the experiment proceeded as if there were no changes at all" (Burke, 1952, p. 136). Although this example is not a clear case of change blindness because the observers were not asked whether they had detected the change on every trial (i.e., the subjective, retrospective report might be inaccurate), it hints at the possibility that observers might not automatically encode, retain, and compare the features of moving objects and that they might fail to notice changes to occluded objects.

Another early study looked more directly at the ability to detect changes by asking observers to detect differences in the positions of dots in two sequentially presented displays (French, 1953). An array of dots appeared for 3 seconds and after a variable-length delay, another pattern appeared and subjects were asked to judge whether the patterns were the same or different. Overall, observers made errors on approximately 30% of trials, with a greater number of missed changes than falsely reported changes (a standard response bias found in many change detection studies). The use of a brief blank interval served to eliminate the visual transient that would have occurred had the second array immediately followed the first. This approach presages many of the current approaches to studying change blindness (see Rensink, 2002)—more recent studies have also used simple dot or letter arrays in a change detection task with the goal of exploring the capacity of visual short-term memory (e.g., Pashler, 1988; Phillips, 1974; Pollack, 1972). All of these studies suggest that change detection can be difficult, even with relatively simple displays and even when observers are actively looking for changes (Simons & Mitroff, 2001). Many behavioral studies of change detection in the 1960s and 1970s similarly focused on the ability to notice differences in displays across a temporal gap (Cermak, 1971; Dirks & Neisser, 1977; Hochberg, 1968; Mandler & Ritchey, 1977; Mandler & Robinson, 1978; Newcombe, Rogoff, & Kagan, 1977), typically finding far less than perfect performance. For example, Hochberg (1968) found that observers struggled to detect changes to inverted and negative faces provided that the delay between the original and changed image was about 1 second.

During the same period, an entirely independent literature on eye movements also provided evidence for change blindness. Research on eye movements and visual representations focused on the quantity and precision of the information retained from one fixation to the next. For example, many studies addressed the ability to detect object displacements that occurred during a saccadic eye movement in an effort to determine how precisely observers can remember the exact spatial location of an object from one fixation to the next and what information they use to do so. An extensive series of studies over a period of three decades found substantial evidence for change blindness in displacement detection (Bridgeman, Hendry, & Stark, 1975; Deubel, Schneider, & Bridgeman, 1996; Ditchburn, 1955; Henderson, 1997; Li & Matin, 1990a,b, 1997; Mack, 1970; Wallach & Lewis, 1965). In the absence of a stable landmark in the display (see Hayhoe, Lachter, & Feldman, 1991 for evidence of integration in the presence of a landmark), observers show poor detection when, during a saccade, the target of their saccade shifts by up to 10% of the saccade length (e.g., Li & Matin, 1990a,b; Mack, 1970). More recent work shows that observers also fail to notice shifts or expansions of the entire display if they occur during an eye movement (Currie, McConkie, Carlson-Radvansky, & Irwin, 2000; McConkie & Currie, 1996), even when the displays consist of photographs of natural scenes.

Contemporaneous to these studies of displacement detection, research on eye movements in reading also produced evidence for change blindness (e.g., McConkie & Zola, 1979). One central issue in the reading literature was determining what information from nonfixated words contributes to reading performance. By using saccade-contingent display changes, the information available on any given fixation could be controlled precisely (Blanchard, Pollatsek, & Rayner, 1989; McConkie & Rayner, 1975; McConkie, Zola, Blanchard, & Wolverton, 1982; Pollatsek, Lesch, Morris, & Rayner, 1992; Pollatsek & Rayner, 1992). The display might include a shifting window of visibility in which letters were visible only in and around fixation, but were masked elsewhere. When the reader saccaded to a new location, additional words were revealed and the previously fixated words were masked. In this "moving window" technique, as long as approximately 4 letters to the left and 15 letters to the right of the currently fixated word are visible, reading speed and comprehension are essentially normal (Rayner & Pollatsek, 1987)—all other letters on the page can be replaced by Xs with no decrement in reading. Interestingly, when only the fixated word is visible, reading rate and comprehension are reduced. The information gained on one fixation provides a preview of words that will be fixated next, and this information is retained across the saccade to facilitate processing on the next fixation (Blanchard et al., 1989). Most studies using this technique did not explicitly assess change detection—instead they focused on what information was used on each fixation. However, the fact that observers could read at effectively normal speeds despite the changes hints that they might not have noticed the changes at all. At a minimum, the changes did not disrupt performance.

A few studies of the benefits of an unfixated word did informally consider awareness of changes. In one paradigm, observers initially fixate the center of a screen and a word is presented away from fixation (either peripherally or parafoveally). Observers initiate an eye movement to the word, and during the saccade, the word is replaced with a target word that observers are asked to name (see Rayner, McConkie, & Ehrlich, 1978; Rayner, McConkie, & Zola, 1980). In general, a preview of the same word or a visually similar word produces considerably faster processing of the target word than does a random letter string or an asterisk (Rayner et al., 1978). Interestingly, observers generally do not report noticing the change from preview to target. The same blindness to changes occurs when observers are required to name a picture that initially appears away from fixation but changes to a new picture or even a new background during the saccade (e.g., Boyce & Pollatsek, 1992). Although all of these studies are consistent with change blindness, none was focused on change blindness per se, and most measured change detection performance only indirectly.

One study, however, was designed specifically to illustrate the extent of change blindness across saccades. McConkie and Zola (1979) asked subjects to read text in AlTeRnAtInG cAsE, and during every eye movement, they changed the case of every letter on the display. When the changes were contingent on eye movements, observers were able to read the text at the same rate they would have if there had been no changes, and they rarely noticed anything different. In contrast, observers who simply watched the displays from behind the observers noticed the changes and were unable to read the text efficiently because the constant changes were disruptive—when the changes were not contingent on eye movements, they produced large transient signals that presumably disrupted reading. This study was anomalous in that it was the only one of that era that was designed to demonstrate the magnitude of change blindness. Not until the 1990s did the field begin a systematic exploration of the extent and pervasiveness of change blindness across eye movements (e.g., Grimes, 1996; McConkie & Currie, 1996).

Despite this varied and fairly extensive early evidence for change blindness, the findings were not synthesized into a coherent description of the phenomenon (Rensink, 2002). Prior to the 1990s, research on eye movements and visual short-term memory generally did not cross-pollinate. Moreover, even within the eye movement literature, evidence from studies of displacement detection was not integrated with evidence from studies of reading and priming. Only later were findings of saccade-contingent change blindness completely integrated with findings of poor change detection across temporal gaps and other forms of visual disruption (e.g., Henderson, 1997; Irwin, 1991, 1992a,b; Rensink et al., 1997; Simons & Levin, 1997).

V. Early Evidence from Other Disciplines

In addition to the early empirical literature on change detection, several other fields have considered failures of change detection. Perhaps the clearest example comes from the development and analysis of the art of filmmaking. The task faced by early film makers was similar to that faced by psychologists studying how the visual system integrates information across a saccade: how does the visual system combine information from sequential views? The earliest films did not have to address this issue. They typically portrayed a single, discrete event that took place in a single location. Essentially, such films were the equivalent of a video recording of a stage performance. Filmmakers set up their camera in front of a performance, started the camera, and then stopped it when the performance was complete. Boxing matches were a popular topic for the first films because all of the action was constrained to the ring and the timing of the match was well defined in advance—an entire round could be filmed in a single take. During the first two decades of the twentieth century, however, Edwin Porter, D. W. Griffith, and others realized that they could present a more interesting story by editing together different views of a scene. Changing views allows the filmmaker to emphasize a subcomponent of the scene such as an actor's emotional reaction. For example, Griffith edited together wide-angle shots of the entire scene with close-up shots that could accentuate subtle emotions that were invisible in the wider shots. The use of multiple views as well as other innovations such as cross-cutting (e.g., alternating shots of narratively linked actions in different locations) allowed film to distinguish itself from its theatrical origins by reducing the reliance on broad, caricatured gestures as the sole vehicles for conveying emotions and intentions. These techniques also provided a unique method of story telling that no other art form could duplicate.

Although the use of multiple views and cross-cutting allows viewers to see different aspects of a scene, the introduction of these techniques raised a new practical question: How could these views be edited together so that audiences would perceive them as a coherent whole rather than as a jumble of unrelated images? To answer this question, filmmakers needed to become astute observers of viewers' cognitive capabilities and limits. Griffith obsessively watched audience reactions to his films from the projection booth, and, based on their reactions, he repeatedly reedited the films between screenings. Over the next 40 years, filmmakers honed their careful observations into a set of traditions and principles that underlies most of the editing techniques used today. Soviet filmmakers Lev Kuleshov and V. I. Pudovkin were among the first to attempt to formalize some of the links between film and psychology by conducting a number of experiments that are well known to students of film history. For example, in one, they combined shots from many distinct locations to give the impression of a single location (for more information, see Levin & Simons, 2000). Even though the individual shots were entirely unrelated, by combining them in a consistent way, viewers were none the wiser. Griffith, Kuleshov, Pudovkin, and others found that as long as viewers related each shot to a global understanding of the scene, and provided that none of the cuts from one scene to another produced any unnatural motion of elements in the scene (i.e., the edit did not cause apparent motion of an object in the scene from one view to the next), observers would interpret it correctly and would not be confused by the cut. Pudovkin (1929/1970) and later theorists described the need to motivate a new view, suggesting that each view should answer a question posed by the previous view. For example, if an actor looks off-screen, the audience is induced to ask "why is he looking there?" The next shot should be a close-up of the target of the actor's gaze because that will answer the audience's question. In that way, separate shots can become a coherent whole.

Although most filmmakers and theorists focused on how to make scenes appear consistent across a cut, they also found that some kinds of consistency were not necessary. Kuleshov was well aware that audiences generally do not detect inconsistencies in actor's clothing or body positions across cuts: "when we ... shoot the constituent parts of a scene at different times, or insert a filmed element of one scene into another, we sometimes have to disregard small inconsistencies in the costume of an actor.... Convincing montage makes the audience overlook such effects" (Kuleshov, 1987/1920, p. 44). Since then, many other filmmakers have commented on the surprising degree to which audiences fail to detect visual inconsistencies (see Dmytryk, 1984). For example, Dmytryk notes that "if the cut is dramatically correct, it is remarkable how often the bad match will be completely unnoticed by the viewer" (1984, p. 44; in the same passage, Dmytryk describes how the viewer's center of interest influences noticing, an effect later explored empirically by Rensink et al., 1997). Evidence for change blindness from motion pictures extends even to failures to notice changes to central, attended objects. For his 1977 film, "That Obscure Object of Desire," Luis Buñuel's first choice for a female lead, Maria Schneider, proved unreliable due to a drug habit. Because production was underway by the time Buñuel discovered this problem, he decided to replace Schneider with two actresses, Angela Molina and Carole Bouquet. In editing the film, Buñuel alternated the two actresses across scenes, in part to symbolize how the male lead actor did not see the true nature of his lover. By the end of the film, one actor was replaced by the other within a single scene with a delay of only a few seconds, but some audience members reportedly never noticed the switch (Buñuel, 1983). Hochberg's (1986) review of psychological research relevant to motion picture perception considered a number of similar examples of poor change detection, and used these examples to conclude that visual memory is "sketchy" and highly schematic. These reports from film history were among the primary inspirations for our more recent work on change blindness in motion pictures (Levin & Simons, 1997; Simons, 1996).

The notion that visual memory is limited and change detection poor has even been incorporated into manuals designed to train script continuity supervisors, the people responsible for avoiding mistakes or changes from one shot to the next in movies (Miller, 1999; Rowlands, 2000). Perhaps more than any other profession, continuity supervisors are practiced at trying to detect subtle changes. They, if anyone, should be able to rely on visual memory for detecting changes from one scene to the next. However, as manuals teaching continuity supervision note, visual memory is limited and nobody can detect all differences without memory aids. For example, aspiring continuity supervisors are advised to use memory aids such as photographs and copious notes to help record the details of each shot: "you can mentally retain a host of details. But there is good reason for profusely jotting clues on the script page while a performance is in progress" (Miller, 1999, p. 88). Miller (1999) also notes that "it is humanly impossible and patently unnecessary for you to simultaneously watch and note every detail in a scene. The mark of a competent continuity supervisor is . . . knowing what is important to observe for matching purposes. By the same token, knowing when it is *not* necessary to match certain details proves invaluable" (p. 177). Similarly, Rowlands (2000) notes that "good continuity is not *just* being good at observation. It is knowing what is important to observe" (p. 88). Rowlands recommends assigning priority to the largest moving object in a scene because "a viewer's attention will be drawn to it" (p. 93). She also notes the need to attend to the main characters, any actor who is speaking, and unusually bright colors. All of these suggestions reflect an intuitive model of attention capture, and they entail an implicit acknowledgment that the capacity of attention is limited. Continuity supervisors cannot attend to every aspect of a scene, so they should focus most on those features that audience members are likely to notice—namely, those features that attract attention.

Evidence from the history of filmmaking and from continuity supervision provide a rich source of intuitions about perception and visual memory precisely because they are based on decades of observation and experimentation. The practical requirements of filmmaking are a natural test-bed for theories of visual memory and attention, one that has been relatively untapped by psychologists. Filmmakers wrote about change blindness and continuity well before systematic empirical work on visual integration in the cognitive psychology literature. Moreover, their ideas about the sketchiness of visual memory often predated similar claims in the psychology literature. An exploration of other practical disciplines would likely reveal similar insights. For example, successful magicians need to understand how their actions can divert attention. They must be aware of the selectivity and limits of attention, and they certainly use this knowledge (whether it is implicit or explicit) to induce change blindness in their audiences (see, for example, Bruno, 1978).

VI. Theoretical Predictions (or Postdictions) of Change Blindness

As in the development of filmmaking, theoretical discussions of change blindness within the psychological literature typically followed from evidence of change blindness rather than predicted it. One of the primary theoretical inferences drawn from recent findings of change blindness is that we lack a detailed internal representation of our visual world that is preserved from one view to the next (e.g., Rensink, 2000b). The notion of sparse representations is one variant of the idea that the world can serve as an "outside memory" (O'Regan, 1992). According to the "outside memory" hypothesis, the visual world need not be represented internally because it can be accessed at will simply by looking. Much as a computer can rely on virtual memory to give the appearance of a greater amount of physical RAM, people can rely on the external world as a storehouse for visual information, thereby reducing the need to rely on internal representations of the world (Rensink, 2000a,b). If this outside memory is seamlessly integrated into perception, observers likely would be unaware of its existence, leading to the mistaken assumption that they have represented the world internally. Consistent with this notion, people do tend to overestimate the amount of information that they retain and compare from one view of a scene to the next (Levin, Momen, Drivdahl, & Simons, 2000).

Variants of the "outside memory" hypothesis have served as a catalyst for much of the current research on change detection and change blindness. In fact, the major ongoing controversies in the field all focus on the amount and nature of the information that is represented when change detection succeeds and fails (Simons, 2000a). For example, a number of studies have claimed to support evidence for implicit change detection despite explicit change blindness (Fernandez-Duque & Thornton, 2000; Smilek, Eastwood, & Merikle, 2000; Thornton & Fernandez-Duque, 2000; Williams & Simons, 2000), but others suggest that such representations might not exist (Mitroff & Simons, 2002; Mitroff, Simons, & Franconeri, 2002). The recent surge of interest in the outside memory hypothesis was certainly bolstered by findings of change blindness. As for the empirical approaches to studying change detection, however, the ideas predated the recent change blindness literature (e.g., see Irwin, 1991, for claims about change blindness and saccadic integration).

Perhaps the most prominent theorist whose views were consistent with the outside memory hypothesis was James Gibson. According to Gibson, because perception must occur over time, visual representations in memory are unnecessary (e.g., Gibson, Kaplan, Reynolds, & Wheeler, 1969). More importantly for the present purpose, Gibson argued that the information needed for perception was available in the visual world and that perceivers simply learned to "pick up" that information (Gibson, 1966, 1986/1979). Accordingly, they need not store the information internally because it continues to exist externally. Although Gibson did not discuss change detection explicitly, his view is certainly consistent with the phenomenon of change blindness. If a change were introduced surreptitiously into a scene, observers would have no way to compare the changed version to the original version—the information for perception is external, and that information would be changed. Unless the change led to a difference in how the observer would interact with the world (i.e., the *affordances* of the environment), no change would be perceived.

Gibson was not the first nor the last to promote the idea of perceiving without representing. Stroud (1955) argued for a similar position before Gibson (see also Shallice, 1964), and a number of authors have argued for limited internal representations since then (e.g., Brooks, 1991; Dennett, 1991; Irwin, 1991; O'Regan, 1992). Dennett (1991) explicitly discussed how the idea of change blindness follows from the hypothesis of minimal representations. However, his predictions were based on empirical evidence of failed change detection garnered from the saccade-contingent change detection studies discussed earlier.[1] Although most of these early theorists did not discuss change blindness explicitly, researchers studying transsaccadic integration did consider the consequences of limited visual memory for real world scene perception. For example, Irwin noted that one implication of limited transsaccadic memory is that "the world could change in many ways during a saccade without the viewer noticing it" (Irwin, 1991, p. 453). However, these earlier generalizations did not anticipate the extent of change blindness for complex scenes or all the means of producing change blindness in scenes.

Although many theorists before the recent surge of research on change blindness had adopted the "limited representations" idea, this minimalist view was not universally accepted. Competing models of visual perception were and still are often based on the idea that vision works by reconstructing an internal model of the visual world. This idea, at least on its surface, seems inconsistent with change blindness. If observers have a complete internal representation, why would they fail to detect changes to the scene—they could readily compare what they see to what they stored. Although few researchers argue for a complete internal representation, the idea that we reconstruct the world internally has a long history (see Lindberg, 1976). In fact, Gibson's assertion that we do not store the contents of the world internally was considered radical precisely because most models of perception assumed that perception operates by constructing an internal representation of the world (e.g., Breitmeyer, Kropfl, & Julesz, 1982; Marr, 1982; McConkie & Rayner, 1976; Trehub, 1991). Thus, change blindness

---

[1]Note that Dennett did predict change blindness for nonmeaningful changes to the sequencing of an event in a motion picture. However, as discussed above, film theorists noted the existence of change blindness decades earlier.

might have been predictable on the basis of limited-representation views of perception, but it did not follow naturally from other prevalent theories.

Interestingly, change blindness could occur regardless of whether visual memory is sparse or complete (Simons, 2000a). Change blindness is frequently used as the primary evidence in support of sparse representations on the basis of the face validity of the idea that limited representations should lead to change blindness (e.g., O'Regan & Noë, 2001; Rensink et al., 1997; Simons & Levin, 1997). However, observers could fail to detect changes even if they fully represented both the pre- and postchange scenes, provided that they never compared those representations. If so, change blindness is logically consistent with both sparse and dense representations, and findings of change blindness do not provide a direct test of the "outside memory" idea.

Successful change detection requires an internal representation of the original state of a changing object and a comparison of that representation to the changed state. When observers successfully detect a change to a scene, we can be certain that they represented sufficient details from each view and compared the two views. Consequently, we can infer the minimum amount of information that they must have retained for that level of change detection performance. If observers lacked internal representations, they would be unable to detect changes. Thus, findings of change blindness seem consistent with the idea that we lack complete and detailed internal representations of our visual world. However, findings of change blindness do not logically require the absence of representations. That is, change blindness can occur even if observers do have a complete and accurate representation of the changed object or feature (Angelone, Levin, & Simons, 2001; Simons, 2000a; Simons, Chabris, Schnur, & Levin, 2002). Change blindness can also occur if observers fail to compare an existing representation to the changed object (Scott-Brown, Baker, & Orbach, 2000) or if they fail to access the changed features that they have represented (e.g., Hollingworth & Henderson, 2002; Simons et al., 2002). Given that sparse representation theories did not actually predict change blindness, these findings provide no direct test or even support for the theory.

VII.   A Narrative Account of the Recent History of Change Blindness

The spark that ignited much of the recent interest in change blindness was a 1992 presentation at the Vancouver Cognitive Science Conference by John Grimes (1996). Grimes extended work on saccade-contingent changes in reading and picture priming to the perception of photographs of natural scenes. In these studies, observers viewed photographs on a computer monitor in order to take a subsequent memory test. As they were studying the images, periodically, during a saccade, some aspect of the scene was changed. Observers knew that changes might occur and were told to press a key whenever they noticed a change. Interestingly, observers often missed large changes to the scenes even though they were intently studying the details for a later memory test. All observers failed to notice when the height of a "prominent building in a city skyline" was increased by 25% and 100% failed to notice "two men exchange hats . . . of different colours and styles." And, perhaps most strikingly, 50% failed to notice when "two cowboys sitting on a bench exchanged heads!" This was the first empirical report of change blindness using photographs rather than words or simple drawings, and it suggested that change blindness might be more pervasive than previously thought.

This dramatic finding might have been sufficient to kindle a renewed interest in the phenomenon of change blindness. However, the presentation itself had an even greater impact. For his talk, Grimes compiled a video to illustrate the nature of the changes he used. The video showed what the observers had seen, illustrating several of the more dramatic changes. Given that the changes were not contingent on saccades during the presentation, audience members should have been able to notice them, and most did. However, for each change, some audience members missed the joke—they did not see the change. Grimes created the video to illustrate how obvious the changes were when they were not contingent on saccades, but it had an entirely different result. Many audience members actually experienced change blindness for the same changes. How did this happen? Perhaps the most obvious explanation is that for some observers and for some changes, the change happened to occur during an eye movement. Given that we move our eyes several times each second and that each eye movement lasts for 30–50 ms, by chance, some of the changes would coincide with an eye movement, causing some audience members to experience the same saccade-masked changes experienced by Grimes' actual subjects.

This conference presentation produced two results, one empirical and one sociological. The empirical innovation, although not theoretically ground-breaking, underlies much of the current interest in change blindness: Grimes' use of photographs of natural scenes extended the study of change detection from words, line drawings, and dot patterns to more complex, naturalistic displays. This was the first evidence that change blindness generalizes to more natural viewing conditions and that it might be a pervasive aspect of how we see the world. The sociological consequence of the talk was that several people in the audience were inspired to study change blindness, and they set out to explore the mechanisms underlying the failure to detect changes across saccades.

Over the next few years, several laboratories independently began to produce evidence for change blindness, both for simple objects and for photographs of natural scenes. Perhaps the most important innovation was the realization that change blindness for natural scenes can occur in the absence of saccades. Much of the early work on change blindness relied on saccades as a way to introduce changes without producing a detectable transient signal. Unfortunately, the equipment needed to produce saccade-contingent changes was prohibitively expensive for most laboratories, especially for exploratory work. Consequently, Ronald Rensink, Susan Blackmore, and others began to explore ways of inducing change blindness without the need for sophisticated eye tracking equipment (Blackmore, Brelstaff, Nelson, & Troscianko, 1995; Rensink et al., 1997). They hypothesized that the reason saccade-contingent changes often produce change blindness is that the saccade disrupts processing, acting much like a visual mask. Essentially, the visual world is blurred on the retina as the eyes move. This blur serves as a visual disruption, and it is the disruption, not the eye movement itself, that is responsible for change blindness. To test this hypothesis, the saccade was replaced with a briefly flashed blank screen. This "blank" served as a visual disruption of approximately the same duration as a saccade (in this case, 80–120 ms).

As discussed above, many other studies had used a single flashed blank screen in change detection tasks (Cermak, 1971; Dirks & Neisser, 1977; Hochberg, 1968; Mandler & Ritchey, 1977; Mandler & Robinson, 1978; Newcombe et al., 1977; Pashler, 1988; Phillips, 1974; Simons, 1996). These new change blindness studies, however, explicitly linked studies using a blank screen to studies using saccade-contingent changes (Blackmore et al., 1995; Rensink et al., 1997). Moreover, Rensink et al. (1997) presented the change repeatedly, always separated by a blank screen, and used detection time rather than accuracy as the primary dependent measure of change detection (see Hochberg, 1968, for an earlier use of this paradigm). For changes made during this flicker, observers often are change blind for many seconds before eventually finding the change. Perhaps more importantly, observers recognize that they cannot readily detect changes. In prior studies, observers had only one opportunity to detect a change, and if they missed it, they could not be certain whether a change had actually been present on that trial. In contrast, in the flicker task, observers are well aware of their inability to find the change. Moreover, once they do find the change, they are often surprised by how obvious it was.

About the same time that Rensink and colleagues developed the flicker task, we began to link the growing empirical literature on scene perception to the extensive knowledge base derived from filmmakers. As noted above, motion pictures provided some of the earliest demonstrations of the existence of change blindness and discussions of film editing contained some of the first descriptions of the phenomenon. Filmmakers are well aware of the difficulty of keeping all aspects of a scene constant from one camera shot to the next. Consequently, editing mistakes are a part of most motion pictures, even today's more expensive and sophisticated productions. To see this for yourself, the next time you are bored with a movie you rented, choose a cut in the motion picture (a change in camera angle) and watch it repeatedly, while trying to notice each detail. You are likely to be able to spot errors whenever the scene was not filmed from all camera angles simultaneously. During normal viewing, however, most observers do not notice errors in motion pictures. Instead, people perceive continuous, uninterrupted events, and the visual details seem to fall by the wayside (Levin & Simons, 1997).

We set out to explore the detection of editing mistakes more systematically by creating motion pictures with intentionally error-filled editing. Our primary question was whether observers would detect such errors, but we were also interested in how people experienced the events as continuous in the face of such errors. Not surprisingly, our studies confirmed what filmmakers have long known—viewers rarely notice changes to the objects and features in a scene when the changes occur across a cut or pan. In fact, even when the central object in a scene changes, people often fail to notice, provided that the overall meaning of the scene is unchanged (Levin & Simons, 1997; Simons, 1996). In one set of studies, we directly explored Buñuel's anecdotal report of change blindness for the central actor in a film (Buñuel, 1983). In our short films, a single character performed a simple action such as standing up and answering a phone. The films contained a single cut, during which the actor playing the character unexpectedly was replaced by a different person wearing similar, but different clothing. We found that approximately two-thirds of observers did not notice anything change (Levin & Simons, 1997).

All of these lines of research, including work on saccade-contingent changes in reading and scene perception, changes during blank intervals and other disruptions, and motion picture perception converged at a 1994 workshop on scene perception hosted by Nissan Cambridge Basic Research. This small meeting was attended by people working on saccade-contingent changes as well as by people studying visual integration across eye movements and by those studying scene perception in general. This workshop included the first public presentations of the flicker technique as well as the "mudsplash" technique in which changes coincide with the presentation of arbitrary "splats" on the display (O'Regan, 1999; Rensink, O'Regan, & Clark, 2000). It also included our preliminary work on change detection in motion pictures (Levin & Simons, 1997; Simons, 1996). The workshop highlighted the rapid acceleration of research on change blindness and it illustrated the extent to which different disciplines all provided evidence for change blindness. Since that time, interest in the phenomenon of change blindness has increased rapidly, in part because the experimental techniques are accessible and because the phenomenology is surprising to those who have not heard about the effects (Levin et al., 2000). Several review articles on change blindness have appeared in the years since the mid-1990s (Henderson & Hollingworth, 1999a; Rensink, 2000a,b, 2002; Simons, 2000a; Simons & Levin, 1997) and a special issue of *Visual Cognition* addressed both empirical and theoretical issues in change blindness research (Simons, 2000b). Evidence for change blindness has also become part of a larger dialogue about the limitations of attention and memory, and the phenomenon has been linked to other independently studied forms of "blindness" such as inattentional blindness (Mack & Rock, 1998), repetition blindness (Kanwisher, 1987), and the attentional blink (Shapiro, Arnell, & Raymond, 1997).

VIII.   Why Is Change Blindness Interesting?

In what respects are more recent demonstrations of change blindness novel or interesting? Prior empirical work on change detection often suggested the existence of change blindness, some theoretical frameworks for perception proposed the idea of sparse representation long before recent findings of change blindness, and evidence from outside academics clearly demonstrated the phenomenon. Given this body of early work, what distinguishes the current research? Why, given what we already knew, are these findings surprising? Recent findings of change blindness are surprising for at least five reasons.

A.   CONVERGENCE OF LITERATURES

Although evidence for change blindness existed in several literatures long before the recent swell of interest in the phenomenon, these disparate findings were not integrated until the 1990s and the phenomenon itself was not considered to be the central topic of study. For example, eye movement studies typically focused on reading or saccadic integration and not on change detection. Evidence for change blindness in these early studies was typically noted as an afterthought rather than as the primary finding of the studies. These studies were focused on theoretical questions about reading and visual integration, and they used change detection as a tool to address these questions. They were less interested in studying change detection or change blindness per se. Consequently, prior to the past decade, no attempts were made to integrate evidence of change blindness from these otherwise disparate areas. The upsurge of interest in change blindness arose in part when findings from these literatures were combined with a direct focus on failures to detect changes across a number of paradigms (Rensink, 2002).

B. INCONSISTENT PREDICTIONS OF CHANGE BLINDNESS FOR COMPLEX SCENES

Not all prior theoretical views were consistent with the existence of change blindness in complex, realistic scenes. Almost all studies of change detection prior to the 1990s used simple line drawings, words, or dot arrays as stimuli. In part, this reluctance to use natural scenes came both from the lack of tools needed to study change detection in scenes and from the difficulty in asking precise empirical questions in a well-controlled form with complex images. However, the lack of direct empirical extensions of early findings from simple displays to natural scenes does not, in itself, make work with natural scenes interesting. What does is that some views would actually predict better change detection with complex scenes than with simple, artificial ones. For example, observers show poor detection of the displacement of a dot during a saccade when it shifts less than 10% of the length of the saccade (Li & Matin, 1990a). However, when additional stable landmarks are added to a display, detection becomes accurate (Matin, 1986). Accordingly, the results of these studies would not necessarily predict change blindness in complex scenes because the scene provides a rich, stable spatial structure—the amount of stable information far exceeds that provided by a single additional dot. Yet, change blindness across saccades can actually be greater for natural scenes (McConkie & Currie, 1996). Similarly, Hochberg (1968) found change blindness for inverted or polarity-reversed drawings of faces, but not for upright faces. This finding implies that familiarity or experience in viewing a display improves the internal representation, thereby making change detection likely. The more readily interpretable a display, the better the internal representation. This view also would predict relatively good change detection for scenes because they are readily understandable and are replete with meaning. Thus, evidence for change blindness with simple displays does not automatically lead to predictions of change blindness for natural scenes, and in some cases it even leads to opposite predictions.

An anecdote from our early work on change blindness for movies and real-world events illustrates the reluctance many researchers had to generalize from simpler displays to more complex ones. When we first reported our evidence of change blindness for the central actor in a brief motion picture, one of our colleagues commented that the results were due to the nature of the displays. Specifically, watching videos is a fundamentally passive activity, and observers might not take an active role in perceiving the displays. Based on this logic, our colleague predicted that this result would never happen in a real-world interaction because that would demand active participation of the subject. Yet, observers do miss changes to the identity of a conversation partner in the real world (Simons & Levin, 1998). Thus, even when confronted with evidence for change blindness in a dynamic, rich motion picture, he was unwilling to predict the existence of change blindness in the real world. The unwillingness to make the inferential leap from a dynamic video to the real world emphasizes the difficulty of making the even larger leap from simple displays to complex ones. In hindsight, of course, the finding of real-world change blindness follows naturally from evidence for change blindness in movies, and it seems implausible that people could ever have thought otherwise. Similarly, evidence for change blindness in scenes seems to follow logically from failures to detect changes to simple displays. Even when current findings seem obvious on the basis of past findings, in hindsight, at the time, opposite predictions were equally possible and perhaps more plausible. Similarly, theoretical arguments for incomplete internal representations of the visual world are entirely consistent with more recent evidence for change blindness, but prior to the 1990s (e.g., Irwin, 1991), none of these models explicitly predicted the existence of change blindness in scenes.

C. INCREASED FACE VALIDITY OF GENERALIZATION

The use of rich, complex displays including photographs, motion pictures, and even real-world events increases interest in change blindness because it provides face validity to the phenomenon. This increased naturalism emphasized the generality and importance of earlier theoretical and empirical results. Theoretical arguments for sparse representations in real-world perception based on evidence from studies using words or dot arrays might well be valid, but the inference is more natural from change blindness in complex scenes. Failing to detect a small displacement of an isolated dot during a saccade and failing to notice two people switching heads seem qualitatively different, even if the mechanisms underlying both examples are identical. The generalization *seems* unmerited even if, in reality, it is legitimate. If anything, the parallel results with simple and complex displays validates the use of simple displays to infer how the visual system operates in the real world.

D. ABILITY TO EXPERIENCE CHANGE BLINDNESS

The newer tasks developed to measure change blindness are often inherently entertaining for observers because they reveal the extent of our own change blindness. Searching for a repeating change in a scene is an enjoyable challenge, and change blindness is sufficiently prolonged that observers can experience the phenomenon in a single trial. The use of tasks that allow any viewer to experience the effect highlights both the magnitude of the effects and their potential generality to real-world perception. Much of the early work on change detection and evidence for change blindness was limited to computer-based paradigms that required precise control over the timing and nature of the displays. Moreover, many of these paradigms were designed such that observers were change blind, but never realized this until they were told later (see Hochberg, 1968, for an exception). In contrast, many more recent tasks allow the observer to experience their inability to find changes (Rensink et al., 1997; Simons, Franconeri, & Reimer, 2000).

E.   FINDINGS WITH COMPLEX SCENES ARE MORE COUNTERINTUITIVE

At their essence, recent examples of change blindness are interesting because they are surprising. Indeed, people unfamiliar with research on change blindness vastly overestimate their ability to detect changes (Levin et al., 2000). Moreover, the magnitude of the overestimation of change detection ability seems larger for real-world materials. In a typical experiment illustrating this overestimate, subjects read a scenario describing a change and viewed images illustrating the changes. They then were asked whether they would have seen these unexpected changes had they actually participated in the task. For example, one scenario described a change in which an actor's scarf disappears across a cut in a movie (from Levin & Simons, 1997). None of the subjects in our original experiment reported seeing the change. In sharp contrast, 90% of subjects in a different study predicted that they would have detected the change. This sort of metacognitive error is robust—subjects make comparable overestimates when predicting their own performance and that of others (Levin et al., 2000), and their estimates are equally inaccurate when they are based on still photographs or the actual videos used in the original experiments (Levin et al., 2002). We refer to these misestimates as "change blindness blindness" (CBB)—people are blind to the extent to which they show change blindness, a metacognitive error similar to other previously documented misunder-standings of real-world memory (e.g., see Wells, 1984).

1.   Explaining Change Blindness Blindness

One relatively subtle misunderstanding that might account for CBB is a belief that changes attract attention, perhaps due to the existence of a perceptual transient (O'Regan, Rensink, & Clark, 1999). Given that most change blindness experiments take pains to avoid such transients, these misestimates could be a relatively unsurprising misunderstanding of the conditions necessary to produce transients. To test this possibility, Levin et al. (2002) asked subjects to estimate their ability to detect immediate changes as well as changes in which the pre- and postchange views were separated in time by up to an hour. Subjects were asked to imagine that they were watching a movie on their VCR and were interrupted by a phone call that they had to answer in a different room. Upon returning, they started the VCR on the next shot and saw the postchange view. If the metacognitive error results from a belief that a perceptual transient will attract attention to the change, then these delays should make that belief irrelevant, thereby reducing CBB. Across three experiments, adding a delay led to no reduction in estimates of change detection, even when the interruption was illustrated by a video of a model experiencing it. In fact, few subjects even mentioned memory for visual information as a motivating factor in explaining their predictions for performance in the delay condition. Accordingly, CBB does not appear to result from an explicit belief in a high-capacity memory for visual detail.

If CBB is not based on mistaken beliefs about transients or beliefs in memory for visual detail, then why do people think they can see these changes? One possibility is that beliefs about visual attention predict CBB. Young children mistakenly believe that attending to one part of the world allows them to see other things in the scene as well (Flavell, Green, & Flavell, 1995). Children apparently conceptualize visual attention as more of a lamp than a spotlight, so that orienting attention to some part of a scene "illuminates" all of it. Although this developmental research implicitly assumes that adults possess the "correct" spotlight model of attention, even adults might overestimate the extent to which looking at one thing allows awareness of other things. When large groups of subjects were asked to judge the breadth of visual attention and to predict change detection success, those who believed in broad and inclusive visual attention also showed greater CBB (Levin, 2001). For example, subjects who indicated that they would see a painting's frame while looking at the painting were more likely to predict successful change detection. Similarly, subjects who believe they typically look at a large percentage of a scene at a glance also showed greater CBB.

Change blindness blindness might also reflect a deeper metacognitive error in which people coopt knowledge about other forms of representation to help reason about visual representations (Levin & Beck, in press). One other extensively studied form of representation, particularly with children, involves beliefs about the knowledge of other social agents. In a standard "false belief" task, a child and a puppet witness an object being hidden in one of two locations. The puppet then leaves the room, and the object is moved to the other hiding place. The puppet then returns, and the child is asked where the puppet will look for the object. Children younger than 4 years old tend to report that the puppet will search for the object in its new location—they have not assimilated the fact that the puppet was out of the room when the hiding place changed. This finding implies that young children lack a fundamental understanding of the difference between representations of the world and the true state of the world. However, by age 4, children can reason about what other agents know. The false belief task and the change detection prediction task have a number of important elements in common. In both, the subjects is asked to reason about the degree to which someone will (1) experience a visual scene, (2) represent it, and (3) be able or unable to appreciate the degree to which is has changed. If older children and adults understand the difference between representations of the world and the true state of the world, why do they succumb to CBB? Why do they fail to recognize that change detection requires representations that are similarly dependent on the perceiver's limited opportunity to assimilate the world? What is it about the change detection task that leads people astray? These questions are particularly compelling given the finding that adults succumb to CBB even when the pre- and postchange views are separated by a temporal disruption, a condition that parallels the false belief procedure in which the model leaves the room while the change occurs.

One possibility is that in the false belief task, the role of representation is made clear not only by the fact that the puppet had to sample the visual world, take that sample from the room in the form of an internal representation, and bring it back to complete the task, but also because once the puppet returned it could not resample the world to check its representation. The child must consider the puppet's representation because the puppet cannot see into either hiding place. In contrast, in the change blindness task, the returning perceiver can resample the world, so the role of representations is less explicit. Accordingly, understanding of the need for representations might be overwhelmed by the immediacy and availability of the visual world (for a related analysis based on intentional theory of mind, see Levin & Beck, submitted). In other words, observers tend to rely on what they currently see rather than referring to information retained in memory, even when using their representations would lead to better performance. For example, in a visual search task in which the display is constant across trials and the target of the search is indicated on each trial, observers could perform efficiently by memorizing the display and searching for the target in their memory representation. However, they adopt the less efficient strategy of using visual search whenever the display remains visible (Wolfe, Klempen, & Dahlen, 2000).

IX. Conclusions

Regardless of the true explanation for CBB, the phenomenon shows that people misunderstand important aspects of vision and visual memory, and that these misunderstandings can lead them astray when predicting their own performance and the performance of others. Mismatches between intuitions and performance are often precisely those for which psychological science is most warranted and relevant. Within psychology, such mismatches serve as an informal guide to help decide what represents an interesting problem for research. Change blindness is interesting to the extent that it deviates from intuitions—both of researchers and of those unfamiliar with the empirical literature—about change detection.

Outside the discipline, this principle has been formalized, and it can be crucial in justifying the impact of our science. One of the clearest examples of such a formalization are the rules for admitting expert testimony in court. These stipulate that the testimony provide information that is "beyond the ken of the ordinary juror" (see Brigham & Bothwell, 1983; Deffenbacher & Loftus, 1982, for a discussion of these rules with respect to testimony about the accuracy of eyewitness memory). Consequently, judges may disallow expert testimony if what they intend to say is consistent with intuition. In fact, this is precisely what happened to one of our colleagues who was set to testify about change blindness![2] Clearly, *insisting* that change blindness is not consistent with intuition will be of little help—as scientists we should be expected to document this assertion empirically.

The metacognitive error of CBB also has practical implications. For example, when driving, we tend to assume that we will automatically detect a change to the color of a stoplight or that we will notice when the car in front of us begins braking. Fortunately, we often do notice those changes, but not necessarily because they draw attention. Rather, we likely notice them because we are actively looking for them (see Folk, Remington, & Johnston, 1992). Relying too much on the assumption that changes draw attention, however, might lead drivers to focus on other activities such as talking on a phone. If these other activities detract sufficiently from their attention to the road signals and surroundings (e.g., Strayer & Johnston,

---

[2]This example might present an interesting case of hindsight bias. If the judge was aware of change blindness, he might have found it difficult to believe that anyone else would believe that they would detect changes. In other words, the judge may have demonstrated "change blindness" blindness! In the absence of such knowledge, research on change blindness blindness does demonstrate that change blindness is counterintuitive.

2001), they might well miss the change. Demonstrations of change blindness are often surprising and interesting because they highlight the degree to which our assumptions can be wrong.

REFERENCES

Angelone, B. L., Levin, D. T., & Simons, D. J. (2002). Representation and comparison failures in change blindness. Submitted.

Blackmore, S. J., Brelstaff, G., Nelson, K., & Troscianko, T. (1995). Is the richness of our visual world an illusion? Transsaccadic memory for complex scenes. *Perception, 24*, 1075–1081.

Blanchard, H. E., Pollatsek, A., & Rayner, K. (1989). The acquisition of parafoveal word information in reading. *Perception and Psychophysics, 46*(1), 85–94.

Boyce, S. J., & Pollatsek, A. (1992). Identification of objects in scenes: The role of scene background in object naming. *Journal of Experimental Psychology: Learning, Memory, and Cognition, 18*(3), 531–543.

Breitmeyer, B. G., Kropfl, W., & Julesz, B. (1982). The existence and role of retinotopic and spatiotopic forms of visual persistence. *Acta Psychologica, 52*(3), 175–196.

Bridgeman, B., Hendry, D., & Stark, L. (1975). Failure to detect displacement of the visual world during saccadic eye movements. *Vision Research, 15*(6), 719–722.

Brigham, J. C., & Bothwell, R. K. (1983). The ability of prospective jurors to estimate the accuracy of eyewitness identifications. *Law and Human Behavior, 7*(1), 19–30.

Brooks, R. A. (1991). Intelligence without representation. *Artificial Intelligence, 47*, 139–159.

Bruno, J. (1978). *Anatomy of misdirection.* Baltimore: Stoney Brook Press.

Buñuel, L. (1983). *My last sigh.* New York: Alfred A. Knopf.

Burke, L. (1952). On the tunnel effect. *Quarterly Journal of Experimental Psychology, 4*, 121–138.

Cermak, G. W. (1971). Short-term recognition memory for complex free-form figures. *Psychonomic Science, 5*(4), 209–211.

Currie, C. B., McConkie, G. W., Carlson-Radvansky, L. A., & Irwin, D. E. (2000). The role of the saccade target object in the perception of a visually stable world. *Perception and Psychophysics, 62*(4), 673–683.

Deffenbacher, K. A., & Loftus, E. F. (1982). Do jurors share a common understanding concerning eyewitness behavior. *Law and Human Behavior, 6*, 15–30.

Dennett, D. C. (1991). *Consciousness explained.* Boston: Little, Brown.

Deubel, H., Schneider, W. X., & Bridgeman, B. (1996). Postsaccadic target blanking prevents saccadic suppression of image displacement. *Vision Research, 36*(7), 985–996.

Dirks, J., & Neisser, U. (1977). Memory for objects in real scenes: The development of recognition and recall. *Journal of Experimental Child Psychology, 23*(2), 315–328.

Ditchburn, R. W. (1955). Eye-movements in relation to retinal action. *Optica Acta, 1*, 171–176.

Dmytryk, E. (1984). *On film editing: An introduction to the art of film construction.* Boston: Focal Press.

Fernandez-Duque, D., & Thornton, I. M. (2000). Change detection without awareness: Do explicit reports underestimate the representation of change in the visual system? *Visual Cognition, 7*(1/2/3), 323–344.

Flavell, J. H., Green, F. L., & Flavell, E. R. (1995). The development of children's knowledge about attentional focus. *Developmental Psychology, 31*, 706–712.

Folk, C. L., Remington, R. W., & Johnston, J. C. (1992). Involuntary covert orienting is contingent on attentional control settings. *Journal of Experimental Psychology: Human Perception and Performance, 18*(4), 1030–1044.

French, R. S. (1953). The discrimination of dot patterns as a function of number and average separation of dots. *Journal of Experimental Psychology, 46*, 1–9.

Gibson, J. J. (1966). *The senses considered as perceptual systems.* Boston: Houghton Mifflin.

Gibson, J. J. (1986/1979). *The ecological approach to visual perception.* Hillsdale, NJ: Erlbaum.

Gibson, J. J., Kaplan, G. A., Reynolds, H. N. J., & Wheeler, K. (1969). The change from visible to invisible: A study of optical transitions. *Perception and Psychophysics, 5*, 113–116.

Grimes, J. (1996). On the failure to detect changes in scenes across saccades. In K. Akins (Ed.), *Perception (Vancouver Studies in Cognitive Science)* (Vol. 2, pp. 89–110). New York: Oxford University Press.

Hayhoe, M., Lachter, J., & Feldman, J. (1991). Integration of form across saccadic eye movements. *Perception, 20*, 393–402.

Henderson, J. M. (1997). Transsaccadic memory and integration during real-world object perception. *Psychological Science, 8*(1), 51–55.

Henderson, J. M., & Hollingworth, A. (1999a). High-level scene perception. *Annual Review of Psychology, 50*, 243–271.

Henderson, J. M., & Hollingworth, A. (1999b). The role of fixation position in detecting scene changes across saccades. *Psychological Science, 10*(5), 438–443.

Hochberg, J. (1968). In the mind's eye. In R. N. Haber (Ed.), *Contemporary theory and research in visual perception* (pp. 309–331). New York: Holt, Rinehart & Winston.

Hochberg, J. (1986). Representation of motion and space in video and cinematic displays. In K. R. Boff, L. Kaufman, & J. P. Thomas (Eds.), *Handbook of perception and human performance* (pp. 22.21–22.64). New York: John Wiley and Sons.

Hollingworth, A., & Henderson, J. M. (2002). Accurate visual memory for previously attended objects in natural scenes. *Journal of Experimental Psychology: Human Perception and Performance, 28*, 113–136.

Irwin, D. E. (1991). Information integration across saccadic eye movements. *Cognitive Psychology, 23*, 420–456.

Irwin, D. E. (1992a). Memory for position and identity across eye movements. *Journal of Experimental Psychology: Learning, Memory, and Cognition, 18*(2), 307–317.

Irwin, D. E. (1992b). Visual memory within and across fixations. In K. Rayner (Ed.), *Eye movements and visual cognition* (pp. 146–165). New York: Springer-Verlag.

James, W. (1950/1891). *The principles of psychology* (Vol. 1). New York: Dover.

Kanwisher, N. (1987). Repetition blindness: Type recognition without token individuation. *Cognition, 27*, 117–143.

Kuleshov, L. (1987/1920). *Selected works: Fifty years in films.* (D. Agrachev & N. Belenkaya, Trans.). Moscow: Raduga Publishers.

Levin, D. T. (2001). *Visual metacognitions underlying change blindness blindness and estimates of picture memory.* Poster presented at the Vision Sciences Society, Sarasota, FL.

Levin, D. T., & Beck, M. R. (in press). Thinking about seeing: Spanning the difference between metacognitive failure and success. In D. T. Levin (Ed.) Thinking and seeing: Visual metacognition in adults and children. Westpart, Conn: Greenwood/Praeger.

Levin, D. T., Drivdahl, S. B., Momen, N., & Beck, M. R. (2002). False predictions about the detectability of unexpected visual changes: The role of beliefs about attention, memory, and the continuity of attended objects in causing change blindness blindness. *Consciousness and Cognition, 11*, 507–527.

Levin, D. T., Momen, N., Drivdahl, S. B., & Simons, D. J. (2000). Change blindness blindness: The metacognitive error of overestimating change-detection ability. *Visual Cognition, 7*, 397–412.

Levin, D. T., & Simons, D. J. (1997). Failure to detect changes to attended objects in motion pictures. *Psychonomic Bulletin and Review, 4*(4), 501–506.

Levin, D. T., & Simons, D. J. (2000). Perceiving stability in a changing world: Combining shots and integrating views in motion pictures and the real world. *Media Psychology, 2*, 357–380.

Li, W., & Matin, L. (1990a). The influence of saccade length on the saccadic suppression of displacement detection. *Perception and Psychophysics, 48*(5), 453–458.

Li, W., & Matin, L. (1990b). Saccadic suppression of displacement: Influence of postsaccadic exposure duration and of saccadic stimulus elimination. *Vision Research, 30*(6), 945–955.

Li, W., & Matin, L. (1997). Saccadic suppression of displacement: Separate influences of saccade size and of target retinal eccentricity. *Vision Research, 37*(13), 1779–1797.

Lindberg, D. C. (1976). *Theories of vision from Al-Kindi to Kepler.* Chicago: University of Chicago Press.

Mack, A. (1970). An investigation of the relationship between eye and retinal image movement in the perception of movement. *Perception and Psychophysics, 8*(5-a), 291–298.

Mack, A., & Rock, I. (1998). *Inattentional blindness.* Cambridge, MA: MIT Press.

Mandler, J. M., & Ritchey, G. H. (1977). Long-term memory for pictures. *Journal of Experimental Psychology: Human Learning and Memory, 3*(4), 386–396.

Mandler, J. M., & Robinson, C. A. (1978). Developmental changes in picture recognition. *Journal of Experimental Child Psychology, 26*(1), 122–136.

Marr, D. (1982). *Vision: A computational investigation into the human representation and processing of visual information.* San Francisco: W.H. Freeman.

Matin, L. (1986). Visual localization and eye movements. In K. R. Boff, L. Kaufman, & J. P. Thomas (Eds.) *Handbook of perception and human performance: Sensory processes and perception* (Vol. 1, pp. 20.21–20.45). New York: Wiley.

McConkie, G. W., & Currie, C. B. (1996). Visual stability across saccades while viewing complex pictures. *Journal of Experimental Psychology: Human Perception and Performance, 22*, 563–581.

McConkie, G. W., & Rayner, K. (1975). The span of effective stimulus during a fixation in reading. *Perception and Psychophysics, 17*, 578–586.

McConkie, G. W., & Rayner, K. (1976). Identifying the span of the effective stimulus in reading: Literature review and theories of reading. In H. Singer & R. B. Ruddell (Eds.) *Theoretical models and processes of reading* (2nd ed., pp. 137–162). Newark, DE: International Reading Association.

McConkie, G. W., & Zola, D. (1979). Is visual information integrated across successive fixations in reading? *Perception and Psychophysics, 25*(3), 221–224.

McConkie, G. W., Zola, D., Blanchard, H. E., & Wolverton, G. S. (1982). Perceiving words during reading: Lack of facilitation from prior peripheral exposure. *Perception and Psychophysics, 32*(3), 271–281.

Miller, P. P. (1999). *Script supervising and film continuity* (3rd ed.). Boston: Focal Press.

Mitroff, S. R., Simons, D. J. (2002). Changes are not localized before they are explicitly detected. *Visual Cognition, 9*, 937–968.

Mitroff, S. R., Simons, D. J., & Franconeri, S. L. (2002). The siren song of implicit change detection. *Journal of Experimental Psychology: Human Perception and Performance, 28*(4), 798–815.

Newcombe, N., Rogoff, B., & Kagan, J. (1977). Developmental changes in recognition memory for pictures of objects and scenes. *Developmental Psychology, 13*(4), 337–341.

O'Regan, J. K. (1992). Solving the 'real' mysteries of visual perception: The world as an outside memory. *Canadian Journal of Psychology, 46*(3), 461–488.

O'Regan, J. K., Deubel, H., Clark, J. J., & Rensink, R. A. (2000). Picture changes during blinks: Looking without seeing and seeing without looking. *Visual Cognition, 7*, 191–212.

O'Regan, J.K., & Noë, A. (2001). A sensorimotor account of vision and visual consciousness. *Behavioral and Brain Sciences, 24*(5), 939–1031.

O'Regan, J. K., Rensink, R. A., & Clark, J. J. (1999). Change-blindness as a result of "mudsplashes." *Nature, 398*(6722), 34.

Pashler, H. (1988). Familiarity and visual change detection. *Perception and Psychophysics, 44*(4), 369–378.

Phillips, W. A. (1974). On the distinction between sensory storage and short-term visual memory. *Perception and Psychophysics, 16*, 283–290.

Pollack, I. (1972). Detection of changes in spatial position: III. Dot number or dot density? *Perception and Psychophysics, 12*(6), 487–491.

Pollatsek, A., Lesch, M., Morris, R. K., & Rayner, K. (1992). Phonological codes are used in integrating information across saccades in word identification and reading. *Journal of Experimental Psychology: Human Perception and Performance, 18*(1), 148–162.

Pollatsek, A., & Rayner, K. (1992). What is integrated across fixations? In K. Rayner (Ed.), *Eye movements and visual cognition: Scene perception and reading* (pp. 166–191). New York: Springer-Verlag.

Pudovkin, V. I. (1929/1970). *Film technique.* Random House: New York.

Rayner, K., McConkie, G. W., & Ehrlich, S. F. (1978). Eye movements and integrating information across fixations. *Journal of Experimental Psychology: Human Perception and Performance, 4*, 529–544.

Rayner, K., McConkie, G. W., & Zola, D. (1980). Integrating information across eye movements. *Cognitive Psychology, 12*, 206–226.

Rayner, K., & Pollatsek, A. (1987). Eye movements in reading: A tutorial review. In M. Coltheart (Ed.), *Attention and performance: XII The psychology of reading* (pp. 327–362). London: Erlbaum.

Reichardt, W. (1961). Autocorrelation, a principle for the evaluation of sensory information by the nervous system. In W. A. Rosenblith (Ed.), *Sensory communication* (pp. 303–317). New York: Wiley.

Rensink, R. A. (2000a). The dynamic representation of scenes. *Visual Cognition, 7*, 17–42.

Rensink, R. A. (2000b). Seeing, sensing, and scrutinizing. *Vision Research, 40*, 1469–1487.

Rensink, R. A. (2002). Change detection. *Annual Review of Psychology, 53*, 245–277.

Rensink, R. A., O'Regan, J. K., & Clark, J. J. (1997). To see or not to see: The need for attention to perceive changes in scenes. *Psychological Science, 8*(5), 368–373.

Rensink, R. A., O'Regan, J. K., & Clark, J. J. (2000). On the failure to detect changes in scenes cross brief interruptions. *Visual Cognition, 7*, 127–146.

Rowlands, A. (2000). *The continuity supervisor* (4th ed.). Oxford, UK: Focal Press.

Scott-Brown, K. C., Baker, M. R., & Orbach, H. S. (2000). Comparison blindness. *Visual Cognition, 7*, 253–267.

Shallice, T. (1964). The detection of change and the perceptual moment hypotheses. *British Journal of Statistical Psychology, 17*(2), 113–135.

Shapiro, K. L., Arnell, K. A., & Raymond, J. E. (1997). The attentional blink: A view on attention and a glimpse on consciousness. *Trends in Cognitive Sciences, 1*, 291–296.

Simons, D. J. (1996). In sight, out of mind: When object representations fail. *Psychological Science, 7*(5), 301–305.

Simons, D. J. (2000a). Current approaches to change blindness. *Visual Cognition, 7*, 1–15.

Simons D. J. (2000). (Ed.) *Change blindness and visual memory: A special issue of the journal Visual Cognition.* Hove, UK: Psychology Press.

Simons, D. J., Chabris, C. F., Schnur, T. T., & Levin, D. T. (2002). Evidence for preserved representations in change blindness. *Consciousness and Cognition, 11*, 78–97.

Simons, D. J., Franconeri, S. L., & Reimer, R. L. (2000). Change blindness in the absence of a visual disruption. *Perception, 29*, 1143–1154.

Simons, D. J., & Levin, D. T. (1997). Change blindness. *Trends in Cognitive Sciences, 1*(7), 261–267.

Simons, D. J., & Levin, D. T. (1998). Failure to detect changes to people in a real-world interaction. *Psychonomic Bulletin and Review, 5*(4), 644–649.

Simons, D. J., & Mitroff, S. (2001). The role of expectations in change detection and attentional capture. In L. R. Harris & M. Jenkin (Eds.) *Vision and attention* (pp. 134–154). New York: Springer-Verlag.

Smilek, D., Eastwood, J. D., & Merikle, P. M. (2000). Does unattended information facilitate change detection? *Journal of Experimental Psychology: Human Perception and Performance, 26*(2), 480–487.

Spelke, E. S. (1990). Principles of object perception. *Cognitive Science, 14*, 29–56.

Strayer, D. L., & Johnston, W. A. (2001). Driven to distraction: Dual-task studies of simulated driving and conversing on a cellular telephone. *Psychological Science, 12*(6), 462–466.

Stroud, J. M. (1955). The fine structure of psychological time. In H. Quastler (Ed.) *Information theory in psychology: Problems and methods* (pp. 174–207). Glencoe, IL: Free Press.

Thornton, I. M., & Fernandez-Duque, D. (2000). An implicit measure of undetected change. *Spatial Vision, 14*(1), 21–44.

Trehub, A. (1991). *The cognitive brain.* Cambridge, MA: MIT Press.

Wallach, H., & Lewis, C. (1965). The effect of abnormal displacement of the retinal image during eye movements. *Perception and Psychophysics, 1*, 25–29.

Wells, G. L. (1984). How adequate is human intuition for judging eyewitness testimony. In G. L. Wells & E. F. Loftus (Eds.) *Eyewitness testimony* (pp. 256–272). Cambridge, UK: Cambridge University Press.

Williams, P., & Simons, D. J. (2000). Detecting changes in novel, complex three-dimensional objects. *Visual Cognition, 7*, 297–322.

Wolfe, J. M., Klempen, N., & Dahlen, K. (2000). Post-attentive vision. *Journal of Experimental Psychology: Human Perception and Performance, 26*(2), 693–716.

INDEX

A

Action
  as attentional glue, 254–257
  automatic, stimulus-cued, 237–241
  categorical, 227–228
  conceptual/semantic route to
    neural substrates for, 248–250
    from vision, 230–231, 234–235, 241–243
  coupling of, to vision, attention and, 257–259
  direct route to, from vision, 225–250
    evidence for, from normal
      participants, 232–237
    nature of, 237–243
    neural substrates for, 248–250
    neuropsychological evidence for, 228–232
  effects on perception, 250–251
  intention for
    and action-related frames of reference, 252
    and attention to action-related
      properties, 251–254
    and perceptual processing, 250–251
  invoked from action parts, 243
  location for, attention to visual
    stimuli at, 251
  optic aphasia and, 228–230
  perceptual knowledge and, 241–242
  prehensile, 227–228
  retrieval of
    convergent route model for, 243–248
      neural substrates for, 248–250
    dual-route account of, 244–248
    image size decision task and, 250
    neural substrates for, 248–250
  and semantic (context) decisions to words

and pictures, 234–235
semantic dementia and, 230–231
support for, by holistic perceptual
  codes, 243
visual apraxia and, 231–232, 243
visual attention and, in visual
  neglect, 252–253
Action errors
  distractor capture effects and, 239–241, 257
  as evidence for direct route from vision to
    action, 232–234, 257
Affordance effects
  and change detection, 305
  and potential for action, in normal
    participants, 235–237
Agnosia, visual, 4, 11–13, 227–228
Ambiguous figures
  interpretation of, 44–45
  reinterpretation of, inhibition of, 44–45
Anarchic hand syndrome, 237–241, 257
Aphasia, optic, 228–230, 248
Apraxia
  and actions invoked from action parts, 243
  cross-modal input in, and convergent route
    for action retrieval, 247–248
  visual, and action, 228, 231–232
Ataxia, optic, 227–228
Attention. *See also* Visual attention
  action-related, intention for action
    and, 251–254
  and coupling of vision and
    action, 257–259
  interactive models of, 158–159
  preattentive versus focal, 158–159
  two-stage models of, 158–159, 160–162

CONTENTS OF RECENT VOLUMES

Volume 41